Lecture Notes in Computer Science 14793

Founding Editors

Gerhard Goos
Juris Hartmanis

The series Lecture Notes in Computer Science (LNCS), including its subseries Lecture Notes in Artificial Intelligence (LNAI) and Lecture Notes in Bioinformatics (LNBI), has established itself as a medium for the publication of new developments in computer science and information technology research, teaching, and education.

LNCS enjoys close cooperation with the computer science R & D community, the series counts many renowned academics among its volume editors and paper authors, and collaborates with prestigious societies. Its mission is to serve this international community by providing an invaluable service, mainly focused on the publication of conference and workshop proceedings and postproceedings. LNCS commenced publication in 1973.

Marta Kristín Lárusdóttir · Bilal Naqvi ·
Regina Bernhaupt · Carmelo Ardito ·
Stefan Sauer

Editors

Human-Centered Software Engineering

10th IFIP WG 13.2 International Working Conference, HCSE 2024
Reykjavik, Iceland, July 8–10, 2024
Proceedings

 Springer

Editors
Marta Kristín Lárusdóttir ⓘ
Reykjavik University
Reykjavik, Iceland

Bilal Naqvi ⓘ
Lappeenranta University of Technology
Lappeenranta, Finland

Regina Bernhaupt ⓘ
Eindhoven University of Technology
Eindhoven, The Netherlands

Carmelo Ardito ⓘ
LUM Giuseppe Degennaro University
Casamassima, Italy

Stefan Sauer ⓘ
Paderborn University
Paderborn, Germany

ISSN 0302-9743   ISSN 1611-3349 (electronic)
Lecture Notes in Computer Science
ISBN 978-3-031-64575-4   ISBN 978-3-031-64576-1 (eBook)
https://doi.org/10.1007/978-3-031-64576-1

This Springer imprint is published by the registered company Springer Nature Switzerland AG
The registered company address is: Gewerbestrasse 11, 6330 Cham, Switzerland

If disposing of this product, please recycle the paper.

Foreword

The 10th International Working Conference on Human-Centered Software Engineering, HCSE 2024, was held at Reykjavik University, Iceland. HCSE is a biennial, single-track, working conference organized by the IFIP Working Group 13.2 on Methodology for User-Centred System Design. HCSE aims to bring together researchers and practitioners interested in strengthening the scientific foundations of user interface design, examining the relationship between software engineering and human–computer interaction and how to strengthen human-centered design as an essential part of software engineering processes. Previous events were held in Salamanca, Spain (2007); Pisa, Italy (2008); Reykjavik, Iceland (2010); Toulouse, France (2012); Paderborn, Germany (2014); Stockholm, Sweden (2016); Sophia Antipolis, France (2018); virtual (2020); Eindhoven, The Netherlands (2022); and now again Reykjavik (2024).

HCSE 2024 focused on recurring topics such as innovative methods for human-centered and participatory design and software engineering, modeling approaches, usable security, and the balancing of multiple properties in development, but also on emerging areas like immersive environments and augmented/virtual/mixed reality, low-code development and human-centered AI. Altogether, it looked at how software engineering is changing perspective when it comes to the focus on users.

The HCSE 2024 program included contributions from Australia, Austria, Belgium, Brazil, Czech Republic, Estonia, France, Finland, Germany, Greece, Iceland, Italy, Malta, The Netherlands, Norway, Slovakia, Sweden, and the UK to name a few. All contributions were peer-reviewed and received at least three reviews. The Program Committee consisted of 23 experts (including General and Track Chairs) from ten different countries. In total, HCSE 2024 accepted six full research papers and five late-breaking results, with an acceptance rate of 43%. Five posters and four demos were also accepted for inclusion in the conference program. Additionally, three PhD student discussion forum papers were accepted, a new format at HCSE. This was an open forum during the conference where PhD students, supported by a poster, briefly presented their research work and the topic of discussion, and received individual and detailed feedback on their PhD work and future perspectives. Our sincere gratitude goes to the members of our Program Committee who devoted countless hours to providing valuable feedback to authors and ensuring the high quality of HCSE 2024's technical program.

The program was organized in six technical sessions including the demonstration, poster, and PhD Student discussion forum. The program started with a keynote given by Grischa Liebel of Reykjavik University. Another keynote was contributed by Yasemin Acar of Paderborn University. The conference program is available at https://www.hcse-conference.org/.

HCSE 2024 was supported by Reykjavik University, Springer, and IFIP's Technical Committee on Human–Computer Interaction (IFIP TC13) whose generous support was essential for making HCSE 2024 special and successful! Finally, our thanks go to all the authors who actually did the research work and especially to the presenters who sparked inspiring discussions with all the participants at HCSE 2024.

For further information about past and future events organized by IFIP WG 13.2, its members and activities, please visit the website http://ifip-tc13.org/working-groups/working-group-13-2/.

We thank all contributors and participants for making HCSE 2024 a special and fruitful conference!

July 2024

Marta Kristín Lárusdóttir
Bilal Naqvi
Regina Bernhaupt
Carmelo Ardito
Stefan Sauer

IFIP TC13 –

http://ifip-tc13.org/ Established in 1989, the International Federation for Information Processing Technical Committee on Human–Computer Interaction (IFIP TC13) is an international committee of 37 IFIP Member national societies and 11 Working Groups, representing specialists of the various disciplines contributing to the field of human-computer interaction (HCI). This field includes, among others, human factors, ergonomics, cognitive science, computer science and design. INTERACT is the flagship conference of IFIP TC13, staged biennially in different countries in the world. The first INTERACT conference was held in 1984, at first running triennially becoming a biennial event in 1993.

IFIP TC13 aims to develop the science, technology and societal aspects HCI by encouraging empirical research, promoting the use of knowledge and methods from the human sciences in design and evaluation of computing technology systems; promoting better understanding of the relation between formal design methods and system usability and acceptability; developing guidelines, models and methods by which designers may provide better human-oriented computing technology systems; and, cooperating with other groups, inside and outside IFIP, to promote user-orientation and humanization in system design. Thus, TC13 seeks to improve interactions between people and computing technology, to encourage the growth of HCI research and its practice in industry and to disseminate these benefits worldwide.

The main orientation is to place the users at the centre of the development process. Areas of study include: the problems people face when interacting with computing technology; the impact of technology deployment on people in individual and organisational contexts; the determinants of utility, usability, acceptability and user experience; the appropriate allocation of tasks between computing technology and users, especially in the case of autonomous and closed-loop systems; modelling the user, their tasks and the interactive system to aid better system design; and harmonizing the computing technology to user characteristics and needs.

While the scope is thus set wide, with a tendency toward general principles rather than particular systems, it is recognised that progress will only be achieved through both general studies to advance theoretical understanding and specific studies on practical issues (e.g., interface design standards, software system resilience, documentation, training material, appropriateness of alternative interaction technologies, guidelines, the problems of integrating multimedia systems to match system needs and organisational practices, etc.).

IFIP TC13 also stimulates working events and activities through its Working Groups (WGs). The WGs consist of HCI experts from around the world, who seek to expand knowledge and find solutions to HCI issues and concerns within their domains. The list of current TC13 WGs and their area of interest is given below:

- WG 13.1 (Education in HCI and HCI Curricula) aims to improve HCI education at all levels of higher education, coordinate and unite efforts to develop HCI curricula and promote HCI teaching.
- WG 13.2 (Methodology for User-Centered System Design) aims to foster research, dissemination of information and good practice in the methodical application of HCI to software engineering.
- WG 13.3 (Human Computer Interaction, Disability and Aging) aims to make HCI designers aware of the needs of people with disabilities and older people and encourage development of information systems and tools permitting adaptation of interfaces to specific users.
- WG 13.4/WG2.7 (User Interface Engineering) investigates the nature, concepts and construction of user interfaces for software systems, using a framework for reasoning about interactive systems and an engineering model for developing user interfaces.
- WG 13.5 (Resilience, Reliability, Safety and Human Error in System Development) seeks a frame- work for studying human factors relating to systems failure, develops leading edge techniques in hazard analysis and safety engineering of computer-based systems, and guides international accreditation activities for safety-critical systems.
- WG 13.6 (Human-Work Interaction Design) aims at establishing relation- ships between extensive empirical work-domain studies and HCI design. It will promote the use of knowledge, concepts, methods and techniques that enable user studies to procure a better apprehension of the complex interplay between individual, social and organisational contexts and thereby a better understanding of how and why people work in the ways that they do.
- WG 13.7 (Human–Computer Interaction and Visualization) aims to establish a study and research program that will combine both scientific work and practical applications in the fields of Human–Computer Interaction and Visualization. It will integrate several additional aspects of further research areas, such as scientific visualization, data mining, information design, computer graphics, cognition sciences, perception theory, or psychology, into this approach.
- WG 13.8 (Interaction Design and International Development) aims to support and develop the research, practice and education capabilities of HCI in institutions and organisations based around the world taking into account their diverse local needs and cultural perspective.
- WG 13.9 (Interaction Design and Children) aims to support practitioners, regulators and researchers to develop the study of interaction design and children across international contexts.
- WG 13.10 (Human-Centred Technology for Sustainability) aims to promote research, design, development, evaluation, and deployment of human-centred technology to encourage sustainable use of resources in various domains.
- WG 13.11/12.1 (Human-Centred Intelligent Interactive Systems), established under the auspices of both TC13 (HCI) and TC12 (AI), aims to shift the focus to how AI can empower humans and support their endeavours. By developing scientific foundations for Human-Centred Intelligent Interactive Systems, it emphasises the human side of the interaction between people and AI.

Further information is available at the IFIP TC13 website: http://ifip-tc13.org/.

IFIP WG 13.2 Members

Officers

Chair

Regina Bernhaupt   Eindhoven University of Technology, The Netherlands

Vice-chair

Carmelo Ardito   LUM Giuseppe Degennaro University, Italy

Secretary

Stefan Sauer   Paderborn University, Germany

Members

Balbir Barn	Middlesex University London, UK
Cristian Bogdan	KTH Royal Institute of Technology, Sweden
Birgit Bomsdorf	Fulda University of Applied Sciences, Germany
Jan Borchers	RWTH Aachen University, Germany
John Carroll	Penn State University, USA
Bertrand David	École Centrale de Lyon, France
Anke Dittmar	University of Rostock, Germany
Xavier Ferre	Universidad Politécnica de Madrid, Spain
Holger Fischer	Atruvia AG, Germany
Peter Forbrig	University of Rostock, Germany
Tom Gross	University of Bamberg, Germany
Jan Gulliksen	KTH Royal Institute of Technology, Sweden
Anirudha Joshi	IIT Bombay, India
Kati Kuusinen	Technical University of Denmark, Denmark
Rosa Lanzilotti	University of Bari Aldo Moro, Italy
Marta Kristín Lárusdóttir	Reykjavik University, Iceland
Célia Martinie	Paul Sabatier University, France
Syed Bilal Naqvi	Lappeenranta University of Technology, Finland
Philippe Palanque	Paul Sabatier University, France

Organization

General Conference Chairs

Marta Kristín Lárusdóttir Reykjavik University, Iceland
Bilal Naqvi Lappeenranta University of Technology, Finland

Technical Paper Chairs

Carmelo Ardito LUM Giuseppe Degennaro University, Italy
Regina Bernhaupt Eindhoven University of Technology, The
  Netherlands
Stefan Sauer Paderborn University, Germany

Demos and Posters Chair

Bilal Naqvi Lappeenranta University of Technology, Finland

Discussion Forum for PhD Students Chair

Marta Kristín Lárusdóttir Reykjavik University, Iceland

Program Committee

Balbir Barn Middlesex University London, UK
Birgit Bomsdorf Fulda University of Applied Sciences, Germany
John Carroll Penn State University, USA
Anke Dittmar University of Rostock, Germany
Peter Forbrig University of Rostock, Germany
Jan Gulliksen KTH Royal Institute of Technology, Sweden
Anirudha Joshi IIT Bombay, India
Rosa Lanzilotti University of Bari Aldo Moro, Italy
Célia Martinie Paul Sabatier University, France
Philippe Palanque Paul Sabatier University, France
Fabio Paternò ISTI-CNR, Italy

Antonio Piccinno	University of Bari Aldo Moro, Italy
José Luís Silva	Instituto Universitário de Lisboa, Portugal
Alistair Sutcliffe	University of Manchester, UK
Ricardo Tesoriero	University of Castilla-La Mancha, Spain
Jan Van den Bergh	Hasselt University, Belgium
Marco Winckler	Université Côte d'Azur, France
Enes Yigitbas	Paderborn University, Germany

Additional Reviewers

Angela Lombardi   Politecnico di Bari, Italy

Local Organizing Committee

Marta Kristín Lárusdóttir	Reykjavik University, Iceland
Anna Sigríður Islind	Reykjavik University, Iceland
Grischa Liebel	Reykjavik University, Iceland
Ioana Visescu	Reykjavik University, Iceland

Web and Publicity Team

Ioana Visescu   Reykjavik University, Iceland

Supporters and Partners

Supporters

HÁSKÓLINN Í REYKJAVÍK
REYKJAVIK UNIVERSITY

Partners

International Federation for Information Processing

Contents

PhD Student Discussion Forum

Posters

Demos

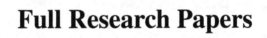

Full Research Papers

Accessibility Knowledge Viewed Through the Lens of the Stakeholders

Dena Hussain[✉] [iD] and Jan Gulliksen [iD]

Media Technology and Interaction Design, School of Electrical Engineering and Computer
Science, KTH Royal Institute of Technology, Stockholm, Sweden
{denah,gulliksen}@kth.se

Abstract. Web accessibility awareness among development teams has increased
with initiatives like the Web Content Accessibility Guidelines (WCAG) and more
user-centered development methods. While this awareness has grown, there is a
need to explore accessibility from diverse stakeholder perspectives when applying
these standards. This study presents findings from a survey of 47 stakeholders who
used an internal customized digital tool with design components like patterns,
principles, and graphic profiles. This study aimed to gain a deeper understanding
of the stakeholders' experiences when developing accessible public web services
with the support of a customized ICT tool. Results show that a knowledge-based
digital platform, which is used for assessing and communicating accessibility
requirements, can streamline the development process and establish a common
baseline for all stakeholders involved in developing accessible public web services.
This research highlights the importance of having a holistic perspective from
various stakeholders on accessibility and the impact of tailored tools in fostering
inclusivity and compliance with web accessibility standards.

Keywords: Digital inclusion · Accessibility · Agile development · Web Content
Accessibility Guidelines · Stakeholder knowledge · Information and
Communication Technologies (ICT)

1 Introduction

Identifying users' needs and reducing the gap between the users' perspective and other
stakeholder perspectives can be challenging. An example of such challenges is when
developing accessible web-based public services that follow the Web Content Accessibility Guidelines (WCAG) [1]. Specifically, when developing accessibility requirements,
which can be challenging due to a) the various user requirements [13], and b) where
direct interaction and involvement of users can be challenging due to limitations in
finding end users to volunteer to participate in the development process of public web
services. According to previous studies [2–4], "*project stakeholders are the direct participants and affected people of the construction projects*". Furthermore, stakeholders are
all those inside and outside an organization who have a vested interest in decisions faced
by the organization in adopting and collaborating to construct projects [5]. Developing

M. K. Lárusdóttir et al. (Eds.): HCSE 2024, LNCS 14793, pp. 3–25, 2024.
https://doi.org/10.1007/978-3-031-64576-1_1

accessibility requirements requires effective collaboration among various stakeholders from different domains [5]. Thus, Information and Communication Technologies (ICT) have been introduced to the development process, to create effective communication and knowledge-sharing [6–8]. Furthermore, using an ICT platform can support the various stakeholders involved in the development process. According to Yang [10], knowledge sharing *"occurs when an individual is willing to assist as well as to learn from others in the development of new competencies"* [9]. Knowledge refers to a related *"set of behaviors, which contribute to knowledge and information sharing and helping others share their knowledge"* [10]. This study aims to examine how organizations address the development of accessibility requirements by using a customized ICT platform for their stakeholders, as a means to create awareness and constructive processes for developing accessible public web services.

2 Aim

This study aims to gain a deeper understanding of the stakeholders' experiences when developing accessible public web services utilizing a customized ICT tool.

3 Background

Accessible web-based services for job-seeking play a vital role in providing equal opportunities for all. These platforms contribute to addressing the digital divide by ensuring that everyone [11], regardless of their background or abilities, has the opportunity to participate in the digital job-seeking landscape [12]. Moreover, various stakeholders play a crucial role in addressing the digital divide and ensuring that public web-based services are accessible to all [13]. To do so, collaborative efforts from these stakeholders are essential in creating an equitable digital landscape [14]. Their perspectives and actions collectively contribute to efforts to create an inclusive digital landscape ensuring that all individuals have the opportunity to benefit from these platforms [11, 15].

3.1 Digital Accessibility

Digital accessibility refers to the process of ensuring that devices and/or services such as web-based services, are available and navigable for individuals with disabilities or other special needs. Moreover, digital accessibility has had a significant impact on society, promoting innovation and societal change. To develop accessibility requirements the World Wide Web Consortium (W3C) [16] issued guidelines to ensure digital content is accessible to individuals with disabilities. These guidelines provide a framework for web developers to create content (WCAG) as a recommendation for designing, developing, and testing a product [17]. Introducing challenges to the various stakeholders involved in the development process such as how accessibility is defined and addressed from the various stakeholders and their perspectives. This can lead to inconsistencies and gaps in accessibility implementation, thus introducing the need for clear communication channels and collaboration among stakeholders.

The digitalization of processes implies adapting to new technological solutions adding advantages to organizations; such new digital technologies embrace ICT systems such as virtualization, mobility, and analytical systems [15, 18]. However, it has also posed challenges related to privacy, security, and the need for digital skills, which results in the problem of the digital divide [14]. Digital accessibility thus is an important aspect when addressing the digital divide [19]. To bridge the digital divide, efforts are being made to improve digital infrastructure and provide access to digital services [11]. It is essential to ensure that all are part of the digital age and that everyone has equal opportunities to benefit from the advantages of digitalization [15, 19]. Therefore, it is important to recognize that the digital divide is not only a matter of inaccessibility but also social, economic, and cultural factors that affect access to ICTs, or their capability to use them effectively [18, 20]. This includes including users of all diverse needs, and disabilities. [21] *"Accessibility is a quality concept that is interpreted differently depending on the design approach used for the development"* [22]. Blyth, defines stakeholder domain knowledge as *"the best source of requirements is domain knowledge, and the best source of domain knowledge is stakeholders. Consequently, requirements can be derived from the domain knowledge owned by the stakeholders"* [4]. This knowledge is often compiled into sets of guidelines. Many attempts are to make collections of guidelines useful when developing, but often the practical advice is a bit too far away to become used in reality. While there are numerous guides for usability and accessibility standards [23], development teams rarely consult these standards and/or guidelines to find immediate solutions [24]. Most guidelines are perceived as complex, difficult to navigate, and filled with extensive information and details, making it challenging to determine what to focus on and what is directly applicable [25]. For instance, resources like the Web Content Accessibility Guidelines (WCAG), international standards, and other references often demand a high level of prerequisite knowledge from stakeholders to fully benefit from their guidance. Therefore, developing accessibility requirements requires various domain knowledge and stakeholder awareness of the challenges associated with the development process. These challenges from a development perspective have been addressed by introducing various user-centered development approaches, such as user-centered design (UCD) [26, 27].

3.2 User-Centered Agile Methods (UCA)

User-centered development (UCD) can be seen as a set of methods, techniques, and processes that puts the user in the center of the development process, to accomplish user satisfaction through the production of usable products that meet the users' needs, based on their use, limitations, and abilities [26]. In addition, the introduction of User-Centered Agile methods (UCA) focuses on creating a shared understanding of both the design content and the design process, which emphasizes collaboration [28]. UCA is guided by knowledge of the end users, their contexts of use, and their needs [11]. However, these methods mentioned require direct contact with the end users, which in many cases is hard to achieve if at all possible and can create challenges. Usability and accessibility often have the same goals or intended outcomes. UCA software development methods provide many qualities that potentially can enhance the opportunities to deliver digital inclusion [29], by creating a flexible coding environment for the developers and creating continuous increment deployments that facilitate the integration of new code [30]. Furthermore, integrating UX design which focuses on the user's needs with activities in an agile environment can create challenges for the developer due to the different stakeholders' domains [30]. The collaboration and expertise of internal stakeholders are crucial in shaping the quality of the end software product, successful communication is fundamental to achieving software quality. A frequent challenge when developing accessibility software is how to efficiently present the essential knowledge to the involved stakeholders in a way that can be applied in the software engineering process [31]. Therefore, this study aimed to conduct a more systematic examination to gain a deeper understanding of a customized ICT toll that effectively served as guidance when developing accessible public web services [32]. In our study, we categorize stakeholders into two main groups, based on their domains and involvement in the development process:

- Development Team (D): This cluster comprises individuals directly involved in ensuring product quality as well as creating and shaping the software. They play crucial roles in ensuring software quality by writing code, testing it, designing user-friendly interfaces, and planning the software's structure and can include Developers, Quality Assurance (QA) Teams, Designers, and Architects.
- Management Team (M): This cluster represents individuals involved directly in the process aspect of software quality. Overseeing the development process, ensuring that it stays on schedule, adheres to quality standards, and coordinates the efforts of the development team. Their role is essential in maintaining software quality through effective project planning and management, which can include Project Managers, Product Owners, and Group leaders.

3.3 Case Setting

The focus of this case study is gaining an understanding of stakeholders involved in utilizing a customized ICT platform when developing public web services in the governmental sector for job-seeking, the Swedish public employment service "Arbetsförmedlingen", which has offices all over the country. The majority of Swedish Public Employment Service organizations' services are managed digitally to make it easier for their clients to manage and gain more control over their situation. A fundamental part of this organization's role is to provide job seekers who find it difficult to enter the labour market with the right tools and thus contribute to preventing exclusion and increasing employment. Therefore, the organization has developed its own customized in-house ICT tool, which is used by all development teams including UX designers, developers, project leaders, and others who work with developing and maintaining the organization's public web services, this customized in-house ICT tool is named "Design System" [33].

3.3.1 The "Design System"

The customized ICT tool "Design System" is one part of a larger handbook publicly available to support the overall development within the Swedish public employment service "Arbetsförmedlingen", which is utilized to create a standardized approach to develop the organization's public web services to meet both the legal requirements and brand guidelines. Moreover, the objective of creating a platform with a digital identity

[34], can be defined as creating a digital platform that has a unique identity, profile, and image, to be used by the organization stakeholders who share a common objective to collaborate and develop accessible services. According to the organization, the design system "*consists of processes, tools, code, and design. It supports tools and processes for streamlining product development, primarily through capabilities that support the daily work performed by developers, designers, and product managers*". As illustrated, the tool is simplistic in its overall layout and features, the following figures below are screenshots from the current platform (See Fig. 1).

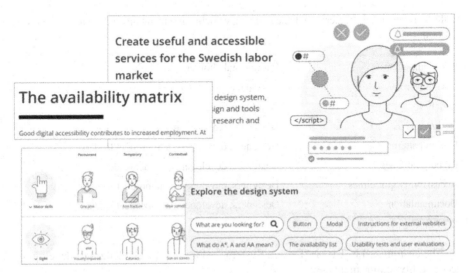

Fig. 1. Translated screenshots from the organization's customized ICT platform "Design System" [33]

Initially reviewing the platform, what can be observed is that the organization's customized platform consists of the following components:

1. Design Patterns: Design and interaction patterns for how interfaces should be designed to solve specific needs, developing design patterns and principles.
2. Design principles: Framework for what a designer should and should not do in different situations, developing design patterns and principles.
3. Graphic profile: Tools and guidelines for how teams work with the Employment Service's brand and graphic profile.
4. Component library: The component library is divided into design and code.
5. Language and translations: Guidelines for how to relate and work with languages other than Swedish.
6. Accessibility guidelines: Knowledge support for how to create solutions for everyone [33].

According to the organization" *Design systems is about designing for scale, making design systematic.*" [...] "*The primary motivations behind organizations embracing design systems encompass efficiency, consistency, scalability, collaboration, accessibility and general cost savings in development and management"*. Furthermore, the organization states that the design system components can be traced back to 2012, and since 2019 a team of 14 has been dedicated to developing and maintaining this customized ICT platform. The design system can be considered as a building block that brings together reusable tools such as components, design patterns, design tokens, processes, and guidelines in one place, creating a common collaborative work environment. The internal stakeholders according to the organization are listed in Table 1 below:

Table 1. Internal stakeholders are dedicated to developing and maintaining this customized ICT platform.

ICT Component	Internal stakeholder
Design Library	Designers
Codebase	Developers
Design tokens	Designers and developers
Design patterns	Designers, developers, and product leaders
Brand guidelines	Designers, developers, product leaders
Accessibility guidelines	Designers, developers, and product leaders
Documentation	Designers, developers, and product leaders

The customized ICT tool, "Design System," addresses the challenges of developing accessibility requirements by:

1. Creating a standardized approach: The tool provides a standardized approach to developing public web services, ensuring that accessibility considerations are integrated into the development process from the outset. By offering predefined templates, design elements, and code snippets that align with accessibility standards, the tool helps developers and designers meet various user requirements without needing extensive prior knowledge.
2. Centralized guidance: The "Design System" serves as a central repository of accessibility guidelines, making it easier for stakeholders to access and implement best practices. Instead of relying solely on individual expertise, developers, designers, and project leaders can refer to the tool for clear and concise guidance on accessibility requirements.
3. Collaboration and feedback: Despite challenges in directly involving end-users, the tool facilitates collaboration among stakeholders by providing a platform for sharing feedback and insights. Through features such as user testing modules or feedback loops, developers and designers can gather input from diverse perspectives, even if direct interaction with end-users is limited.
4. Simplified implementation: Recognizing that accessibility standards like the Web Content Accessibility Guidelines (WCAG) may require specialized knowledge, the

"Design System" aims to simplify implementation by translating complex requirements into practical, actionable steps. By breaking down specific technical terminologies and providing contextual explanations, the tool empowers stakeholders to apply accessibility principles effectively, regardless of their level of expertise.

Overall, the "Design System" aims to bridge the gap between accessibility requirements and stakeholder capabilities, enabling the organization to develop inclusive public web services, despite challenges in user interaction and prerequisite knowledge.

4 Method

The study aims to provide insights into the efficacy of the "Design System" in addressing accessibility challenges and its potential to improve the development of accessible public web services. The following section describes the data collection methods used during this study. With the objective of evaluating the effectiveness of the customized ICT tool, "Design System," in addressing the challenges of developing accessibility requirements for public web services, the study seeks to understand the participants' experiences and perceptions when utilizing this ICT platform to develop accessible web services.

4.1 Data Collection

The data collection process was initiated by investigating the participants/the organization's preferences, for example, the organization's language preference, and if there was a preferred digital survey tool to use. The survey consisted of a combination of closed-ended and Likert-scale questions. The questions were designed to capture participants' perceptions, experiences, and preferences related to their perspectives regarding the ICT platform. An online anonymous survey was conducted based on these three stages, as illustrated in Fig. 2.

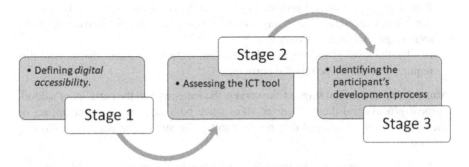

Fig. 2. An overview of the data collection stages

The survey questionnaires were organized based on the three analysis stages and digitally distributed to a total of 250 potential participants via the organization's internal intranet to reach all users of the customized ICT platform.

- **Stage One:** In stage one, the aim was to better understand the participant's characterization of the term *digital accessibility*. Therefore, the first question in the survey introduced several different definitions in the format of a multiple-choice matrix. Here, participants could assess the different definitions using a scale; strongly agree; agree; neutral; disagree; strongly disagree. The definitions included in the survey were:

  a. Uniformity and trust in a digital service.
  b. The extent to which a service can be used by a population with the widest range of characteristics
  c. It is providing equitable opportunity, regardless of a person's abilities or circumstances
  d. It is about compliance with the rules, regulations, or laws of accessibility set forth by organizations, agencies, or communities.
  e. It is the ability to identify and respond to the user's ability to access, understand, or interact fully and productively with a digital service
  f. It is a quality concept that is interpreted differently depending on the design approach used for the development

- **Stage Two**: Moreover, it was important to identify if the participants had experienced developing accessibility requirements in previous and/or current projects, therefore participants were asked if they had experience developing accessibility requirements. Therefore, in the second stage, the main focus was to capture the participant's experiences utilizing the in-house customized ICT platform "Design System", focusing on capturing the participants' perspective of using the tool. To do so, questions focused on assessing the participants' experience about how the platform supported them during the process of developing accessibility requirements, by investigating the following three aspects.

  a. If the level of information provided by the platform supported the participant to understand accessibility requirements.
  b. If the level of information provided by the platform included supported the participants in developing and designing accessibility requirements for web development and design. And if it was easy to use.
  c. Finally, the level of information the platform includes to assess the accessibility requirements developed by the participants.

- **Stage three**: In the final stage of the survey, the focus was on the participant's development process and their perceived roles since both can have a direct impact on the development of accessibility requirements. The survey included the following questions:

  a. What is your current job title/role? The participants were presented with several different job titles and development processes that they could choose from, including roles representing the development team, such as (Software developers, Software architects, UX designers, etc.…) and roles representing the management team, such as (Team leader, Project manager, System administrator, IT engineer, etc..).

b. Moreover, participants were asked what development method they used, such as; (Agile, Lean, waterfall, Human-centered design, User experience design, etc...).
c. Questions regarding the platform that could be affected based on the participants' role include:

- If the platform supports the participant in assessing the finalized accessibility requirements developed.
- If the platform supports the participant's communication during the development process.

4.2 Data Analysis

An inductive quantitative analysis was performed, conducting quantitative research method often translates into the use of statistical analysis to create a connection between what is known and what can be learned through research [35]. Whereas, collecting and analysing data using quantitative strategies requires an understanding of the relationships among variables using either descriptive or inferential statistics [36, 37], allowing the narrative or theory to emerge from the raw data and coming up with new theories, ideas, or concepts [38]. Given the diverse sample of participants, subgroup analyses were used [39] to explore potential significant patterns within specific subgroups based on their roles. The collected data was systematically organized into datasets and subjected to an inductive analysis of quantitative data [40, 41]. Deriving patterns, and themes from the data [42], for instance, to capture how accessibility requirements are developed, the data sets were grouped based on several different factors such as a) the participant's role in the organization, b) the participant's experiences utilizing the in-house customized ICT platform "Design System", and finally c) the development processes used by the participants, allowing for the emergence of new understandings from the data itself. The following section describes the analysis process of each data set and the coded themes generated.

1. **The participant's role in the organization:** it was important during the survey to capture the various stakeholders' roles that utilize this ICT platform and their role in the organization. The aim of capturing and creating a data set based on the participant's role was to understand their perspective of the tool and if it supports them during the development process of accessibility requirements. To do so participants were given a predefined list of roles. However, they were allowed to fill in their roles if needed in addition to elaborating on the details of the individual roles and their domains.
2. **The participant's experiences:** The second data set focused on the participant's experiences utilizing the in-house customized ICT platform "Design System" about their roles and how they assessed the platform based on their domain and understanding of accessibility requirements. Furthermore, accessibility requirements are developed based on various guidelines and legal requirements regarding digital accessibility and are therefore developed based on various components that are facilitated, analysed, formulated, and tested by various stakeholders, thus the stakeholder's use of the ICT platform can vary according to their domain.
3. **The development process used:** Since accessibility requirements are developed in different stages of the development process this means each stakeholder has a specific

impact on the development process and therefore the process used can have an impact on the stakeholders' experience using the tool.

Figure 3 illustrates an overview of the coding themes generated to create clusters of data, which are discussed in the results section of this study. Identifying the stakeholder's knowledge and domain can influence their level of awareness and understanding of requirements when developing accessibility qualities.

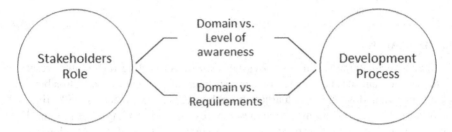

Fig. 3. The analysis process of the main data sets grouped and potential interdependencies between stakeholders' roles and the development process.

This approach allowed for a better understanding of variations and similarities between different fields and provides insights into the impact of field-specific factors on the survey outcomes, thus based on the two stakeholder clusters mentioned in the background section, results were grouped and analysed based on the perspectives of the development stakeholder cluster (D) and the management stakeholder cluster (M).

5   Results

As mentioned previously this case study is based on investigating a current in-house customized national organization ICT platform, which is used by various development teams consisting of various stakeholders, focusing on developing public web-based service. Creating a toolbox, which includes different components, design patterns, design tokens, and clarifications and information to support the stakeholder's understanding of why these components are important to have in addition to how to use them. During this study it was important to analyse the survey results based on understanding and capturing the different stakeholders' perspectives concerning their needs by using a customized ICT platform, hence to reach 250 participants 47 users of the platform responded, representing 18.8%. As mentioned in the method section the stakeholders were clustered into two main groups, the development stakeholder group, and the management stakeholder group, as illustrated in Table 2.

5.1   Stakeholder Domain vs Level of Awareness

The initial question in the survey was aimed at gaining an understanding of the different participants' experiences based on their domain while developing accessibility

Table 2. Overview of participants that were included in the study, grouped and categorized into two main clusters.

Development Cluster (D)		Management Cluster (M)	
Participants role	No.	Participants role	No.
Accessibility Expert	1	Agile change management	1
IT Engineer	2	Business Developer	1
Service designer	1	Educational producer	2
User experience (UX) analyst	4	Group leader	2
UX designers	17	Intranet content coordinator	1
Software Developer	8	Product owner	1
Software developer; UX designer	2	Project manager	4
Sub Total	35		12
Total			47

requirements. Hence capturing the participant's perspective on the definition of digital accessibility in the initial stages was important, the definitions included in the survey and response percentages are presented in Table 3.

Table 3. Participant responses rate to statements regarding digital accessibility perceptions.

Statements	Absolutely Agree	Agree	Neutral	Disagree	Absolutely Disagree
A. Uniformity and trust for a digital service	25.5%	46.8%	19.1%	6.4%	2.1%
B. The extent to which a service can be used by a population with the widest set of characteristics	53.2%	36.2%	6.4%	2.1%	2.1%
C. It provides equal opportunities, regardless of a person's abilities or conditions	78.7%	19.1%	2.1%	0.0%	0.0%
D. It is about compliance with the rules, regulations, or laws for accessibility specified by organizations, authorities, or associations	61.7%	23.4%	14.9%	0.0%	0.0%
E. It is about the ability to identify and respond to the user's ability to access, understand or fully productively interact with a digital service	66.0%	27.7%	4.3%	0.0%	2.1%

(*continued*)

Table 3. (*continued*)

Statements	Absolutely Agree	Agree	Neutral	Disagree	Absolutely Disagree
F. It is a quality concept that is interpreted differently depending on which design method is used for development	19.1%	34.0%	19.1%	8.5%	19.1%

Based on the definitions that all stakeholders "absolutely agreed", "agreed", "neutral", "disagreed", or "absolutely disagreed" are illustrated in Fig. 4. What can be established is that the majority absolutely /strongly agreed on options C = 78.7%, D = 61.7%, and E = 66%. Based on the data representing the definitions that all stakeholders absolutely and strongly agreed on. They defined digital accessibility as providing equitable opportunity, regardless of a person's abilities or circumstances, and complying with the rules, regulations, or laws of accessibility set forth by organizations, agencies, or communities. Furthermore, it is the ability to identify and respond to the user's ability to access, understand, or interact fully and productively with a digital service, extending to which a service can be used by a population with the widest range of characteristics.

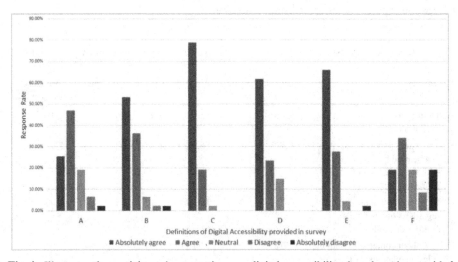

Fig. 4. Illustrates the participants' perspectives on digital accessibility, based on the provided definition in Table 3 based on the provided scale in the survey.

Moreover, it was important to identify if the participant had worked with accessibility requirements before, as the survey indicated that the majority (62.2%) of participants had experience developing accessibility requirements. As illustrated in Fig. 5, the survey results focused on capturing the participants' experiences working with accessibility requirements based on the two main clusters representing the stakeholder's role; development cluster (D) and management cluster (M). What was realized is that 98% of all the participants have had some experience working with accessibility requirements. Moreover, 100% of the management cluster had a level of experience, while only 2% of the development cluster had never worked with accessibility requirements.

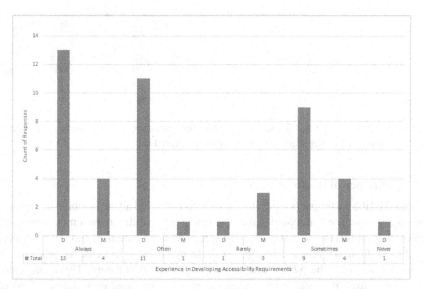

Fig. 5. Participants' experiences working with accessibility requirements based on the two main clusters representing the stakeholder's role; development cluster (D) and management (M).

5.2   Stakeholder Domain vs Requirements

The objective of the following section is to capture the participants' experiences utilizing the tool based on their roles and responsibilities, focusing on the platform's ability to support users in why and how to develop accessibility requirements. Furthermore, experience using an ICT tool varies from user to user and this can depend on various factors such as years of working experience and stakeholder's role. What was observed in the survey data is that the majority of the participants (66%) with a score between the ranges 8 to 10 indicated that the platform's information regarding how to develop accessibility requirements is efficient as illustrated in Fig. 6. Further analysis of the 66% based on the stakeholder clusters illustrates that 71% (25 out of 35 development clusters represented the highest scores in total. In the Management Cluster, only 6 out of 12 felt that the platform supported their ability to understand how to develop accessibility features, this may indicate that the platform supports only the development stakeholder's domain effectively.

5.3   Stakeholder Role vs Domain Knowledge

When investigating the customized tool from a knowledge support perspective two questions were asked as mentioned in the method section which were:

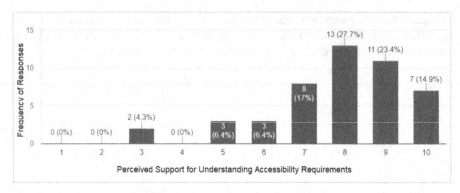

Fig. 6. Participants' responses when asked if the platform supports their ability to understand how to develop accessibility requirements and their perceived support.

5.3.1 Sufficiency of the Information Included

We first asked the participants if they thought the tool covered all the essential information regarding information that would make developing accessibility requirements sufficient. The survey discloses that a total of (57.4%) agreed with the statement and (19%) strongly agreed (See Table 4) When investigating these numbers in more detail what can be realized is that from the 57.4% that agreed 46.8 were developers. The management cluster had a high percentage of neutral opinions (8.5%) and only the development cluster stakeholders disagreed with the tool providing sufficient information. This can indicate that the information the tool provided focuses on product quality and thus does not support the stakeholders involved the supporting the product process. Moreover, when investigating this subgroup deeper, what can be revealed is that 25 out of 37 indicated that they use an agile development process, which overall supports changes in requirements and focuses on individual roles over processes.

Table 4. Stakeholders' responses when asked if the tool provided them with sufficient information when developing accessibility requirements.

Response options	Cluster response rate %		Total %
	D	M	
Absolutely agree	12.8%	6.4%	19.1%
Agree	46.8%	10.6%	57.4%
Disagree	8.5%	0%	8.5%
Neutral	6.4%	8.5%	14.9%

5.3.2   Feasibility of the Information Included

The second stage focused on asking the participant if the information in the platform was easy to follow, the survey illustrates that 49% of the participants assessed the platform with a score between the ranges of 8 to 10 (See Fig. 7). When analysing these results what was found is that from the 49%, 38.30% of the participants were from the development cluster (D), while only 11% were from the management cluster (M). Moreover, 49% of these participants worked with an agile development process, which indicates the impact of working with a development process that adapts to changes and supports the stakeholder's knowledge building.

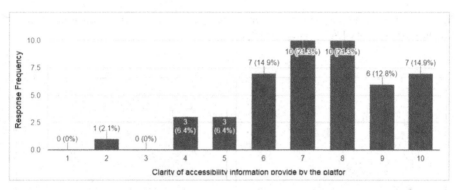

Fig. 7. Participants' response rate of the platform when asked if the information provided on the platform was easy to use and efficient.

Furthermore, it was important to investigate how the tool supports stakeholders to assess the accessibility requirements developed. Therefore, the participants were asked if the platform supported them in evaluating the requirements developed based on the information provided regarding the established WCAG accessibility guidelines. As illustrated in Fig. 8, 72% of the participants gave the platform a score between the ranges 7 to 10, investigating this sub-set further what was indicated is that 51% of this rate was the development cluster (D).

What was also noted was that 72.3% gave the tool a score between the ranges of 7 to 10, and 53.19% of that percentage was from the development cluster. This indicates that the majority of developers rely on the platform to support their role when utilizing the WCAG guidelines and translating these guidelines into accessibility specifications. This can be interpreted as either the platform lacking details that support this stakeholder group and/or the current WCAG standards being viewed as a challenge for this specific stakeholder group. Moreover, this suggests that there is room for improvement in the customized ICT tool to support the stakeholders when assessing accessibility requirements (See Fig. 9).

These key results suggest a generally positive perception of the platform's effectiveness in supporting accessibility development and evaluation, with the majority of participants expressing agreement or strong agreement across various aspects, as illustrated in Table 5.

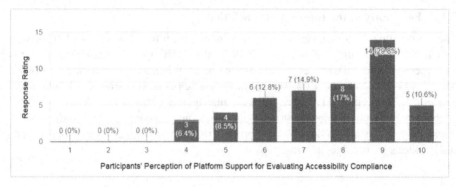

Fig. 8. The participants' response rates when evaluating the information provided on the platform regarding the established WCAG accessibility.

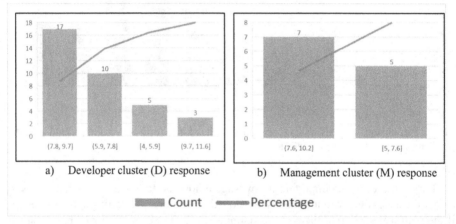

a)   Developer cluster (D) response   b)   Management cluster (M) response

Count ━━━Percentage

Fig. 9. Pareto chart illustrating the individual clusters' response when evaluating the information provided regarding the established WCAG accessibility is effective

Table 5. A summary of the key results from the survey data regarding participant reflections regarding the platform.

Survey questions focusing on the platform	Absolutely agree	Agree	Neutral	Disagree
• Does this platform support your ability to understand how to develop accessibility requirements?	21.28%	57.45%	17.02%	4.26%
• Does the platform provide you with sufficient information about accessibility requirements for web design and development?	17.02%	55.32%	19.15%	8.51%

(*continued*)

Table 5. (*continued*)

Survey questions focusing on the platform	Absolutely agree	Agree	Neutral	Disagree
• Do you find the information about accessibility requirements provided on the platform easy to follow?	19.15%	55.32%	19.15%	6.38%
• Does this platform support your ability to evaluate what you have developed to be in line with established accessibility guidelines?	21.28%	55.32%	21.28%	2.13%

6 Stakeholder Domain vs. Development Process

Participants were asked if the platform supported them in assessing the development process and if it supported stakeholders' communication, the overview response indicates that 72.3% = 53.2% (D) + 19.1% (M) rate the platform between 7 to 10, specifying that the platform supports in having better communication with other stakeholders regarding accessibility requirements. Investigating this sub-group in more detail what was established is that 94% of this sub-group used either Agile or user-centered processes, where 71% = 53% (D) + 18% (M) used Agile processes and 24% = 18% (D) + 6%(M) used UCD process (See Fig. 10).

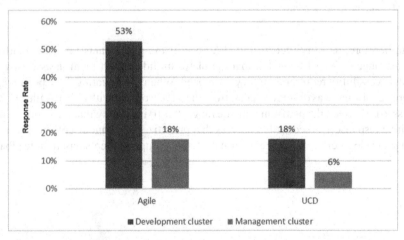

Fig. 10. Participants' response rate when asked if the platform supported them in assessing accessibility requirements, based on their cluster groups' development team (D), the management team (M), and the development process.

This indicates that the platform is providing means for various stakeholders to discuss and assess accessibility requirements, in addition to supporting their individual needs in evaluating how they develop accessibility requirements based on their roles and responsibilities. Furthermore, when analysing this data based on the main data set (quality vs process, the two main cluster groups, $62\% = 45\%$ (D) + 17% (M) of these participants worked with an agile process, while $30\% = 23\%$ (D) + 6% (M) used a user-center design approach (UCD), leaving 9% using mixed methods such as waterfall (See Fig. 11).

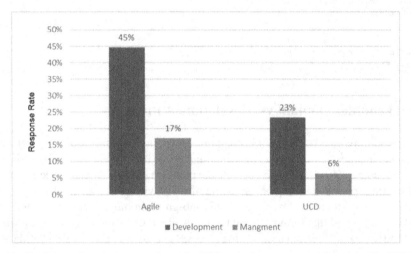

Fig. 11. Participants' response rate when asked if the platform supported them in evaluating how they develop accessibility based on their cluster groups' development team (D), the management team (M), and the development process.

Furthermore, as illustrated in Fig. 12, 66% of the participants rated the platform with the range of 7 to 10 and felt that the platform did support them in assessing the various accessibility requirements they developed. When investigating these percentages in more detail what was observed is that from the 91% working with either Agile or UCD process, 61.2% rated the platform with the range 7 to 10 indicating that the majority with a positive response worked with a process that prioritizes continuous collaboration and iterative development, emphasize the use of iterative improvements based on feedback.

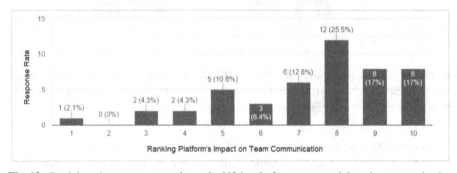

Fig. 12. Participant's response rate when asked if the platform supported them in communicating accessibility requirements during the development process.

All of these are essential for incorporating accessibility requirements into the process of developing publicly accessible web services. In summary, when assessing how the platform supports the development process as listed in Table 6, the majority of participants felt that the ICT platform supported the development process.

Table 6. Summary of survey data assessing if the ICT tool supported the various stakeholders during development the process.

Survey questions focusing on the platform	Overall response percentage rate (%)
Does this platform support your ability to assess whether you are Done with accessibility requirements during the development process?	70.1%
Do you feel that this platform improves communication between you and your team when developing accessibility requirements?	67.8%

7 Discussion

The need for inclusive platforms for job-seeking aims to create an environment that fosters diversity, equity, and accessibility for job seekers of all backgrounds. In this discussion, we will explore the key benefits, challenges, and implications of inclusive job-seeking platforms. This study aimed to gain a better understanding of ICT tools for accessibility, their role in the knowledge building for the stakeholders, and their effect when developing accessibility requirements. It was particularly important in this study to understand if these platforms interfere with the stakeholders' creativity. To do so we conducted a survey study among developers working with accessibility requirements in the Swedish Employment Service. The survey data on participants' perceptions of digital accessibility reveals a consensus on several key discussion points as listed in Table 7.

Firstly, there's a strong emphasis on the need for digital services to be uniformly accessible and trustworthy, underlining the importance of consistency and reliability in digital offerings. Additionally, participants overwhelmingly agree on the necessity of inclusivity, stressing that digital accessibility should cater to a wide range of characteristics to ensure equal opportunities for all users, regardless of their abilities or conditions. While there's recognition of the importance of complying with accessibility regulations, there's also a call for discussions on whether legal requirements suffice or if higher standards should be set to enhance accessibility further. Moreover, the acknowledgment of user-centered design principles highlights the importance of understanding and responding to user needs in creating accessible digital experiences. However, the data also reveals different views and perspectives on certain aspects of digital accessibility, which require further exploration. Overall, these findings underscore the multifaceted nature of digital accessibility and the ongoing efforts needed to ensure inclusivity and usability for all users. When investigating the data generated during this case study various factors can

Table 7. Summary of key discussion points based on the survey data provided.

Discussion Point	Summary
Uniformity and Trust	Participants emphasized the importance of digital services being uniformly accessible and trustworthy
Inclusivity	There's consensus on the necessity of digital accessibility catering to a wide range of characteristics, highlighting the importance of inclusivity
Equal Opportunities	The overwhelming agreement indicates a commitment to providing equal opportunities in digital spaces regardless of abilities or conditions
Compliance with Regulations	While adherence to accessibility regulations is recognized, responses open a discussion on whether legal requirements suffice or if higher standards should be set
User-Centered Design	Recognizing user abilities and designing accordingly is crucial, suggesting a focus on user-centered design to ensure accessibility
Interpretation and Quality	Differences in interpreting accessibility indicate a need for clarity and consistency in defining and implementing accessibility standards
Divergent Views	Instances of disagreement and neutrality highlight varying perspectives on what constitutes effective digital accessibility

impact the development process of accessibility requirements, including the stakeholders' domain and development process used. What can be concluded is that there is a clear dependency between the stakeholder role and the development process when investigating the stakeholder's experience utilizing the platform. Based on the analysis method, the themes identified include the majority of the participants reporting positive experiences with agile processes. Alongside various accessibility guidelines and development standards, the complexity of accessibility requirements can overwhelm stakeholders. Thus, a customized platform focusing on specific product needs can support effective development processes. Creating a common knowledge base platform for assessment and communication proves efficient in aiding development, as indicated by this study. Furthermore, Agile and User-Centered Design (UCD) processes are crucial in supporting accessibility requirements. UCD places users with diverse needs at the center, fostering an understanding of their requirements. By integrating accessibility considerations early, UCD helps create inherently accessible products, reducing the need for costly retrofits. These processes serve as effective frameworks for embracing accessibility in development, leading to more accessible digital solutions. Survey results show positive reviews for the organization's customized ICT platform covering various aspects of developing accessible web services.

8 Conclusion

Inclusive platforms for job seeking not only provide practical tools for finding employment but also contribute to a larger movement towards a more equitable and inclusive digital world. By breaking down barriers and promoting diversity, these platforms help create a society where individuals have the opportunity to participate and succeed in the job market. In conclusion, the survey data presents a comprehensive snapshot of participants' perspectives on digital accessibility, highlighting both areas of consensus and points of divergence. The overwhelming agreement on the importance of uniformity, inclusivity, and equal opportunities underscores a shared commitment to creating digital spaces that are accessible to all users, which seemed to be a unanimous perspective for the various stakeholders included. However, the recognition of divergent views suggests a need for ongoing dialogue and collaboration to address varying perspectives and ensure that accessibility efforts are comprehensive and effective. Therefore, stakeholders need to prioritize user-centered design principles and work towards understanding accessibility standards. With different concerns and interdependencies between different stakeholders, it is important to acknowledge the various factors that could add to the challenges of developing accessible public web services. Thus, creating customized ICT platforms that include the various standards and information required for all involved in a project, can support both knowledge sharing and creating a reference point, leading toward effective collaboration among the various types of stakeholders involved. Based on the results of the presented case study, what can be concluded, is that utilizing a customized ICT platform that focuses on providing information that supports various stakeholders developing accessible web service, creates a positive impact on the stakeholders' performance by supporting both various domains and various processes. Creating awareness among stakeholders on the importance of understanding the relationship and interactions between development processes, and accessibility requirements. Future work includes further opportunities to analyse and investigate ICT platforms utilized in similar organizations. In conclusion, creating accessible public web services is not only a legal requirement but also a moral and practical imperative. It ensures that all individuals, regardless of their abilities, can fully participate in the digital world. By prioritizing accessibility, organizations can reach a wider audience and contribute to a more inclusive and equitable society.

Acknowledgments. We would like to thank Arbetsförmedlingen (The Swedish Employment Service) for opening up their activities and letting us research their accessibility practices. Especially we would like to thank all respondents of the survey for their invaluable contribution to the research. A special thank you to Elisabeth Aguilera, the Chief Accessibility Officer (CAO), and Magnus Brodén Product Manager of Design Systems, The Swedish Employment Agency for their collaboration.

References

1. Caldwell, B., et al.: Web content accessibility guidelines (WCAG) 2.0. In: WWW Consortium (W3C), vol. 290, pp. 1–34 (2008)
2. Mok, K.Y., Shen, G.Q., Yang, R.J.: Addressing stakeholder complexity and major pitfalls in large cultural building projects. Int. J. Project Manage. 35(3), 463–478 (2017)
3. Mok, K.Y., et al.: Investigating key challenges in major public engineering projects by a network-theory based analysis of stakeholder concerns: a case study. Int. J. Project Manage. 35(1), 78–94 (2017)
4. Blyth, A.: Using stakeholders, domain knowledge, and responsibilities to specify information systems' requirements. J. Organ. Comput. Electron. Commer. 9(4), 287–296 (1999)
5. Ryan, M.J.: 1.2. 2 the role of stakeholders in requirements elicitation. In INCOSE International Symposium. Wiley Online Library (2014)
6. Wei, C.-P., et al.: Finding experts in online forums for enhancing knowledge sharing and accessibility. Comput. Hum. Behav. 51, 325–335 (2015)
7. Huang, Y., et al.: Exploring the impact of information and communication technology on team social capital and construction project performance. J. Manag. Eng. 36(5), 04020056 (2020)
8. Ipe, M.: Knowledge sharing in organizations: a conceptual framework. Hum. Resour. Dev. Rev. 2(4), 337–359 (2003)
9. Yang, J.T.: The impact of knowledge sharing on organizational learning and effectiveness. J. Knowl. Manag. 11(2), 83–90 (2007)
10. Ahmadi, A., et al.: High-performance, knowledge sharing and ICT skills. Hum. Syst. Manag. 37(3), 271–280 (2018)
11. Vassilakopoulou, P., Hustad, E.: Bridging digital divides: a literature review and research agenda for information systems research. Inf. Syst. Front. 1–15 (2021)
12. Fisk, R.P., et al.: Healing the digital divide with digital inclusion: enabling human capabilities. J. Serv. Res. 10946705221140148 (2022)
13. Johansson, S., Gulliksen, J., Gustavsson, C.: Disability digital divide: the use of the internet, smartphones, computers and tablets among people with disabilities in Sweden. Univ. Access Inf. Soc. 20(1), 105–120 (2021)
14. Cullen, R.: Addressing the digital divide. Online Inf. Rev. 25(5), 311–320 (2001)
15. Vartolomei, V., Avasilcai, S.: Challenges of digitalization process in different industries. Before and after. In: IOP Conference Series: Materials Science and Engineering. IOP Publishing (2019)
16. Web Content Accessibility Guidelines (WCAG) 2.1 (2021). https://www.w3.org/TR/WCAG21/
17. Abuaddous, H.Y., Jali, M.Z., Basir, N.: Web accessibility challenges. Int. J. Adv. Comput. Sci. Appl. (IJACSA) (2016)
18. Arroyo, L.: Implications of digital inclusion: digitalization in terms of time use from a gender perspective. Soc. Incl. 8(2), 180–189 (2020)
19. Jamil, S.: From digital divide to digital inclusion: challenges for wide-ranging digitalization in Pakistan. Telecommun. Policy 45(8), 102206 (2021)
20. Robinson, L., et al.: Digital inclusion across the Americas and Caribbean. Soc. Incl. 8(2), 244–259 (2020)
21. Kulkarni, M.: Digital accessibility: challenges and opportunities. IIMB Manag. Rev. 31(1), 91–98 (2019)
22. Persson, H., et al.: Universal design, inclusive design, accessible design, design for all: different concepts—one goal? On the concept of accessibility—historical, methodological and philosophical aspects. Univ. Access Inf. Soc. 14, 505–526 (2015)

23. Hakala, H.: A Digital Society for All–Defining Accessibility Practices in Agile Software Development (2019)

24. Westin, M.: The municipal challenges of the accessibility act: a study of the challenges in compliance with the Swedish act on accessibility to digital public service within Swedish municipalities (2022)

25. Persson, J.S., et al.: Agile software development and UX design: a case study of integration by mutual adjustment. Inf. Softw. Technol. **152**, 107059 (2022)

26. Larusdottir, M.K., et al.: UCD sprint: a fast process to involve users in the design practices of software companies. Int. J. Hum.–Comput. Interact. 1–18 (2023)

27. Gulliksen, J., et al.: Key principles for user-centred systems design. Behav. Inf. Technol. **22**(6), 397–409 (2003)

28. Brhel, M., et al.: Exploring principles of user-centered agile software development: a literature review. Inf. Softw. Technol. **61**, 163–181 (2015)

29. Kropp, E., Koischwitz, K.: Experiences with user-centered design and agile requirements engineering in fixed-price projects. In: Ebert, A., Humayoun, S.R., Seyff, N., Perini, A., Barbosa, S.D.J. (eds.) UsARE 2012/2014. LNCS, vol. 9312, pp. 47–61. Springer, Cham (2016). https://doi.org/10.1007/978-3-319-45916-5_4

30. Jurca, G., Hellmann, T.D., Maurer, F.: Integrating agile and user-centered design: a systematic mapping and review of evaluation and validation studies of agile-UX. In: 2014 Agile Conference. IEEE (2014)

31. Ciflikli, C., Kahya-Özyirmidokuz, E.: Enhancing product quality of a process. Ind. Manag. Data Syst. **112**(8), 1181–1200 (2012)

32. Ruby, S., Copeland, D.B., Thomas, D.: Agile web development with rails 6. Pragmatic Bookshelf (2020)

33. Design System (2023). https://designsystem.arbetsformedlingen.se. Accessed 03 May 2023

34. White, O.: Digital identification: a key to inclusive growth (2019)

35. Jebb, A.T., Parrigon, S., Woo, S.E.: Exploratory data analysis as a foundation of inductive research. Hum. Resour. Manag. Rev. **27**(2), 265–276 (2017)

36. Soiferman, L.K.: Compare and Contrast Inductive and Deductive Research Approaches. Online Submission (2010)

37. Kamil, M.L.: The current state of quantitative research. Read. Res. Q. **39**(1), 100–107 (2004)

38. Yom, S.: From methodology to practice: Inductive iteration in comparative research. Comp. Pol. Stud. **48**(5), 616–644 (2015)

39. Gulliksen, J., et al.: Making a difference: a survey of the usability profession in Sweden. In: Proceedings of the Third Nordic Conference on Human-Computer Interaction (2004)

40. Williams, T.A., Shepherd, D.A.: Mixed method social network analysis: combining inductive concept development, content analysis, and secondary data for quantitative analysis. Organ. Res. Methods **20**(2), 268–298 (2017)

41. Sánchez-Algarra, P., Anguera, M.T.: Qualitative/quantitative integration in the inductive observational study of interactive behaviour: impact of recording and coding among predominating perspectives. Qual. Quant. **47**, 1237–1257 (2013)

42. Goddard, W., Melville, S.: Research methodology: An introduction. Juta and Company Ltd. (2004)

CM-DIR: A Method to Support the Specification of the User's Dynamic Behavior in Recommender Systems

Carla A. Martins[1], Carina Dorneles[1], Ankica Barišić[2] (iD),
Thiago Rocha Silva[3] (iD), and Marco Winckler[2]([✉]) (iD)

[1] Federal University of Santa Catarina, Florianópolis, Brazil
[2] Université Côte d'Azur, CNRS, Inria, I3S, Nice, France
{Ankica.Barisic,Marco.Winckler}@univ-cotedazur.fr
[3] The Maersk M. Moller Institute, University of Southern Denmark,
Odense, Denmark
thiago@mmmi.sdu.dk

Abstract. This paper introduces CM-DIR (Conceptual Model - Dynamicity and Interaction in Recommender Systems), a method that we have originally devised to help with the description of dynamic user behavior in Recommender Systems (RS). The identification of user behavior change is paramount to optimize RSs to face new contexts of use and adapt their user interface accordingly. Capturing dynamic user behavior is, however, not an easy task and most RS systems do not take this information into account during the requirements engineering process. The proposed method leverages user and Behaviour-Driven Development (BDD) stories and extends them to describe dynamicity. The method has been evaluated with a panel of experts through semi-structured interviews and the results suggest that the CM-DIR is necessary and comprehensible and that the proposed extension allows flexibility and adaptability while ensuring informative specifications.

Keywords: User Stories · Behaviour-Driven Development (BDD) · Requirements Specification · Recommender Systems · User Behavior

1 Introduction

A Recommender Systems (RS) is a type of adaptive systems that uses information about the user interaction (such as clicking on items, browsing history, page revisiting, purchase history, likes, etc.) as an input to an algorithm that recommends a set of items that might match users' interest. In that, RSs system might help users to discover new items and/or to find again items previously seem that are still relevant. RSs are largely employed nowadays, from reading content to web services [2, 15, 32], and play an essential role in helping users with decision making processes, such as what items to buy, what music to listen to, what news to read, etc. In all these processes, user interaction is a key component for the

M. K. Lárusdóttir et al. (Eds.): HCSE 2024, LNCS 14793, pp. 26–46, 2024.
https://doi.org/10.1007/978-3-031-64576-1_2

system to respond satisfactorily in recommending items [1]. While the accuracy of the predictions is a core research question, the design of user interaction and the user interaction with RSs also have a strong impact on users' assessment of the recommendations and their overall experience of using the system [42].

Time of interactions is a core factor for understanding the users preferences. As we shall see in Fig. 1, user interactions are characterized by periods of use (the so-called sessions) alternated by periods of non-use. While the analysis of *sequences of interactions* in a user session reveals the dialog between the user and the interactive system, the analysis of interactions across sessions allows the identification of *patterns of user behaviour*. In a longer run, it is also possible to observe the evolution of these patterns and then characterize the *dynamic user behavior* [34].

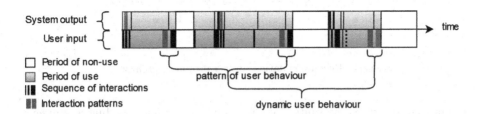

Fig. 1. General scheme of user interaction and behaviour changing overtime.

There may be countless reasons for a behavior change, and not all are worthy of interest. However, discovering behavior changes that make sense to the user allows the development of more flexible and valuable RSs. For recommendation algorithms, the problem is neither collecting information about the user interactions or detecting patterns, but rather to make sense of changing characteristics of the users.

A clear understanding of users needs along the time might be used to improve algorithms, thus preventing useless recommendations such as illustrated by Fig. 2 where the RS proposes (at T2) the very same product that users just bought (at T1).

Researchers have shown that taking into account the temporal properties of datasets leads to improvements in rating prediction and ranking. Hence, analyzing the contextual nature of user feedback shows promise for performance improvement [11]. In this scenario, the system could, for example, adapt more effectively to the dynamic behavior of the user, which can be identified in some situations that consider the user behavior, the external context, or even periods of time.

Whilst many RS's algorithms value information about interaction as a mean to determine the recommendations, little is known about how to identify, specify, and use dynamic behaviors as part of the users requirements for tuning the recommendations. Indeed, as we shall see in Sect. 2, there is a gap in the RS literature in terms of methods for specifying how user interactions should affect

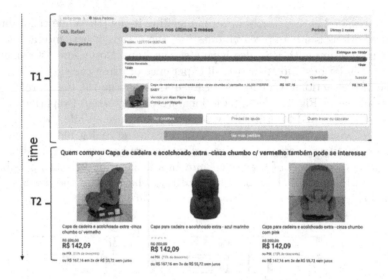

Fig. 2. Recommendation after a product purchase.

recommendations; so that, quite often, the only way of understanding recommendations is to look at the code source documentation (if any) of RS algorithms. For that, this paper presents a method called CM-DIR (Conceptual Model – Dynamicity and Interaction in Recommender Systems). The method CM-DIR aims to assist requirements analysts and software developers with the specification of *user dynamic behavior* and their use for creating recommendations prior to the implementation of RS algorithms. The CM-DIR method proposes a few extensions to Behaviour-Driven Development (BDD) stories [24,29] to support the specification of *user dynamic behavior*. It was specially devised to address the following premises:

- To detect and to cope with ambiguous and/or conflicting recommendations;
- To inform which users' actions on the user interface, and more specifically *patterns of user behaviour*, must be taken into account to formulate recommendations;
- To prevent code source reading (of RS algorithms) as the sole way of understanding recommendations;
- To cope with of the evolution of all aspects surrounding recommendation systems (such as requirements, recommendations, user interface design, user behaviour, and system technology) that are prone to evolve over time.

The rest of the paper is organized as follows: Sect. 2 presents the review of the literature. The Sect. 3 introduces the theoretical framework of the method as well as the extension proposed for the user and BDD stories. Then, preliminary results of an evaluation of the method based on structure interviews with domain experts are presented in Sect. 4 and discussed with respect to the related work in Sect. 5. Lately, Sect. 6 concludes the paper and discusses future work.

2   Overview of User Interaction and RSs

The literature often divide RSs into three main approaches based on filtering methods: content-based (CB), collaborative filtering (CF), and hybrid (Hybrid). Content-based methods generate recommendations by relying on attributes of items and users, such as age, sex, job type, and other personal information. On the other hand, item attributes are descriptive information that distinguishes individual items. Collaborative filtering methods focus on the historical interactions of users with the items to generate recommendations. Historical interactions of users with items can be a product purchase, listening to a song, rating a product, watching a movie, clicking on a news article, and similar. Finally, the hybrid approach combines previous ones to obtain a recommendation with fewer drawbacks than the others, which most large platforms use [27].

Users can interact with a RS either implicitly or explicitly. The action is explicit when the user selects or rates an item on the interface [12]. On the other hand, the interaction is implicit when the relevance of an item is based on the user history, such as the number of clicks, number of page visits, the number of times some user played a song, and so on, i.e., the number and time in which the implicit interaction occurs may represent the interest of users [2,39]. Compared to the explicit interaction, the implicit interaction is much more expressive as hardly users provide explicit *feedback*, only 15% of users according to [39].

Some works consider time as a crucial factor in defining user preferences [7,9,14,22,25], as it serves as a basis for calculating values of variables used as measures to define preferences, such as time of permanence in certain items and navigation time and the number of actions repetitions over time [14]. Over time, the relative order of the clicked items can also reflect the detailed trajectories of the change of interest of a given user [9]. An SR also needs to consider the evolution of the user based on their needs, not just their personal preferences that are variable over time [25]. A RS can work on generating logs that mark the frequency and duration of occurrence of user interactions [7]. The logs are available on the server, browser, or proxy, and scores are assigned, which can be used to calculate the subsequent recommendations [22].

Other works in the literature propose metrics to measure user interaction with the interface in several dimensions [7]. The metrics assess user interaction, and the values measured serve as a parameter to filter and eliminate unnecessary information and recommend what is important [13,35]. The metrics defined are simple, such as permanence time, number of visits, purchases made, the favorite topic, favorite content, and session duration [6]. Misztal-Radecka et al. [20] propose another set of metrics, and the idea is to build archetypes that serve as a structure in predicting new interactions, influencing the SR. In [6], the authors define the following items for this measurement: (a) total interaction time (in minutes); (b) favorite topic (ordered list of topics); (c) favorite content (ordered list of contents); (d) session duration (ordered list of content/duration pairs); (e) comments (number); (f) direct feedback (number of "starts"); (g) repetitive readings (number of iterations); (h) session length/content length.

In addition to the time variable, user interaction actions are influenced by the context in which the user is inserted. The context may restrict the [21] item selection actions. For example, in [26], the authors mention that depending on the environment in which they are, the user selects a style of music, or in [37], the authors show that depending on the context, the explanatory text of a document recommendation can be better detailed. In the analyzed studies, few studies considered the user's context at the moment of interaction.

It is possible to identify the user interaction that contributes to the enhancement of the interface for using the recommendations, investing in the placement of the items to be chosen, and explaining the recommended items [37]. For this, a structure can be defined in the interface/document body, and attributes can be used to understand user interaction by reviewing the text or selecting the item. Feedback on such information begins to influence future review propositions [38].

User interaction may also influence RSs through the sequential interaction of the user in the selection (or not) of items, with the entire interaction being stored over time. After the interaction is captured, it is modeled with complex relationships for understanding implicit data recommendation [23]. In this case, the idea is to use the dynamic elements of interaction and time that contribute to the possibility of variation in the result of the recommendations.

When the contexts influence item selection, there is a personalization of the recommendations for which such interactions are mapped [26]. In this case, the dynamic elements worked are interaction and context, which may significantly influence the variation of selection results of the recommendations. Some studies [19,40] deepen the specialization of user interaction learning to feedback to the RS and, thus, contribute to the precision of future item propositions.

Regarding user interaction, [23] exemplified a way called Sequential Implicit To Explicit (SITE), which directly models both types, item sequence and sequential user interactions with an item, to capture user interaction. The SITE method uses two continuous phases in a single task to model the several types of interactions as action sequences. Therefore, it is possible to model complex relationships among the user interactions with an item. It is also possible to capture the evolution of user preferences over time, exploring sequence items with which they interacted in the past.

3   The CM-DIR Method

The CM-DIR method was conceived to capture scenarios describing temporal aspects of the context of use, to specify the user dynamic behaviour, and to show which aspects of RSs should be modified (specially the user interface) to address user needs. The method also aims at capturing in the process the various influences of variables internal (desires and needs) and external to the user. In general, user interaction is directly connected to the variations in the decision to choose the recommended item, such as time, context, and the change of interests that impact interaction.

3.1   A Motivating Example

To illustrate one of the dynamic behaviors that our method aims to capture, consider the following motivating example related to a searched item. Julia majors in psychology and, for four semesters, have bought books and read articles in this topic. However, she changed her degree to dentistry and the subjects of her interest therefore changed. This dynamic change in behavior cannot be predicted by the current system, which keeps recommending the old subjects. In order to reduce the learning curve, the description of scenarios formalising *user dynamic behavior* is built using and extensions of the method Behaviour-Driven Development (BDD) [24,29]. This behavior change could be easily specified by our method as (the proposed extensions are highlighted in lime):

As a student, **I want** to remove the course of psychology <**interaction 1**>

Context: study

OR dentistry <**interaction 2**>, **OR** physiotherapy <**interaction 3**>,

OR computing <**interaction 4**>

At time 1: <sequence>

So that I can keep information of interest <**interaction 5**>

Scenario: Course change

Given I do not use the course of psychology <**interaction 1**>

Context: study

OR dentistry <**interaction 2**>, **OR** physiotherapy <**interaction 3**>,

OR computing <**interaction 4**>

At time 1: <sequence>

When I select dentistry <**interaction 5**>

And I present a new course <**interaction 6**>

Then the system relates it to the available content <**interaction 7**>

As we shall see, the use of BDD contemplates the indication of time, context, the user's specific object of desire, and the implicit interaction. A dictionary is then provided to specify the interactions on the user interface that capture such behaviors.

Dictionary:

interaction 1 : <uncheck> do not send information about the unchecked course.

interaction 2, 3, and 4 : <check> be able to select one of the options to receive information.

interaction 5 : <confirm> to present selected item to which content will be sent.

interaction 6 : <present check> selected component.

interaction 7 : <combo list> with information to be sent.

3.2   Conceptual Elements of CM-DIR

The method includes a conceptual model that describes the main concepts used for defining dynamic behavior variables and a stepwise process for mapping dynamic user behaviors to the (desired) adaptation of the user interface. The CM-DIR covers a set of concepts that determine the dynamic aspects of the user interactions with RSs. These concepts are presented in Fig. 3.

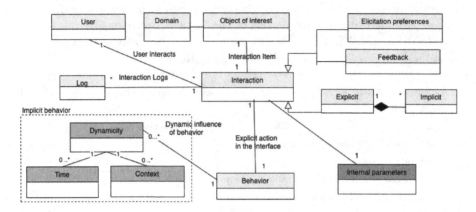

Fig. 3. Core concepts in the conceptual model of dynamicity and interaction with RS.

The conceptual model used for describing the dynamic behavior is organized around the concept of user's "Interaction". This concept can be implemented either as "Elicitation preference" (when the user specify the preference prior to interacting with the system, like by defining preferred settings) or a "Feedback" (when users tell their preferences while interacting with the system, like by giving a positive mark for a recommendation). An interaction may be explicit or implicit. A user interaction is often counted as an explicit behavior, but some implicit behavior, such as waiting times, can be computed to determine the outcomes. The objects of interest of a user (item/product/feature) and the application domain are also specified as part of the conceptual model as they determine which objects will be affected by the recommendations. The interaction may represent dynamic behavioral issues related to the elapsed time and the context in which the user is.

The term "time" encapsulates the dynamics of the behavior which can be expressed as a sequence, a moment, and/or a period that describe the timeliness relevance of information for the user. Therefore, time is a core concept that will be used in the definition of the RS specifications. In addition, the user interaction is related to the internal system configuration parameters that process input variables to the system from the interface. With these concepts mapped, it is possible to provide conceptual support in identifying the dynamicity depicted by the user behavior with the system interface.

3.3   A 3-Stages Method

The CM-DIR method encompasses three stages (Fig. 4), namely: (1) Requirements Gathering and Specification, (2) Requirements Analysis and Presentation, and (3) Interface Modeling. They are based on consolidated requirements processes such as CMMI [31] with an addition of dynamicity. Stage 1 (Requirements Gathering and Specification) focuses on identifying dynamic information about user behavior. Stages 2 and 3 are specifically designed to exploit the specification of requirements, respectively, for the presentation of requirements to the development team and for guiding the design of the user interface of RSs.

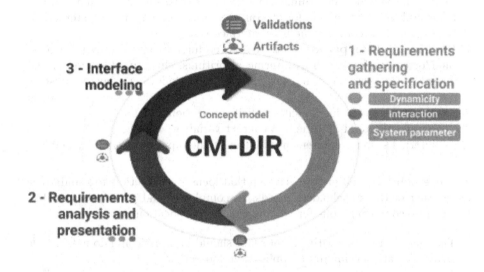

Fig. 4. Overview of the steps of the CM-DIR method.

The specification is key to prevent the ambiguities not only in terms of the description of the requirements but also in terms of how requirements are expected to be implemented in the user interface. Notice that the method (see Fig. 4) also includes a validation step, which must be performed with the stakeholders at the completion of each stage to ensure that their needs and expectations are aligned with the generated artifacts. The following sections describe in detail the three stage of the method.

3.4   Requirements Gathering and Specification

Requirements Gathering is a step that aims at identifying requirements that might encompass changes in the user behaviors. For that we need to:

1. **Identify the dynamicity**: behaviors are identified through (explicit/ implicit) interactions with objects of interest in a context of use. The variable

interactions depend on the context of use. For the variable time, it tells the timely relevance of information. The following tasks are sought to help to identify these variables:
- identify behaviors that generate explicit interactions on the interface;
- note the time (moment/sequence/period) of events causing a behavior change;
- check all context of use to identify a change in the users' interest with objects (ex. items, features, products).

2. **Identify interactions**: In this step, the temporal dynamicity (ex. sequence of interactions) associated with the behavior is also identified. Stakeholders must be consulted to determine the relevant associations, as it is not possible to generalize an interaction for all contexts of use. Then, for each interaction, the expected outcome on the user interface is described.

3. **Identify system parameters**: this cover internal system's requirements (and/or constraints) such as filtering algorithms, clustering techniques, and format of the system outputs (ex. ranking). The following elements must be considered:
- parameters used in explicit/implicit interactions;
- parameters used by time and context variables;
- internal system requirements that meet the inputs/outputs of variables.

Requirements Specification is a step that focuses on practices to standardize the writing of the stakeholders' needs, as completely and generic as possible. These are recommendations for writing generic specifications:

- The user interactions with the interface should be generic and do not include terms that are specific to an application domain.
- Always assume that a user interface is the main source of information, where dynamic user behavior can be captured and the recommendations presented to the user.
- For each specification of behavior, we consider one object of interest at time.
- The attributes of the object interests must encompass information about the context. Hence, it is possible to relate items with the same context and differentiate contexts in which the user may choose.
- The variables time, context, and object of interest work together with behavior, but only time and context are optional in a specification.

Moreover, the notation to be used should be sufficiently flexible to accommodate the scenario with two or more options, express the context in which the item belongs, and work on the time variables and definition of the interaction that may add value with the defined implicit interaction. As for the formalism of specification, we extend two widely known techniques (user stories [5] and BDD scenarios [24]) in order to meet the use of the dynamic variables of time, context, and behavior. The proposed template with the dynamicity extensions (including a dictionary of controlled vocabulary) is presented below:

As a <persona>, **I want** <feature> **<interaction>**

Context: <product attribute or item under specification>

AND/OR <resource> **<interaction>**

At time t: <sequence, period, moment>

So that <benefit> **<interaction>**

Scenario: <title>

Given <condition c> **<interaction>**

Context: <product attribute or item under specification>

AND/OR <condition c+1> **<interaction>**

At time t: <sequence, period, moment>

When/And <action> **<interaction>**

Then/And <outcome> **<interaction>**

Dictionary:

interaction i : <interaction component on the user interface>

The following conventions apply to the template:

- Parameters of objects of interest as item/feature/product: (1) the name of the item, (2) the context, and (3) when the item will be shown again.
- Interaction dictionary: indicates which interaction component will capture the behavior that will be translated into explicit/implicit interaction. It must contain the identification and description of the meaning of the capture by the system.
- Re-redisplay settings are specified according to the operators presented in Table 1, including the options on the interface (symbolizes the options presented on the interface in which the user will take the action), the user actions (the attitude of the user towards the options available on the interface, which may be viewing, purchasing, evaluating, etc.), and the expected behavior of the system according to the specification (behavior expected by the system according to the defined specification of !OR, OR, !AND, and AND).
- Time: it is used to define the classification of time to be considered, as follows: **Sequence** – used when it is necessary to consider the order in which the items undergo an action. For example, when a user selects a sequence of items (such as the books), other users with similar profile will receive the same recommendation. **Period** – when a period of time for which an action is performed on an item. For example, in the case that a user selects a car seat cover and the RS waits for one or two years to provide a new recommendation of the same item. **Moment** – (progression) the exact moment in which an action is performed on an item. For example, at moment T1, a user goes onto a page to look at book options and does not execute anything on the page until

moment T2. Depending on the time, different definitions may be considered, such as the user giving up or not finding what they need. These parameters may be used together or separately. It is possible to consider situations in which the information is provided through explicit interaction or as a result of processing an implicit interaction.

Table 1. Re-redisplay according to the action.

Operator	Options	User Actions	Behavior
!OR	1|..|n	2	Fetches what was not selected
OR	1|..|n	2	Fetches what was selected
!AND	1|..|n	Any option	Do not display anything
AND	1|..|n	Any option	Display everything

When a user story presents itself dynamically, several options are presented to the user, enabling the construction of various test scenarios. The importance of knowing if the story is dynamic is related to the number of necessary scenarios that must be created for testing, considering that there may be different times to understand the behavior. Each option in the interface is considered a test scenario. The keywords are repeated in BDD, but now with the aim of specifying all possible test conditions. The tests address one or more options selected through explicit interaction, which we may use in the dynamic capture of behavior by identifying implicit interactions (keyword interaction).

3.5   Requirements Analysis and Presentation

In this phase, all the specifications created by the RS analysts (including user stories and BDD templates) are organized and classified to facilitate the access to recommendations. The goal is to have a representation that all project participants may use to allow the joint analysis of the identified requirements, the possible existence of conflicts, duplicity, ambiguity, and other points that need to be unified or separated into new ones. During the analysis, the characteristics presented in the first stage about the dynamic user behavior in the face of systems are taken into account.

We suggest that the specifications must grouped according to their purpose. If the requirements specified are too high level and need to be detailed, then organized by similarity. In addition, dependencies are identified if they are too complex and may also be prioritized according to the interest in delivery.

3.6   Interface Modeling

This stage foresees the construction of wireframes of the interfaces considering the behaviors identified and represented by the Interaction Components. Interaction components that capture the dynamicity of user behavior must be visible in the wireframe. The specification of the interaction and the use on the interface are described at the beginning of this section. At this step, the low-fidelity screens are validated with the stakeholders to ensure the achievement of satisfaction in the delivery of the developed product. Once the wireframe is created, we proceed to a second validation to unify requirements and eliminate possible ambiguities.

4   Evaluation

The method was assessed using semi-structured interviews of about 1 h via video conference with seven independent experts (four from industry and three from academia), who evaluated the feasibility, ease of use, and completeness of the method. The analysis of interview data was inspired by Silva et al. [28]. The questions used, data colled, the analysis are available in a data repository [18].

4.1   Participants

Table 2 shows the profile of participants that were selected in a convenience sample to take part in the study. All participants had a higher education in computer science and/or software and are knowledgeable about BDD.

Table 2. Participant's profile

ID	Gender	Education	Professional Experience	Role
P1	Female	Master's	17y	Requirements Analyst
P2	Male	Postgraduate	14y	Solutions Architect
P3	Male	Postgraduate	18y	UX Designer
P4	Male	Postgraduate	20y	Engineer
P5	Female	PhD	22y	Research Engineer
P6	Male	PhD	20y	Researcher
P7	Male	Bachelor's	6y	Full-Stack Developer

4.2   Procedure

The interviews followed the presentation of: (i) the goals of the study and overview of the method CM-DIR; (ii) concepts of interaction; (iii) concepts with dynamic characteristics (dynamic behaviour, time, context); (iv) review of user stories; (v) extensions for user stories; (vi) illustrative examples; (vii) the three stages of the CM-DIR method emphasizing the extensions; (viii) an example using the extended user and BDD stories; (ix) questions requesting participants to elaborate a user/BDD story including dynamicity using the proposed extension; (x) a post-questionnaire; and (xi) debriefing. The questions used in the post-questionnaire are: **(Q1)** *Is it clear why the conceptual model is needed? For the method as a whole? Why?*, **(Q2)** *Do the proposed concepts in the model reflect the reality? Why?*, **(Q3)** *Does it make sense for you that the conceptual model only covers the first step of the method?*, **(Q4)** *Do you consider that both user story and BDD appropriate techniques to address the dynamic aspects of recommender systems? Would you use another type of specification?*, **(Q5)** *How intuitive is the proposed specification?*, and **(Q6)** *Do you consider that the method encompasses all the necessary steps to address the presented problem? Do you think more specification is needed for implementation purposes?*.

4.3 Results

Proposal Conformity and Provided Suggestions. We explored how participants perceived and used the various concepts (as described in the step ii and iii of the interview) to create an example using the extended user/BDD story (step ix). Figure 5 illustrates the participants' adherence to each item. Certain evaluation items exhibited deviations in adherence to issues and recommendations.

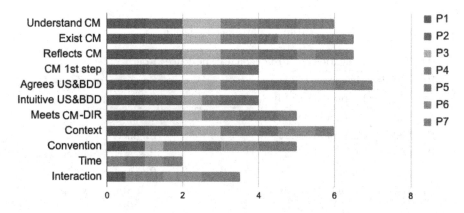

Fig. 5. Participants adherence to proposed conceptual model (CM).

Below, we elaborate the key findings, identifying areas for improvement and issues that could be addressed through adjustments to the proposed specification extension. The recommendations were detailed as follows:

1. Adequacy of a conceptual model (i,ii,iii)
    – *Understand CM* (Understanding of the presented model): It is not clear how the specified requirements are used in all the stages of the CM-DIR method

- *Exist CM* (Enhancing a need for the existence of CM).
- *Reflects CM* (The presented concepts in the model reflect the reality): More details would to facilitate design and testing, in particular how to concurrently combine time and context or to allow them to occur independently.
- *CM 1st step* [4]: Two participants expressed the opinion that the conceptual model should be applied in the second phase, emphasizing its relevance in reflecting the subsequent steps of the CM-DIR. Additionally, its use in requirements validations was highlighted.

2. Standard US and BDD (iv, v)
   - *Agrees US and BDD* (The technique presented is suitable for use with user stories and BDD).

3. CM-DIR (vi, vii, viii)
   - *Intuitive US and BDD* (The proposal is intuitive): Enhance the comprehension of the connections between the conceptual model and the CM-DIR method. Refine the representation of e-commercial and E, as they symbolize the same concept and may lead to confusion. Improve the clarity of convention symbols. Propose an extension that integrates the use of US and BDD in tandem.
   - *Meets CM-DIR* (The proposal is suitable to solve the problem raised about dynamism): Include a reference to tests in this context. Additionally, address the lack of detail regarding the utilization of UX design, as this information can impose limitations.

4. Use of the extended specification item (ix)
   - *Context* - All participants utilized the concept of context, with two employing phrases or expressions to define it. Enhance the guidance for defining context with a particular emphasis on using language suitable for the specification within a pre-defined scenario.
   - *Convention* - In one instance, no convention symbol was selected, and in another case, two symbols were employed. The latter scenario provides an opportunity to examine the feasibility of using multiple symbols simultaneously.
   - *Time* - In three specifications, the progression time and the time for re-displaying options on the interface were not indicated. Four other specifications provided partial information on time, encompassing aspects like the presentation of re-presentation time, definition of the moment, definition of the progression, and, in one case, the parameters (sequence, moment, and period) were left undefined.
   - *Interaction* - In three cases, there was no definition provided for interaction. Two cases partially outlined the interaction, while two other cases presented a comprehensive definition of interaction.

Analysis of Answers. Figure 6 summarizes the answers during the post-interview, step (x). Concerning *Q1* and *Q2*, five participants confirmed the need for a conceptual model, and they agreed on that the presented model accurately mirrors the reality. Two participants noted areas for potential enhancement in the conceptual model. Regarding $Q3$, four participants suggested alternatives for using the conceptual model into other phases of the CM-DIR method in order to facilitate validations across stages, fostering testing, and UX design. Conversely, three participants contend that confining the use of the conceptual model solely to the initial stage of the method is sufficient.

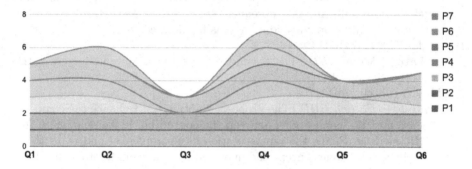

Fig. 6. Participants' answers to evaluation questions.

As for $Q4$, there was unanimous agreement among all participants asserting that BDD adequately captures the dynamic issues posed by the proposed model. Addressing $Q5$, unanimous positive feedback was received, with all interviewees expressing ease and intuitiveness in utilizing CM-DIR and its BDD extensions. Notably, three participants provided constructive suggestions aimed at refining the specification. Concerning $Q6$, the suggestions are towards going into more detail on UX design and testing.

Problems While Elaborating Examples. During the interviews, participants were asked to write sample of requirements (step ix). Figure 7 shows a summary of problems detected on participants' specifications.

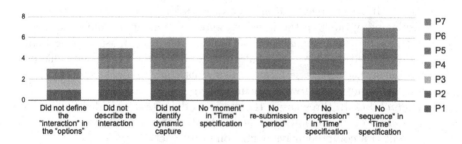

Fig. 7. Problem detected when using the proposed specification.

Hereafter we provide the list of the suggestions received to improve the CM-DIR method, as follows:

1. *Missing the definition of the 'interaction' in the 'options'* - Three participants did not define this parameter, possibly because explicit known interaction components are limited to clicks and selections, thus restricting the concept of dynamic behaviour captured through interaction.

2. *Did not describe the interaction* (Detailed explanation of how the interaction works - should include the explicit interaction used and how it is presented on the screen and received by the behavior screen) - Five participants did not provide descriptions of interactions, whether they used them or not. Some participants may have hastily included them directly into the specification without utilizing the dictionary.

3. *Did not identify dynamic capture* (Report on how the explicit dynamic user behavior will be interpreted by the explicit interaction) - Six participants did not address this capture aspect, indicating a need for more guidance on how to approach this task.

4. *Missing the option 'moment' in the 'Time' specification* (Information supporting the capture of information to generate implicit interaction) - Six participants did not define the moment of option selection. This was possibly due to the recommendation strategy outlined in the specification, which may not have required the use of this parameter. The moment parameter is not mandatory.

5. *No re-submission 'period'* (The definition of this time is linked to how the convention should function at each time) - Six participants did not utilize this specification, as their individual specification ideas did not pose a problem for the presentation of repeated items in a short period.

6. *No 'progression' in the 'Time' specification* (The progression time considers the situation of parameters defined at each moment of the specification) - Some participants defined T1, but the existence of Tn is necessary to identify dynamic variation. Based on the specifications and the conceptualization of projecting the same specification expressed at different times with different outcomes, it is assumed this might not be straightforward for those evaluating it.

7. *No 'sequence' in the 'Time' specification* (Considers the sequence in which items were selected or should be presented) - Although not a mandatory parameter, it provides information on implicit interaction to enhance the accuracy of recommending the next options.

Summary of Results. Overall, the findings from the interviews were quite encouraging. The majority of improvements suggested by participants are related to the use of the conceptual model. Participants suggested alternative examples that could be more intuitive for illustrating the method. Concerning the use specification, participants suggested clarifying when mandatory items (such as actions related to time progression and the period linked to conventions) are required. They also prompted the importance of defining interactions.

The proposed extension offers flexibility. For dynamic specifications, it must include behavior, options, convention, and at least one of the other parameters (interaction, context, or time). If any mandatory parameter is unspecified, the user story converts to the default use thus ensuring user-friendly specifications. Despite some participants' specifications lacking certain parameters, the dynamism is preserved, indicating the resilience and adaptability of the method.

In evaluating participant responses, a consensus among five participants underscores the need for a conceptual model reflecting behavior, context, time, and product. Some suggest integrating this model across CM-DIR phases for usability, while others find its application limited to the initial stage sufficient. Unanimous agreement asserts that BDD effectively addresses dynamic issues. While feedback on CM-DIR and BDD extensions was positive, there is an emphasized need for detailed explanations on UX design and testing.

In the evaluation of our approach, several limitations were also identified and should be discussed. First, the evaluation was constrained by the limited number of participants involved, which may impact the generalizability of the findings. Another notable limitation is the lack of experience of participants in handling dynamic requirements. Despite the flexibility of not requiring the simultaneous use of all parameters, there is a challenge in defining and managing the multitude of parameters involved. This complexity could potentially hinder the ease of implementation and usability of the approach.

5   Discussion and Related Work

The conception of our method was based on a prior systematic literature review (SLR) on requirements engineering techniques for RSs. During the stage of analysis of the works in the literature, we initially sought proposals that took into account user behavior in the face of RSs.

Most studies on RSs focus on the performance of recommendation algorithms. In general, only a few examples of recommendation algorithms use variables related to *sequence of interaction* over time [13,16,19,20,23] or *pattern of user behaviour* related to the context [26,37]. *Dynamic user behavior* changes over time is not take into account [11].

We did not find any prior work with a proposal to formalize the requirements specification that reflected the dynamicity of user behavior. Therefore, we reviewed the scope of this study and sought to analyze some works that considered the user interaction actions in RS as these are systems in which the user interaction has a direct effect on the accuracy of the recommendations made. These works were classified into three groups: *(i)* preference elicitation, including works that captured interactions at the time when user preferences were not known; *(ii)* indication of preferences in the results, indicating user feedback and including works that considered capturing interactions when the system was already calibrated with some preferences; and *(iii)* hybrid, including works that used an approach that considered the two previous cases.

Works such as [10,26,35] require use preference to be elicited clearly, in which case the most mentioned action was "selecting". Other important preferences, represented by interactions such as "view" [10], "visit" [13] and "check" [20] are related to the action of seeing something interesting, so it may be chosen and marked as a preference. As much as confirming what is observed through behavior is necessary, walking this path implicitly brings information of interest. Interactions of "editing" and "accessing" items appeared in only a few studies [20, 33], but have their functions in setting preferences. These interactions, combined with other ones, present relevant implicit information that may contribute to calibrating the systems, either with other interactions or with dynamic variables that support the flexibility of RSs functioning.

In the second group, concerning the indication of preferences in the results, the most recurring interaction actions were "rate product" or "categorize items" [17, 20, 30, 41] which indirectly make it possible to evaluate the purchased product. The "evaluate items" action [4, 17] also appeared as a user interaction. The "comment" [38] and "like" [3] actions were the least frequent from the preference results according to the works surveyed.

Finally, in the third group - the hybrid one [3, 16, 23, 36, 40], the interactions to be defined are implicitly captured at different moments and screens, and each moment will have its interaction.

Similar to other works, CM-DIR shares the overarching goal of addressing accuracy in recommendations. However, its distinctive feature lies in emphasizing precision improvement while building recommender systems.

This work is not alien to the problems reported in the Fogg Behavioral Model (FBM) [8]. The FBM asserts that three factors must occur at the same time for a person to perform a target behavior: the person must (1) be sufficiently motivated, (2) have the ability to perform the behavior, and (3) be triggered to perform the behavior. Despite the fact that the FBM has been demonstrated useful to support the analysis and design of recommendation systems by explaining the factors that affect the change in user behavior, it does not specify which elements of the user interface of RS systems are affected by the user behaviour change. In that sense, the CM-DIR method provides an complimentary notation that can finely describe the behaviour change on the system.

6   Conclusion

This paper introduced CM-DIR, a method that aims to guide requirements analysts and developers in building systems that must consider dynamic user behavior. Exploring the aspect of dynamism in user behavior corroborates studies already carried out in the literature, in which a deficiency was detected in investigating the problem [11]. Our proposed solution extends user and BDD stories by adding new elements to reflect the dynamism of user behavior in RSs, thus allowing interaction actions to be captured and treated more accurately. Our method was evaluated with a panel of experts, and the results proved promising because the participants responded positively to the approach, indicating that the problem is relevant and the solution is quite feasible.

In future work, the focus will be on refining the structure of user stories and BDD to enhance intuitiveness, with specific consideration of retaining only dynamism in BDD. The need for using certain parameters in conjunction, like

Period and Convention, will be clarified. Additionally, the extension will involve the application of time parameters to each interface option. Further investigation will delve into the intricate details of defining interaction to better support the work of UX design. Furthermore, efforts will be directed towards improving the model to align with the requirements of phases 2 and 3 in the CM-DIR method.

Acknowledgements. Partial support for this research was provided by the National Council for Scientific and Technological Development (CNPq) under Grant for graduate scholarship, Process Nr. 131014/2021-8 - GM GD 2020.

References

1. Bobadilla, J., Ortega, F., Hernando, A., Gutiérrez, A.: Recommender systems survey. Knowl.-Based Syst. **46**, 109–132 (2013). https://doi.org/10.1016/j.knosys.2013.03.012
2. Cao, Z., Qiao, X., Jiang, S., Zhang, X.: An efficient knowledge-graph-based web service recommendation algorithm. Symmetry **11**(3) (2019). https://doi.org/10.3390/sym11030392
3. Chang, J., et al: Sequential recommendation with graph neural networks, pp. 378–387. Association for Computing Machinery, New York (2021)
4. Chong, S., Abeliuk, A.: Quantifying the effects of recommendation systems. In: 2019 IEEE International Conference on Big Data (Big Data), pp. 3008–3015 (2019)
5. Cohn, M.: User Stories Applied: For Agile Software Development. Addison-Wesley Professional, Boston (2004)
6. Crespo, R.G., Martínez, O.S., Lovelle, J.M.C., García-Bustelo, B.C.P., Gayo, J.E.L., de Pablos, P.O.: Recommendation system based on user interaction data applied to intelligent electronic books. Comput. Hum. Behav. **27**(4), 1445–1449 (2011). https://doi.org/10.1016/j.chb.2010.09.012
7. Feng, M., Peck, E., Harrison, L.: Patterns and pace: quantifying diverse exploration behavior with visualizations on the web. IEEE Trans. Visual Comput. Graphics **25**(1), 501–511 (2019). https://doi.org/10.1109/TVCG.2018.2865117
8. Fogg, B.: A behavior model for persuasive design. In: Proceedings of the 4th International Conference on Persuasive Technology. Persuasive 2009. Association for Computing Machinery, New York (2009). https://doi.org/10.1145/1541948.1541999
9. Gan, M., Xiao, K.: R-RNN: extracting user recent behavior sequence for click-through rate prediction. IEEE Access **7**, 111767–111777 (2019). https://doi.org/10.1109/ACCESS.2019.2927717
10. Guo, S., Li, C.: Hybrid recommendation algorithm based on user behavior. In: IEEE 9th Joint International Information Technology and Artificial Intelligence Conference (2020)
11. Jawaheer, G., Weller, P., Kostkova, P.: Modeling user preferences in recommender systems: a classification framework for explicit and implicit user feedback. ACM Trans. Interact. Intell. Syst. **4**(2), 1–26 (2014)
12. Jawaheer, G., Weller, P., Kostkova, P.: Modeling user preferences in recommender systems: a classification framework for explicit and implicit user feedback. ACM Trans. Interact. Intell. Syst. **4**(2) (2014). https://doi.org/10.1145/2512208

13. Jianjun, M.: Research on collaborative filtering recommendation algorithm based on user behavior characteristics. In: 2020 International Conference on Big Data Artificial Intelligence Software Engineering (ICBASE) (2020)

14. Kang, S., Jeong, C., Chung, K.: Tree-based real-time advertisement recommendation system in online broadcasting. IEEE Access **8**, 192693–192702 (2020). https://doi.org/10.1109/ACCESS.2020.3031925

15. Kong, X., Mao, M., Wang, W., Liu, J., Xu, B.: VOPRec: vector representation learning of papers with text information and structural identity for recommendation. IEEE Trans. Emerg. Top. Comput. **9**(1), 226–237 (2021). https://doi.org/10.1109/TETC.2018.2830698

16. Koren, Y., Bell, R., Volinsky, C.: Matrix factorization techniques for recommender systems. Computer **42**(8), 30–37 (2009)

17. Liu, T., at al: Sorrrs: social recommendation incorporating rating similarity and user relationships analysis. In: 2020 7ª International Conference on Information, Cybernetics, and Computational Social Systems (ICCSS) (2020)

18. Martins, C.A.: Research evaluation information - CM-DIR - mendeley data (2023). https://doi.org/10.17632/ddmvrdc4sc

19. Meshram, R., et al: Monte Carlo rollout policy for recommendation systems with dynamic user behavior. In: International Conference on COMmunication Systems NETworkS (2021)

20. Misztal-Radecka, J., Indurkhya, B.: Persona prototypes for improving the qualitative evaluation of recommendation systems. In: Adjunct Publication of the 28th ACM Conference on User Modeling, Adaptation and Personalization, pp. 206–212 (2020)

21. Mo, Y., Chen, J., Xie, X., Luo, C., Yang, L.T.: Cloud-based mobile multimedia recommendation system with user behavior information. IEEE Syst. J. **8**(1), 184–193 (2014). https://doi.org/10.1109/JSYST.2013.2279732

22. Neelima, G., Rodda, S.: Predicting user behavior through sessions using the web log mining. In: 2016 International Conference on Advances in Human Machine Interaction (HMI), pp. 1–5 (2016). https://doi.org/10.1109/HMI.2016.7449167

23. Nguyen, T., Ngo Van, L., Than, K.: Modeling the sequential behaviors of online users in recommender systems. In: Artificial Intelligence and Machine Learning for Multi-Domain Operations Applications II (2020)

24. North, D.: Introducing BDD (2006). http://dannorth.net/introducing-bdd/

25. Ortiz Viso, B.: Evolutionary approach in recommendation systems for complex structured objects. In: Fourteenth ACM Conference on Recommender Systems, RecSys 2020, pp. 776–781. Association for Computing Machinery, New York (2020). https://doi.org/10.1145/3383313.3411455

26. Gao, Q., Ma, P.: Graph neural network and context-aware user behavior prediction and recommendation system research. Comput. Intell. Neurosci. (2021)

27. Ricci, F., Rokach, L., Shapira, B.: Recommender systems: techniques, applications, and challenges. In: Ricci, F., Rokach, L., Shapira, B. (eds.) Recommender Systems Handbook, pp. 1–35. Springer, New York (2022). https://doi.org/10.1007/978-1-0716-2197-4_1

28. Rocha Silva, T., Winckler, M., Bach, C.: Evaluating the usage of predefined interactive behaviors for writing user stories: an empirical study with potential product owners. Cogn. Technol. Work **22**, 437–457 (2020)

29. Rocha Silva, T.: Ensuring the consistency between user requirements and task models: a behavior-based automated approach. Proc. ACM Hum.-Comput. Interact. **4**(EICS) (2020). https://doi.org/10.1145/3394979

30. Saranya, A.S., et al: Social recommendation system using network embedding and temporal information. In: 5º International Conference on Computing, Communication and Security (ICCCS) (2020)
31. SEI: CMMI® for development version 1.2 improving processes for better products. Pittsburgh, Pensilvânia, EUA: Carnegie Mellon University (2006)
32. Setty, V., Hose, K.: Event2vec: neural embeddings for news events. In: SIGIR 2018. Association for Computing Machinery, New York (2018). https://doi.org/10.1145/3209978.3210136
33. Shibamoto, E., et al: A recommendation system of sightseeing places based on user's behavior of taking and editing photos. In: IEEE Pacific Rim Conference on Communications, Computers and Signal Processing (PACRIM) (2019)
34. Shin, D.: How do users interact with algorithm recommender systems? The interaction of users, algorithms, and performance. Comput. Hum. Behav. **109**, 106344 (2020)
35. Walek, B.: Creating adaptive web recommendation system based on user behavior. J. Phys. Conf. Ser. **933**, 012014 (2018)
36. Widiyaningtyas, T., et al.: User profile correlation-based similarity (UPCSim) algorithm in movie recommendation system. J. Big Data **8**(1), 52 (2021)
37. Xu, X., et al: Understanding user behavior for document recommendation. In: Proceedings of the Web Conference 2020. ACM (2020)
38. Yang, Z., Zhang, M.: TextOG: a recommendation model for rating prediction based on heterogeneous fusion of review data. IEEE Access **8**, 159566–159573 (2020)
39. Yi, P., et al: An optimization method for recommendation system based on user implicit behavior. In: 2015 5º International Conference on Instrumentation and Measurement, Computer, Communication and Control (2015). https://doi.org/10.1109/IMCCC.2015.326
40. Zheng, L., et al: Joint deep modeling of users and items using reviews for recommendation. In: 10th ACM International Conference on Web Search and Data Mining (2017)
41. Zhou, D., et al.: Novel SDDM rating prediction models for recommendation systems. IEEE Access **9**, 101197–101206 (2021)
42. Ziegler, J., Loepp, B.: Interactive recommendation systems. In: Vanderdonckt, J., Palanque, P., Winckler, M. (eds.) Handbook of Human Computer Interaction, pp. 1–29. Springer, Cham (2020). https://doi.org/10.1007/978-3-319-27648-9_54-1

Facilitating Development of Accessible Web Applications

Giulia Causarano[1] and Fabio Paternò[2]([⊠]) [iD]

[1] University of Pisa, Pisa, Italy
g.causarano@studenti.unipi.it
[2] CNR-ISTI, HIIS Laboratory, Pisa, Italy
fabio.paterno@isti.cnr.it

Abstract. Today, more than 60% of websites on the Internet are created and run using content management systems (CMS), and this rate is constantly increasing. Thus, it has become important to ensure that these platforms support and promote web accessibility for all. While in traditional software engineering approaches, the accessibility validation is carried out at the end of the process, often with the support of external validators, it would be important to support Web developers during the actual development process while the content is defined. The work described in this paper addresses the possibility of supporting web accessibility while developing websites with WordPress, the currently most used CMS. For this purpose, we report on the design and development of a plugin to evaluate the accessibility of pages created with this popular platform. The developed plugin aims to provide WordPress users with open, useful and effective accessibility evaluation support capable of filling the gaps in current practices.

Keywords: Web content management systems · Accessibility · Plugin

1 Introduction

Making the Web accessible benefits not only individuals but also businesses and society. Accessibility is important for several reasons: accessibility promotes effective digital inclusion, allowing a wide range of individuals to participate in digital society actively; when websites are accessible, they can be used by a wider audience, which is crucial for companies and organisations that want to reach as many users as possible, increasing communication and interaction opportunities; accessibility practices often improve the overall usability of websites, which benefits all users, including those without disabilities, by making the browsing experience smoother and more intuitive; offering an accessible digital environment can be a competitive advantage, showing a commitment to equity and attention to the needs of a wide variety of users; and in many jurisdictions, some laws and regulations require web accessibility (for example, the WAD directive [5] has indicated that all European countries should also monitor the accessibility of web and mobile applications).

© IFIP International Federation for Information Processing 2024
Published by Springer Nature Switzerland AG 2024
M. K. Lárusdóttir et al. (Eds.): HCSE 2024, LNCS 14793, pp. 47–62, 2024.
https://doi.org/10.1007/978-3-031-64576-1_3

All such factors have increased the complexity of the validation of Web applications, which consequently requires considerable effort and can be rather tedious if performed manually. For such reasons, interest in automatic support of accessibility validation has increased, even if it is well-known that not all the guidelines for accessibility can be automatically performed [9], and direct user feedback is still necessary.

Automated tools play a key role in ensuring the accessibility of websites, as they help operators collect and analyse data on the actual application of guidelines, detect non-compliance and provide relevant information on how to address possible problems. Furthermore, although not all accessibility requirements can be automatically validated, the use of automatic tools can significantly speed up the evaluation work, allowing even individuals inexperienced in the subject to obtain an understandable overview of the accessibility of a specific website. Indeed, several tools for automatic accessibility validation have been put forward by both commercial (e.g. Siteimprove, Lighthouse) and research organisations (e.g. QualWeb[1], MAUVE++[2]).

To date, a popular choice for creating websites is using content management systems (CMS), particularly useful tools as they allow anyone, including people, without advanced programming knowledge, to create websites. Content management systems offer a cost-effective solution for a wide range of users, ranging from beginners to professional web developers. One of their strengths is their ease of use for users, who do not have to worry about the "technical subsystem" (such as databases and programming). They are an organised set of tools to facilitate and control the management and publication of web content practically and efficiently. Furthermore, they provide centralised management of information, a factor that guarantees immediate and synchronised availability from all access points. Originally developed as a blogging system, WordPressis currently the most used CMS software in the world to power websites of various types, including personal blogs, corporate sites, online stores/communities, and much more. The first version of the software dates back to 2003; over the years, the versatility of this tool and the large community of developers dedicated to the project have transformed WordPress into a complete CMS with thousands of plugins, widgets and themes. The popularity of WordPress undoubtedly comes from its ease of use, but an equally crucial aspect is its expandability. In fact, the very core of WordPress is based on its API (Application Programming Interface), which allows developers to quickly and effectively customise the application they are implementing, based on their specific needs.

Consequently, it is important that all CMSs that allow access to information via the Internet must ensure that the published content is accessible. However, it may be problematic to perform the accessibility validation only at the end of the development process since it may then require numerous changes in order to satisfy it. Thus, it would be useful to support Web developers during the actual development process while the content is defined, exploiting the customisation features provided by WordPress through specific plugins. To know if a website is accessible it is necessary to evaluate its compliance with the specific standards, the WAI WCAG guidelines[3]. It is helpful to remember that to ensure this compliance, assessments should start from the site's design and continue in

---

[1] http://qualweb.di.fc.ul.pt/.

[2] https://mauve.isti.cnr.it/.

[3] https://www.w3.org/WAI/standards-guidelines/wcag/.

subsequent iterations, up to the final delivery. The goal of the accessibility assessment is to find out whether all people can use a website and, in addition, to provide useful feedback to promote future design and implementation changes that improve the usability of the site. While no WordPress plugin can solve all accessibility problems, these tools can automate the evaluation process, helping developers identify problems, fix them, or provide guidance on fixing them; some of these plugins are more geared towards checking and reporting errors, while others focus on the end-user experience, allowing them to customise accessibility. Regardless of the specific features and functionality offered, more or less complete, CMS plugins for evaluating accessibility are potentially valuable tools for ensuring that a website complies with accessibility standards and can be used easily by people, regardless of their skills. While some CMS accessibility plugins have been proposed they still suffer from some limitations in terms of usability and functionality, thus we decided to design a new one, which also exploits the functionalities of an external accessibility validator. In particular, we chose to integrate the plugin with the MAUVE++ validator [6], which is an open tool with a large community (currently 4795 registered users) and is currently used to monitor accessibility of all the Italian public administration websites[4].

In the paper, after discussing related work, we present the design of the proposed solution, how it has been implemented, and the feedback received in a first user test. Lastly, we draw some conclusions and indications for future work.

2   State of Art

Evaluating Web accessibility is becoming a complex activity because, on the one hand, the websites become richer and richer in interactive elements, and, on the other hand, the accessibility guidelines become increasingly refined to address all potential problems, thus requiring checking and monitoring many details across the pages of a website. Accessibility validation is a process that cannot be fully automated [12], however, to simplify the monitoring, analysis, detection, and correction of website accessibility problems, many automatic and semi-automatic tools have been proposed over the years (e.g. [3, 11]) to help in this regard. Such tools can radically differ according to various aspects [1], from the coverage of accessibility guidelines to how tools interpret and to what extent they can support the considered guidelines, to the way such tools present their results, including errors and warnings (which require manual intervention to be evaluated). In addition, validators can even provide different results when evaluating the same Web content [2], also due to some ambiguities in the description of the guidelines themselves [8]. They sometimes are not clear about what they actually validate; thus, there is a need to make such tools more transparent [7], and better consider their users [13]. Several studies on accessibility tools have been carried out as well. For example, a detailed study on the results of automatic Web accessibility evaluation provided by several tools is reported in [2], which considered support for only WCAG 2.0 guidelines and analysed eight popular and free online automated Web accessibility evaluation tools, finding significant differences among them in terms of various aspects. More recently,

---

[4] https://accessibilita.agid.gov.it/.

Burkard et al. [4] compared four commercial monitoring accessibility tools (SiteImprove, PopeTech, aXe Monitoring and ARC Monitoring), by evaluating them on only five Web pages according to criteria such as coverage of the Web pages, success criteria, completeness, correctness, support for localisation of errors, and manual checks. In another recent study, accessibility experts [10] performed an analysis and comparison of some accessibility assessment tools freely available as Chrome browser extensions, to evaluate their quality. Eight tools best known to developers were chosen and compared based on their features, usability and the results of the evaluation of ten websites. The analysis and comparison results demonstrated that the individual tools were inadequate to ensure full compliance with the WCAG guidelines.

We have analysed some of the most popular plugins for evaluating the accessibility of WordPress sites. The objective was to identify any gaps present in the currently available plugins and the most appreciated features to propose an alternative tool that could overcome these gaps and combine the advantages recognised in the analysed tools within a single solution. The tools to be analysed were selected starting from those in the WordPress plugin directory. The selection criteria considered how individual plugins were launched, the type of evaluation report provided and the evaluation environment presented to the user. The analysis and comparison made it possible to detect the strengths and weaknesses of the individual tools, allowing us to draw an overall picture of the features to consider in the development of a new plugin for WordPress users. Since the result of the selection was a large list of tools, we have focused on four plugins, each representing a distinct type of "accessibility evaluation plugin", which differ in their methods of initiation, type of report and evaluation context, and were selected to examine their strengths and weaknesses. The comparison was conceived with a dual purpose: to recognise the characteristics that make these plugins useful and to identify limitations and gaps, in order to collect the information necessary for the design of an improved solution. In the following we synthesise the results of the analysis of the four WordPress plugins.

Accessibility Checker[5]. Strengths: automatic scanning even during editing, when saving content or publishing it; accessibility report always visible at the end of the page; easy access to documentation via icons; indication of the line of code involved; results are aggregated by error. Weaknesses: error information is not very detailed and complete; it does not allow users to visually identify the problematic element on the page; it is not very understandable for users without computer skills; it can make errors in judgment after editing and updating the content.

Accessibility by Audioeye[6]. Strengths: real-time monitoring of the entire site; comprehensive and detailed accessibility dashboard and report; automatically fix common errors; detailed explanations on solving problems that require human support; provides an accessibility toolbar available on every page. Weaknesses: it requires creating an AudioEye account and purchasing a subscription; evaluation is performed only after publishing the site; evaluation dashboard is visible only from the supplier's website.

---

[5] https://it.wordpress.org/plugins/accessibility-checker/

[6] https://it.wordpress.org/plugins/accessibility-by-audioeye/

WP ADA Compliance Check[7]. Strengths: the scans are activated by clicking on easily recognisable buttons; scanning is available during editing; accessibility report in tabular format, sorted and comprehensible; detailed information and easy-to-follow instructions; easy access to documentation via links in each row of the table; it indicates the line of code involved for each error encountered. Weaknesses: it does not allow users to visually identify the problematic element on the page; the results are not aggregated by error; the evaluation in the editor is not very intuitive; the position of the button to start is not immediately identifiable; it requires the 'settings' block to be opened at each new evaluation; the report available in the editor is decentralised, inconvenient to consult and does not provide access to the documentation.

Editorially Accessibility Checker[8]. Strengths: it provides immediate feedback; It allows users to visually identify the problematic element within the page by inserting in-line icons; it automatically scans content during editing and indicates the total number of errors via icons; it allows users to scroll through the alerts easily using the 'previous' and 'next' buttons; it provides a complete description for each problem and suggestions on how to resolve it. Weaknesses: it is aimed exclusively at content authors without IT and accessibility skills; it detects only the most common editorial errors; it uses many icons on the page, which creates clutter and confuses the user; it places warnings above corresponding page elements, limiting their visibility; it does not provide a summary report; it must be integrated with additional tools aimed at developers, to ensure full accessibility of the contents.

The information derived from the comparative analysis was used to define the main characteristics to be considered in designing the new plugin to guarantee its usefulness and effectiveness, successfully complementing the current tools available.

One point for developing the plugin was to connect it to the functionalities of an already existing validation tool. For this purpose, we have chosen the MAUVE++ tool, which is currently used for large-scale validations [6]. Such a tool helps analyse Web applications' compliance with the WCAG 2.0 and WCAG 2.1 guidelines (conformity levels A, AA and AAA). Among the main features of MAUVE++ it is worth mentioning: it supports the validation of both static and dynamic content, it can simulate Web access of various types of devices when performing the validation, it provides the possibility of evaluating, in addition to a single page, also entire websites, including their PDF content, the techniques and the success criteria supported are indicated transparently. In addition, several members of the community of MAUVE++ asked for integrated support in WordPress to facilitate their work in developing accessible Web applications.

3   The Design of the Proposed Solution

The MAUVE++ plugin was designed with the goal to propose a robust alternative for evaluating web accessibility on WordPress, capable of overcoming the limitations found in existing plugins and providing a satisfactory and effective user experience In addition, there was the aim of providing a natural extension of the accessibility capabilities of the

---

[7] https://it.wordpress.org/plugins/wp-ada-compliance-check-basic/

[8] https://it.wordpress.org/plugins/editorially-accessibility-checker/

selected mother platform, while preserving visual and functional continuity. To simplify the process of selecting the features to include in the design of the plugin, a series of objectives to be achieved have been defined:

- Universal usability: develop a tool that is easily understandable and suitable for every type of user, from inexperienced IT editors to professional developers;
- Usefulness and effectiveness: guarantee maximum accessibility of the contents created with WordPress from the initial phase of their creation and during each modification phase, simplifying and consequently encouraging the evaluation of the contents;
- Functional homogeneity with MAUVE++: maintain functional homogeneity with the MAUVE++ platform, allowing users to take advantage of the features offered by the platform without having to access it;
- Completeness and simplicity: facilitating consultation and error resolution, providing complete results that are easily accessible, identifiable and include the necessary documentation.

Such objectives played a key role in outlining the requirements of the plugin. The plugin characteristics related to the startup mode, the type of report provided and the evaluation environment were selected by carefully evaluating the strengths and weaknesses of the plugins analysed. This approach allowed us to adopt best practices and avoid the limitations observed in the panorama of web accessibility tools available on WordPress.

The conceptual design process of the MAUVE++ plugin begins with identifying its functional requirements, i.e. the characteristics that the tool should possess and the functions that it should be able to perform, each defined according to the set objectives.

To pursue the first objective, 'universal usability', we chose to support multiple views on its results. The first is the 'end-user' view which, combined with the 'live preview' functionality, allows all users to receive understandable information regarding the accessibility, regardless of their level of IT experience. The second is the 'web developer' view, designed primarily for developers and users with expertise in the field, as it provides access to the source code highlighting the problematic parts. This choice aims to ensure that the plugin is accessible and understandable for a wide range of users, from those new to content editing to those with more advanced skills in web development.

Achieving the second objective, 'usefulness and effectiveness', represented an interesting challenge to address. To determine the most suitable evaluation environment so that the plugin was perceived as a useful tool and guaranteed high performance during the entire process of creating a website, we informally gathered feedback from accessibility stakeholders, and performed some informal tests in two evaluation contexts that emerged from the analysis of the existing plugins: the 'in-page' evaluation, conducted during the content editing phase within the WordPress editor, and the 'online' evaluation, which is performed after the content itself has been published. A preliminary version of the plugin was therefore developed, focused on evaluating the accessibility of the contents after their publication (following the model of many plugins examined). After developing the plugin's framework, this first version was modified and adapted to work within the WordPress editor. Analysing the two evaluation contexts, we concluded that the effectiveness of the plugin would have been maximised if the evaluation had been performed during the editing phase, allowing users to evaluate the accessibility of the contents before publication. Consequently, it was decided to eliminate the post-publication evaluation option, considering it redundant, and not very profitable since there are already tools for that type of validation.

Functional and visual homogeneity with the MAUVE++ platform was achieved by implementing the distinctive graphic and behavioural aspects of the reference external platform in the plugin. These include the tabular organisation of the evaluation results, grouped according to the violated success criteria, the consistent use of colours and struc-tures to those present in the parent platform, to differentiate errors and warnings within the source code, as well as the ability to visually identify errors within the evaluated content.

The last objective established, to guarantee the "completeness and simplicity" of the tool, was achieved by creating an intuitive and communicative user interface. In fact, we strategically positioned the evaluation report at the bottom of the evaluated page, ensuring constant access without interfering with the workflow or being invasive. In addition, it was decided to provide within the report all the information necessary for the user to understand and resolve errors or warnings; these include: the indication of the success criterion violated and the related technique; a descriptive summary of the error detected; the number of occurrences identified for each error/warning; the documentation necessary to resolve each error/warning; a preview of the corresponding HTML element; the possibility of visually identifying the error within the content, highlighted by a red frame for immediate understanding; a direct reference to the corresponding code line, appropriately highlighted by a raised frame, to facilitate consultation. This arrangement and presentation of information ensures that users have everything they need for a clear and complete assessment, contributing to the ease of use and quick understanding of the tool.

After having defined the basic requirements of the MAUVE++ plugin, which were essential to ensure that the final result conformed to the objectives, we focused on defin-ing further features that distinguished the tool developed from the other solutions present in the WordPress plugin directory. Following an in-depth analysis of the strengths and weaknesses of the existing plugins, the characteristics related to the launch mode, the type of report and the evaluation environment were then outlined. As regards the first feature, the activation of scanning via an easily recognisable button is a useful element found in existing tools; while among the weak points, there was the not immediately recognisable position of the activation button, and the confusion generated by those plu-gins automatically showing the results on the page and did not provide for the start by explicit user request. To simplify the use of the plugin, we chose to insert a clearly iden-tifiable start button at the top of each evaluated page/post to improve the user experience by providing intuitive access to the plugin's functionality.

It was also planned to hide the start button after its selection, so as not to disturb the user by interfering with content editing, and to show it again, in a side window, following the first update of the content, which thus becomes convenient and non-invasive (see Fig. 1). In this way, the user can re-evaluate the updated contents by clicking the button again, or perform a new evaluation at a later time. This solution optimises user interaction with the plugin, offering flexibility and user control in the activation and re-evaluation of content.

Fig. 1. Updated content evaluation window

Regarding the type of report returned by the plugin, we took into consideration the fact that the tabular format was the most used by the accessibility assessment tools analysed, as it allows for easy consultation and effectively organises all the necessary information. Therefore, we chose to adopt a table to clearly present the results returned by the plugin, grouping them by the violated success criterion (see Fig. 2), which is shown below the live preview of the Web application user interface. This approach allowed us to provide the user with an overview of the number of errors detected, thus addressing one of the weaknesses identified in current solutions. In addition, we chose to insert the accessibility report inside a multi-tab box and to allocate a second tab of the box to the 'web developer' view.

This design allows the user to easily navigate between these two views, offering a dual option for examining the data: by consulting the table or by viewing errors directly within the source code. The 'web developer' view displays an error/warning box followed by the line of code responsible for the problem and provides the same information reported in the table view, including access to the related documentation (see Fig. 3).

The 'web developer' view has been further optimised to make consultation more immediate and smooth by introducing the easy scrolling option. This allows the user to quickly view errors detected in the code using the scroll keys, 'previous' and 'next', enabled after clicking the 'view results' button.

As previously mentioned, the environment chosen to allow users to evaluate the accessibility of content during its creation is the Gutenberg block editor, default in WordPress starting from version 5.0. This choice is driven by the desire to make accessibility checking convenient and immediate for the user, eliminating the need to go elsewhere on the site or visit external platforms, such as MAUVE++, to view accessibility results.

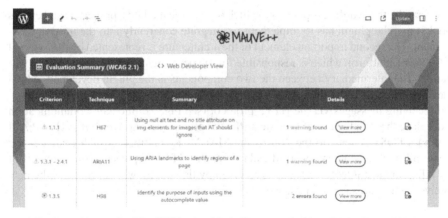

Fig. 2. The 'evaluation summary' view

Fig. 3. 'Web developer' view

To determine the optimal presentation of the accessibility report within the WordPress editor, we analysed various solutions, and we decided to insert the accessibility report into a metabox at the bottom of the page to provide efficient and convenient access. Thus, in the MAUVE++ plugin the data returned from the external validation engine are placed in a metabox at the bottom of the page, ensuring constant visibility and facilitating consultation without disturbing the user's workflow. Furthermore, after activating the accessibility validation plugin, the user is automatically redirected to the metabox. This behaviour makes the system's state immediately visible, showing the user the impact of the validation and facilitating the user's understanding of how the tool works. This feature is more usable with respect to what is provided in Accessibility Checker, which inserts the accessibility report inside the metabox but without providing a clear indication of where to find it.

The resulting architecture is described in Fig. 4. One important element of every plugin's architecture is the host application, which is the software that provides the environment in which the plugin operates. In the context of the MAUVE++ plugin this role is covered by the WordPress platform, which defines the methods, properties and events (hooks) that the plugin has to implement to integrate coherently into the hosting environment. The second important element of the architecture is represented by the external MAUVE++ platform, which is responsible for the performance of the accessibility validation. The intermediary between the two components is the plugin developed, which manages the communication between WordPress and the MAUVE++ platform, sending and receiving messages via the HTTP protocol (see Fig. 5). In detail, communication takes place through the use of specific APIs: the plugin uses the WordPress HTTP API to send a POST request to the API of the MAUVE++ platform, which evaluates the accessibility of the content received and returns the HTTP response, with the results of the validation in JSON format; this is received by the plugin, which processes the data received and returns it within the WordPress interface.

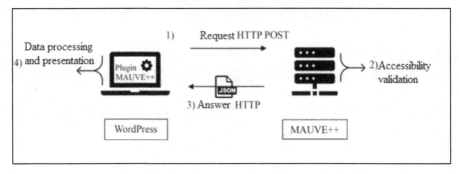

Fig. 4. Overall solution architecture

To start interacting with the MAUVE++ platform, the user has to select the start button, labeled MAUVE++, which is automatically inserted into the WordPress editor after activating the plugin, according to the methods detailed in the following. This button allows the user to trigger, when desired, the execution cycle of the MAUVE++ plugin. The plugin executive cycle works as follows (see Fig. 5):

1. Inserting the metabox: when the user clicks the MAUVE++ button, the plugin inserts a new metabox into the WordPress editor, intended to host the accessibility assessment report.
2. Communication with MAUVE++ sending the HTTP request to the API of the MAUVE+ platform, including the code of the content to be evaluated.
3. Data Processing: After retrieving the returned accessibility report from MAUVE++, the plugin proceeds with the manipulation of the received object, with the aim of extracting only the relevant information to show to the user.
4. Data return: at the end of its operating cycle, the plugin returns the data processed within the previously inserted metabox, allowing its viewing by the user.

The design of the MAUVE++ plugin is carefully designed to ensure consistency with the user experience offered by the reference platform. For this reason, the colours, icons and graphic elements of the interface recall those present in the MAUVE++ environment, adapting their layout to the new context of the WordPress editor. The results of

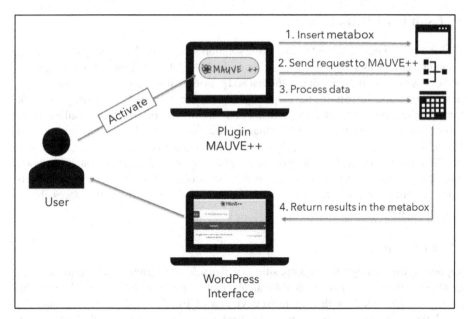

Fig. 5. Execution cycle of the plugin

the accessibility evaluation are presented in different ways to satisfy different types of users. The "live preview" view (see Fig. 6 left) shows the errors in the user interface by highlighting the problematic element with red borders, while the "web developer" view highlights the errors in the code (see Fig. 6 right).

Fig. 6. Live preview (left) and web developer (right) views highlighting an error

4   Usability Evaluation

We have carried out a user test to assess the solution's usability. To recruit participants, a communication was sent to the mailing list of the MAUVE++ platform, informing them of the possibility of participating in the test and providing information on the characteristics of the test and the solution developed. Since we were interested in receiving feedback from people with various backgrounds, among those who offered their availability to participate in the test, providing information regarding professional qualifications and familiarity with the WordPress CMS, we selected users with different levels of IT skills. Finally, considering the desire to propose a useful tool for all WordPress content authors, regardless of their experience in accessibility or the tools used, we also extended the invitation to some people who had never used the MAUVE++ platform or other accessibility assessment tools.

4.1   Participants

Regarding the demographic composition of the selected sample, the group of users involved in the test is characterised by an age that varies between 23 and 57 years; the average was 37 years, with a standard deviation of 10.6, 13 males and 2 females. In detail, the following user groups were involved: ten users registered on the MAUVE++ platform (of these, four declared that they exclusively use the MAUVE++ platform while six users declared that they also use other accessibility assessment tools); five users who had never used the MAUVE++ platform (of these, two declared that they had never used an accessibility assessment tool while three users indicated the use of alternative tools such as Wave, w3c validator and vscode).

As for the level of IT competence of the selected users, all test participants stated that they surf the web every day or more; 46.7% of them have very good programming experience, i.e. advanced/professional knowledge, while 20% declared they have no programming experience. Regarding knowledge and experience in using WordPress, 20% of the selected users have never used this CMS, while 13.3% claimed to have extensive knowledge of all the tool's features.

4.2   User Test Design

To ensure that all users performed the same tasks while interacting with identical content, a test WordPress page was created, specially populated with a series of accessibility errors. They had to perform five tasks, one for each significant activity that can be carried out via the plugin. Each task was associated with a success criterion and the maximum time within which the task should have been completed; usually between 3 and 5 min, depending on the complexity of the task. Below is the list of tasks and the associated success criteria identified for the user test of the MAUVE++ plugin:

- Task 1. "Access the 'Usability Test' page in editing mode and perform the accessibility assessment by activating the MAUVE++ plugin".
  The task is completed when the accessibility assessment report is displayed. Success criterion: the user recognises the function of the 'MAUVE++' button and presses it to start the accessibility assessment. Maximum time: 3 min.

- Task 2. "Starting from the accessibility evaluation report, display on the page one of the elements that violated the success criteria 1.1.1 - 1.3.1 - 4.1.2".
  The task is completed when one of the problematic elements is selected and highlighted on the page. Success criterion: The user locates the table row corresponding to the indicated criteria, presses the "view more" key to consult the details of each problematic element and recognises the function of the element "view on page", selecting it to view the element. Maximum time: 3 min.
- Task 3. "Display the element that violated success criterion 1.4.3 on the page, correct the error using the WordPress toolbar, save the new content by updating and evaluate the modified content again".
  The task is concluded when a new content evaluation is carried out following the changes made. Success criterion: the user views the indicated element on the page, modifies it and updates the content; after the update, the user uses the side window to re-evaluate the content. Maximum time: 5 min.
- Task 4. "Starting from the accessibility evaluation report, identify one of the elements that generated the warning for success criterion 2.5.3 in the source code and then return to the evaluation report".
  The task is finished when one of the problematic elements appears in the source code, and the user returns to the report screen. Success criterion: The user recognises the function of the icon (view on code), selects it to view one of the elements indicated within the source code; subsequently, clicks the 'go back to summary' button to return to the initial position. Maximum time: 3 min.
- Task 5. "Identify one of the elements that generated a warning for a success criterion of your choice and find the useful documentation to correct it".
  The task is completed when the documentation page associated with the chosen warning is displayed. Success criterion: the user chooses a warning element as desired and displays it on the page; next, the user identifies and selects the icon (help) to access the associated documentation page. Maximum time: 3 min.

All users selected for the test were contacted individually, and an appointment was made with each of them, lasting a maximum of 30 min. After making the individual appointments, each user received the materials necessary for carrying out the test: the folder containing the MAUVE++ plugin files, the default "Usability Test" page, to be imported into their WordPress environment, and a document introduction which explains the purposes and methods of the test, as well as providing detailed instructions for installing the required materials. Each user was also asked to consent, or not, to the audio and video recording of the test session, clarifying the methods through which such recordings would be managed while respecting privacy.

At the end of the test, users filled in a questionnaire divided into three parts. The first section presents a series of questions to gather general information on the users involved in the test: name, surname, gender, age, educational qualification, programming experience/on WordPress/with software evaluation tools. Accessibility, frequency of use and type of tools used. The second one was the System Usability Scale (SUS). The third section aims to acquire data regarding the level of user satisfaction. Different aspects of the plugin, commonly considered in the web context, are presented, and users are asked to express their satisfaction with each aspect. These aspects include ease of use, graphic quality, pleasantness and speed of interaction, ease of reading, exhaustive content, completeness of data, and overall usefulness. The last two questions in this section are open-ended and are aimed at gathering feedback regarding the three elements of the plugin that the users liked most and least.

4.3 Results

Based on the data collected (task completion times and errors), it is possible to state that, in general tasks were completed within the expected times. Figure 7 shows the task completion times. The calculated confidence intervals are relatively wide, especially for task 3, indicating considerable variability between users. This variability, however, is related to the level of IT competence of the users involved. Task 3 required the modification of an element of the page through the use of the tools offered by WordPress and, for this reason, was performed with particular difficulty by those who had little or no experience in using it, two of them were even unable to complete the task. However, the users who completed the task performed the operations foreseen in a short time, easily identifying and using the plugin. This factor made it possible to note that the significant amount of time used to perform task 3, and the failures were not attributable to the usability of the plugin, but rather to the skills of the test participants. A different situation, however, applies to task 5, for which the same number of failures was recorded and a relatively high execution time. Unlike task 3, task 5 made it possible to detect a usability problem in the developed solution. Although the average completion time of the activity was less than the allocated maximum time, this task raised several doubts among users who, in some cases, verbally expressed their difficulties in achieving the goal during the testing session. Through the observation of users, the collection of feedback and the analysis of completion times, it was possible to identify and correct the usability problem that would otherwise have been overlooked: the icon for accessing the documentation associated with an error was unclear: one user misunderstood it believing it was associated with the documentation of the entire plugin, and two users even did not notice it, failing the task.

In general, we note that the number of errors committed for each task was very limited. It is important to underline that only two of these errors can be directly attributed to the usability of the plugin, demonstrating good overall efficiency in its use.

Regarding the SUS, the average score was 74, with a 95% confidence interval, scores vary between a minimum of 65.9 and a maximum of 82.1.

In the open questions, we also asked them to indicate the aspects that they liked most and least. The users indicated as most appreciated aspects: the possibility of having both a preview of the user interface and access to the associated code; the support for problem finding (direct link to the errors identified, both in the editor and at code level), speed and ease of use, graphic appearance of the plugin, highlighting of errors, intuitiveness of the interface, the possibility of carrying out accessibility checks within the editor, clarity and completeness of the results.

In the least favourite aspects, some users indicated ambiguity, low recognisability of the documentation icon, lack of indications for switching from 'end-user' to 'web developer' view, and unintuitive correlation between the HTML element and the corresponding error box in the "web developer" view.

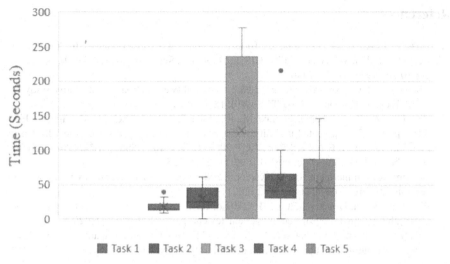

Fig. 7. Task completion time

5 Conclusions and Future Work

The results effectively respond to the objectives initially set and lay solid foundations for further research and optimisation, aimed at expanding and giving continuity to the work carried out. The user test of the plugin confirmed the solution's usability, allowing the identification of a small design issue related to the access to the error documentation, which was promptly resolved. We have provided a useful tool to better support current practises in Web development by allowing accessibility checking while the content is being created in the most popular CMS platform, exploiting a powerful open external accessibility engine and overcoming the usability limitations of previous plugins.

Future work can further improve the performance and expand the functionality of the developed component, starting, for example, with the integration of other features or services, such as the contrast control feature, which evaluates the contrast ratio between background and foreground colours, ensuring that it complies with standards. Other features that could represent a further strong point of the developed plugin include, for example, the visual overview of the analyses conducted and the results obtained or the reference to the WCAG techniques successfully evaluated and those that cannot be evaluated. In future developments, particular attention will be paid to managing compatibility with other WordPress plugins and editors. The project's upcoming goals include the official publication of the plugin and its release as a finished product.

In conclusion, the work presented constitutes a further step towards advancing web accessibility, aimed at improving the online experience, promoting awareness of the importance of universal access and ensuring that all web users can fully and equitably enjoy the vast range of content available on the internet.

Disclosure of Interests. The authors have no competing interests to declare that are relevant to the content of this article.

References

1. Abascal, J., Arrue, M., Valencia, X.: Tools for web accessibility evaluation. In: Yesilada, Y., Harper, S. (eds.) Web Accessibility. HIS, pp. 479–503. Springer, London (2019). https://doi.org/10.1007/978-1-4471-7440-0_26
2. Abduganiev, S.G.: Towards automated Web accessibility evaluation: a comparative study. Int. J. Inf. Technol. Comput. Sci. (IJITCS) **9**(9), 18–44 (2017)
3. Beirekdar, A., Keita, M., Noirhomme, M., Randolet, F., Vanderdonckt, J., Mariage, C.: Flexible reporting for automated usability and accessibility evaluation of web sites. In: Costabile, M.F., Paternò, F. (eds.) INTERACT 2005. LNCS, vol. 3585, pp. 281–294. Springer, Heidelberg (2005). https://doi.org/10.1007/11555261_25
4. Burkard, A., Zimmermann, G., Schwarzer, B.: Monitoring systems for checking websites on accessibility. Front. Comput. Sci. **3**, 2 (2021)
5. EU Commission. Directive (EU) 2016/2102 of the European Parliament and of the Council (2016). https://eur-lex.europa.eu. https://eur-lex.europa.eu/eli/dir/2016/2102/oj
6. Iannuzzi, N., Manca, M., Paternò, F., Santoro, C.: Usability and transparency in the design of a tool for automatic support for web accessibility validation. Univ. Access Inf. Soc. 1–20 (2022)
7. Manca, M., Palumbo, V., Paternò, F., Santoro, C.: The transparency of automatic web accessibility evaluation tools: design criteria, state of the art, and user perception. ACM Trans. Access. Comput. **16**(1), 1–36 (2023)
8. Pelzetter, J.: A Declarative model for web accessibility requirements and its implementation. Front. Comput. Sci. **3**, 605772 (2021)
9. Power, C., Freire, A., Petrie, H., Swallow, D.: Guidelines are only half of the story: accessibility problems encountered by blind users on the web. In: Proceedings of the SIGCHI Conference on Human Factors in Computing Systems, pp. 433–442. ACM (2012)
10. Santos, T., Duarte, C.: Comparing accessibility evaluation plug-ins. In: W4A 2020: Proceedings of the 17th International Web for All Conference, pp. 1–11 (2020)
11. Schiavone, A.G., Paternò, F.: An extensible environment for guideline-based accessibility evaluation of dynamic web applications. Univ. Access Inf. Soc. **14**(1), 111–132 (2015)
12. Vigo, M., Brown, J., Conway, V.: Benchmarking web accessibility evaluation tools: measuring the harm of sole reliance on automated tests. In: Proceedings of the 10th International Cross-Disciplinary Conference on Web Accessibility, pp. 1–10 (2013)
13. Yesilada, Y., Brajnik, G., Vigo, M., Harper, S.: Exploring perceptions of Web accessibility: a survey approach. Behav. Inf. Technol. **34**(2), 119–134 (2015)

GaLaPaGoS: A Design Pattern for Sustainability of ICT Interactive Software and Services

Shola Oyedeji[1]($\boxtimes$) (iD), Mikhail O. Adisa[1] (iD), Ahmed Seffah[2] (iD), Felipe Leon Coello[1], and Bilal Naqvi[1] (iD)

[1] LUT University, Lappeenranta, Finland
{shola.oyedeji,mikhail.adisa,felipe.leon,Syed.Naqvi}@lut.fi
[2] Zayed University, Dubai, United Arab Emirates
ahmed.Seffah@zu.ac.ae

Abstract. ICT is an enabler for sustainable development and contributes to sustainability problems arising from different human activities aided by ICT interactive software and services. Consequently, these ICT-aided activities contribute to a vast amount of electronics and paper package waste at different stages of production, usage, and disposal. Some of these wastes can be attributed to a lack of understanding from ICT designers on how to design ICT interactive software and services for a green user experience. This paper explores design patterns as a tool to capture and incorporate sustainability concerns into the design of ICT interactive software and services for green user experience, where users become more conscious of the sustainability impacts of their actions. The Design science research method was applied to create and validate three sustainability design patterns. The results show that the proposed design patterns can guide ICT designers to engage and influence user behavior toward sustainability awareness.

Keywords: ICT · Green UX · Sustainability awareness · persuasive technology · e-waste · eco-feedback · repair · reuse

1 Introduction

The concern for sustaining our world is increasing worldwide [1] and the importance of sustainability is highlighted by the United Nations Sustainable Development Goals (SDGs) [2]. Human activities and actions are central to some of the sustainability problems today with the continuous usage of Information and Communication Technology (ICT) and software systems, which have led to the disposal of different electronic waste (e-waste) [3] and paper waste. For example, in Europe, 16 tons of materials (glass, plastic, wood, papers, etc.) are used per person yearly, out of which 6 tons become waste. From this total of 2.5 billion tons, only a limited (albeit increasing) share (36%) was recycled, with the rest landfilled or burned, of which some 600 million tons could be recycled or reused [4]. According to E-waste Monitor, 50 million tons of e-waste are generated annually [5] of which a sizeable proportion is related to ICT. Figure 1 illustrates that e-waste is mostly generated in developed countries and transferred to developing countries in Africa and Asia, where e-waste management is still a problem [6].

© IFIP International Federation for Information Processing 2024
Published by Springer Nature Switzerland AG 2024
M. K. Lárusdóttir et al. (Eds.): HCSE 2024, LNCS 14793, pp. 63–83, 2024.
https://doi.org/10.1007/978-3-031-64576-1_4

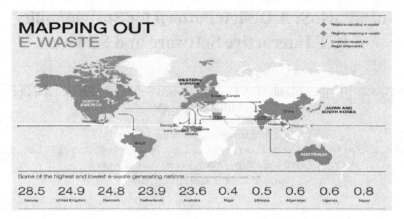

Fig. 1. The global E-waste statistics on e-waste generated by nations adapted from [5]

An investigation for Sunday's Dateline [7] found that varieties of old electronic equipment were discarded in what was once a picturesque wetland of Ghana, West Africa, without proper waste management. Research outcomes, as presented in [6, 8–10], show increased concerns and efforts toward proper ICT e-waste management in developing and developed countries [11] through extended producer responsibility (EPR) and efficient recycling facilities but less research on user behavioral change towards waste reduction (e-waste and paper waste) aided by user interaction with ICT interactive software and services. The US Environmental Protection Agency reported that humans are at the center of waste generation [12] as most of their activities impact sustainability (environmental, social, individual, and economic). As such, ICT interactive software and services play a significant role in waste reduction (e-waste and paper waste). Therefore, there is a need to investigate how to design sustainably and develop ICT interactive software and services to support user behavior towards reducing waste and emissions and promote a mindset change towards repair, reuse, and recycling options among users.

The following scenario is an elaborate typical problem of user experience with current ICT interactive software and services:

"Many mobile phone devices and computers we buy are packaged in nice and very attractive boxes. What do we do with boxes after buying and using the devices? What do we do with the device at the end of life (EOL)? The user experience (UX) analysis shows that the boxes may stay in users' drawers for years, or users may trash them. Also, the device at the EOL might be disposed because of bad parts. What if the manufacturer has a Web service that provides users with information about alternative ways of using the device parts at EOL and the benefits of reusing the box used in packaging the device? UX analysis again shows that users may not access it and thus never read this information. Then the question is, how do we design the accessibility and the attractiveness of the Web service for green user experience (green UX)?"

From the context of this research, green UX refers to the effectiveness of user interaction with interactive ICT software and services in creating user awareness about their environmental and societal impacts on sustainability. It entails how well ICT interactive software and services support change in user behavior toward reducing resource wastage and encouraging repair, reuse, and recycling. From the above scenario, green UX will be that whenever a user opens the box and starts the device, the web service is integrated into the device setup operations. As part of the setup service, the device tells the user how to easily reuse the package box, the device at the end of life, provides the environmental benefits of reuse with different alternative options, and uses eco-feedback to educate users about their actions while using the device. This will ensure that the new interactive service setup in devices facilitates the incorporation of sustainability elements into the design loop. Currently, the way ICT interactive software and services are designed affects sustainability, which has an impact on the users, society, and environment [13]; [14] because every line of code in software systems and services has the financial, technical, moral, ethical implication that shapes human behavior [15].

This study addresses the research question: "What design tool can support the design of interactive software and services for green UX?" The goal is to investigate ways to support software development practitioners (designers, developers, architects, programmers, product managers, product owners, and CTOs) in designing interactive ICT software and services for green UX (creating user consciousness about their impacts on sustainability) through design patterns. There is evidence of patterns being used as a powerful and useful tool to solve different reoccurring problems, such as interaction design patterns [16], Navigation in Large Information Architectures [17], UI patterns [18], and Usable Security Patterns [19]. The sustainability design patterns created in this research are called GaLaPaGoS (GAmified LAnguage of PAtterns for GlObal Sustainability) for green UX. This paper is structured as follows: Sect. 2 provides background information. Section 3 details the research design. Section 4 presents the research execution with results. Discussion and threat to validity are in Sect. 5. Concluding remarks in Sect. 6.

2 Background

Design and engineering of ICT interactive software and services for green and sustainability have focused more on energy efficiency and CO_2 emission [20] [21] without consideration of green UX. The lack of attention towards green UX in the design of ICT solutions for waste reduction has continuously led to an increase in waste generation annually because one-half of all e-waste comes from users of ICT interactive software and services [5]. In today's society, where ICT is an important element, software systems have a significant role in achieving sustainability [22] and supporting most of the sustainable development goals (SDGs) [2] through green UX, especially SDG 12 (Ensure sustainable consumption and production patterns). Research conducted by [23] indicated the importance of user engagement in interactive software design through an art-inspired tangible eco-feedback system that engages users emotionally, influencing users to be more energy-conscious. Persuading users and influencing their behavior toward green and sustainability can be achieved through patterns. According to a study

[24], technology and patterns can be used to persuade users to be more environmentally aware. Another research [25] described how the application of patterns can provide awareness of social influence in the persuasive systems design (PSD) model. The patterns proposed by [25] are components of social stimuli such as competition, recognition, and cooperation with the potential to influence human behavior.

Fogg's model for understanding human behavior shows the importance of embedding social stimuli into a design pattern and states that behavior is characterized by three factors, namely motivation, ability, and triggers [26]. These factors play a huge role in influencing human behavior and social stimulus as defined and used in a design patterns study for social influence [25]. Different patterns presented by Lockton et al. [27] also show the effectiveness of influencing behavior through design that considers social stimuli. The complexity of understanding humans is the major challenge designers face in designing systems for human behavioral change [28]. According to Gabrielsen [28], the strategies for designing for sustainability include the use of persuasive technology, behavior steering, and eco-feedback. Furthermore, Colmant et al. [29] research shows that green software and technologies have tremendous potential for reducing world CO_2 emissions with improved software energy efficiency on multi-core systems. However, this potential of reducing CO_2 emissions through green software and technologies will not be achievable without consideration for UX with different ICT interactive software and services. Despite the high number of studies on green technologies and software, there has been less research advancement toward designing green technologies, software systems, and services to influence and persuade users to become more conscious of their impact based on interaction with different ICT solutions. Additionally, to consider making users green based on ICT interactive software and services, sustainability perspectives should be considered about green technologies and services by designing and developing solutions that adapt to its users [30]. The need to design better technology interfaces that engage humans in civic actions was identified by [31] in an attempt 'to design the next generation of "digital soapboxes" where they emphasize (1) the importance of designing better tools that connect, exchange and dialogue with users and (2), the need to utilize the capabilities of new technologies. There are three distinctions where sustainability has a relation with green Information Technology (IT) [32]:

- Greening IT systems and usage, such as developing software systems and services that support user action to consume less energy
- Using IT to support environmental sustainability, one example is helping citizens to reduce their resource consumption and wastage, encouraging reuse (upcycling), and recycling.
- Using IT to create awareness about the impacts of users' actions on sustainability.

As such, these different studies show the need to incorporate green UX in the design of interactive ICT software and services because green UX will aid better changes in user habits, which over time can support user behavior towards sustainability (creating user consciousness about their impacts on sustainability, decrease in resource wastage such electronic and paper waste) with good eco-feedback on their action.

3   Research Design

This research is grounded in the overall design science research methodology (DSRM) [33] that provides the process of iteratively creating and testing artifacts, which were applied in this research to solve problems of green UX in ICT interactive software and services. Figure 2 provides an overview of how the three design science research cycles (Relevance Cycle, Design Cycle, and Rigor Cycle) from [33] were applied in the study.

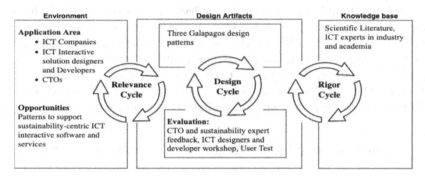

Fig. 2. Design science research cycles adapted from Murugesan and Gangadharan [33]

- **Relevance Cycle**: The relevance cycle initiates design science research within the context of finding solutions to the challenge of persuading and influencing positive user behavior towards sustainability (creating user consciousness about their impacts on sustainability and decreasing electronic and paper waste) because of the usage of different ICT interactive software and services. The relevance cycle (contextual environment) is connected to the design cycle (construction of artifact) to ensure a better evaluation of the created artifacts and determine whether additional iterations of the relevance cycle are needed in this design science research.
- **Rigor Cycle**: Design science research requires knowledge based on scientific theories that provide a foundation for the research work. Within this research, the rigor cycle covers studying past knowledge on sustainability problems of ICT interactive software and services with artifacts (tools, processes, guidelines) that already exist to tackle the problem of persuading and influencing positively user behavior towards sustainability through user sustainability awareness.
- **Design Cycle**: This is the heart of design science research because this cycle of research activities iterates more rapidly between the construction of an artifact, its evaluation, and subsequent feedback to refine the design artifacts based on the feedback. The design cycle in this research covers activities such as workshops and evaluation of all the created artifacts with software development practitioners in the industry.

4   Research Execution and Results

This section covers the creation and validation of the design patterns (GaLaPaGoS design pattern) by software development practitioners and end-users testing prototypes created based on GaLaPaGoS design pattern to support green UX.

4.1 Relevance Cycle 1: Problem Identification

Research results from literature studies in the background section highlight different problems for designing ICT interactive software and services to support positive user behavior towards reducing waste (electronic and paper waste) and user consciousness about their impacts on sustainability. Therefore, a full-day participatory pattern workshop [34] with software development practitioners was organized. Table 1 provides the background details (Job title and years of experience) of the software development practitioners (workshop participants) from different companies in the industry.

Table 1. Background of workshop participants from different companies

No	Job Title	Years of Experience
1	CTO	13
2	UX Lord	11
3	Programmer	8
4	UI Designer	6
5	ICT Engineer	5
6	DevOps Manager	5
7	Software Developer	4
8	IT Manager	4
9	Business Analyst	4

The researchers (authors) acted as facilitators and participants in the workshop. The first phase of the workshop focused on identifying design challenges related to green user experience (UX) in ICT interactive software and services. The workshop participants highlighted several key issues. Firstly, they noted a lack of practical guidelines and design tools suitable for integrating green UX into the design process. Existing sustainability guidelines were considered impractical for business environments because it is time-consuming and not economically feasible. Moreover, the workshop participants emphasized the need for practical examples demonstrating how sustainability can be effectively translated into design elements of interactive software and services to enhance user consciousness of their sustainability impacts. Additionally, they highlighted a gap in incorporating sustainability into software development and design practitioners education and training. Regarding resource waste from user interactions with

ICT interactive software and services, major concerns included excessive printing leading to paper and energy waste in companies, electronic waste from discarded devices
(computers, smartphones, tablets, etc.) and packaging waste from e-commerce activities. Addressing these challenges requires the development of design tools that support
designers in creating green UX solutions while considering business constraints and
sustainability complexities.

Next Action: Develop a tool to support and educate ICT interactive software and
services designers to design ICT interactive software and services for green UX.

4.2   Rigor and Design Cycle 2: Development of Artifacts (Patterns)

The second phase of the workshop involves co-designing solutions for all identified
green UX problems in interactive software and services. Researchers and workshop
participants explored persuasive design tools to support green UX and concluded that
design patterns serve as a structured template to support designers of ICT interactive
software and services for green UX. This led the researchers to introduce participatory
pattern workshop [34] guidelines to facilitate different design narratives with the workshop participants on ICT interactive software and services for green UX. This resulted in
the creation of three GaLaPaGoS design patterns (Improved packaging, green printing,
and electronic lifecycle extension). Table 2 outlines the pattern template used in creating
the three GaLaPaGoS design patterns by the researchers and workshop participants.

Table 2. Patterns template adapted from participatory pattern workshops resource kit [34]

Pattern content	Description
Name	Naming is important. Think of a short, catchy phrase that captures the essence of your pattern
Summary	Try to capture the essence of the pattern in 2–3 sentences. Focus on function - what it does, not how it is built
Illustration	Metaphoric or inspirational image, which captures the spirit of the pattern
Problem	What is the problem that this pattern addresses? What does it try to achieve?
Context	When and where is this pattern most relevant?
Solution	Describe the core of the solution in such a way that it can be directly implemented a million times without doing the same thing twice
Diagram	A structural or narrative graphic that supports the detailed description of the solution
Related Patterns	List other patterns related to this one under categories such as component, assisting, conflicting, uses this, etc.

4.2.1 The Electronic Lifecycle Extension Pattern

The Electronic Lifecycle Extension pattern, as detailed in Table 3, focuses on electronic waste, which is a global ecological issue because of the increase in the amount of e-waste from increased usage of different electronic devices [35] to access different ICT interactive software and services for our daily activities.

Table 3. GaLaPaGoS pattern template for electronic lifecycle extension pattern

Pattern Name	Electronic Lifecycle Extension
Context/Intent	This pattern showcases how to repair hardware components (screen, battery, memory, processor) to avoid disposal of usable electronics, and when an electronics device is damaged, usable components are recommended for reuse by the person in need of such components
Problem	Electronics are disposed of even when components (screens, chips, metals, plastics) are still working or can be repaired
Forces	• Relatively new electronics such as cell phones are replaced by new ones often within 6 months to 2 years • Electronic components have a long life expectancy • Materials are not biodegradable and hard to extract
Solutions	• Show the life expectancy of components • If some component in an electronic device is damaged, suggest repair/replacement • Provide guides to repair your cell phone • Provide sources where to find parts • Encourage repair with motivational phrases • Provide solutions if repair is not effective
Consequences	• Fewer electronics are disposed off in the environment • Increased life expectancy of electronics • Users become more aware of their environmental impact • Reduced environmental pollution

The electronic lifecycle extension pattern supports the reuse of electronic components (screen, battery, memory, processor) to reduce the disposal of usable electronics, and if disposed of, reuse recommendations for a person in need of those components should be available.

4.2.2 The Green Printing Pattern

Printing is a function in ICT interactive software and services that serve as a source of paper waste in companies and homes. However, the consequential effects of printing have cross-boundary impacts on the environment: trees used in producing papers, energy consumed in printing and reprinting the same documents, paper wastage and hardware resources (printers) used in printing, the exploitation of forests to obtain pulp for the paper, to the use of inks that pollutes the environment. Billions of tons of paper are used worldwide (Statistic Brain Research Institute, 2016) and the number keeps growing due to the availability and reduced prices of printers and paper in the world.

Table 4. GaLaPaGoS pattern template for green printing pattern

Pattern Name	Green Printing
Context/Intent	This pattern is to reduce/stop printing unless necessary
Problem	Large sums of documents are printed unnecessarily generating a huge waste of resources (paper and ink) and having a negative impact on the environment
Forces	• The document size is large and is widely used, and almost every person in the organization wants to print • The document is in colours, 1 face, spaces between lines and margins are wide • Oversized images that take up much space
Solutions	• Disable by default the print button • If a user insists on printing, display a warning • Show leader board/point reward system • Finally allow print but with print, settings changed
Consequences	• Users print less • Fewer resources are consumed

Table 4 provides details of the green printing pattern centered on the design problems associated with printing in different interactive software and services which can be used by designers of green UX to reduce paper waste and make users aware of their sustainability impacts from printing.

4.2.3 Improved Packaging Pattern

This pattern aims to support the design of an online shopping experience where users are given choices of using less paper packaging and shown how to reuse their package boxes for the alternative purpose of reducing paper waste that comes from online shopping.

The improved packaging pattern (See Table 5) targets those in charge of the technological and business logic of online shops to help reduce the amount of paper packaging waste from shopping online.

Next Action: Apply the three GaLaPaGoS design patterns to test effectiveness in supporting design decisions of ICT interactive software and services for green UX.

Table 5. GaLaPaGoS pattern template for improved packaging pattern

Pattern Name	Improved Packaging
Context/Intent	This pattern displays how to reduce unnecessary extra packing when ordering items online
Problem	Due to the convenience of online shopping, more people are buying items online, which increases the amount of packaging used for shipping those items
Forces	• Any item bought online has its own packing plus the packaging for shipping • People tend to buy items separately • Some materials (plastic) are not biodegradable • The package is disposed off without recycling or reuse
Solutions	• When purchasing the item online, show the types of packaging available for shipping, and pre-select less packaging, thus a cheaper option • Attach instructions to conserve the packaging and reuse them as gift boxes • Display instructions to encourage recycling • Encourage the devolution of packages for further use in other shipping
Consequences	• Use only necessary packages when sending items • More reused packages within online shopping • Customers reuse packages for other purposes

4.3   Relevance Cycle 3: Testing of the Artifacts by Developers

This section provides results demonstrating the applicability of GaLaPaGoS design patterns to support green UX by designing sustainability-centric interactive ICT software and services. Four software developers with more than five years of experience were recruited from different companies to work together and apply the three GaLaPaGoS design patterns for the redesign of any interactive software or service of their choice.

4.3.1   Green Printing Pattern

A daily activity that is related to ICT in every workplace and household is printing. Printing activities involve different resources, such as hardware, software, and paper. The four developers applied the green printing pattern to reduce unnecessary printing and create user awareness about paper wastage from printing. Google Docs and Microsoft Word documents were used case for the design of a mock-up solution. Figure 3 shows the design mock-up based on a green printing pattern where users are informed of their printing activities about natural resources (trees) and their CO_2 emissions.

This interface provides users with a statistical overview of their printing activities and educates them about their impacts on sustainability and the environment through the information in the dashboard (CO2 emission, rank in the company, and relating the printed documents to trees killed in the forest). The four developers indicated that the green print pattern can be applied to these scenarios to promote green UX:

1. The first scenario is when the user wants to reprint an already printed document, a pop-up tip from the interface tells the user there are two or three pages that have

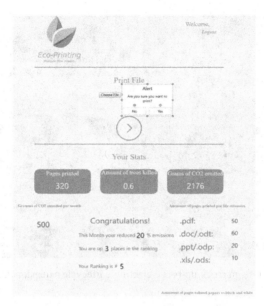

Fig. 3. Design mock-up based on green printing pattern

changed since the last time a user edited that same document and asks if the user wants to reprint only pages that have changed.

2. The second scenario is that when users want to print with color, a tip from the interface informs users to print only colored pages.

3. Finally, the dashboard gives user statistics about the percentage of their printing and the number of pages, which equals a certain amount of killed trees, to create awareness about their environmental impacts.

Feedback from Developers: Add to the green pattern template solution: "alert users of oversized images" and "tips for users to reduce image size".

4.3.2   Electronic Lifecycle Extension Pattern

All our modern-day life requires the use of different electronic devices or electrical equipment such as phones, computers, tablets, and screens. The developers used the electronic lifecycle extension pattern to create a mock-up design (see Fig. 4) for supporting an extension of electronic device lifespan that can be incorporated into electronic device apps like mobile phones, computers, and tablets to create user awareness about how to repair, reuse and replace components of electronic devices.

According to the four developers, the application of the Electronic Lifecycle Extension pattern in the design and development of ICT solutions can guide end-users on how to repair, reuse, and fix parts of the electronics instead of disposing the electronic device, which in the long term will help reduce the ecological footprint of ICT waste.

Fig. 4. Design mock-up-based electronic lifecycle extension pattern

Feedback from Developers: Extend this pattern or create another pattern that can aid diverse alternatives for reusing electrical components at the end of the life cycle for other purposes.

4.3.3 Improved Packaging Pattern

One major source of waste comes from items used in packaging products. Items such as cardboard, plastic, and special foams are used to package products that will later become waste.

Fig. 5. Design mock-up based on green printing pattern

Though logistics have improved with the use of ICT technology for improved delivery [24], it has increased waste due to poor packaging. The software developers created a mock-up design (see Fig. 5) for online stores like Amazon and eBay using the improved packaging pattern as a guide. The four developers stated that by applying the improved packaging pattern, the design mock-up in Fig. 5 is one example of how those in charge of the technological aspect of online retail stores can design purchase experience to inform users on how to reuse package boxes and charge extra for packaging to discourage unnecessary packaging waste.

Feedback from Developers: Create another pattern focusing on information display within interactive software and services for green UX that can support user engagement and foster better sustainability awareness.

The design mock-up results from applying the three GaLaPaGoS design patterns show it can serve as a design tool to support designers in adding elements of sustainability to their design decisions for ICT interactive software and services. This can support green UX, where users become aware of their impacts on sustainability.

4.3.4 User Awareness Campaign

The four developers proposed a prototype idea for user awareness called "Save the Planet Campaign," which can be incorporated into a mobile phone and tablet setup to improve user's green UX. The developers combined the electronic lifecycle extension pattern and the improved packaging pattern to design a prototype using Marvelapp [37], an online prototyping tool to explore the Save the Planet Campaign mimicking a new mobile phone setup.

Fig. 6. Mobile phone setup prototype for Save the Planet Campaign Available Online [37]

Figure 6 shows some snapshots of the prototype, and the full version of the Save Planet Campaign prototype is available online [37]. Multinational technology companies like Apple and Samsung that contribute to the problems of e-waste and are leaders in the production and selling of different mobile devices and laptops can incorporate different campaigns similar to the Save the Planet Campaign in their electronic device setup to educate consumers or users of their products about sustainability and alternative reuse options for their electronic devices.

Next Action: Test the prototype (Save the Planet Campaign) and the three design mock-ups with end users to evaluate the effectiveness of supporting green UX among users.

4.4 Relevance Cycle 4: Testing Prototype with End Users

This section details the user experience testing of the Save the Planet Campaign prototype from Sect. 4.3 with end users. The goal is to test the green UX based on user interaction with the prototype. Users were recruited by the researchers (authors) with different usage of ICT and technology needs. The volunteer users were asked the following questions before interacting with the Save the Planet Campaign prototype to gather information about each volunteer user and their habits:

- **Q1:** How many old smartphones do you have but currently do not use?
- **Q2:** What do you do with your old smartphones after you purchase new ones?
- **Q3:** What do you do with your phone package boxes after you purchase a new phone?

The responses from users for each of these questions are detailed in Table 6, with information on each participating volunteer user.

Table 6. Volunteered users information and answers before interacting with the Save the Planet Campaign prototype

Users	Age	Q1	Q2	Q3
User 1	52	2	I sometimes give it to my kids	I throw the package box to trash bin
User 2	50	3	Keep at home for memories	Keep them in the drawer
User 3	47	1	Throw them away since the batteries are usually bad	I save the boxes in my storage room
User 4	45	1	Dispose it off	Usually put in the trash
User 5	33	2	Left it in my drawer at our house	I leave it in my store
User 6	25	2	Put it in my garage storage	Trash them
User 7	23	1	Throw it away in the electronic bin	Put the package boxes in the recycle bin after unboxing new phones
User 8	21	0	Trade in when a new phone is released	Put them in the trash
User 9	20	0	Exchange for a better phone with an improved camera at the phone shop	Give my kid brother to play with it

The user test was conducted on 1st November 2023 with 9 volunteer users to interact and test the mobile phone setup for the Save the Planet Campaign. The volunteer users were provided with the prototype. All 9 volunteer users explored the prototype for an average of 15 min each. The following were verbatim comments from some of the volunteer users that summarize their opinions after exploring the mobile phone setup prototype for the Save the Planet Campaign:

- *Reflecting after this test I realized I can do more to reduce my electronic waste generation which can impact the environment*

- *I learned a lot of interesting ways in how my mobile phone package box and old smartphones can be put to good alternative use. My old smartphone can be a permanent GPS in my car, and in the future, I can use my old phone as a security camera or baby monitor when I have kids.*
- *There are alternative ways to reuse old smartphones. For example, reuse it as artwork, a security camera, and a virtual remote control.*
- *Now I know how to reuse my old mobile phone for useful purposes, not just to throw them away. Also, I got a new idea to use my phone box package as a jewelry holder.*
- *I will transform my phone boxes into jewelry and stationery boxes and use them as a key storage holder for my children and myself.*

The overall comments from the volunteer users indicated that they had learned something new through their experience of interacting with the prototype. However, it is one thing to learn something new and another to put it into daily practice. To test how this experience has influenced the user behavior, we deliberately waited three months to see what has changed in the user behavior.

The second phase of the user test was to identify changes in the user behavior towards alternative usage of old smartphones and phone boxes based on their sustainability awareness through the "Save the Planet Campaign." All the volunteer users were invited back after three months on 1st February 2024 to discuss changes in their usage of old smartphones and alternative reuse of mobile phone package boxes after unboxing new phones. The 9 volunteer users were asked the same questions as in the first phase. Their responses are detailed in Table 7. The responses from the volunteer users (Table 7) show differences in user awareness and behavior (habits) when compared to responses in Table 6. All the volunteer users with at least one old smartphone have put it to alternative reuse (see responses in columns Q1 and Q2 in Tables 6 and 7).

Figure 7 shows an image of reusing an old smartphone as a permanent GPS in the car by volunteer User 1 (on the left), and User 5 shared a picture of reusing an iPhone package box as a jewelry box on the right. The results in this second phase indicate the potential for users to adopt greener habits through a sustainability-focused user experience, facilitated by ICT solutions. However, during our interaction with the volunteer users, we identified convenience as a barrier for transitioning to more sustainable habits as they are accustomed to certain routines in their daily activities.

Some of the volunteer users expressed that their experiences during the first phase (test of the Save the Planet Campaign prototype) provided them with the awareness and knowledge to understand their impacts on sustainability, especially waste generation which prompted them to reconsider some of the daily habits. Therefore, ICT solution designers should take responsibility for integrating sustainability into their solutions to design sustainability-centric interactive software and services because they play a vital role in raising sustainability awareness and influencing user behavior toward sustainability.

Table 7. User test information and answers after prototype testing

Users	Age	Q1	Q2	Q3
User 1	52	1	I mount one of the old Android phones permanently on my car dashboard as a GPS	Phone boxes can be reused as a gift box
User 2	50	1	My old mobile phone now serves as a baby monitor for my grandson and the other as a security camera	As a plastic plant holder
User 3	47	0	I have transformed my old phone into a bedside voice command alarm. I am using the wakeVoice application. I wonder why I did not think of this before now	It can be used as a drawer divider to store small items
User 4	45	0	I use the old smartphone as a second remote control in the house and also use it to stream videos to my LG TV	Used as a stationary box on my kids' table
User 5	33	1	The old smartphone is an awesome wireless mouse and keyboard that uses the unified remote app. I am working on making an artwork and asking my friends to donate their old smartphones	Transformed to Jewelry holder and bracelet Storage
User 6	25	0	Thanks to you (authors) for the ideas in the prototype. Now, I use my two old phones as security cameras for my room and storage using the WardenCam application	Gift box and key holders on the shelve
User 7	23	0	My old phone is now my ghost phone that hackers can't access. I will be using it for any of my bank transactions. I went through the links in the prototype and studied more to learn how to create untraceable phones	Plastic flower vase for home and garden decoration
User 8	21	0	You can use it in several ways, such as a security camera or remote control, or donate it to those in need	Jewelry holder
User 9	20	0	Use it as a cheap alternative to GoPro with phone mounts	Stationary divider for pens, pencils, and a gift box

User 1   **User 5**

Fig. 7. User 1 Shared an image of reusing an old smartphone as a permanent GPS in a car, and User 5 Shared an image of reusing a phone box as a jewelry box.

5 Discussion and Threat to Validity

5.1 Discussion

Green user experience involves how well interactions between users of different ICT interactive software and services create user awareness about their impacts on sustainability. The GaLaPaGoS design patterns serve as a tool to support ICT designers in incorporating green and sustainability concerns into the design of ICT interactive software and services. User awareness about the current ecological problems has increased end users' demand for sustainability in ICT products and services [38]. The design of user experiences centered on green UX with sustainability can offer more value to users and companies. The GaLaPaGoS design patterns from this research support such design to aid more awareness about the ecological issues of our society and support design for change in user habits towards sustainability.

Several studies on persuasive technologies and patterns as reported in [24, 25] have explored self-centered values to influence user behavior. However, this approach can be counterproductive to sustainability efforts since self-enhancement persuasive technology often prioritizes personal benefits over fostering empathy-driven, long-term sustainable behaviors through technology [24]. In contrast, the GaLaPaGoS design patterns provide designers of interactive software and service a template for effectively engaging users to raise sustainability awareness and promote a sense of care for the environment. The findings from the developers and user test in Sects. 4.3 and 4.4 further illustrate that implementing the Galapagos design patterns can support design for green UX to foster internal motivation for sustainability among users for long-term sustainable behaviors.

Additionally, ICT interactive software and services for green UX covering user interactions and their awareness about their impacts on sustainability are less investigated. The challenge for software development practitioners, as expressed in the Participatory Pattern Workshop, is that most ICT designers and developers interested in sustainability lack concrete examples and tools that can demonstrate how sustainability is translated into design decisions in ICT solutions for green UX. Furthermore, to promote sustainability consciousness among users, interactive ICT software and services companies have the responsibility to incorporate means of gathering sustainability and green requirements for their ICT solutions to improve user sustainability awareness. The negative UX-based discovery approach is one method for gathering sustainability and green requirements[39]. However, there are fewer green UX patterns to support designers in incorporating those sustainability requirements in interactive software and service design. The GaLaPaGoS design patterns are created to address these design issues.

5.2 Threat to Validity

- **Construct Validity:** To mitigate threats to construct validity, the research question was based on the results of the participatory pattern workshop with ICT practitioners from industry and academic publications related to the design of ICT interactive software and services for green UX.
- **Internal Validity:** The GaLaPaGoS design patterns were co-created by the authors and ICT practitioners in a participatory pattern workshop by analyzing problems of green UX from literature combined with industry challenges for green UX in ICT interactive software and services.
- **External Validity**: The GaLaPaGoS design patterns were validated by software developers and end users outside the participatory pattern workshop to ensure the generalizability of the results. The GaLaPaGoS design patterns show promising value in guiding the design of ICT interactive software and services for sustainability awareness among end users. However, Green UX requires more than the three patterns covered in this paper. We acknowledge a need for more testing of GaLaPaGoS design patterns by software development practitioners from different domains to collect data for improving and extending GaLaPaGoS design patterns. This will be done in future work to improve the generalization of results.

6 Conclusion

Green UX design is a new topic area, and there is no well-known best practice for ICT designers or software developers. Most developers and designers do not understand how and what it means to design, develop, and engineer ICT interactive software and services for green UX. These are the reasons for developing design patterns to capture best practices to guide software development practitioners during the design of ICT interactive software and services for green UX. Incorporating sustainability and green UX considerations in the design of ICT interactive software and services will facilitate sustainability awareness among users and ignite their consciousness about their impacts while using different ICT solutions.

The three GaLaPaGoS design patterns, the design mock-ups created by software developers and tested by recruited users, demonstrate a real example of how designers can raise sustainability awareness among the end users at different stages of interactive ICT software and services. Based on the feedback from the developers, we observed that there is a need to create more patterns that guide and support designers of interactive software and services in presenting information within their design solution in a way that supports sustainability awareness and encourages reuse among users. One central and challenging problem is making the users of ICT interactive software and services aware of their negative actions toward the environment. This consists of exploring avenues to incorporate green UX and foster research towards making sustainability the core of ICT interactive software and services design. As part of plans for future work, we will improve the three GaLaPaGoS design patterns based on the feedback and organize a second participatory pattern workshop with software development practitioners to co-design and evaluate new patterns.

References

1. Jiang, S., Jakobsen, K., Jaccheri, L., Li, J.: Blockchain and sustainability: a tertiary study. In: 2021 IEEE/ACM International Workshop on Body of Knowledge for Software Sustainability (BoKSS), p. 1 (2021). https://github.com/SINTEF-SE/P4C/blob/main/Scopus202012ana lysis.pdf
2. United Nations: Sustainable Development Goals, pp. 8–23 (2000). https://www.un.org/sustai nabledevelopment/sustainable-development-goals/. Accessed 23 June 2022
3. Needhidasan, S., Samuel, M., Chidambaram, R.: Electronic waste – an emerging threat to the environment of urban India. J. Environ. Health Sci. Eng. **12**(1), 36 (2014). https://doi.org/10. 1186/2052-336X-12-36
4. Didier, B.: Understanding waste streams Treatment of specific waste, no. July (2015)
5. Bel, G., et al.: A New Circular Vision for Electronics Time for a Global Reboot. Geneva (2019)
6. Emmanouil, M.-C., Stiakakis, E., Vlachopoulou, M., Manthou, V.: An analysis of waste and information flows in an ICT waste management system. In: 6th International Conference on Information and Communication Technologies in Agriculture, Food and Environment (HAICTA 2013), pp. 157–164. Elsevier B.V. (2013). https://doi.org/10.1016/j.protcy.2013. 11.022
7. SBS: E-Waste Hell. http://www.sbs.com.au/news/dateline/story/e-waste-hell. Accessed 14 June 2021
8. Osibanjo, O., Nnorom, I.C.: The challenge of electronic waste (e-waste) management in developing countries. Waste Manage. Res. **25**(6), 489–501 (2007). https://doi.org/10.1177/ 0734242X07082028
9. Taghipour, H., et al.: E-waste management challenges in Iran: presenting some strategies for improvement of current conditions. Waste Manage. Res. **30**(11), 1138–1144 (2012). https:// doi.org/10.1177/0734242X11420328
10. Gollakota, A.R.K., Gautam, S., Shu, C.M.: Inconsistencies of e-waste management in developing nations – Facts and plausible solutions. J. Environ. Manage. **261**, 110234 (2020). https:// doi.org/10.1016/j.jenvman.2020.110234
11. Khetriwal, D.S., Kraeuchi, P., Widmer, R.: Producer responsibility for e-waste management: key issues for consideration - learning from the Swiss experience. J. Environ. Manage. **90**(1), 153–165 (2009). https://doi.org/10.1016/j.jenvman.2007.08.019
12. US EPA: Wastes | What are the trends in wastes and their effects on human health and the environment? (2022). https://www.epa.gov/report-environment/wastes. Accessed 14 Nov 2022
13. Becker, C., et al.: Sustainability design and software: the karlskrona manifesto. In: Proceedings of the 37th International Conference on Software Engineering, vol. 2, pp. 467–476 (2015). https://doi.org/10.1109/ICSE.2015.179
14. Oyedeji, S.: Software Sustainability by Design. Lappeenranta-Lahti University of Technology LUT (2019)

15. Chitchyan, R., et al.: Sustainability design in requirements engineering: state of practice. In: 38th International Conference on Software Engineering Companion (ICSE 2016), pp. 533–542 (2016). http://eprints.hud.ac.uk/28747/

16. van Welie, M., Traetteberg, H.: Interaction patterns in user interfaces. In: Seventh Pattern Languages of Programs Conference, pp. 13–16 (2000)

17. Van Duyne, D.K., Landay, J.A., Hong, J.I.: The design of sites : patterns, principles, and processes for crafting a customer-centered web experience, p. 762 (2003)

18. Tidwell, J.: UI Patterns and Techniques. Designing Interfaces, First Ed (2005)

19. Naqvi, B., Porras, J., Oyedeji, S., Ullah, M.: Towards identification of patterns aligning security and usability. In: Abdelnour Nocera, J., Parmaxi, A., Winckler, M., Loizides, F., Ardito, C., Bhutkar, G., Dannenmann, P. (eds.) INTERACT 2019. LNCS, vol. 11930, pp. 121–132. Springer, Cham (2020). https://doi.org/10.1007/978-3-030-46540-7_12

20. Dick, M., Naumann, S.: Enhancing software engineering processes towards sustainable software product design. In: 24th International Conference on Informatics for Environmental Protection (EnviroInfo 2010), vol. 2010, pp. 706–715 (2010)

21. Erdélyi, K.: Special factors of development of green software supporting eco sustainability. In: Proceedings of IEEE 11th International Symposium on Intelligent Systems and Informatics-SISY 2013, pp. 337–340 (2013). https://doi.org/10.1109/SISY.2013.6662597

22. Oyedeji, S., Shamshiri, H., Porras, J., Lammert, D.: Software sustainability: academic understanding and industry perceptions. In: Wang, X., Martini, A., Nguyen-Duc, A., Stray, V. (eds.) ICSOB 2021. LNBIP, vol. 434, pp. 18–34. Springer, Cham (2021). https://doi.org/10.1007/978-3-030-91983-2_3

23. Seifert, J., Bayer, A., Rukzio, E.: PointerPhone: using mobile phones for direct pointing interactions with remote displays. In: Kotzé, P., Marsden, G., Lindgaard, G., Wesson, J., Winckler, M. (eds.) INTERACT 2013. LNCS, vol. 8119, pp. 18–35. Springer, Heidelberg (2013). https://doi.org/10.1007/978-3-642-40477-1_2

24. Knowles, B., Blair, L., Walker, S., Coulton, P., Thomas, L., Mullagh, L.: Patterns of persuasion for sustainability. In: Proceedings of the Conference on Designing Interactive Systems: Processes, Practices, Methods, and Techniques, DIS, pp. 1035–1044 (2014). https://doi.org/10.1145/2598510.2598536

25. Oduor, M., Alahäivälä, T., Oinas-Kukkonen, H.: Persuasive software design patterns for social influence. Pers Ubiquitous Comput **18**(7), 1689–1704 (2014). https://doi.org/10.1007/s00779-014-0778-z

26. Fogg, B.: A Behavioral Model for Persuasive Design. Persuasive Technology Lab (2009). http://scholar.google.co.uk/scholar?start=60&q=persuasive+design&hl=en&as_sdt=0,5#17

27. Lockton, D., Stanton, N.A.: Design Intent behaviour through design (2010). designwithintent.co.uk

28. Gabrielsen, K.R.: Designing Human Behavior sustainable habits (2005)

29. Colmant, M., Rouvoy, R., Seinturier, L.: Improving the energy efficiency of software systems for multi-core architectures. In: Proceedings of the 11th Middleware Doctoral Symposium, MDS 2014 - co-located with ACM/IFIP/USENIX 15th International Middleware Conference, pp. 2–5 (2014). https://doi.org/10.1145/2684080.2684081

30. Adaji, I., Adisa, M.O.: A review of the use of persuasive technologies to influence sustainable behavior. In: Adjunct Proceedings of the 30th ACM Conference on User Modeling, Adaptation and Personalization, pp. 317–325. ACM, New York (2022). https://doi.org/10.1145/3511047.3537653

31. Foth, M., Agudelo, L.P., Palleis, R.: Digital soapboxes: towards an interaction design agenda for situated civic innovation. In: UbiComp 2013 Adjunct - Adjunct Publication of the 2013 ACM Conference on Ubiquitous Computing, pp. 725–728 (2013). https://doi.org/10.1145/2494091.2495995

32. Murugesan, S., Gangadharan, G.R.: Harnessing Green IT: Principles and Practices, pp. 1–22 (2012)
33. Hevner, A., Chatterjee, S.: Design Research in Information Systems. Springer, New York (2010). https://doi.org/10.1007/978-1-4419-5653-8
34. Mor, Y., Winters, N., Warburton, S.: Participatory Pattern Workshops kit (2010). http://www.lkl.ac.uk/niall/Resource-Kit-Handbook-DRAFT.doc
35. Alblooshi, B.G.K.M., Ahmad, S.Z., Hussain, M., Singh, S.K.: Sustainable management of electronic waste: empirical evidences from a stakeholders' perspective. Bus Strategy Environ **31**(4), 1856–1874 (2022). https://doi.org/10.1002/BSE.2987
36. Statistic Brain research Institute: Paper Use Statistics – Statistic Brain
37. Marvelapp: Marvelapp: Save the Planet Campaign. https://marvelapp.com/prototype/5f0bhba/screen/82429776
38. Kramer, K.-L.: User Experience in the Age of Sustainability (2012). https://doi.org/10.1016/b978-0-12-387795-6.00001-9.
39. Condori-Fernandez, N., Lago, P.: Characterizing the contribution of quality requirements to software sustainability. J. Syst. Softw. **137**, 289–305 (2018). https://doi.org/10.1016/j.jss.2017.12.005

Prototyping Cross-Reality Escape Rooms

Sebastian Krois[✉][iD] and Enes Yigitbas[iD]

Paderborn University, Paderborn, Germany
{sebastian.krois,enes.yigitbas}@uni-paderborn.de

Abstract. With more and more applications exploring the possibilities of AR and VR, some applications do not stay inside one reality but operate cross-reality. We propose the concept of a cross-reality escape room, where one player is in the real world interacting with real objects and one player is in a virtual world. They have to work together to solve a series of puzzles to complete the game. The actions one player does on their side can directly affect the other player's world. Besides the concept of cross-reality escape rooms, we also provide an end-user editor to create such games. The editor aims to enable non-technical users, like designers for conventional escape rooms, to create their own cross-reality escape room, including creating and positioning objects and integrating and configuring a logic flow that drives the application. This allows virtual objects to be configured as well as real-life objects.

To evaluate the concept and editor, twelve participants in groups of two first played a demo escape room and used the editor to create part of a room themselves. They were asked to give quantitative and qualitative feedback for both parts. With a score of 55.17 out of possible 63 on the Game User Experience Satisfaction Scale (GUESS)-18, we can say, that players like the demo room, we created. Combined with results from open feedback sessions, the players liked the concept, and that cross-reality adds value to the concept of escape rooms. However, there is still potential to improve. For the editor, we received mixed results, that depend heavily on the individual users. During semi-structured interviews, we could also create a list of improvements for future versions.

1 Introduction

Augmented Reality (AR) and Virtual Reality (VR) have evolved to be part of our everyday lives. Apart from industrial [6,12,22] or medical [10,23] applications, AR and VR are increasingly used in the entertainment sector. In particular, more and more video games utilize AR and VR to enable a direct movement of the player for physical games or use increased immersion to amplify the experience of a story. Those games' concepts can be specifically designed for VR, or they can be adapted from components present in the real world. One concept that would fit the latter category, is the idea of a virtual escape room. An escape room is a game, where players are locked in a room and need to solve a series of puzzles to win. Many escape rooms and their puzzles are designed to resemble a

M. K. Lárusdóttir et al. (Eds.): HCSE 2024, LNCS 14793, pp. 84–104, 2024.
https://doi.org/10.1007/978-3-031-64576-1_5

specific scenario. Some typical scenarios include, for example, secret laboratories or fictional crime scenes [14]. With VR, we can create worlds and scenarios that are beyond the possibilities of the real world. The scenario can be set on distant planets or incorporate gameplay mechanics, like flying, which are not possible to realize in conventional escape rooms. But real-life (R) escape rooms have one big advantage over VR ones. Solving puzzles allows the interaction with several haptic objects like chests, locks, and other props. To integrate that in VR, Hanus et al. added passive haptics to a VR escape room where players wear a VR Head Mounted Display (HMD) and interact with replicas of the provided props [9].

Communication and teamwork are also two big parts of escape rooms. To solve the puzzles, players need to describe the problem and work together with their team to find the solution. Some puzzles are designed in a way that demands players to be in different positions while communicating what they see.

Although some projects already cover different types of mixed and cross-reality games, most of them consider games where players are in the same room, use AR devices to get more information and hints or add haptics to VR applications. Only a few projects cover the interaction of players divided into R and VR. Therefore, we propose the concept of a cross-reality escape room that combines the real with the virtual world, where one part of the players use virtual reality to find themselves in distant worlds or bygone times to experience things not possible in the real world, while the other part is in a real escape room containing realistic and haptic objects to interact with. The players (in R and VR) have to collaborate to reach a common goal and win the game together. They need to find ways to communicate with each other. The actions of one side can affect what happens on the other. In R, there are objects that are connected to the virtual environment, so they can react to the actions of the VR player.

However, the conception and implementation of (cross-reality) escape rooms are cumbersome and complex and many stakeholders do not have the experience and technical knowledge to create such a game on their own. Escape room designers have experience in creating settings, stories, and puzzles for escape rooms. But to create an escape room that operates in R and VR, both sides need to be developed. Developing a VR application requires expertise that escape room developers do not necessarily possess. Creators do not only need those skills isolated, but they need to know how to combine them to realize the concept and vision created for the escape room game. To create such a game, we create an end-user editor, with which users can create their own cross-reality escape rooms. We also used the editor to create a demo application to test the editor and concept. With those concepts in mind, we can create applications for entertainment purposes, but explore other domains as well. For example, educational escape rooms are used to teach students while maintaining their motivation, or researchers can study the social interaction of groups in stressful situations. Those examples can be adapted to create meaningful applications using cross-reality. Additionally, with the editor at hand, teachers and researchers can create/change their game without the need to develop a whole new application.

In this paper, we focus on two main research areas. The first is to evaluate whether the concept of cross-reality escape rooms can be beneficial to the players' experience. Second, we create and evaluate a tool to create such a game. To the best of our knowledge, there is no escape room available, which combines the real world with the virtual world. There are escape rooms in real life and in virtual worlds for entertainment and research purposes (c.f. Sect. 3.1), and there have been different projects exploring the possibilities of cross-reality (c.f. Sect. 3.3). But since no project that creates an escape room that builds on top of cross-reality exists yet, we have formulated our first research question.

RQ1: Can cross-reality enhance the escape room experience?

Before we are able to evaluate such an escape room, we first need to design and build it. That task is iterative and can be time-consuming. The room itself needs to be built and decorated according to the chosen setting and different puzzles need to be created, tested, and integrated. Next, test groups play in the room. It is improved based on their feedback and the creators' observations. Here, the puzzles often need to be adjusted and the positions of objects inside the room need to be changed. With that, a new iteration starts until the creators and playtesters are satisfied with the results. When considering an escape room that operates cross-reality, the software component adds another layer of complexity. In addition to dealing with the objects in the real room, the virtual reality part needs to be developed and changed. As VR development requires a multitude of tools and experience, it is challenging for escape room designers to create and adjust it. Additionally, once created, the room is static and a major effort is required to change it. To simplify the development of cross-reality escape rooms, we want to develop an application that enables non-developers to quickly design and test a configuration of the escape room. With that in mind, we formulate the second research question.

RQ2: How can we enable easy prototyping of cross-reality live-escape rooms?

Escape room designers are the core subject of our research, as we want to enable them to create a cross-reality escape room. That implies to follow a user-centered design [1] approach. We need to define clearly which exact requirements users have for an application that supports them in design. To not limit the application to escape room designers, we gather requirements from multiple user groups, e.g. *game designers* and *escape room gamemasters*. With that, we aim to get a deeper understanding of what our application needs to look like. With that, we get the first sub-question to answer **RQ2**.

RQ2.1: Which requirements do different user groups have for a tool to build such games?

Once the application is developed, we evaluate it in three steps. The first is to find out how the users interact with the editor. Here, we deduce patterns they use and detect problems or well-working features.

RQ2.2: How do users approach building a cross-reality escape room?

Next, we evaluate the usability and workload. When designing an application with which users are supposed to interact, we need to design it as usable as possible. Especially when we start a new iteration of the development process, or if we make changes to the editor, it is helpful if we possess a measurement for its usability. We compare future versions to the first one to determine if the usability was improved or if further changes are necessary. The same holds for the workload, when using an application, the workload should be as low as possible. That results in the third sub-question.

RQ2.3: What is the usability of the editor and the workload using it?

Finally, we need to know what works well and what does not. With the knowledge gained during the evaluation, we can start a new iteration of the design science research process to get closer to solving the problem at hand. To build a foundation for that, we state the following subquestion.

RQ2.4: How can the tool be improved during future iterations?

To answer these RQs, the rest of the paper is structured as follows. In Sect. 2, we present the requirements users have for a tool to create cross-reality escape rooms. Followed by that is Sect. 3, where we present related works. In Sect. 4, we present the architecture of the application during the game and edit modes. The evaluation of the game and tool is presented in Sect. 5. Finally, we conclude or work and give an outlook on future work in Sect. 6.

2   Requirements

To determine the requirements users have for an artifact helping them to create an escape room. We performed interviews with six different potential user groups. For every user group, two persons were asked. After presenting them with the concept, we conducted the interviews with *escape room designers* and *gamemasters* working at a local escape room facility. Additionally, we interviewed two *video game designers* from our university's GamesLab. *Escape room players*, *VR gamers*, and *VR application developers* were recruited from friends and colleagues. We asked the participants what is important for real-life escape rooms, desktop, and VR games based on their area of expertise. Afterwards, we presented the concept of cross-reality escape rooms using VR and R and asked them about potential ideas of what an editor should look like, so they can use it to create their own cross-reality escape room. The main focus of the interviews was identifying the requirements the user groups have when they are supposed to design a VR/R escape room themselves. As different people have different requirements and ideas, there were many statements only made by a few or only a single user. To focus on the most important ones, we only consider statements made by at least four participants. It should be noted that we do not consider requirements on the hardware side which are related to the craftsmanship of creating real-life elements in an escape room. We grouped the resulting statements into four requirements (R)s.

R 1: Build the Escape Room. This first group of requirements focuses on the creation of the virtual level. For the final result, the virtual level will be connected to the real world. For the VR level, all objects present there need to be created and configured. Users can select which objects to create, and which position and rotation they have. Additionally, they need to create or configure the logic of the escape room, meaning they control what players have to do in order to progress in the story That logic also needs to apply to R elements connected to the virtual level. For visual objects and logic creation, the users required an easy-to-use editor. There, users also need an asset catalog that provides easy access to visual assets as well as puzzle assets. Those assets should be good-looking to support the player's immersion in the story. Support for non-technical R elements is not considered at this point, as those objects are common for escape rooms and do not introduce additional complexity.

R 2: Create the (VR) Gameplay. Some requirements focus on the gameplay, especially in VR. For example, players (of both realities) should be able to communicate with each other, at least by using some kind of voice chat. To introduce players to the escape room, they need an introduction with a story that tells them what to do and why. Users need a tool for creating and integrating such an introduction. Considering the virtual reality part, players need to be able to control the application. They need to move around and interact with the virtual elements. The virtual environment does not need to be realistic and can contain elements that do not exist or are possible in real life. It is important, that the movement and interaction feel natural and are easy to learn.

R 3: Specify the Puzzles. Puzzles are the main elements in an escape room, so they need to be created and specified. As described above, we need some assets with which puzzles can be added to the game. As we operate in cross-reality, we need to provide puzzles or puzzle templates that require players from different realities to work on them simultaneously. To make that possible, we also need assets or modules for the R room, which can be configured and connected to the game. To guide users, and not overwhelm them with the possibilities, the editor should allow the creation of sequential puzzles, in which solving one puzzle unlocks the next puzzle or room.

R 4: Dynamically Adjust the Game. For real-world escape rooms, there is a gamemaster observing the player's progress. Gamemasters can then give hints to the players or manually mark a hard puzzle as solved so that the players can continue. Another version of the same principle is to provide adjustable difficulty which can be set to fit the player's needs.

Even though some users required those functions, they are out of scope for this thesis. We want to provide a prototypical implementation of a cross-reality escape room editor. Extending the runtime with control options for gamemasters is a topic for future work.

3   Related Work

This paper combines aspects of *escape rooms, virtual reality escape rooms, prototyping for augmented/virtual reality,* and *cross reality.* To the best of our knowledge, there is no approach covering all those areas. In this chapter, we present recent works covering at least one of the areas used by our approach.

3.1   Escape Rooms

When considering escape rooms, there are conventional (real) ones, where all players are in a physical room to solve puzzles. In addition to that, there exist digital escape rooms, where the game is played virtually.

Real World Escape Rooms. In recent years there is a growing interest in commercial escape rooms for entertainment purposes.

With the growing interest, researchers also explored the potential of escape rooms for research and educational purposes. In 2017, Pan et al. observed several escape room playthroughs and interviewed the players to analyze their behavior during the game [18]. They found out that players can practice their collaboration and communication skills in escape rooms and they suggest to design rooms so they actively teach those skills. Additionally, environments like escape rooms allow investigation of a variety of social aspects of the players' interactions. Another dimension is educational escape rooms (EERs). Here, the main goal is to teach or deepen knowledge in a specific area. That can be applied to a wide range of target audiences or topics. Avargil et al. developed an EER to teach chemistry subjects to high school students [2]. The goal of their escape room is to assess the student's knowledge of the provided topics.

Digital Escape Rooms. In addition to the real-world escape rooms, there are also projects creating digital (desktop and virtual reality) escape rooms. Here, designers can even better transfer the users to other worlds that are not bound to the laws of reality. One commercial example is the previously mentioned *Escape the Lost Pyramid* by Ubisoft, where multiple players wear VR HMDs and are transferred to the past to explore and escape an old Egyptian pyramid. In addition to those commercial products, there are also multiple educational escape rooms researchers proposed for virtual reality. One such example is the ARI escape room by DeCusatis et al. [7]. They created a digital escape room for desktop computers (not VR) for cybersecurity awareness. Here, the player controls a robot that walks through a space station. Christopoulos et al. developed a virtual reality escape room to teach students how enzymes operate under different conditions and circumstances [5]. One disadvantage of virtual reality is that the surroundings of a player are only virtual, i.e. all objects players interact with are virtual and do not provide haptics. To tackle this problem, Hanus et al. created a multiplayer VR escape room including passive haptics, where players need to escape a medieval dungeon [9]. Virtual objects which are important to solve the riddles have real-life representations with which the users have to interact.

3.2 Augmented Reality Escape Rooms

To combine the real and the virtual world in the escape room domain, some approaches use AR. For example, Estudante et al. created an escape room to fight fake news [8] and Paraschivoiu et al. [19] created a game to teach different chemical topics. The authors of both projects used a smartphone or tablet to display virtual objects and interactions with bots to guide users through the experience. In the real world, the used markers which, after being scanned, revealed more information and puzzles about the specific topic. The games are designed for one player in [8] and max three players in [19]. All players are in the same reality (AR) and do not utilize haptic elements besides paper.

3.3 Cross Reality

There are multiple ways to use cross-reality. Many of the approaches search to enable users in different realities to work in the same (virtual) world while also being in the same physical place. That can be done using a CAVE-like installation with some users standing in and some standing outside the cave or using displays to show parts of the virtual world [4,15]. With the use of cross-reality technology, people can use different devices to collaborate from different realities. They are also not bound to the same physical space, they can work together from different locations as well. Here, they can use different devices to access the same virtual environment [11], or a fixed set of devices, like a VR headset and an tablet [21]. Some works in the area of cross-reality research also explore the escape room domain. For example, McCready et al. developed LabXscape [16], a cross-reality escape room where three users, each in one either augmented reality, virtual reality, and on a desktop computer. They aimed to analyze the player experience in a cross-reality escape room focusing on determining aspects that increase the player experience. This paper focussed on the concept and the development of the application, and an in-depth analysis of their user study is to be published.

3.4 Prototyping for Augmented, Virtual, and Cross Reality

In addition to the works presenting an application that is used on their own, there is also a class of works providing a framework for prototyping AR, VR, and XR applications. One such framework is *360proto* by Nebeling and Madier [17]. They provided a suite of tools to emphasize paper prototyping for AR and VR applications. One way of paper prototyping is to use equirectangular grids to create or paint scenes on a 2D sheet of paper, which is then transformed into a 360° view where users can look around.

Speicher et al. created the 360theatre [20], which combines live-streamed paper prototypes with a Wizard of Oz approach (humans acting as the application) in VR as well as AR. For VR scenarios, a level can be created as a three-dimensional diorama with a 360° camera placed inside. Users wear a cardboard VR headset with a smartphone that receives a video stream from the camera.

To go one step further than paper prototyping, FlowMatic by Zhang and Oney [24] can be used. The framework allows users to design their applications while being immersed in VR. Here, they can access models which can be placed in the scene. In contrast to many other VR authoring frameworks, FlowMatic offers a visual logic editor directly in VR. Here, users can access objects in the scene as well as add new objects.

One work targeting end-user prototyping for cross-reality applications is presented by Bellucci et al. [3]. With their X-Reality toolkit, they offer a suite of tools to quickly prototype cross-reality applications. They include an editor for the virtual world as well as for real world objects using mirco controllers.

3.5 Discussion

As seen above, there is a wide range of works in the different areas we cover in this paper. There are positively received real-life and virtual reality escape rooms for entertainment and education as well as cross-reality applications that explore the potential of different combinations of realities, devices, and segmentation of space. But there is no approach combining R with VR or AR in a way where the interaction with elements in their respective reality directly affects the element in the other's reality. To the best of our knowledge, there exists no approach in research or the industry, where the concept of cross-reality interactions is applied to the escape room domain. There is also a wide range of prototyping and authoring tools for AR, VR, and cross-reality that could be used to create an escape room application. None of those tools enables the creation of a cross-reality escape room that satisfies the requirements derived from the user interviews (Sect. 2).

4 Architecture

We first create an editor that fulfills the requirements (**R1-R3**) presented in Sect. 2. We do not consider **R4** at this point, as tools for the gamemaster are out of scope for this paper. We use the editor later to create a demo version of a cross-reality escape room.

4.1 High-Level Architecture

Figure 1 shows a very high-level concept of the application's architecture. All VR objects (orange), and some R objects (green) are connected to an underlying server (purple) which holds the game state and updates all objects accordingly. The virtual level and the configuration of the R objects (dark blue) are saved and loaded by the server. A puzzle is a combination of multiple objects, so all puzzles happening at the virtual level are also saved and loaded using the configuration. Everything happening only in R is not part of the application or configuration, they need to be stored separately. The application is divided into a play and an edit mode.

The play mode offers all the features needed to load a level and let players interact with it. With that, they can play the game and we fulfill **RG2**.

To also satisfy **RG1**, we created the edit mode. It provides the tools needed to create and save such a level. Users can move freely in the level and place objects where they want them to be.

At the top, we have the players (pink) who interact with the application. One player uses a VR application where they can interact with the virtual level, and one player is in R interacting with the real elements in the escape room. For creating cross-reality puzzles, and, thus, satisfying **RG3**, the editor allows the creation of logic connections. A logic connection allows one object to invoke an action on another object. To give an example, imagine we have a button that is logically connected to a door. When

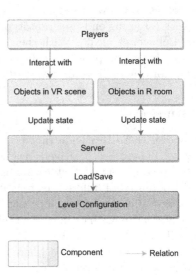

Fig. 1. High-Level Concept (Color figure online)

the button is pushed, it uses the connection to tell the door it should open. That also holds for R elements, when a VR button is pressed, there can be a logical connection to a real-life chest. After the button is pressed the chest opens. We provide a set of real-life objects which are connected to the application. Their behavior can be configured by the editor just like interactive virtual elements.

4.2 In Game Architecture

Figure 2a shows an overview of the application in play mode. During the game, there are two players who are depicted pink in the diagram. Each of them has a way to interact or at least see the virtual level. This is achieved via the devices in yellow . The VR player wears an HMD to see the virtual level and uses controllers to interact with the objects in the scene. The R player cannot interact with the objects but uses a laptop acting as a camera display to see the virtual world. The scene consists of different objects (orange). Most of these objects do not have logic (light grey), like walls or decoration objects. Here, we can make another distinction between static and dynamic objects. Static objects

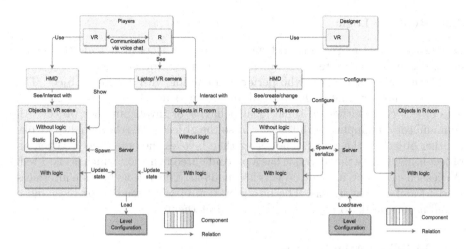

Fig. 2. (a) In Game Mode Concept Overview. (b) Editor Concept Overview (Color figure online)

are placed once and will not move, e.g., a wall. Dynamic objects, however, can be grabbed and moved by the player and also simulate physics. An example is a cup that can be picked up and thrown through the room. In addition to the objects without logic, there are some objects with logic (red). A door is an example of an object with logic that can be opened with a command, e.g. a button sending the signal to open the door when pressed. That can be opened with a command, e.g. a button, which can send the signal to open the door. When a game is started, the server (purple) loads the configuration (dark blue) and spawns the objects accordingly. The R player is able to interact with objects in R (green). Similar to virtual objects, they may have logic. But in this case, the definition of "logic" is different from the one used for virtual objects. In R, the objects *with logic* only include objects that are connected to the server. Like the VR. objects with logic, they communicate with the server to send or receive input. R objects without logic (blue) are not connected to the server. For example, assume there are two chests in R. One with a padlock and one with a magnetic lock. The chest with the padlock is not considered an object with logic, as no interaction with the server is required to open the chest. The chest with the magnetic lock, however, is a logic object, as the chest will only open once the server sends the open command. With that, we described all elements contained in the play mode.

4.3   Runtime Logic

During the game, players interact with the logic objects in R and VR. Those objects, however, can interact with the player or with other objects.

There is always a player who performs an action with one logic object. The object can now evaluate what the player did and decide on how to proceed. The object could either do some local behavior or invoke another object. All communication happens with the server, so the object sends the signal to invoke another object to the server. The server then invokes the next object. When an object is invoked by the server, it has a preconfigured behavior, which is executed. With such a concept, all logic objects are modular. The objects provide interfaces to send and receive signals. The interpretation of what sending or receiving a signal *means* needs to be done by every object themselves.

4.4   In Editor Architecture

The editor focuses on the virtual level. The real level needs to be built neverthe-less, but that is not part of our tool. Even though the edit mode is planned to be used by one person, we decided to use the same infrastructure with a server (purple) as in the play mode. With this, we do not need to create another appli-cation for the editor and it can be easily extended, such that multiple designers can work together to design a room. The server can load an existing configura-tion (dark blue) or create a new one. The current state of the level can always be saved. When a level is loaded in edit mode, the server spawns the objects (orange) similar to play mode. Contrarily to the game mode, the user can edit those objects. This means objects can be deleted or moved around. Also, the user has access to a library of objects which can be inserted into the level. To configure the objects with logic (red), they provide connection interfaces that can either send a signal (a button that sends a signal when it is pressed) or receive a signal (a door that can open). Those interfaces can be connected, and some basic operations (e.g. AND, which requires two signals to proceed) can be configured. Here, we can also connect the R objects with logic in the same way. Representations of those objects can be spawned, which are not shown in the game, but provide the same connection interfaces as virtual objects. With those tools, a designer can build the virtual room and fully configure the virtual as well as the real objects with logic to provide the game flow. The resulting application is displayed in Fig. 3.

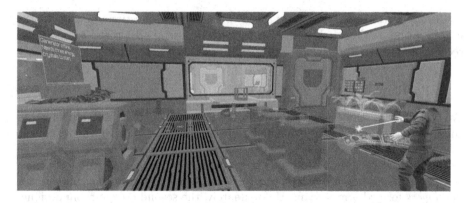

Fig. 3. VR-Editor for Prototyping Cross-Reality Escape Rooms (Color figure online)

5   Evaluation

After the description of the design and development of an editor for cross-reality escape rooms based on the end-user requirements, we used this editor to create a demo escape room game so we could also evaluate the concept itself.

The study was divided into two phases. In the first phase, the group played the demo cross-reality escape room. In the second phase, users were provided with the same room they played in before, but parts of the level were missing. Each user had to rebuild a missing section with our editor while the second user could observe and help. The whole session took between three and four hours, the participants received no monetary compensation.

First, the participants are presented with the concept and procedure we will follow during the evaluation. Then, they played the demo game we created. The two players were located in different rooms, so they could only communicate via voice chat. During the game, the players were supervised and, similar to conventional escape rooms, provided with hints when they got stuck on a puzzle. After playing the game, they were asked to fill out a questionnaire asking for demographics, experience with VR and escape rooms, player satisfaction, and presence. After answering the questionnaires, the participants had the opportunity to describe their experiences and give open feedback. After a short break, we started the second phase. We explained to the users that they were provided with an incomplete version of the escape room they played earlier. Each user got the task of rebuilding one part of the room. The other user could observe and supervise the other during their task. Before the participants started editing, we provided them with a short tour of the editor, briefly explaining the available tools and objects. Now, the R player started editing their part of the level, followed by the second user. Both users had the opportunity to add decorative elements as they wanted. For mandatory objects and logic, we provided them with a blueprint of how the room should look and how the puzzles should work. But they had to figure out for themselves how to implement the logic in the editor.

After they finished, they were asked to answer two questionnaires about the usability and workload. Finally, we performed a semi-structured interview to receive qualitative feedback.

5.1 Participants

We conducted a study with the user groups presented in Sect. 2. We planned to conduct the study with the participants from the initial interviews, but due to scheduling difficulties, we had to change some participants. The *VR gamer* and *escape room player* groups had the same participants, the *escape room gamemaster* and *escape room designer* groups had one member exchanged, and the *VR developers* formed a new team. Unfortunately, the second escape room designer could not attend the study. Instead, the remaining designer teamed up with an experienced gamemaster. We had 12 participants (6 female, 6 male) with the majority (83%) in the 20–30 age range and varying experience with VR applications and escape rooms.

5.2 Demo Cross Reality Escape Room

To answer **RQ1:** *Can cross-reality enhance the escape room experience?*, we first look at the player satisfaction, and analyze the open feedback afterwards. To measure, how "good" the game is, we used the Game User Experience Satisfaction Scale (GUESS)-18 questionnaire by Keebler et al. [13]. It contains 18 questions with which the areas *usability, narratives, play engrossment, enjoyment, creative freedom, audio aesthetics, personal gratification, social connectivity,* and *visual aesthetics* are covered. For the analysis, an area is called a *subscale*. All questions need to be answered on a seven-point Likert scale. Even though the questionnaire was designed to evaluate video games, we decided to use it for the R part as well because the R part contains all the elements covered in the questionnaire too.

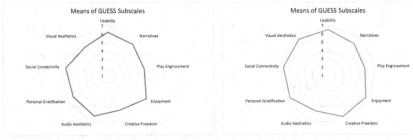

(a) GUESS-18 Subscales VR Players   (b) GUESS-18 Subscales R Players

Fig. 4. GUESS-18 Subscales

We can see, that usability, enjoyment, and social connectivity achieved very high values. The results for narrative, creative freedom, audio aesthetics, personal gratification, and visual aesthetics are a bit lower but still high. Play engrossment achieved the lowest value. The usability is higher for R than for VR. The only interaction with a digital interface users make is with the laptop, where they only need to click on a button, so we expect high usability as there are not many options to make an error. Second, they only interact with elements common in our everyday lives, so there is not much that can cause problems. That differs in VR. Here the players have more interaction with the application itself. Some players had problems with precise teleportation or the virtual buttons' sensitivity. That is one factor reducing the usability values. For the narratives, play engrossment and enjoyment, both parts reported similar values. The players are introduced to the story with a video in the beginning, but we did not include elements referring to the story during the game, which could increase those values. For both sides, the enjoyment achieved the highest value, 6.5, indicating that both players liked the game. The R players reported higher creative freedom than the VR players. To broaden the creative freedom of the VR player, adding more possibilities for interactions with objects could help as well as allow the combination of objects. Both players heard background music and a sound when e.g. a door or chest opened. But those sounds "happen" in the virtual world, so the audio aesthetics are perceived better by VR players. To enhance the experience for the R player, we should integrate sound cues into their actions in R as well. Personal gratification and social connectivity are perceived as similarly high. Considering the visual aesthetics, the R players liked the visual elements more. In VR, we used low-poly models. In another iteration, we could switch to a more realistic look to compare if players like that more.

After the players answered the questionnaires, they had the opportunity to give verbal feedback on the game without being guided by the supervisor. Both players were present during those sessions. After analyzing the feedback, we drew the following conclusions.

Improve the Other Side's Ingegration

With the camera, R users can get a good understanding of what happens in VR. But all information for the other direction needs to be communicated by the R user. We need to avoid one player feeling cut off from the other player's world. The escape room designers proposed to use a hologram representing the current puzzle the R player is working on. Also, the current progress of a puzzle being solved in R should be displayed. Additionally, using a different model for the camera representation and allowing the R player to control it in some way could increase the feeling of collaboration with another person and, thus, increase the social presence. When not allowing the R player to freely move in the virtual scene, we need to make the camera movement easier for the VR player. In the current state, the VR player always needs to carry the R player with them making the collaborative work exhausting. The game and escape room designers proposed to integrate a button to instantly retrieve the camera. For the same reason, the rendered image needs to be accurate with the representation's position, as it is inconvenient for the VR users to correct the camera position multiple times because the rendered image differs from the preview. This impedes to include the R player in the virtual level.

Keep the Story Alive. The story is the driving force behind the player's actions. Hence, we created a video to set the initial motivation so players want to start the game. Especially the game and escape room designers suggested embedding story elements into the game, such that the "space pirates become a real danger" (P2). In VR, spaceships could fly in the sky or the ground control in R gets warnings about the decreasing oxygen levels. Additionally, story-related events could happen, for example, space pirates attack the station and the light gets turned off for some time.

5.3   Editor

To answer **RQ2:** *How can we enable easy prototyping of cross-reality live-escape rooms?*, we first needed to know, which requirements users have. They are described in Sect. 2, with which we already answered **RQ2.1:** *Which require-ments do different user groups have for a tool to build such games?* To answer **RQ2.2:** *How do users approach building a cross-reality escape room?*, we observed the users building the escape room. With the idea of a blueprint at hand, all users started by creating the rooms using walls and doors. That was inconvenient, as all walls need to be placed manually. Many users also had prob-lems finding the correct position for the wall. The process of creating rooms and placing walls needs to be easier and faster so users can focus on the feeling, details, and puzzles. For objects other than walls, our editor seemed to work well. Users spawned the required object and moved it to its position. As they were in VR, just like a player, they often adjusted the position so it would feel right during the game. The logic elements were also placed when they designed the interior. After all elements were placed, they created the logic connections as the last step.

With that knowledge at hand, the editor could be extended to support this workflow. A highlight option for logic objects that are created but not connected yet could be integrated. Now, users can stick to the workflow but we help them in the last phase when they connect the logic elements.

Next, we look at the usability and workload ratings by the users to answer **RQ2.3:** *What is the usability of the editor and how high is the workload using it?*. Figure 5a shows the SUS score distribution for all users. We can see, that the editor received very mixed results with the lowest value being 27.5 and the highest 95. Throughout all scores, the standard deviation is 17.47 with a mean value of 69.58 and a median of 75. The user producing the lowest score of 27.5 stated directly after completing the questionnaire that they were not able to use the editor properly, as they had multiple problems with virtual reality itself. Even when not moving, they experienced simulator sickness. In VR, they could not see their real hands and thus had problems deciding which side was left or right. The general mental overload led to the condition that they could not remember any controls or focus on the task. For the workload, Fig. 5b shows the results for all players. Similar to the SUS score, we have a wide range of different values. The lowest value is 14, and the highest is 77. The mean workload is 39.83, the median is 38.5, and the standard deviation for all workloads is 17.25.

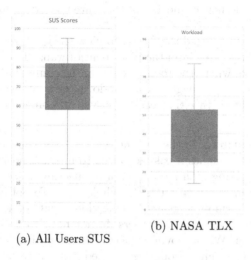

(a) All Users SUS   (b) NASA TLX

Fig. 5. SUS and TLX Scores

The highest workload value of 77 was reported by the same user rating the lowest SUS score due to problems with VR.

We received very mixed results for the usability and workload, so we cannot make a general statement about RQ2.3 at this point. Receiving mixed results means that some users can use the system well and some can not. We want the editor to be easy and accessible to as many users as possible, so we use the insights gathered during the observations and interviews to determine suggestions on how to improve the editor. After that, we need to repeat the study to evaluate the impact. Those suggestions are the answer to the last question. **RQ2.4:** *How can the tool be improved during future iterations?*

Slowly Teach Users. Especially when using the editor, the majority of users reported they were struggling with the controls at the beginning. But, after getting used to it, they had no problems using the editor. The controls could be slowly taught to the users, so the overwhelming feeling in the beginning disappears. Two types of support were requested. The game designers and escape room players suggested showing hints explaining certain features, and the escape room gamemasters suggested a tutorial before the task started. The tutorial could either guide the users through a simple task or motivate them to try everything out as they cannot break anything.

Allow External Tools. The editor aims to be very simple, so users with low technical knowledge can use it. For this reason, we designed the logic editor in a very simple way. Most users liked the level of complexity and especially the easy configuration of R elements. But when users need to add very complex logic elements, there should be an option to configure and import the logic object from a script or another artifact produced by an external editor. That element can then be accessed like all other elements in the editor. Currently, we as developers of the editor, could add new elements but there are no options for users to create a new element.

Next, four groups requested the option to view the level from a different perspective. The idea originates from the placement of walls. Two groups proposed using an external tool where the room layout can be configured and loaded into the VR editor. One group suggested a top-down view of the level, where the layout could be painted. In either case, the wall placement is made using an external tool.

Quality of Life Features. In the current version, logic connections need to be dragged by hand. That makes it easy for users to understand which objects are connected. When working on a large level or connecting objects far away, users need to drag the connection through the whole area. To optimize the process, we need an option to remotely create a connection. That connection should still be visible and editable by hand but users do not need to walk the whole way to make a connection. When moving objects, the menu belt can block the ray when objects near the ground should be selected. Currently, users need to move away from that spot to try it from a different angle. It is still possible to move all objects, but it would be easier if the menu could be deactivated.

Add More Assets. The editor currently only consists of a small asset library. To create bigger games, we need more assets available. Additionally, there should be an option for users to upload their custom models. Like with the logic elements, developers of the editor could easily add new assets.

5.4   Limitations and Threats to Validity

For our evaluation, we only had twelve participants. When analyzing the date for the game, we could see trends in the data, but with no statistically significance. The usability and workload analysis of the editor, did not reveal a trend. We need to extend our study with a higher number of users. Especially, we need a more escape room designers to investigate the practical use of our tool.

We only considered building the VR side of the game. The users were presented with a complete concept and blueprint for the room to build. We did not investigate how we (can) support designers when the *design* the room. For that, we also need a higher number of escape room designers. In that case, we also need longer or more building sessions to give them enough time for the design.

The game as well as the editor should be tested on a more diverse user group as well. Most of our participants were aged 20–30. Especially older people who are not used to use technologies like VR could have different requirements for using the application.

6   Conclusion and Future Work

Escape rooms and cross-reality applications have been part of research projects for some time. Until now, no project combined those two areas. Therefore, we were the first to explore this new area. To create such an experience, we needed a tool with which the virtual level and the connections to the real world can be configured. The currently supported setting for the VR level is a space station where the VR player is located. Together with the ground control (R player), they must repair the oxygen generators so everybody in the space station survives. With the editor, objects can be spawned, moved, and deleted. We included objects with and without logic. Objects with logic can be connected with other logic elements to control the game. To combine the two realities, players used a voice chat for communication. We created real elements that can be connected to the logic in-game. To evaluate the game and editor, twelve users from six user groups (escape room designers, escape room gamemasters, escape room players, VR developers, VR gamers, and game designers) first played a game we created and used the editor to complete a provided level.

Conclusion. We found that the idea of adding cross-reality elements to an escape room was liked by the players, they reported a fun experience (GUESS-18 mean $\mu = 55.17$, standard deviation $\sigma = 5.27$) and that adding cross-reality adds value to an escape room game. But still, there is potential to fuse the two sides stronger together, e.g. by better integrating what happens on the R side into the VR side. Additionally, we need to keep the story alive during the game, not only explain it in the beginning. When using the editor, users reported very mixed results regarding usability (mean SUS score $\mu = 69.58$, standard deviation $\sigma = 17.47$) and workload (mean $\mu = 39.83$, standard deviation $\sigma = 17.25$). They liked the possibility to edit the level while being in there like the players would do, but for creating the room's layout they demanded additional tools to simplify that task. Users stated the logic editor is easy to learn but still allows for the creation of complex logic. The configuration of real-life elements and their integration in the game does not require different actions than only virtual objects. However, we could create a list of suggestions to improve the editor for the next version. While designing the game and observing users playing it, we also gained some experience with designing puzzles for a cross-reality escape room. The most important thing is to design puzzles in a way that both sides are needed to solve them. Otherwise, the player on one side will start working on a puzzle alone while the second player either has to wait or work on something else alone. We were focusing on combining the two realities, we must emphasize the work across the realities. Generally speaking, there is always a *puzzle*, which results in a *solution*. The solution needs to be entered somewhere to continue in the game. To solve a puzzle, players need the puzzle itself and, optionally, hints on how to solve it. We tried to spread those components across the different realities. A simple example is that the player in VR has a puzzle that they can only solve by using a hint available in R. Once the VR player solved the puzzle, its solution needs to be entered in R. This concept can be extended so that not only information is transferred across the realities. As an example of that, we integrated the object scanner, with which objects can be transferred from R to VR.

Future Work. The results for the usability and workload of the editor are mixed and we could not identify a trend. Future work should extend the study with a larger number of users to retrieve significant results. As the current version only acts as a demo of the concept, we only included basic elements to create puzzles with. To create a more advanced game, we need to include more complex elements and puzzles. Additionally, we can integrate pre-configured puzzles, so users do not need to create them from scratch. We described how assets are created and added to the editor. With that, more assets of the same setting could be added, or we could explore new settings with a new set of assets. When doing so, the editor could be extended such that users can choose the setting for their game. We did not include the requirements from gamemasters (**R4**), in the current version. Integrating tools for gamemasters and evaluating new possibilities for helping and supervising could be done in the future. We can also investigate different variations of the concept, currently, the players are physically separated. There are different cross-reality applications where the players are in different realities but in the same physical space. That could be adapted to our escape room concept. Additionally, we can create an escape room that features a transitional-cross reality. All users could wear an HMD and are located in a real escape room scenario. To get the required hints, they need to change the reality they operate in. For example, could a box in R be locked with a number lock, the number is written on the wall near the box but only visible in VR. With our concept, we also opened a new research area. Cross-reality escape rooms can be used as a tool for different types of research. Pan et al. [18] observed players in conventional escape rooms to find out how people collaborate. Such a study could be repeated in the cross-reality escape room to determine if there is a difference in how players behave if they are in the real or virtual world. This could be extended to evaluate multiple aspects of social behavior when parts of the players are in the real- and virtual world.

References

1. Abras, C., Maloney-Krichmar, D., Preece, J.: Introduction and History (2004)
2. Avargil, S., Shwartz, G., Zemel, Y.: Educational escape room: break dalton's code and escape! J. Chem. Educ. **98**(7), 2313–2322 (2021). https://doi.org/10.1021/acs.jchemed.1c00110
3. Bellucci, A., Zarraonandia, T., Díaz, P., Aedo, I.: End-user prototyping of cross-reality environments. In: Proceedings of the Eleventh International Conference on Tangible, Embedded, and Embodied Interaction, TEI 2017, pp. 173–182. Association for Computing Machinery, New York (2017). https://doi.org/10.1145/3024969.3024975
4. Chan, L., Minamizawa, K.: FrontFace: facilitating communication between HMD users and outsiders using front-facing-screen HMDs. In: Proceedings of the 19th International Conference on Human-Computer Interaction with Mobile Devices

and Services, MobileHCI 2017, pp. 1–5. Association for Computing Machinery, New York (2017).https://doi.org/10.1145/3098279.3098548

5. Christopoulos, A., Mystakidis, S., Cachafeiro, E., Laakso, M.J.: Escaping the cell: virtual reality escape rooms in biology education. Behav. Inf. Technol. 1–18 (2022)

6. Ciprian Firu, A., Ion Tapîrdea, A., Ioana Feier, A., Drăghici, G.: Virtual reality in the automotive field in industry 4.0. Mater. Today Proc. **45**, 4177–4182 (2021).https://doi.org/10.1016/j.matpr.2020.12.037. https://www.sciencedirect.com/science/article/pii/S2214785320397224. 8th International Conference on Advanced Materials and Structures - AMS 2020

7. DeCusatis, C., et al.: A cybersecurity awareness escape room using gamification design principles. In: 2022 IEEE 12th Annual Computing and Communication Workshop and Conference (CCWC), pp. 765–770 (2022). https://doi.org/10.1109/CCWC54503.2022.9720748

8. Estudante, A., Dietrich, N.: Using augmented reality to stimulate students and diffuse escape game activities to larger audiences. J. Chem. Educ. **97**(5), 1368–1374 (2020). https://doi.org/10.1021/acs.jchemed.9b00933

9. Hanus, A., Hoover, M., Lim, A., Miller, J.: A collaborative virtual reality escape room with passive haptics. In: 2019 IEEE Conference on Virtual Reality and 3D User Interfaces (VR), pp. 1413–1414 (2019). https://doi.org/10.1109/VR.2019.8798241. ISSN: 2642-5254

10. Ivanov, V.M., et al.: Practical application of augmented/mixed reality technologies in surgery of abdominal cancer patients. J. Imaging **8**(7) (2022) https://doi.org/10.3390/jimaging8070183. https://www.mdpi.com/2313-433X/8/7/183

11. Jorge, J., Belchior, P., Gomes, A., Sousa, M., Pereira, J., Uh, J.F.: Anatomy studio II a cross-reality application for teaching anatomy. In: 2022 IEEE Conference on Virtual Reality and 3D User Interfaces Abstracts and Workshops (VRW), pp. 441–444 (2022). https://doi.org/10.1109/VRW55335.2022.00097

12. Joshi, S., et al.: Implementing virtual reality technology for safety training in the precast/ prestressed concrete industry. Appl. Ergon. **90**, 103286 (2021). https://doi.org/10.1016/j.apergo.2020.103286. https://www.sciencedirect.com/science/article/pii/S0003687020302349

13. Keebler, J.R., Shelstad, W.J., Smith, D.C., Chaparro, B.S., Phan, M.H.: Validation of the GUESS-18: a short version of the game user experience satisfaction scale (GUESS). J. Usability Stud. **16**(1) (2020)

14. Krekhov, A., Emmerich, K., Rotthaler, R., Krueger, J.: Puzzles unpuzzled: towards a unified taxonomy for analog and digital escape room games. Proc. ACM Hum.-Comput. Interact. **5**(CHI PLAY), 269:1–269:24 (2021). https://doi.org/10.1145/3474696

15. Mai, C., Rambold, L., Khamis, M.: TransparentHMD: revealing the HMD user's face to bystanders. In: Proceedings of the 16th International Conference on Mobile and Ubiquitous Multimedia, MUM 2017, pp. 515–520. Association for Computing Machinery, New York (2017). https://doi.org/10.1145/3152832.3157813

16. McCready, M., Covaci, A., Tabbaa, L.: LabXscape: a prototype for enhancing player experience in cross-reality gameplay. In: 2022 IEEE International Symposium on Mixed and Augmented Reality Adjunct (ISMAR-Adjunct), pp. 183–187 (2022). https://doi.org/10.1109/ISMAR-Adjunct57072.2022.00041. ISSN: 2771-1110

17. Nebeling, M., Madier, K.: 360proto: making interactive virtual reality & augmented reality prototypes from paper. In: Proceedings of the 2019 CHI Conference on Human Factors in Computing Systems, CHI 2019, pp. 1–13. Association for Computing Machinery, New York (2019). https://doi.org/10.1145/3290605.3300826

18. Pan, R., Lo, H., Neustaedter, C.: Collaboration, awareness, and communication in real-life escape rooms. In: Proceedings of the 2017 Conference on Designing Interactive Systems, DIS 2017, pp. 1353–1364. Association for Computing Machinery, New York (2017). https://doi.org/10.1145/3064663.3064767
19. Paraschivoiu, I., Buchner, J., Praxmarer, R., Layer-Wagner, T.: Escape the fake: development and evaluation of an augmented reality escape room game for fighting fake news. In: Extended Abstracts of the 2021 Annual Symposium on Computer-Human Interaction in Play, CHI PLAY 2021, pp. 320–325. Association for Computing Machinery, New York (2021).https://doi.org/10.1145/3450337.3483454
20. Speicher, M., Lewis, K., Nebeling, M.: Designers, the stage is yours! Medium-fidelity prototyping of augmented & virtual reality interfaces with 360theater. Proc. ACM Hum.-Comput. Interact. 5(EICS), 205:1–205:25 (2021). https://doi.org/10.1145/3461727
21. Thoravi Kumaravel, B., Nguyen, C., DiVerdi, S., Hartmann, B.: TransceiVR: bridging asymmetrical communication between VR users and external collaborators. In: Proceedings of the 33rd Annual ACM Symposium on User Interface Software and Technology, UIST 2020, pp. 182–195. Association for Computing Machinery, New York (2020). https://doi.org/10.1145/3379337.3415827
22. Yigitbas, E., Krois, S., Gottschalk, S., Engels, G.: Towards enhanced guiding mechanisms in VR training through process mining. In: Paljic, A., Ziat, M., Bouatouch, K. (eds.) Proceedings of the 18th International Joint Conference on Computer Vision, Imaging and Computer Graphics Theory and Applications, VISIGRAPP 2023, Volume 2: HUCAPP, Lisbon, Portugal, 19–21 February 2023, pp. 152–159. SCITEPRESS (2023). https://doi.org/10.5220/0011651600003417
23. Yigitbas, E., Krois, S., Renzelmann, T., Engels, G.: Comparative evaluation of AR-based, VR-based, and traditional basic life support training. In: 2022 IEEE 10th International Conference on Serious Games and Applications for Health(SeGAH), Sydney, Australia, 10–12 August 2022, pp. 1–8. IEEE (2022). https://doi.org/10.1109/SEGAH54908.2022.9978596
24. Zhang, L., Oney, S.: FlowMatic: an immersive authoring tool for creating interactive scenes in virtual reality. In: Proceedings of the 33rd Annual ACM Symposium on User Interface Software and Technology, UIST 2020, pp. 342–353. Association for Computing Machinery, New York (2020). https://doi.org/10.1145/3379337.3415824

What is Needed to Apply Sentiment Analysis in Real Software Projects: A Feasibility Study in Industry

Alexander Specht[1]($\boxtimes$)(iD), Martin Obaidi[1](iD), Lukas Nagel[1](iD), Marek Stess[2], and Jil Klünder[1](iD)

[1] Software Engineering Group, Leibniz University Hannover, Hannover, Germany
{alexander.specht,martin.obaidi,lukas.nagel,
jil.kluender}@inf.uni-hannover.de
[2] metanoy GmbH, Althütte, Germany
marek.stess@metanoy.tech

Abstract. Due to the increasing size of software projects, they usually require team work and a sufficient amount of communication, which can influence team mood. However, this communication is often not adequate by means of tone and language. Sentiment analysis tools can be used to prevent this problem by investigating the mood conveyed by text-based communication. Most studies aim to improve or develop sentiment analysis tools for a better prediction of the sentiments raised by a specific communication behavior. The tools were often tested in a small experimental group settings (e.g. academia or open-source), but only very few studies applied the tools in industrial software projects.

In this paper, we focus on the feasibility and usefulness of a state-of-the-art sentiment analysis tool in industrial settings. We conducted a user study over 4 months, in which twelve practitioners used a sentiment analysis tool and received weekly information on the sentiments conveyed with their text-based communication in group chats. This way, we evaluated the general feasibility of sentiment analysis in industry. Afterwards, we conducted an interview study with six of the twelve participants to get feedback. This way, we validated the insights gained from the user study and evaluated whether the application of sentiment analysis is useful in industrial software projects. We also investigated which improvements are necessary in order to increase the usefulness of sentiment analysis. Every participant reported that such a tool is suited for the use in software projects. However, they also pointed out some improvements that are required to increase its usefulness. These improvements include explanations, dashboards, and sarcasm detection.

Keywords: Software project · social aspects and behaviors · sentiment analysis · feasibility study

1 Introduction

Most software projects require collaboration: The members of the development team need to collaborate with other team members as well as with other persons

© IFIP International Federation for Information Processing 2024
Published by Springer Nature Switzerland AG 2024
M. K. Lárusdóttir et al. (Eds.): HCSE 2024, LNCS 14793, pp. 105–129, 2024.
https://doi.org/10.1007/978-3-031-64576-1_6

involved in the project such as the customer [19,27,34,41,50]. This leads to an increasing need for social interactions in software development that often go along with issues and problems (e.g., [10,32,55]). To analyze these problems, over the years, different techniques emerged (e.g., in meetings [20,23]).

Sentiment analysis can be used to investigate communication [44,52,60]. A sentiment analysis tool analyzes texts in reviews, comments, or text-based communication according to the conveyed polarity [2,4,59]. That is, the tool analyzes which feeling a sentence may evoke on the receiver's side. In most cases, the tool distinguishes between *positive, negative,* and *neutral* statements [4,15,59] instead of distinguishing between different emotions [21,42,58]. For example, analyzing the communication in a group chat allows conclusions on the current mood in a team. Analyzing textual input before a message is sent allows the sender to adjust their message should it be unintentionally negative [46].

In research, sentiment analysis has been applied to software projects, for example to analyze comments on Stack Overflow (e.g., [3,37,51]), GitHub (e.g., [12,17,31,35,36]), text-based communication [33,57], or in meetings [13]. However, so far, the feasibility of such kind of analysis has not been scientifically investigated in industrial settings. Integrating sentiment analysis in the daily workflow of industrial software projects is necessary to evaluate its usefulness in real software projects. Such an evaluation should be performed before conducting theoretical research on improving sentiment analysis in experimental settings that could be transferred to industry. According to recent research [38,40], it is likely that the analysis of text-based communication according to its polarity is relevant and meaningful for software projects (e.g., in order to avoid unfriendly communication or to enable interventions in extreme cases), but to the best of our knowledge, it is not yet clear whether this kind of analysis is feasible and, if so, whether it is useful.

In this paper, we want to close this research gap by investigating the feasibility and usefulness of sentiment analysis of text-based communication in an industrial setting. As the idea of real-time sentiment analysis (i.e., the tool analyzes a text before it is sent) is not yet validated to be used in a real-world setting [46], we focused retrospective sentiment analysis in this feasibility study. In this case, at specific points in time, e.g., in the end of each week, the team receives feedback on their communication of the last week, and can improve the communication in the upcoming week. The study presented in this paper consisted of two steps:

(1) We evaluated the *feasibility of sentiment analysis* using a user study in an industrial setting with twelve practitioners from one company who used a sentiment analysis tool, the SEnti-Analyzer [13,15], over a period of four months. They were free to decide how frequently they used the tool, ranging from just running in the background to regularly assessing the feedback.

(2) Afterwards, we validated the feasibility (i.e., the results of the user study) and investigated the *usefulness of sentiment analysis* in an interview study with a subset of six participants from the twelve practitioners that participated in the user study. During the interviews, they reported on the

usefulness of such an analysis, opportunities for the future, and what needs to be improved.

Based on the user study and the interview study with practitioners, we can draw conclusions on the general feasibility of sentiment analysis in industry by showing a possibility of how it can be integrated in the daily workflow of a team. We can also draw conclusions on the usefulness of such tools. More concretely, our results point to the general usefulness of raising the awareness for the relevance of how a team communicates. We also observe some potential for improvement, including explanations ("why is my message negative?"), dashboards ("how did our communication change over time?"), and sarcasm detection (sarcastic or ironic statements are most often misclassified).

Structure. The rest of the paper is structured as follows: In Sect. 2, we present related work and background details. The study design, research question and data basis is introduced in Sect. 3. The results are presented in Sect. 4 and discussed in Sect. 5 with an interpretation and take aways. The paper is summarized in Sect. 6.

2   Background and Related Work

For the field of software engineering, there are several sentiment analysis tools that differ regarding their intended use case, as well as data sets that can be used to train these tools.

Schroth et al. [46] present a tool that allows real-time analysis of sentiments in software projects. They evaluated the concept in a use case by conducting an experiment with participants from industry. They focused on how a real-time sentiment analysis system can theoretically be integrated into the daily work of developers. The case study showed the usefulness of such a tool. However, Schroth et al. [46] did not integrate the tool in a development team's daily work and, hence, did not evaluate it in a real-world setting, but only in a hypothetical situation. Whiting et al. [55] analyzed developers' chats for their sentiments in Amazon MTurk, using the sentiment analysis tool Vader [16]. Their goal was to increase the viability of the online context for software development teams through a concept of constantly anonymously changing teams and maintaining the best constellation. El-Halees [9] presents a model to extract knowledge from opinions to improve subjective software usability. To analyze subjective usability reviews, the author used SentiStrength [48]. Werner et al. [54] analyzed support tickets of the company IBM to be able to prevent a possible escalation. They were able to show that the sentiments of escalated tickets differ from those of non-escalated tickets. Islam and Zibran [18] developed SentiStrength-SE, which is a customized version of the lexicon-based tool SentiStrength [48]. They added a domain-specific dictionary, implemented ad hoc heuristics to correct observed misclassifications, and considered SE-specific contexts. Hence, this tool does not need retraining and already has some domain-specific customization. Islam and Zibran [18] compared SentiStrength-SE with SentiStrength on technical texts and observed an improved performance. Calefato et al. [4] developed Senti4SD, another sentiment analysis tool tailored to software development, and thus enabled training and classification of models specific to the SE domain. To do this, they used a specialized word lexicon in combination with a support-vector machine. With this approach, they were able to classify an input document in one of the three polarities *positive, negative,* and *neutral.* Zhang et al. [59] compared the performance of different pre-trained neural network models with the performance of tools using more classical machine learning approaches. These included neural network models like BERT [7] and five other existing tools including SentiStrength-SE [17]. They evaluated the classification accuracy of all these tools and models on many of the data sets. The evaluation revealed that the performance of the tools changes depending on the test data set [59]. The authors observed that the RoBERTa model [30] most often had the highest average F1-scores among the pre-trained transformer models [59]. Novielli et al. [35] conducted a cross-platform study to investigate to what degree tools that have been trained for one platform (e.g. GitHub) perform on other platforms (e.g. Stack Overflow). They used three data sets and four tools and concluded that supervised tools perform significantly worse on platforms they were not trained on. In these cases, a lexicon-based tool performs better across all platforms.

Several papers highlight the need of domain adaptation to the field of SE (cf. [2,4–6,8,17]), leading to some SE specific data sets. They were often crawled from freely available sources such as open-source software projects [36,37] or app reviews [53]. The systematic mapping study about sentiment analysis in SE by Obaidi et al. [40] as well as the systematic literature review about opinion mining in SE by Lin et al. [28] show an overview of the data sets used. Novielli et al. [37] collected 4,800 questions asked on the question-and-answer site Stack Overflow and assigned the emotions *love, joy, anger, sadness, fear,* and *surprise* to each sentence of the collected communication data [37]. Afterwards, they labeled these sentences based on the emotions with three polarities *positive, negative* and *neutral.* This labeling process was done by a majority decision of three raters. Another gold standard data set crawled from the collaborative development website GitHub was developed by Novielli et al. [36]. This data set contains over 7,000 sentences manually annotated by polarities. Similar to the Stack Overflow data set [37], they first assigned emotions to each sentence and labeled polarities based on these emotions. The sentences were extracted from textual contributions to pull requests and commits, i.e., changes made by developers to public code in different projects [36]. Lin et al. [29] collected 1,500 discussions on Stack Overflow tagged with Java. Five authors labeled the data using a web application they built. No emotion model or guidelines for labeling were mentioned in the paper. Their initial sentiment assignment ranged from -2 to $+2$, but for further analyses, they merged the negative and the positive numbers to create the three classes *negative (−2, −1), neutral (0),* and *positive (+1, +2).* Uddin et al. [51] developed a data set which consists of 4,522 sentences from 1,338 Stack Overflow posts on API aspects. The authors did not use an emotion model or other guidelines. However, their coding guide includes an example sentence for each polarity with focus on the opinion expressed in the text. Ahmed et al. [2] built a data set which includes negative and non-negative documents. Thus, it is a binary-class data set. The documents consist of multiple comments. They were collected from 20 open-source projects that do tool-based code reviews supported by the same tool (e.g. Gerrit).

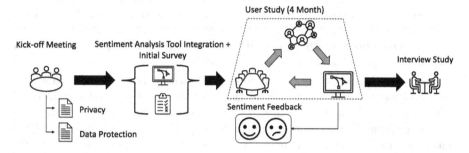

Fig. 1. Timeline for our feasibility study. The integration takes place in Microsoft Teams.

3 Study Design

In the following, we present our research design with the research goal and research questions, the data handling and analysis. Figure 1 presents the general process for our feasibility study.

3.1 Research Goal and Research Questions

This paper aims to *investigate the feasibility of sentiment analysis in industrial software projects and analyze the usefulness of applying sentiment analysis in such contexts*. In particular, we are interested in answering the following research questions:

> **RQ1: Is sentiment analysis feasible in industrial software projects without disturbing the team members?**

We first want to check whether the assumption that applying sentiment analysis is feasible in industrial settings is correct. In this case, feasibility also includes not disturbing the team members by smoothly integrating the analysis in the development team's daily workflow.

> **RQ2: What advantages can sentiment analysis provide for project teams in industry?**

In a next step, we want to evaluate the usefulness of sentiment analysis in a specific project context. Knowing possible advantages emerging from the use of sentiment analysis in practice can further motivate other teams to apply sentiment analysis in their team.

The first two research questions can be best answered if a project team uses a sentiment analysis tool over a longer period of time. This allows to get first-hand feedback that is not based on any thought experiments or hypothetical situations. Such a setting further allows us to pose the third research question:

> **RQ3: How does using the tool influence the participants?**

This research question allows us to evaluate whether the use of such a tool has a positive or negative impact on the team or single persons according to their perception. In addition, to go beyond feasibility, we want to provide an overview of adjustments or opportunities for improvement of sentiment analysis to increase the likelihood that teams will benefit from its application. Thus, we pose the following research question:

> **RQ4: What adjustments or improvements need to be made to sentiment analysis tools to increase their benefits and applicability?**

By answering this research question, we opt for a list of requirements that should be taken into account when improving sentiment analysis tools.

3.2   The Case Company

Answering our research questions requires a team of practitioners that are willing to use sentiment analysis in a real context in their daily work. Applying sentiment analysis necessitates a tool running at least in the background, analyzing anonymized text-based communication. Overall, our feasibility study requires a company with a sufficient number of practitioners that are willing to use such a tool. At *metanoy*[1] a rather young company, we found these requirements being fulfilled. Due to previous collaborations (not with *metanoy*, but with the CEO), there was sufficient trust on both sides to conduct the research.

metanoy is a German company with a focus on information technology, in particular on digital transformation based on Azure Cloud[2]. The company has 20 employees with different skills and tasks, including requirements engineering, process design, user experience, user interface design, software development, and software architecture. Due to the size of the company its atmosphere is rather informal and relaxed. The employees work fully remote and have full technical equipment in their home office setup (e.g. monitors, smartphone). To connect with other colleagues face-to-face they have several events in the year.

---

[1] For more information, please visit https://metanoy.tech/en/.
[2] https://azure.microsoft.com/de-de.

3.3 Overview of the Study

Our study consisted of four parts that are visualized in Fig. 1. The study started with an *Initial Kick-Off Meeting* in which we explained the general process and purpose of the feasibility study. We explained the core idea of sentiment analysis and our research goal. We further used this meeting to sensitize the team for data protection. We drew attention to the fact that we (researchers) will access neither their text-based communication at any point in time, nor the results of the sentiment analysis. The analysis is limited to group chats in which all (actively or passively) participating team members agree to apply sentiment analysis.

Afterwards, we sent an *Initial Survey* to the subset of employees who indicated interest in participating in the study. We used this initial survey to get some information about demographics, general expectations of the participants regarding sentiment analysis, as well as their attitude towards such kind of analyses.

In the third part of our study, we conducted a *User Study*. We deployed a sentiment analysis tool, namely the SEnti-Analyzer [15], to the team's server and asked the team to use the tool for a period of four months. This integration is further explained in the next section. Roughly spoken, the tool was integrated in Microsoft Teams[3], the main communication tool at *metanoy*, as a bot. This bot was added to all group chats in which all team members agreed upon using it. The bot ran completely in the background, only providing feedback once at the end of a week.

We ended the feasibility study with an *Interview Study* in which six team members participated voluntarily. The participants gave feedback on the user study, their experiences with sentiment analysis, and opportunities for future improvements.

3.4 Used Tool: The SEnti-Analyzer

For the sentiment analysis in the team, we needed a sentiment analysis tool usable in German and English, as the mainly used language at *metanoy* is German with a high amount of English phrases. As several papers have shown [2–4,6,8,47], besides selecting the correct language, there is a need for software engineering specific tools in order to retrieve reliable results when they are applied in such technical contexts. As a third requirement, the tool had to be integrated into Microsoft Teams.

To the best of our knowledge, the SEnti-Analyzer [15] is the only tool that satisfies all these requirements, i.e., it allows German and English input, is validated in a technical context in German and English, we got access to the source code and were able to adjust it such that it could be integrated into Microsoft Teams.

---

[3] https://www.microsoft.com/en-gb/microsoft-teams.

The text-based analysis of the SEnti-Analyzer [15] was validated in two different ways. First, the authors calculated the accuracy of the tool using two predefined labels of sentiment analysis datasets: A GitHub gold standard dataset from Novielli et al. [36] with 7122 entries and a Stack Overflow dataset from Lin et al. [29] with 1500 entries [15]. Both datasets were given in full to the SEnti-Analyzer as input for validation without any prior training of the tool with the data. The accuracy of the SEnti-Analyzer was 79.8% for the Stack Overflow dataset and 72% for the GitHub dataset [15].

Second, the predicted labels from the SEnti-Analyzer were compared with the labels from participants of a survey [14,39]. In the online survey, 94 participants labeled a total of 96 statements [14,39]. The 96 statements were taken from the two previously mentioned datasets GitHub [36] and Stack Overflow [29] with 48 statements each (with the split 16-16-16 negative-neutral-positive). The median label of the participants was then compared with the predicted label from SEnti-Analyzer and also with the author labels [15]. Overall, the SEnti-Analyzer agreed with the participants 63.5% and with the authors of the data sets 64.6% [15].

Therefore, we opted for the SEnti-Analyzer [15] developed by Herrmann and Klünder [13]. In Fig. 2, a schematic presentation of the used implementation of the SEnti-Analyzer is presented. The tool was initially developed for analyzing meetings with an implementation of one sentiment analysis tool [13]. To improve its accuracy, more tools, e.g. BERT, were integrated [15]. In the current implementation, a written message is sent to the SEnti-Analyzer, where an ensemble (cf. Fig. 2) of state-of-the-practice tools is implemented. After sending the message to the tool, the tool calculates two medians of the polarities "positive", "neutral", and "negative" based on different sentiment analysis tools. One median is based on machine learning tools and the other considers lexicon-based tools. The output is generated by a probability of the two medians (cf. technical report [15]). The result presents a positive, negative or neutral feedback and will be sent to the user.

To make sentiment analysis feasible, we adjusted the tool to be integrated into Microsoft Teams which is the participating team's standard communication system. The tool was designed to analyze the text-based communication in dedicated group channels. For our study, we use the German version of the SentiAnalyzer, which was evaluated in a study by Herrmann [13]. As written before, the tool works as ensemble of several sentiment tools and the single tools were evaluated in the associated papers (BertDE [11] and GerVader [49]).

All users with access to these channels were asked beforehand if they agree with the study. Every single team member allowed us to integrate the SEnti-Analyzer as a bot to the group channel. Over a period of four months, the participants retrieved automated feedback on a weekly basis including the communication's sentiment score, which was in our case positive, negative, and neutral, for each channel they used in Microsoft Teams. The rest of the time, the bot was silent, analyzing the communication in the background.

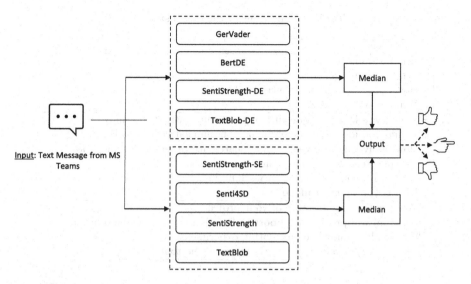

Fig. 2. Schematic presentation of the SEnti-Analyzer. It contains an ensemble of multiple sentiment analysis tools. The used language for analysis in the tool were German and English. The figure is based on the report [15] and were modified for our purpose.

3.5   Data Collection

In the following, we present each step in which we collected data in more detail. The initial survey started in April 2022 and the interviews were conducted after a period of four months in which the participants of the company used our tool.

Initial Survey. Twelve team members participated in the initial survey that was realized online via MS Forms. This tool was used as the team's work is based on the Microsoft tool suite. The survey consisted of questions on the demographics (experience, role, and similar) and on the attitude towards communication and such kind of analysis. The majority of the questions was answered on an ordinal or on a 5-Point-Likert scale, one was a single choice selector, and the age was another single choice selector with 10 point intervals. An overview of the questions is presented in Table 1.

Sentiment Data. Our tool analyzed the sentiment of the communication data of each group chat. Only the study participants were able to see the resulting sentiment score. The tool presented the results only on their devices. The experimenters, did not retrieve any data from the tool as the analysis method was subject to our research and not the sentiments of the team.

Interview Study. After 4 months, we conducted an interview study to get feedback on the usefulness of sentiment analysis in industrial context. Participation in this interview study was on a voluntary basis. Six of the twelve initial

Table 1. Questions of the initial survey.

	Questions
General	What is your occupation?
	What is your age?
	How many year of experience you have?
	What is your gender?
Communication	Would you identify yourself being communicative? (textual)
	Would you identify yourself being communicative? (verbal)
	How many times do you communicate with others at a typical day?
	Do you prefer to work in teams?
	Do you have experience with working in teams?
	How is your current mood?
Study	What is the current state of your project
	The tool will provide a supportive function for team collaboration.
	The study sounds like an exciting experiment.
	I hope to gain valuable insights by using the tool.

team members participated. The semi-structured interviews were conducted in German, the native language of study participants and authors of this paper, and followed the guideline presented in Table 2. The interviews had an average length of 20 min.

3.6   Data Availability

The data we collected partially contains highly sensitive information on communication behavior and similar. We did receive the consent to publish the company's name in line with this paper, but we did not get the consent to publish the data collected during our study. This includes the interview transcripts, the sentiment data, and the results of the initial survey.

3.7   Data Pre-processing and Analysis

For our analysis, we used a tool to transcribe the interviews automatically and performed a manual check on the generated transcripts manually. In line with Saldana et al. [43], we performed open and selective coding. That is, the codes emerged from the interview transcripts, but we only coded parts of the interviews we considered relevant, i.e., parts that contained information helping answer our research questions. We started with open coding and assigned codes to the statements made in the interviews. For example, in response to the question *Do you think the tool can be used in practice?*, we received the answer "I think maybe in stressful situations, e.g. projects, where we have a deadline and we have to finish it fast, there I can imagine to use a tool, because I think the communication could be fast more negatively." For this example, we assigned the following codes: *stressful situations, deadlines, communication could quickly become negative*. Based on answers of the six interviewees who each answered

Table 2. Interview guideline

	Questions	RQ
General	What is your occupation?	
	How many years of experience do you have (occupation)?	
	Do you work remote?	
Communication	Would you identify yourself being communicative?	
	Could you give some examples for or describe your typical communication behavior?	
	How many times do you communicate with others at a typical day?	
	Do you prefer to work alone or in teams?	
	How important do you consider mood?	
	Did you have situations where negative mood was noticeable?	
	Did you have situations where positive mood was noticeable?	
Mood in Study	What sentiment was presented by the tool (average)?	RQ1
	Do you think that the presented sentiment is your personal self-perceived sentiment?	RQ1
	Do you trust the results of the tool?	RQ1
	Were the results comprehensible?	RQ1
	Do you think, you are now more aware of your personal mood?	RQ1, 2
Study Design	What was your opinion about the study?	
	Could your opinion be confirmed?	
	Have you changed your opinion?	
	Do you think that such a tool is necessary?	RQ2
	Do you think, the team collaboration has changed?	RQ3
	Do you think the tool can be used in practice?	RQ1
Tool Feedback	Where do you think, can this tool be used?	RQ1, 2
	Was the study an interesting new experience?	
	What do you think about the presentation of the tool?	RQ1
	What do you dislike about the study?	RQ4
	What do you like about the study?	RQ2
	Would you use the tool in future?	RQ1,4

28 questions, we retrieved a total of 168 codes. We summarized and abstracted these codes into categories and aggregated them. For example, for the question *What sentiment was presented by the tool (average)?*, we aggregated "frequently positive" and "sometimes positive" to "two participants reported that the tool returned a regular positive feedback". In the last step, we classified the codes into the five core categories presented on the left side of Table 2, namely "general", "communication", "mood in study", "study design", and "tool feedback".

4   Results

In this section, we present the results of the feasibility study.

4.1 Overview of the Project Team

The initial survey allowed us to get an overview of the team members that participated in the feasibility study. Although not all team members participated in the survey, the results show the team's diversity.

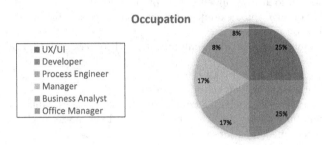

Fig. 3. Our participants have different occupations with a focus on information technology.

Of the twelve participants, five identified as female and seven as male. The participants hold different occupations: Three participants in our initial survey are UX/UI designer and another three are developers. Two reported being process engineers and two are managers. In addition, one business analyst and one office manager participated in the initial survey (cf. Fig. 3).

All participants reported to be between 20 and 40 years old with a mean of 2.91 years of experience (min: 1, max: 9, standard deviation: 2.84).

In the initial survey, we asked the participants questions about their team collaboration, sentiment and goals for the study: Three out of twelve assumed that the tool would support the team collaboration. The others took a neutral stance. As for their own sentiment, eleven out of twelve claimed that they were positively thinking. Nine of the twelve participants expected the study/tool to be profitable, three were neutral. We also asked our participants about their communication behavior: Seven participants reported communicating frequently via text-based communication channels. In contrast, ten participants reported that they frequently communicate with others verbally. Furthermore, eleven of the twelve participants indicated that they communicate daily or hourly with others at work. We also asked about the experience in different team constellations, e.g. larger or smaller teams. Nine of them reported some or a lot of experience in working in a team. All of them claimed to enjoy working in teams. Most participants (11) reported a more positive mood and one a more negative mood at the time they finished the survey compared to the beginning. The last results of our initial survey show that the most (11) think that the study could have a supporting function for their teams and all expected that the study would be an exciting experiment. For the last question *I hope to gain valuable insights by using the tool* nine out of twelve agreed and the remaining three partially agreed.

4.2 Feasibility Study

After the initial survey, the twelve participants and other team members who agreed (they don't filled out the survey), used the SEnti-Analyzer integrated as a bot in dedicated group channels Microsoft Teams. All members in these groups were informed about the integration of the bot. The bot silently "observed" the communication, analyzing every statement that was sent via the respective group channel. This way, it was possible to perform a sentiment analysis without disturbing the team. The only active part of the bot was to send a report at the end of each week, reporting the aggregated polarity on the team level of the whole communication in the group.

This procedure of integrating the sentiment analysis as a bot makes sentiment analysis feasible in real settings, as the bot does not disturb the team members and does not frequently draw their attention to the analysis they agreed upon.

4.3 Interview Study

To gain further insights into the feasibility of sentiment analysis in real software projects, we conducted an interview study (cf. Fig. 1).

Out of the twelve participants of the initial survey, six agreed upon partic-ipating in the interview study after being part of the feasibility study for four months. The other participants reported time constraints or simply no interest in participating in the interview study. As we did not want to force them to participate, we respected their decision and opted for six participants. However, the fact that half of the initial participants did not want to report on their experiences introduces some threats to validity that we discuss below.

Four interview participants identified as male and two as female. Regarding their occupation (cf. Table 2), two specify being *Business Managers* or *Full-Stack Developers*. We also interviewed one *Assistant to the Management* and one *UX/UI-Designer*. They reported having between 1 year and 13 years of work experience (M = 6.17; SD = 4.3) and all work remotely.

Communication Behaviour of the Participants. All participants describe themselves as being communicative: They often use messaging services, write mails or news, discuss with colleagues, or communicate about other topics. Each participant described that they have many (online) meetings. In their daily tasks, they also prefer to work in a group rather than working alone. The two developers explained that some tasks, e.g., programming, are easier to perform alone to stay focused. In addition, three participants report that they have to communicate more than others because of their position which includes talking to clients or sending more e-mails. In the next part, the participants were asked to estimate how much time they spend communicating with colleagues per day. Answers ranged from two to six hours (M = 3.83, SD = 1.67).

In addition to their communication behavior, we wanted individual feedback from our participants about "mood" in general. All participants consider mood being an important aspect in order to finish a project successfully. Furthermore, we asked them if (and in which situations) they have experienced situations in which negative or positive sentiments were present. The answers regarding negative sentiments included situations in which private problems influenced the professional context, messages with a negative impact, miscommunication, or changes of group members. However, playing some games in the lunch break or sitting together and talking can improve the mood.

Mood in the Study. In the next part of the interview, we focused on the mood of the participants during the study (cf. Table 2). Due to data protection and anonymization, we did not collect the results of the SEnti-Analyzer for our analysis. These results were only reported to the team after being aggregated on the team-level. Thus, we asked our participants which sentiment polarity, on average, was presented by our tool. All participants answered that the most frequent sentiment was neutral with a tendency towards a positive sentiment. We subsequently wanted to know if their personal perception coincided with the sentiment reported by the tool. For most of the time, the participants agreed with the SEnti-Analyzer, one of the participants even reported fully agreeing with the results. However, some participants reported that irony was not correctly detected. Five out of six participants trusted the results, with the sixth participant reporting missing information to be the reason for no ultimate trust. This missing information included, for example, which phrases impacted the overall score to a large extent. Each participant reported that, in general, the results were comprehensible. One participant would have preferred another scale for the results, e.g., a softer scale from -1.00 to 1.00, which might be a better option to see tendencies. This way, situations can be avoided where the mood "neutral" is displayed, but it remains unclear whether it is neutral with a tendency towards positive or towards negative, or with no tendency at all. To check whether the tool has an impact to their personal perception of their sentiment, we ask them whether the tool has increased their awareness. Three participants answered that it has a little impact and that they had re-read e-mails or messages and reflected the results. As the tool only gave feedback in retrospect, one participant missed some useful functions to use the tool more productively. Overall, the provided feedback points to a general feasibility of sentiment analysis in industrial settings.

Feedback on the Tool. In the following, we present the results from the last part of the interview study, namely feedback on the study and the tool (cf. Table 2). In particular, we asked the participants to provide concrete feedback on the tool and to report on functionality they missed. This also includes requested changes in order to further increase the tool's usability.

Each participant reported that they liked the experiences made during the user study and considered the study to be a successful experiment. However, two participants reported that, in a company, it is generally not necessary to use a sentiment analysis tool due to the professional setting. Two participants reported that, in the case company, the general mood is "not negative". Nevertheless, two participants reported that using such a tool can help to improve the written communication and that it might reveal problems in communication. Each participant reported that they were euphoric to participate in the study in the beginning. Unfortunately, in at least one case, this euphoria decreased over time due to missing functions of the tool. Regarding the changes in the team collaboration, each of the participants reported that the team collaboration has not increased (as it was already good before), but one mentions being more attentive while writing messages since having participated in the study. As all participants see a practical use case of such a tool, we asked them to provide requirements and improvements for the further development of sentiment analysis tools. The overall feedback on the study is presented in Table 3. For example, the participants criticized that feedback was only given once a week, pointing to the need to provide *realtime sentiment analysis* as presented by Schroth et al. [46].

Table 3. Feedback on the study

Likes	Dislikes
Each participant got new experience about the scientific side of sentiment analysis	Feedback came only on one day, not in real-time
They self-reflect messages they write	No meeting analysis
Exploring how communication can be evaluated	Notification were annoying, e.g. notifications
Everyday life integration for their work-day	Interruption of communication flow
Insights how sentiment can be presented	The explanations were insufficient

Some participants proposed to use continuous *values* rather than three polarity classes. As discussed before, it can be an advantage to use continuous values, e.g. -1.00 to 1.00, to see a trend (e.g. more positive than negative). Another frequently mentioned requirement refers to *explanations*. Every single interviewee reported at least one situation in which they wanted an explanation of why the current rating is presented or which word or phrase has an impact on the results. It is useful to see which word has an impact on the sentiment. For example, such words can be *highlighted* or marked. Further, the participants wanted to know why the tool presented this concrete feedback. In this line, another improvement would be functionality that shows words or phrases which could *increase the rate of positive sentiment* or provide examples for similar words with a less negative polarity.

Besides the application to text-based communication, three participants would like to use the tool in *meetings*, which was the initial use case of the SEnti-Analyzer [13]. The participants would like to get feedback on the group mood in real-time or after the meeting. In addition, there should be an explanation stating why the sentiment is presented and how the affected person can prevent negative results in future. In meetings, there are different kinds of attendees, some of which talk more and or less than others. An integration to analyze the *communication flow* and the participation in the communication would help to balance meetings, so that future meetings could be more productive. A future tool should also have an integration which does not interrupt the *work flow*, e.g., by avoiding annoying notifications or pop-ups. In our study, we opted for weekly notifications, which was acceptable for the study participants. However, the participants consider this highly relevant (as well as an adequate integration) to reduce the number of interruptions. Two participants would have liked a **dashboard** presenting the personal sentiment (including the sentiments over time, sentiments in contrast to last month, and similar) as well as functionality to see the group sentiment or a comparison with other colleagues in an anonymized manner. This feature could be used for project managers to identify problems. Overall, five out of six interviewees would like to continue using the tool in future, but only with the mentioned adjustments. One participants would not continue using it.

5   Discussion

In this section we answer our research questions, discuss our results and present takeaways for future work.

5.1   Answering the Research Questions

Based on our results, we can answer the research questions as follows:

RQ1: *Is sentiment analysis feasible in industrial software projects without disturbing the team members?* The results of a user study over a duration of four months show that sentiment analysis is generally feasible in industrial software settings. When implemented as a bot that silently "observes" the communication in group chats and provides reports on a weekly basis, it does not interrupt the workflow of the users. However, in our study, the participants even wanted more interruptions, for example realized as real-time sentiment analysis that provides feedback when typing a message.

RQ2: *What advantages can sentiment analysis provide for project teams in industry?* Our result shows that participants started self-reflecting their written messages. They pay more attention to the possible effects a message can have and how the message can be interpreted by others. The participants reported on an increasing awareness of the relevance of adequate communication. Some participants stated that they were a bit more attentive while working in teams. It would be more useful if the tool was more active and gave direct suggestions for improvements to maximize the benefit for teams and reveal "poisoned mood". All but one of the participants would use such a tool in future, if the mentioned features were integrated. The participants were fascinated how mood can be measured and they see a positive benefit for their work and other companies in the future.

RQ3: *How does using the tool influence the participants?* According to our results, the collaboration has not changed remarkably, but the team members paid more attention to their mood and their written communication. They also say that they can easily imagine other use cases, e.g., in companies with a less open-minded atmosphere or in which the general mood is negative or where stressful situations fit closely (e.g. deadlines), in which such tools can have a positive effect.

RQ4: *What adjustments or improvements need to be made to sentiment analysis tools to increase their benefits and applicability?* Although the participants see some value in the sentiment analysis, they propose several improvements, including real-time integration for both text-based and verbal communication, and explanations to understand how communication can be improved. These explanations could also be extended by functionality proposing changes to text messages.

5.2   Discussion

Overall, we can summarize the findings of our study as follows:

(1) Sentiment analysis on text-based communication in real software projects is generally feasible.
(2) When sentiment analysis is applied, participants want to improve their communication, even welcoming frequent interruptions by the tool.
(3) Using a sentiment analysis tool increases the awareness for the relevance of communication.
(4) Although the participants see limited usefulness in a professional context with a neutral communication, five out of six would like to continue using the tool.

(1) Integrating sentiment analysis as a bot in group channels is one way to make sentiment analysis feasible in industrial settings. The realization as a bot that silently "observes" the conversation in the group channel and analyzes the communication in the background allows an integration of sentiment analysis in the typical daily workflow. This integration does not require an installation of any software before using the analysis, or the use of a different tool, which was one of the main concerns identified in the study by Schroth et al. [46].
(2) The participants were not fully satisfied with our realization as a bot that provides feedback on a weekly basis. We tried to minimize the interruptions of the workflow by having a bot running in the background that only provides feedback once a week. However, in the interview study, the participants somewhat criticized the sparse feedback. Indeed, they proposed real-time sentiment analysis, providing feedback at each point in time. This is a

different use case of what we intended with our study, allowing the participants to get deeper feedback on how they communicate instead of how the team communicates. For their personal development, they would like more information from the tool, i.e., they wanted to learn about the strengths and weaknesses of their communication. In this case, they welcomed more frequent interruptions.

(3) The fact that applying sentiment analysis raises the awareness for the relevance of communication is an important, but not particularly surprising finding. Research has often shown that it is possible to raise the participants' or team members' awareness by processing their communication (or collaboration, interaction, ...) data and presenting it to the team [22, 24–26]. Increasing the awareness for social aspects in software projects is meaningful [45]. Thus, the results of our study are promising in the way that applying sentiment analysis to team communication can help being more empathetic or aware that the receiver might perceive a message differently than intended by the sender.

(4) The fact that participants wanted to continue using the tool although they see limited usefulness is interesting. Given the neutrality of the communication in an industrial setting, the participants see limited usefulness in applying a sentiment analysis tool. However, given the advantages they experienced on a personal level when using the tool, they would nevertheless continue using it. Another possible explanation for the further use of such a tool is the implementation of benefits. Once there is a dashboard and a more fine-grained score, it is also possible to include some gamification aspects such as "who writes the most friendly messages?". As the participants already reported playing with the tool (regarding the most positive or most negative score) without retrieving any points for these scores, maybe, the participants already thought about such gamified aspects.

However, besides the four findings that are supported by our results, it is even more interesting what we do not see:

(1) None of the participants reported privacy concerns, despite the analysis of their communication.

(2) The participants did not report on huge differences between their perception and the tool's output.

(1) Previous research analyzing social aspects in development teams such as interactions in meetings [23], collaboration in general [22], or communication [46] often needed to deal with privacy concerns. These concerns lead to users who are unwilling to use analysis tools. In particular, when it comes to personal (communication) data, they are concerned about the consequences of the results. Surprisingly, none of the participants of our study mentioned that such kinds of issues reduce the likelihood that they will continue using the tool. We assume that this is due to the fact that the tool was only applied to group chats that are accessible for every person in a company. The communication that needs to be protected in the eyes of our interviewees takes place in private chats that must not be analyzed.

(2) Almost all participants reported on agreeing with the tool's output. This is kind of surprising as the SEnti-Analyzer is trained using pre-labeled data sets, although these data sets often do not meet the perception of individual developers [14]. However, as also argued by Herrmann et al. [14], on a median level, the pre-defined labels meet the "average" developer's perception. As most of the communication in our study was neutral anyway, it is not unlikely that the tool meets the team members' perception. However, the participants' request for explanations highlights that there are cases in which the tool should be able to explain what makes a message positive or negative (or not).

Summarizing, our study shows the potential of sentiment analysis tools to be used in practice. However, several improvements are required that are, as of now, expected to increase the usefulness and applicability of such tools. These expectations need to be proven by future studies after having implemented the new requirements. Nevertheless, if increasing the team members' awareness on the relevance of their communication is the goal of the application in an industrial setting, it is not unlikely that this goal can already be achieved by the current version of the SEnti-Analyzer.

5.3   Threats to Validity

The results of our study must not be over-generalized, as they are subject to some threats to validity. In the following, we discuss these threats to our feasibility study according to Wohlin et al. [56].

Construct Validity. 12 participants took part in the initial survey, but only 6 took part in the interview study. This means that our number of participants may not be sufficiently large, and the number of participants for the interviews was smaller than both the number of participants from the survey and who used the tool. Most of them reported time constraints as the reason for not participating in the interviews. As we did not force them to participate, we respected their decision, ending up with a total of six interviews. We cannot verify whether the practitioners really used the tool as they stated. This way, we wanted to avoid Hawthorne effect [1] and protect the data privacy of our participants. We assured as part of the study that we were not collecting any data from the tool. However, as the participation in the interview study was on a voluntary basis and answering the questions required having used the tool, we only retrieved feedback from participants who made use of the tool.

Internal Validity. The internal validity of our results is threatened by the fact that they could have been affected by participants' boredom or fatigue. To minimize this threat, we ensured that the time for the survey does not exceed 10 min and the interview study does not exceed 30 min. Due to the nature of this user study, our results provide insights from one single company. However, for our selected setting we retrieve feedback over four months and this give us in-depth feedback of the user behavior.

Another threat is that our participants actively volunteered for our interview study. We interviewed only six of the twelve participants. This might have introduced the threat that only participants with a biased opinion about the tool volunteered to be interviewed.

Conclusion Validity. Our survey and interview study asked for self-reports, presenting subjective perceptions of the team. However, our feasibility study was about how the employees felt about an integration of a sentiment analysis tool, because without the acceptance of a tool by the employees, it will be difficult to adopt it. Thus, regarding the usefulness of our tool, subjective measurements are more meaningful and interesting than objective ones. Furthermore, the semantic codes were generated by only one author. To minimize this threat, they were reviewed by another author who completely agreed with the assigned codes. Many participants come from the software engineering field. However, this is a realistic scenario in industry when such a tool is used in a development team. In the interview study, certain questions, such as "Do you prefer to work alone or in a team?" might not have been answered truthfully. However, we made it clear to participants that we were processing the data anonymously. Furthermore, they had the option to opt out of answering a question.

External Validity. The company is very young, so we cannot generalize our results to, e.g., large companies with large teams or teams with older participants. However, we strove to collect feedback on the general applicability and usefulness of sentiment analysis for software projects. Future studies are required to provide more generalizable results. This also includes the context of the team. The team in our study works from home. Thus, we cannot draw any conclusions for hybrid or co-located teams. To strengthen the conclusions and to provide more generalizable results, we plan to conduct further case studies in different settings in the future.

6   Conclusion

Our paper provides insights into the usefulness and applicability of sentiment analysis tools in industry. To the best of our knowledge, this is the first study that covers the industrial perspective after the team has used the tool for four months. We integrated a sentiment analysis tool into the day-to-day business of the team, including weekly feedback about their mood for every group channel in their messaging service.

In our interview study with six participants, we gathered feedback on the tool's usefulness as well as opportunities for improvement. We see a large interest about using a sentiment analysis tool: Five out of six participants would like to continue using the tool in the future if the mentioned features would be integrated, e.g., a dashboard to observe how the team mood evolves over time, a detection for ironic phrases, and the possibility to receive direct suggestions for improvement. A future tool with the mentioned features could be integrated in a long-term study and to gather more information about benefits for sentiment analysis. This appears in particular to be helpful, as none of the participants claimed discrepancies between their own perception and the outcome of the tool, which is a necessary prerequisite to apply the tool in industrial settings.

References

1. Adair, J.G.: The hawthorne effect: a reconsideration of the methodological artifact. J. Appl. Psychol. **69**(2), 334 (1984)
2. Ahmed, T., Bosu, A., Iqbal, A., Rahimi, S.: Senticr: a customized sentiment analysis tool for code review interactions. In: 2017 32nd IEEE/ACM International Conference on Automated Software Engineering (ASE), pp. 106–111. IEEE (2017). https://doi.org/10.1109/ASE.2017.8115623
3. Cabrera-Diego, L.A., Bessis, N., Korkontzelos, I.: Classifying emotions in stack overflow and JIRA using a multi-label approach. Knowl.-Based Syst. **195**, 105633 (2020). https://doi.org/10.1016/j.knosys.2020.105633
4. Calefato, F., Lanubile, F., Maiorano, F., Novielli, N.: Sentiment polarity detection for software development. Empir. Softw. Eng. **23**(3), 1352–1382 (2018). https://doi.org/10.1007/s10664-017-9546-9
5. Calefato, F., Lanubile, F., Marasciulo, M.C., Novielli, N.: Mining successful answers in stack overflow. In: 2015 IEEE/ACM 12th Working Conference on Mining Software Repositories, pp. 430–433 (2015). https://doi.org/10.1109/MSR.2015.56
6. Chen, Z., Cao, Y., Lu, X., Mei, Q., Liu, X.: Sentimoji: an emoji-powered learning approach for sentiment analysis in software engineering. In: Proceedings of the 2019 27th ACM Joint Meeting on European Software Engineering Conference and Symposium on the Foundations of Software Engineering, ESEC/FSE 2019, pp. 841–852. Association for Computing Machinery, New York (2019). https://doi.org/10.1145/3338906.3338977
7. Devlin, J., Chang, M.W., Lee, K., Toutanova, K.: Bert: pre-training of deep bidirectional transformers for language understanding (2019)
8. Ding, J., Sun, H., Wang, X., Liu, X.: Entity-level sentiment analysis of issue comments. In: Proceedings of the 3rd International Workshop on Emotion Awareness in Software Engineering, SEmotion 2018, pp. 7–13. Association for Computing Machinery, New York (2018). https://doi.org/10.1145/3194932.3194935
9. El-Halees, A.M.: Software usability evaluation using opinion mining. JSW **9**(2), 343 (2014)
10. Graziotin, D., Wang, X., Abrahamsson, P.: Happy software developers solve problems better: psychological measurements in empirical software engineering. PeerJ **2**, e289 (2014). https://doi.org/10.7717/peerj.289
11. Guhr, O., Schumann, A.K., Bahrmann, F., Böhme, H.J.: Training a broad-coverage German sentiment classification model for dialog systems. In: Proceedings of the Twelfth Language Resources and Evaluation Conference, pp. 1627–1632 (2020)
12. Guzman, E., Azócar, D., Li, Y.: Sentiment analysis of commit comments in github: an empirical study. In: Kim, S., Pinzger, M., Devanbu, P. (eds.) 11th Working Conference on Mining Software Repositories: proceedings: 31 May–1 June 2014, Hyderabad, India, pp. 352–355. ACM (2014). https://doi.org/10.1145/2597073.2597118

13. Herrmann, M., Klünder, J.: From textual to verbal communication: towards apply-
    ing sentiment analysis to a software project meeting. In: 2021 IEEE 29th Inter-
    national Requirements Engineering Conference Workshops (REW), pp. 371–376
    (2021). https://doi.org/10.1109/REW53955.2021.00065

14. Herrmann, M., Obaidi, M., Chazette, L., Klünder, J.: On the subjectivity of emo-
    tions in software projects: how reliable are pre-labeled data sets for sentiment
    analysis? J. Syst. Softw. **193**, 111448 (2022). https://doi.org/10.1016/j.jss.2022.
    111448

15. Herrmann, M., Obaidi, M., Klünder, J.: Senti-analyzer: joint sentiment analysis
    for text-based and verbal communication in software projects. Technical report
    (2022). https://doi.org/10.48550/ARXIV.2206.10993

16. Hutto, C., Gilbert, E.: Vader: a parsimonious rule-based model for sentiment anal-
    ysis of social media text. In: Proceedings of the International AAAI Conference on
    Web and Social Media, vol. 8, no. 1, pp. 216–225 (2014). https://doi.org/10.1609/
    icwsm.v8i1.14550. https://ojs.aaai.org/index.php/ICWSM/article/view/14550

17. Imtiaz, N., Middleton, J., Girouard, P., Murphy-Hill, E.: Sentiment and polite-
    ness analysis tools on developer discussions are unreliable, but so are people. In:
    Proceedings of the 3rd International Workshop on Emotion Awareness in Software
    Engineering, SEmotion 2018, pp. 55–61. Association for Computing Machinery,
    New York (2018). https://doi.org/10.1145/3194932.3194938

18. Islam, M.R., Zibran, M.F.: Sentistrength-se: exploiting domain specificity for
    improved sentiment analysis in software engineering text. J. Syst. Softw. **145**,
    125–146 (2018). https://doi.org/10.1016/j.jss.2018.08.030

19. Jongeling, R., Sarkar, P., Datta, S., Serebrenik, A.: On negative results when
    using sentiment analysis tools for software engineering research. Empir. Softw.
    Eng. **22**(5), 2543–2584 (2017). https://doi.org/10.1007/s10664-016-9493-x

20. Kauffeld, S., Lehmann-Willenbrock, N.: Meetings matter: effects of team meet-
    ings on team and organizational success. Small Group Res. **43**(2), 130–158 (2012).
    https://doi.org/10.1177/1046496411429599

21. Kaur, A., Singh, A.P., Dhillon, G.S., Bisht, D.: Emotion mining and sentiment
    analysis in software engineering domain. In: 2018 Second International Conference
    on Electronics, Communication and Aerospace Technology (ICECA), pp. 1170–
    1173. IEEE (2018)

22. Klünder, J., Kortum, F., Ziehm, T., Schneider, K.: Helping teams to help them-
    selves: an industrial case study on interdependencies during sprints. In: Bogdan,
    C., Kuusinen, K., Lárusdóttir, M.K., Palanque, P., Winckler, M. (eds.) HCSE 2018.
    LNCS, vol. 11262, pp. 31–50. Springer, Cham (2019). https://doi.org/10.1007/978-
    3-030-05909-5_3

23. Klünder, J., et al.: Do you just discuss or do you solve? Meeting analysis in a
    software project at early stages. In: Proceedings of the IEEE/ACM 42nd Interna-
    tional Conference on Software Engineering Workshops, ICSEW 2020, pp. 557–562.
    Association for Computing Machinery, New York (2020). https://doi.org/10.1145/
    3387940.3391468

24. Klünder, J., et al.: Do you just discuss or do you solve? Meeting analysis in a soft-
    ware project at early stages. In: Proceedings of the IEEE/ACM 42nd International
    Conference on Software Engineering Workshops, pp. 557–562 (2020)

25. Kortum, F., Klünder, J., Brunotte, W., Schneider, K.: Sprint performance fore-
    casts in agile software development-the effect of futurespectives on team-driven
    dynamics. In: SEKE, pp. 94–128 (2019)

26. Kortum, F., Klünder, J., Schneider, K.: Behavior-driven dynamics in agile development: the effect of fast feedback on teams. In: 2019 IEEE/ACM International Conference on Software and System Processes (ICSSP), pp. 34–43. IEEE (2019)
27. Kraut, R.E., Streeter, L.A.: Coordination in software development. Commun. ACM **38**(3), 69–81 (1995). https://doi.org/10.1145/203330.203345
28. Lin, B., Cassee, N., Serebrenik, A., Bavota, G., Novielli, N., Lanza, M.: Opinion mining for software development: a systematic literature review. ACM Trans. Softw. Eng. Methodol. **31**(3), 1–41 (2022). https://doi.org/10.1145/3490388
29. Lin, B., Zampetti, F., Bavota, G., Di Penta, M., Lanza, M., Oliveto, R.: Sentiment analysis for software engineering: how far can we go? In: Proceedings of the 40th International Conference on Software Engineering, ICSE 2018, pp. 94–104. Association for Computing Machinery, New York (2018). https://doi.org/10.1145/3180155.3180195
30. Liu, Y., et al.: Roberta: a robustly optimized bert pretraining approach (2019)
31. Freira, M., Caetano, J., Oliveira, J., Marques-Neto, H.T.: Analyzing the impact of feedback in github on the software developer's mood (2018). https://doi.org/10.18293/SEKE2018-153
32. Graziotin, D., Wang, X., Abrahamsson, P.: How do you feel, developer? An explanatory theory of the impact of affects on programming performance. PeerJ Comput. Sci. **1**, e18 (2015)
33. Nandwani, P., Verma, R.: A review on sentiment analysis and emotion detection from text. Soc. Netw. Anal. Min. **11**(1), 81 (2021)
34. Novielli, N., Girardi, D., Lanubile, F.: A benchmark study on sentiment analysis for software engineering research. In: 2018 IEEE/ACM 15th International Conference on Mining Software Repositories (MSR), pp. 364–375 (2018)
35. Novielli, N., Calefato, F., Dongiovanni, D., Girardi, D., Lanubile, F.: Can we use SE-specific sentiment analysis tools in a cross-platform setting?, pp. 158–168. Association for Computing Machinery, New York (2020)
36. Novielli, N., Calefato, F., Dongiovanni, D., Girardi, D., Lanubile, F.: A gold standard for polarity of emotions of software developers in github (2020). https://doi.org/10.6084/m9.figshare.11604597
37. Novielli, N., Calefato, F., Lanubile, F.: A gold standard for emotion annotation in stack overflow. In: Proceedings of the 15th International Conference on Mining Software Repositories, MSR 2018, pp. 14–17. Association for Computing Machinery, New York (2018). https://doi.org/10.1145/3196398.3196453
38. Obaidi, M., Klünder, J.: Development and application of sentiment analysis tools in software engineering: a systematic literature review. In: Evaluation and Assessment in Software Engineering, EASE 2021, pp. 80–89. Association for Computing Machinery, New York (2021). https://doi.org/10.1145/3463274.3463328
39. Obaidi, M., Nagel, L., Specht, A., Klünder, J.: Dataset: Systematic Mapping Study on the Development and Application of Sentiment Analysis Tools in Software Engineering (2022). https://doi.org/10.5281/zenodo.4726650
40. Obaidi, M., Nagel, L., Specht, A., Klünder, J.: Sentiment analysis tools in software engineering: a systematic mapping study. Inf. Softw. Technol. **151**, 107018 (2022). https://doi.org/10.1016/j.infsof.2022.107018
41. Perry, D.E., Staudenmayer, N.A., Votta, L.G.: People, organizations, and process improvement. IEEE Softw. **11**(4), 36–45 (1994). https://doi.org/10.1109/52.300082
42. Sailunaz, K., Alhajj, R.: Emotion and sentiment analysis from twitter text. J. Comput. Sci. **36**, 101003 (2019)

43. Saldana, J.: The Coding Manual for Qualitative Researchers, vol. 11, no. 440, p. 81. SAGE Publications Ltd., London (2021)
44. Sanei, A., Cheng, J., Adams, B.: The impacts of sentiments and tones in community-generated issue discussions. In: 2021 IEEE/ACM 13th International Workshop on Cooperative and Human Aspects of Software Engineering (CHASE), pp. 1–10 (2021). https://doi.org/10.1109/CHASE52884.2021.00009
45. Schneider, K., Klünder, J., Kortum, F., Handke, L., Straube, J., Kauffeld, S.: Positive affect through interactions in meetings: the role of proactive and supportive statements. J. Syst. Softw. **143**, 59–70 (2018). https://doi.org/10.1016/j.jss.2018.05.001
46. Schroth, L., Obaidi, M., Specht, A., Klünder, J.: On the potentials of realtime sentiment analysis on text-based communication in software projects. In: Bernhaupt, R., Ardito, C., Sauer, S. (eds.) Human-Centered Software Engineering. LNCS, vol. 13482, pp. 90–109. Springer, Cham (2022). https://doi.org/10.1007/978-3-031-14785-2_6
47. Sun, K., et al.: Exploiting the unique expression for improved sentiment analysis in software engineering text. In: 2021 IEEE/ACM 29th International Conference on Program Comprehension (ICPC), pp. 149–159 (2021)
48. Thelwall, M., Buckley, K., Paltoglou, G.: Sentiment strength detection for the social web. J. Am. Soc. Inform. Sci. Technol. **63**(1), 163–173 (2012). https://doi.org/10.1002/asi.21662
49. Tymann, K., Lutz, M., Palsbröker, P., Gips, C.: Gervader-a German adaptation of the vader sentiment analysis tool for social media texts. In: LWDA, pp. 178–189 (2019)
50. Uddin, G., Guéhénuc, Y.G., Khomh, F., Roy, C.K.: An empirical study of the effectiveness of an ensemble of stand-alone sentiment detection tools for software engineering datasets. ACM Trans. Softw. Eng. Methodol. **31**(3), 1–38 (2022). https://doi.org/10.1145/3491211
51. Uddin, G., Khomh, F.: Automatic mining of opinions expressed about APIs in stack overflow. IEEE Trans. Software Eng. **47**(3), 522–559 (2021). https://doi.org/10.1109/TSE.2019.2900245
52. Venigalla, A.S.M., Chimalakonda, S.: Understanding emotions of developer community towards software documentation. In: 2021 IEEE/ACM 43rd International Conference on Software Engineering: Software Engineering in Society (ICSE-SEIS), ICSE-SEIS 2021, pp. 87–91. IEEE Press (2021)
53. Villarroel, L., Bavota, G., Russo, B., Oliveto, R., Di Penta, M.: Release planning of mobile apps based on user reviews. In: 2016 IEEE/ACM 38th International Conference on Software Engineering (ICSE), pp. 14–24 (2016). https://doi.org/10.1145/2884781.2884818
54. Werner, C., Tapuc, G., Montgomery, L., Sharma, D., Dodos, S., Damian, D.: How angry are your customers? Sentiment analysis of support tickets that escalate. In: Fucci, D., Novielli, N., Guzmán, E. (eds.) 2018 1st International Workshop on Affective Computing for Requirements Engineering. IEEE, Piscataway (2018). https://doi.org/10.1109/affectre.2018.00006
55. Whiting, M.E., Gao, I., Xing, M., Diarrassouba, N.J., Nguyen, T., Bernstein, M.S.: Parallel worlds: repeated initializations of the same team to improve team viability. Proc. ACM Hum.-Comput. Interact. **4**(CSCW1), 1–22 (2020). https://doi.org/10.1145/3392877
56. Wohlin, C., Runeson, P., Höst, M., Ohlsson, M.C., Regnell, B., Wesslén, A.: Experimentation in Software Engineering. Springer, Heidelberg (2012). https://doi.org/10.1007/978-3-642-29044-2

57. Xu, G., Meng, Y., Qiu, X., Yu, Z., Wu, X.: Sentiment analysis of comment texts based on BiLSTM. IEEE Access **7**, 51522–51532 (2019). https://doi.org/10.1109/ACCESS.2019.2909919

58. Yadollahi, A., Shahraki, A.G., Zaiane, O.R.: Current state of text sentiment analysis from opinion to emotion mining. ACM Comput. Surv. (CSUR) **50**(2), 1–33 (2017)

59. Zhang, T., Xu, B., Thung, F., Haryono, S.A., Lo, D., Jiang, L.: Sentiment analysis for software engineering: how far can pre-trained transformer models go? In: 2020 IEEE International Conference on Software Maintenance and Evolution (ICSME), pp. 70–80 (2020). https://doi.org/10.1109/ICSME46990.2020.00017

60. Zhang, Y., Hou, D.: Extracting problematic API features from forum discussions. In: Kagdi, H. (ed.) 2013 IEEE 21st International Conference on Program Comprehension (ICPC). IEEE, Piscataway (2013). https://doi.org/10.1109/icpc.2013.6613842

Late-Breaking Results

Allowing for Secure and Accessible Authentication for Individuals with Disabilities of Dexterity

Abbie Price and Fernando Loizides[✉]

Cardiff University, Cardiff, UK
loizidesf@cardiff.ac.uk

Abstract. People living with disabilities of dexterity can be vulnerable to attackers when authenticating using physical input methods, such as when inputting PIN numbers using a keypad at an ATM(Cash Point), due to the extended time these interactions take because of the device's lack of accommodations and accessibility. This makes their input more observable to a potential attacker and thus compromises their security. In addition, when ease of use is severely compromised, this may cause a need to circumvent good security practices for practical usability which further makes these individuals vulnerable to potential attackers. While research in the field of accessible and secure authentication exists, limited work has focused on the unique needs of individuals who have limited to no hand or finger dexterity. This paper proposes an accessible framework for authentication (AAFIDD), that focuses on meeting the needs of this group. We implemented a prototype authentication model and present an initial user study with 7 participants that evaluated the efficacy of this prototype and the framework. Each participant was randomly assigned a PIN and asked to input it using a method reliant on hand-dexterity and then using the prototype gaze-based input. Users were timed and asked to evaluate their experience in terms of ease of use while a researcher attempted to perform an over-the-shoulder attack to evaluate the security. We found that the prototype input method was less likely to be interpreted by an observer than using a mouse to input, while users considered the prototype input method accessible and easy to use.

Keywords: Pupillary Biometrics · Dexterity Disability · Eye-tracking · Security · PIN

1 Introduction and Motivation

In modern society, technology has revolutionized the way people interact with digital systems. However, this digital revolution has also increased the risks of technologies being abused or exploited by criminals. The FBI reports an increase

© IFIP International Federation for Information Processing 2024
Published by Springer Nature Switzerland AG 2024
M. K. Lárusdóttir et al. (Eds.): HCSE 2024, LNCS 14793, pp. 133–146, 2024.
https://doi.org/10.1007/978-3-031-64576-1_7

in victim losses of over \$3 billion[1] compared to the previous year[2], showing the significance of this risk. To combat this danger, scientists and security researchers place more and more emphasis on designing and implementing robust security systems to safeguard user privacy and data - however, this security often does not consider the needs of all individuals in its operation.

The Family Resources Survey[3] estimated that 14.6 million people in the UK are living with a disability of some kind. Of this population, the third most prevalent type of disability for state-pension-age adults and the fourth most prevalent for working-age adults was a disability of dexterity. For many of these individuals, this disability can add significant challenges to their ability to make use of technology which relies solely on finger and hand dexterity. Limitations in the usability of authentication technologies not only make it more prohibitive and time-consuming to perform authentication but also increase the likelihood that people who struggle with these operations may circumvent it in less secure manners when their needs are not met, as found by Lewis and Venkatasubramanian [15]. For example, password-sharing and shoulder-surfing attacks are greater security concerns for individuals for whom authentication is less accessible and more time-consuming. For PIN, password, one-time code and code-via-SMS methods of authentication, the security of individuals with Parkinson's and upper extremity disabilities is uniformly easier to circumvent through reduced search-space entropy or reliance on another individual [11].

An example of this model of authentication is in the use of ATMs, where the user has to insert their bank card and input their PIN on a keypad to verify their identity and access their funds. For individuals with disabilities of dexterity, this interaction can prove problematic in terms of accessibility and security. While ATM keypads have been commonly adapted in the UK to use braille for visually impaired users, there is no such adaptation for individuals with disabilities of dexterity who may struggle or be unable to use the keypad itself. This highlights the lack of provisions in terms of usability and security for individuals with disabilities of dexterity regarding authentication. In response to these lacking provisions, the primary objective of this work is to propose a new method of authentication that takes into consideration the distinct requirements of individuals with disabilities of dexterity in terms of usability and security. Additional objectives are to explore alternate input methods for individuals with disabilities of dexterity, test the accessibility and security of the proposed framework with users, and ultimately evaluate the appropriateness of the framework for use in this context.

---

[1] Federal Bureau of Investigation Internet Crime Report for 2022 - https://www.ic3. gov/Media/PDF/AnnualReport/2022_IC3Report.pdf - accessed February 2024.

[2] Federal Bureau of Investigation Internet Crime Report for 2021 - https://www.ic3. gov/Media/PDF/AnnualReport/2021_IC3Report.pdf - accessed February 2024.

[3] Department for Work and Pensions Family Resources Survey: 2020 to 2021 - https://www.gov.uk/government/statistics/family-resources-survey-financial-year-2020-to-2021/family-resources-survey-financial-year-2020-to-2021#disability-1   - accessed February 2024.

We present a bespoke eye-tracking system and process to allow users with dexterity disabilities to control the entry of their pin code and investigate its efficacy and its vulnerability to over-the-shoulder attacks. Our fully working system and pilot testing give us positive results and a methodology that shows promise to be implemented to encourage accessibility in security design and enable people with dexterity issues to more securely enter their PIN.

2   Related Work

Accessibility is commonly considered to be a neglected need within the field of authentication [10]. While it is best practice to consider accessibility from the outset, solutions are still commonly designed without adequate consideration of the needs of disabled users [21]. However, with the advent of biometric data, there is cause for optimism for some disabled users; for example, a survey of dyslexic users highlighted limitations faced by this user base in creating and remembering passwords but found that biometric methods including face recognition enjoyed higher success metrics [13]. Legislation is also beginning to address the needs of accessibility. In 2006, the United Nations first enshrined in law the minimum standards required for accessibility [18]. The UK agreed to follow these legal guidelines in 2009. First established in 1999, the World Wide Web Consortium (W3C) has created the Web Content Accessibility Guidelines (WCAG) to promote accessibility within web content. Prior to the most recent revision, WCAG did not include many references to authentication but in 2023 WCAG 2.2 was introduced which addressed this need with a success criterion based on Accessible Authentication[4]. However, the criterion is based on avoiding the need for cognitive tests in authentication. This is useful for some disabled users, such as users with cognitive disabilities, but does not assist other forms of disability as greatly such as visual impairments and disabilities of dexterity. While the field is thought to still be in its infancy [21], there have been many innovations to assist with the authentication needs of users with visual impairments. One such example is BendyPass, a novel form of authentication involving the user remembering a series of bends to input on a given bend device [2]. However, this does have some limitations. The study found that there is lower memorability of bend passwords in comparison to traditional passwords, and the practicality relies on flexible phones being introduced in the future [8]. In the case of users with disabilities of dexterity, there are barriers to many of the stages of authentication. One study [17] interviewed eight users with upper extremity impairment (UEI) to discover the nature of these barriers and the workarounds used to bypass them. They suggested voice print or eye gaze approaches would be good opportunities for this user group. However, it called for more research with disabled users in both of these approaches. The researchers discovered that the participants found assistive technology cumbersome and inconvenient to use. They

---

[4] W3C Web Content Accessibility Guidelines 2.2 - https://w3c.github.io/wcag/guidelines/22 - accessed February 2024.

found that security measures for reaching verification, such as pressing 'ctrl-alt-del', were difficult to use and workarounds were found such as using software to automate these button presses.

In particular, biometric-based credentials were found to have barriers. While participants enjoyed fingerprint and facial recognition for their relative speed and ease of use, it was not always possible to use this as fingerprints and faces can fail to register, which caused participants to avoid enabling authentication entirely. One common workaround for authentication used by people with disabilities when there are usability issues is password-sharing [22]. However, this is an imperfect workaround as the increase in usability comes with a reduction in the level of security. Some approaches have countered this by making password sharing almost impossible, such as with the use of image authentication [6]. While this approach could help reduce the cognitive load, which would help users with cognitive disabilities, it is unlikely to help users with disabilities of dexterity as they must still navigate to and select the chosen image. Users with disabilities of dexterity are also likely to be unable to use some approaches designed for individuals with other disabilities, such as BendyPass. Other innovations have been made in the field of accessible authentication for individuals with disabilities of dexterity. One alternate approach to authenticating the wearable Internet of Things (wIoT) devices often used by people with UEI was the use of an accelerometer and a gyroscope to be mounted on the wIoT device, which then analyses the heart to create ballistocardiograms which are fed into convolutional neural networks to authenticate the user. The downside of this approach is that the equal error rate (EER) increases in the time after training; over the course of two months, the EER increased from 4.02% to 10.02% [16]. Another approach which could be useful for people with UEI is breath authentication. One study [3] explored the use of breathing gestures in authentication. The users found that deep breathing was the best gesture to analyse for this purpose. However, this technique is recommended as a secondary modality in a multimodal system rather than a standalone approach. It is also vulnerable to replay attacks and voice conversion attacks. One advantage this study has over previously mentioned studies is that it does not require future technology or external devices, as it uses the microphone of the smartphone or laptop. It seems from this body of research that the most promising advances are in voice print and eye gaze technology. However, voice print recognition has several limitations such as being susceptible to background noise, being easy to spoof, and the issue that users with severe illness or throat problems can find this method difficult to use [7]. One of the earlier studies in eye gaze interaction [5] emphasised the usefulness of the technique in avoiding shoulder surfing attacks and evaluated three different eye gaze interaction methods for PIN entry; gaze gestures, dwell time method, where the dwell time of the eye on the number designates which button should be pressed, and the look and shoot method, which involves pressing a button while looking at the PIN. The look-and-shoot method may be discounted for the purpose of users with UEI, as many users would be unable to press the button. The gaze gestures method is promising as it had the lowest error rate, but users found the method to be unintuitive as the gaze gesture alphabet needed to be learned before use. The study also required a "gesture button" to assist with the gestures, thereby making it less useful for users with UEI. Several multimodal approaches have been attempted with gaze-tracking software. One of these is a 2010 study [9] which focuses on eye gaze upon user-selected points on images. This is promising but does not address the need for eye gaze software to function with legacy passwords and PINs. Another study [20] explores augmenting eye gaze with facial gestures, where eye gaze is used to direct the cursor whereas facial gestures are used to perform actions. This shows a clear accessibility increase over the look-and-shoot method but is not primarily designed for authentication and may be unusable for users whose disabilities affect their ability to use facial recognition, such as the participants in the study previously discussed which interviewed users with UEI [17]. The work displayed at this conference in 2018 by Yigitbas et al [23] presented a model-driven UI development approach for cross-device UIs that included the use of Authentication via VisualPin, a method of gaze-based password input where the user gazes at predefined password symbols and found usability difficulties where testers were unsure of how long to look at a UI element, an issue we could then anticipate and counteract with an audible confirmation chime upon successful input. This paper also significantly differs from Yigitbas' approach to gaze-based authentication in that it does not make use of predefined password symbols. Finally, one study [1] discussed the combination of eye gaze with midair hand gestures. This method performed well in the metrics of input time, error rate, perceived workload, and resistance to observation attacks, but is impossible to use for most users with UEI. We have focused on unimodal eye gaze in this study. The advantage of this is that it can integrate with existing backends. An example of this is the gesture eye gaze methods EyePin and EyePassShapes developed to use at banking ATMs with the aid of an inbuilt camera [4]. However, as previously discussed, gaze gestures have an impact on memorability. One review of the topic praises unimodal methods as easy to use while hands-free [12]. This paper differs from similar work in this area by Manu Kumar [14] in that rather than using the gaze to input an alphanumeric password it uses only the PIN system, and also in that it makes use of a wearable technology - the Pupil Labs Core glasses - as opposed to the Tobii 1750 eye tracker that was used in that study. We also particularly focus on designing and evaluating how this technology may be of use to individuals with disabilities of dexterity.

3   System Description

We define a set of requirements for the system based on a combination of the functionality of eye-tracking and the process of inputting a pin on a standard ATM (Automated Teller Machine). These are also used to base success and inform Key performance indicators when testing. Our requirements (presented in a hierarchical MUST - SHOULD - COULD method) are based on a combination of the literature and expert requirements from accessibility evaluator communications as an initial starting set.

Must

1. Be able to input their PIN using the solution.
2. Be able to connect to the eye-tracking hardware.
3. Be able to collect data from the hardware.
4. Support calibration of the eye-tracking system.
5. Securely store and process the PIN.

Should

1. Be able to input their PIN entirely hands-free.
2. Provide a reliable means of user authentication, minimizing false positives and negatives.
3. Be compatible with a variety of devices and platforms.

Could

1. Receive feedback to let them know about the status of the input method during operation.
2. Integrate with eye biometric data for enhanced security.
3. Support gaze gestures for common tasks (e.g., cancel, submit)

Based on the requirements we built our eye-tracking prototype testing system. We utilized a Pupil Labs w120 e200b binocular eye tracking headset fitted with nose support, two eye cameras, and a world camera connected to the system with USB 3.0. Data recording was achieved using the software Pupil Capture v3.5.1 and the plugins 'Fixation Detector', 'Network API', and 'Surface Tracker' for said software, all with their default settings. For surface detection, it makes use of the AprilTag [19]; specifically, the tag36h11 family of markers. These tags are to be placed in each corner of the display and we are aware of a limitation which is that the apparatus must be located in a well-lit environment for optimal results (See Fig. 1).

The prototype relies on the use of the Pupil eye-tracking glasses (See Fig. 2) to receive gaze fixation data. To do this, the glasses must be set up properly. This is best done in the Pupil Capture software, as it displays what the cameras currently can see, and involves physically adjusting the cameras using the sliding camera arm and ball joint to ensure a good image of the eyes is captured. The world camera can also be angled up and down to align with the user's field of vision.

We make use of the ZeroMQ messaging library to establish a connection to the glasses and subscribe to the 'surfaces' publisher to retrieve gaze data that is related to any surface currently visible with the world camera. The Pupil network API returns information in the 'Surface datum format', an example of which is in the figure below[5]. We are particularly interested in the "fixations_on_surfaces" data, which contains the "confidence" and "norm_pos" fields. The "confidence"

---

[5] Pupil Labs Core Developer Overview - https://docs.pupil-labs.com/developer/core/overview/#surface-datum-format - accessed February 2024.

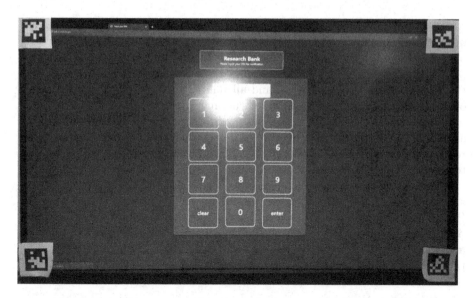

Fig. 1. Tag markers placed on the four corners for more accurate eye-tracking gaze data

Fig. 2. A Pilot Tester Using the Pupil Glasses to Enter a Pin Code

data is a percentage rating on how confident Pupil Capture is with the position. For this prototype, we discounted any fixation with a confidence that was not 100% to maintain accuracy during input. The "norm_pos" data is an X,Y normalized position corresponding to where on the surface the user is currently looking. This is delivered as a percentage ranging from 0 to 1, with percentage (0,0) being the bottom left corner of the surface and percentage (1,1) being top right. These normalized coordinates must be processed by the software to approximate where on the screen the user's gaze is fixed. Our code[6] detects the

---

[6] Can be shared on request.

screen size of the operating device and computes where on the screen the given normalized coordinates correspond. This code makes use of the ZeroMQ messaging library to establish a connection to the glasses and subscribes to the 'surfaces' publisher to retrieve gaze data that is related to any surface currently visible with the world camera. The prototype and all related tests were confirmed to work on a Microsoft Windows 10 computer running Build 19045 with the following hardware. Due to the use of the ctypes module, the prototype will not work on an Apple device as it will be unable to detect the screen size of the device. It requires Python version 3.7.9 or above. We utilized bcrypt to hash PINs prior to storing. The PIN was generated randomly with the Python random.randint function and then passed to bcrypt. bcrypt also generates a random salt with a work factor of 12 (212 iterations) with the gensalt function, then hashes the PIN. The prototype also utilises the bcrypt function checkpw to authenticate, by hashing the user input pin from the keypad with the salt stored in the hash and comparing the computed hash with the stored one. The Process diagram of the high-level functionality and interaction can be seen in Fig. 3.

4   Initial Testing and Findings

For our initial pilot user tests, seven participants were recruited voluntarily. This project received a favorable ethical opinion from the - ANON - Research Ethics Committee per SREC reference COMSC/Ethics/2023/083. Participants attended a test session where they were asked to input a randomly generated PIN in two conditions – the traditional input condition using a mouse and keyboard and the alternate input condition using gaze tracking glasses. Prior to the beginning of the gaze prototype test, users had to wear the Pupil glasses, which required some time to adjust the camera positioning per individual. Participants were timed and notes about the experience were made to identify areas of difficulty or ease, and the researcher attempted to observe the participants' actions to try and discover what had been input. Participants were aware of their observation in this manner. At the end of each of these conditions they were directed to a web-based survey to answer questions evaluating the input method in terms of accessibility, ease of use, and adaptability through a Likert 1–5 rankings, with the opportunity present to expand on their ranking. All participant information was anonymized at the time of submission.

To evaluate the success of the over-the-shoulder attack performed by the researcher, a scoring system was created to compare the digits the researcher suspected were correct and the digits of the actual PIN (See Fig. 4). Where an observed digit matched the similarly placed digit of the actual PIN, a score of 0 was given. Where the observed digit was incorrect, the guessed digit was given an incremental score based on its adjacency to the actual digit to indicate

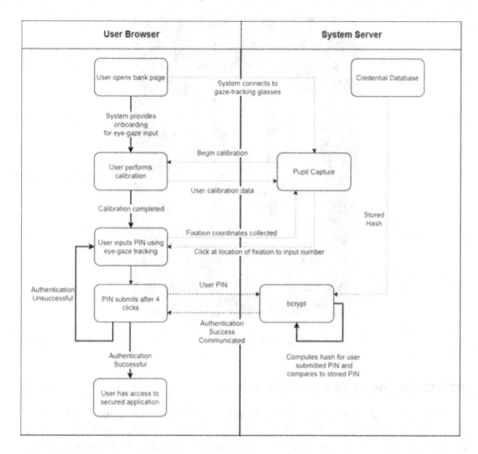

Fig. 3. Process Diagram of the Prototype

the reduction in search-space entropy were someone to attempt to brute force the PIN – for example, knowing that the digit is within the top left region (numbers 1,2,4,5) is a reduction of over 50% of candidates, and so a score of 1 for such a guess indicates that the guess is a significant reduction in security compared a wholly unknown digit. As such, a lower 'PIN proximity score' (PPS) indicates a more successful attempt at the over-the-shoulder attack. There is some variability in this scoring system, as 3 points could only be awarded when a digit was in the top or bottom rows of the keypad. To accommodate this, we used a scaling system that calculated what percentage a score was out of the maximum available, where a lower percentage represented a more accurate attack attempt.

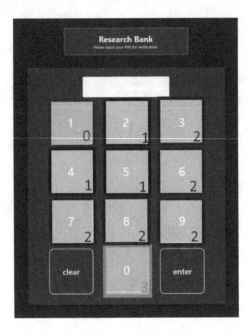

Fig. 4. PIN entry test

4.1   Condition 1: Traditional Input

In the traditional input condition, all participants used the mouse rather than the keyboard and reported that they very quickly understood how to input their PIN thanks to the recognizable input system of a keypad. All participants also gave the highest score for how quickly they could input their PIN and how easy it was to do so with most stating this was related to their regular use of a mouse as an input device. Most participants reported that they understood how to input their PIN with this method quickly or very quickly. They stated that the operation was intuitive and that the explanation was effective. One participant gave a lower score for understanding, stating that the "explanation given was okay, but I didn't understand fully until calibrating". Most participants also reported that this input device was maximally comfortable for their use, although two participants gave slightly lower scores, with one finding the mouse too big for their hands and the other finding this input modality less comfortable than using a touchscreen. Participants also identified multiple limitations of this input method. Most participants considered the operation of the mouse; that it required a suitable flat surface, that its wire could get tangled, that it was slower than a touchscreen; while one participant considered that it was wholly limited by the ability to make use of the mouse. The participants took an average of 2.702 s to input their PIN, with the longest taking 5.043 s due to a need to repeat their input after an incorrect entry. The average PPS was 25.77% with scores ranging from 0%, where the researcher successfully completed the over-the-shoulder attack and could fully observe the user PIN, to 66.67%. The results from the first condition suggest that the design of the website was a suitable analog for an ATM machine, as no participants reported confusion on how to operate the site or input their PIN. The high scores given for speed and ease of inputting their PIN indicates that this group of participants found no difficulties in the operation of a mouse, which is an input method that relies on high hand and wrist dexterity. This is also supported by the time taken for users to input their PIN, with 4 participants taking under 2 s to input their pin, suggesting this is an efficient method of operation when undertaken by familiar and able individuals. The results from the over-the-shoulder attack suggests that this input method is quite susceptible to this attack. It was notably easier to identify the PINs of the users with longer input times compared to those without, with the longest three times at most being only one point away from the correct PIN. This suggests that an extended interaction time while inputting the PIN increases the vulnerability of the user to an over-the-shoulder attack when input with this method. Overall, these results indicate that the participants had no difficulties identifying what they were supposed to do to input their PIN and so the website served as an appropriate ATM analog. The results also suggest that the participants were comfortable inputting their PIN with this input modality, though its resilience to over-the-shoulder attacks is considerably lacking. Input in this manner appears to be comfortable, though the variability of hand size and mouse design gives a degree of variability to this comfort.

4.2 Condition 2 - Prototype Input

In the prototype input condition, most participants reported that they understood how to input their PIN with this method quickly or very quickly. They stated that the operation was intuitive and that the explanation was effective. One participant gave a lower score for understanding, stating that the "explanation given was okay, but I didn't understand fully until calibrating". When asked how quickly they could input their PIN using this input method, participants gave an average score of 2.8, ranging from 2 to 4. When asked how easy it was to input their PIN, they gave an average score of 3.5, ranging from 2 to 5. The most common reason given for this was that it took a long time to input each digit. One participant also stated that it was unclear whether they were successfully inputting their PIN at first, though this changed when they heard the 'click' to confirm input. When asked how comfortable the input method was, participants gave an average score of 3.14, ranging from 2 to 5. Most participants stated that the headset was comfortable, but a major complaint was the time taken to input each digit. Other notable complaints were given by participant 5, who reported that the time taken to adjust the headset to track their eyes appropriately would be uncomfortable if they had to make use of the device multiple times a day, and participant 3 who experienced a particularly lengthy calibration period. Participants identified several limitations of this input method, mentioning the extended input time, sensitivity to head movement, the need for very precise camera placement, and the need for adequate lighting. Two participants also mentioned the limitations of the glasses themselves, stating that the perceived price of the glasses was a limitation and that they felt they would be unsafe wearing the glasses outside because of the mounted camera. The participants took an average of 52.336 s to input their PIN, ranging from 41.329 s to 71.460 s. The average PPS was 66.52%, with scores ranging from 50% to 88.89%. The individual results are presented in the figure below. The results from the second condition survey suggest that while the design of the website was a suitable analog for an ATM, participants reported confusion on how to operate the site. The lower scores given for speed and ease of inputting their PIN compared to the first condition indicate that this input method is more time-consuming than the operation of a mouse. This is also supported by the time taken for users to input their PIN, with one participant taking over a minute, which is a significant increase in authentication time. This may suggest that the prototype is not very competitive in terms of authentication efficiency compared to using a mouse for this group of participants. The results also suggest that the participants were much less comfortable inputting their PIN with this input modality than with the mouse due to the extended time it could take per digit. Participant 5 particularly identified issues during the setup of the eye-tracking glasses which were believed to be due to their hooded eyes. The results from the over-the-shoulder attack suggest that this input method is significantly less susceptible to this attack than in the first condition. It was notably harder to identify the PINs of the users due to the significantly reduced scope of visible movement, especially from behind. The primary indicator for movement became slight adjustments in head tilt and skew which were very subtle when evident. Significantly, no participant's PIN was successfully recovered, with the best score being 50% with participant 4. This suggests that this input method has significantly reduced vulnerability to over-the-shoulder attacks. Overall, these results indicate that the participants had no difficulties identifying what they were supposed to do to input their PIN and so the website served as an appropriate ATM analog. However, the results also suggest that the participants were much less comfortable inputting their PIN with this input modality than with a mouse. The improvements to the PPS score between conditions suggest that the prototype is more resilient against over-the-shoulder attacks than mouse input. The necessity for a setup and calibration were also reported issues with this input method that were not necessary in the prior condition.

5   Conclusions and Future Work

This paper presents the initial stage of work to investigate the efficacy of a more secure way of inputting a PIN number for individuals with dexterity disabilities and limitations. We present a fully operational bespoke eye-tracking solution prototype with custom software. We test the prototype in a pilot test to test for the usability compared to a traditional input system, and the effects of an over-the-shoulder attack with promising results and feedback from the participants. Our system showed promising results and favorable feedback usability-wise from our participants. Currently, our participants were not suffering from any dexterity issues. In future, we aim to expand the test to persons with severe dexterity disabilities to verify further the ecological and external validity of our findings. We are currently building a framework to direct the development of similar systems. We also aim to expand our work to utilize biometric identification of users thus removing the need to insert a bank card for a truly hands-free authentication experience – particularly the use of pupillary biometrics given the technologies utilized in the scope of this project could potentially provide this information.

References

1. Abdrabou, Y., Khamis, M., Eisa, R.M., Ismail, S., Elmougy, A.: Just gaze and wave: exploring the use of gaze and gestures for shoulder-surfing resilient authentication. In: Proceedings of the 11th ACM Symposium on Eye Tracking Research & Applications, pp. 1–10 (2019)
2. Briotto Faustino, D., Girouard, A.: Bend passwords on bendypass: a user authentication method for people with vision impairment. In: Proceedings of the 20th International ACM SIGACCESS Conference on Computers and Accessibility, pp. 435–437 (2018)
3. Chauhan, J., Hu, Y., Seneviratne, S., Misra, A., Seneviratne, A., Lee, Y.: Breathprint: breathing acoustics-based user authentication. In: Proceedings of the 15th Annual International Conference on Mobile Systems, Applications, and Services, pp. 278–291 (2017)
4. De Luca, A., Denzel, M., Hussmann, H.: Look into my eyes! can you guess my password? In: Proceedings of the 5th Symposium on Usable Privacy and Security, pp. 1–12 (2009)
5. De Luca, A., Weiss, R., Drewes, H.: Evaluation of eye-gaze interaction methods for security enhanced pin-entry. In: Proceedings of the 19th Australasian Conference on Computer-Human Interaction: Entertaining User Interfaces, pp. 199–202 (2007)
6. Dhamija, R., Perrig, A.: Deja {Vu–A} user study: using images for authentication. In: 9th USENIX Security Symposium (USENIX Security 2000) (2000)
7. Fatima, K., Nawaz, S., Mehrban, S.: Biometric authentication in health care sector: a survey. In: 2019 International Conference on Innovative Computing (ICIC), pp. 1–10. IEEE (2019)
8. Faustino, D.B., Nabil, S., Girouard, A.: Bend or pin: studying bend password authentication with people with vision impairment. In: Graphics Interface 2020 (2019)
9. Forget, A., Chiasson, S., Biddle, R.: Shoulder-surfing resistance with eye-gaze entry in cued-recall graphical passwords. In: Proceedings of the SIGCHI Conference on Human Factors in Computing Systems, pp. 1107–1110 (2010)
10. Furnell, S., Helkala, K., Woods, N.: Accessible authentication: assessing the applicability for users with disabilities. Comput. Secur. **113**, 102561 (2022)
11. Helkala, K.: Disabilities and authentication methods: usability and security. In: 2012 Seventh International Conference on Availability, Reliability and Security, pp. 327–334 (2012)
12. Katsini, C., Abdrabou, Y., Raptis, G.E., Khamis, M., Alt, F.: The role of eye gaze in security and privacy applications: survey and future HCI research directions. In: Proceedings of the 2020 CHI Conference on Human Factors in Computing Systems, pp. 1–21 (2020)

13. Kelly, N., Petrie, H.: Digital authentication and dyslexia: a survey of the problems and needs of dyslexia people. In: Miesenberger, K., Kouroupetroglou, G., Mavrou, K., Manduchi, R., Covarrubias Rodriguez, M., Penáz, P. (eds.) ICCHP-AAATE 2022. LNCS, vol. 13342, pp. 18–25. Springer, Cham (2022). https://doi.org/10.1007/978-3-031-08645-8_3

14. Kumar, M., Garfinkel, T., Boneh, D., Winograd, T.: Reducing shoulder-surfing by using gaze-based password entry. In: Proceedings of the 3rd symposium on Usable privacy and security, pp. 13–19 (2007)

15. Lewis, B., Hebert, J., Venkatasubramanian, K., Provost, M., Charlebois, K.: A new authentication approach for people with upper extremity impairment. In: 2020 IEEE International Conference on Pervasive Computing and Communications Workshops (PerCom Workshops), pp. 1–6 (2020)

16. Lewis, B., Hebert, J., Venkatasubramanian, K., Provost, M., Charlebois, K.: A new authentication approach for people with upper extremity impairment. In: 2020 IEEE International Conference on Pervasive Computing and Communications Workshops (PerCom Workshops), pp. 1–6. IEEE (2020)

17. Lewis, B., Venkatasubramanian, K.: "i... got my nose-print. but it wasn't accurate": how people with upper extremity impairment authenticate on their personal computing devices. In: Proceedings of the 2021 CHI Conference on Human Factors in Computing Systems, pp. 1–14 (2021)

18. MacKay, D.: The united nations convention on the rights of persons with disabilities. Syracuse J. Int. L. Com. **34**, 323 (2006)

19. Olson, E.: Apriltag: a robust and flexible visual fiducial system. In: 2011 IEEE International Conference on Robotics and Automation, pp. 3400–3407. IEEE (2011)

20. Rozado, D., Niu, J., Lochner, M.: Fast human-computer interaction by combining gaze pointing and face gestures. ACM Trans. Accessible Comput. (TACCESS) **10**(3), 1–18 (2017)

21. Saxena, N., Watt, J.H.: Authentication technologies for the blind or visually impaired. In: Proceedings of the USENIX Workshop on Hot Topics in Security (HotSec), vol. 9, p. 130 (2009)

22. Singh, S., Cabraal, A., Demosthenous, C., Astbrink, G., Furlong, M.: Password sharing: implications for security design based on social practice. In: Proceedings of the SIGCHI Conference on Human Factors in Computing Systems, pp. 895–904 (2007)

23. Yigitbas, E., Anjorin, A., Jovanovikj, I., Kern, T., Sauer, S., Engels, G.: Usability evaluation of model-driven cross-device web user interfaces. In: Bogdan, C., Kuusinen, K., Lárusdóttir, M.K., Palanque, P., Winckler, M. (eds.) HCSE 2018. LNCS, vol. 11262, pp. 231–247. Springer, Cham (2019). https://doi.org/10.1007/978-3-030-05909-5_14

Defining Software Company's KPIs
from Customers' and Employees' Perspectives

Marta Lárusdóttir[1]([⊠]) [iD] and Guðný Lára Guðmundsdóttir[2]

[1] Reykjavik University, Menntavegur 1, 102, Reykjavik, Iceland
marta@ru.is
[2] Annata ehf, Hagasmári 3, 201, Kópavogur, Iceland

Abstract. Customers are the lifeline of software companies. Therefore, it is vital for companies to guarantee customer satisfaction and loyalty. Many research studies have been conducted on employee satisfaction and employee motivation, but these have rarely been connected to software services to customers. In this paper, we describe a case study where performance indicators were defined both from the perspective of the employees and the customers to give some indication of the quality of the services. The case study was conducted in collaboration with an international software company in Iceland where the main author of this paper is an employee. The main results show that the employees agreed that the performance indicators were positive and motivating. The main contribution of the project is in the form of key performance indicators that the employees will hopefully use in the future. The results of the project can be used by other IT professionals that want to define performance indicators for their services from the joint perspective of the customers and the employees.

Keywords: Key Performance Measures · Software Development · Customers Satisfaction

1 Introduction

Software companies often make most of their revenue from providing services to customers. It is therefore important that customers are satisfied and remain loyal to the company. Software people usually do not interact much with the customer and they often do not know what the customer thinks about the service provided or the system they use. The software companies thus often do not have a correct picture of what the customers think and how useful the service or system is. If service personnel are not satisfied at work, customers are not satisfied [1]. It is therefore necessary to consider the job satisfaction and motivation of staff in order to increase customer satisfaction.

Many companies use performance measurements with the overall aim of motivating employees at work. Motivation can be defined as: "a process that directs a person's enthusiasm, passion and resilience in order to achieve their goal." [7]. Motivation has also been defined as: "Having the will to do something" [8]. Objectives linked to metrics are

© IFIP International Federation for Information Processing 2024
Published by Springer Nature Switzerland AG 2024
M. K. Lárusdóttir et al. (Eds.): HCSE 2024, LNCS 14793, pp. 147–159, 2024.
https://doi.org/10.1007/978-3-031-64576-1_8

motivating for intrinsically motivated employees. Goals and metrics can also be used to design a reward system that motivates employees who are more extrinsically motivated. It is important that the reward system is simple, because if it is too complicated, it will not attract the attention of the employees [10]. Company managers need to understand that they can only direct the direction of employees, but not their effort to work. In this way, employees can be steered in the direction that managers want with the right performance measures [11]. Key performance indicators (e. key performance indicators, KPI) are a few measures of how well a company executes its strategic vision (e. strategic vision) [15, 17]. Key performance indicators address the success of a team or group in a company's most important success factors, which need to be clear and known.

Several studies have been conducted on Icelandic companies to analyze what it is that motivates people to continue working. In one study, the Icelandic career motivation list was elaborated and used [12]. Two international surveys were used in another study, to create a questionnaire to be used at one of the biggest banks in Iceland [13]. The third study included measuring job satisfaction at a one of the biggest pharmaceutical companies in Iceland. The results of the study show the importance for companies to monitor the job satisfaction of their employees [14].

The goal of this study is to identify key performance indicators (KPIs) that can be used to set motivational goals that increase job satisfaction and are unrelated to the number of billed hours. In the study, key performance indicators were selected in collaboration with the employees. The employees themselves will be responsible for the KPIs and the goals that can be set based on them. The objective is that job satisfaction and motivation at work will increase, and that the customer experience will be better, through the usage of the KPIs. This project can be useful to other companies with similar software service processes.

This study examines the following research questions:

1. What is the impact of performance indicators on employees working in software services and interacting with customers?
2. What key performance indicators (KPIs) do software services employees choose?
3. How willing are employees to continue using KPIs?

The background literature is briefly described in Sect. 2. The methodology is described in Sect. 3. In Sect. 4, we describe the answers to the research questions. In Sect. 5 we discuss the results briefly and summarise the contribution in the paper.

2   Background

In this section we briefly describe the related work on measuring performance, selecting key performance indicators, and the service of software companies.

2.1   Measuring Performance

Many companies use performance measurements. The purpose of using those has been categorized in eight categories [2]: 1) to evaluate; 2) to control; 3) making a budget; 4) to motivate; 5) to promote; 6) to celebrate; 7) to learn and 8) to improve. According to

Behn [2], all measurements must be based on one or more of these purpose categories since it is no longer sufficient to measure only with regards to the financial goals.

The method Balanced Scorecard [3] was introduced in 1992, when it became clear that looking at financials was not enough to assess a company's performance or to see if they were achieving their goals [4]. The balanced scorecard method suggests that managers look at the company's operations from four perspectives at once. The perspectives are: 1) customers, 2) finance, 3) internal business processes and 4) learning and growth. The Balanced Scorecard assessment is put together in one place (e.g. in one document or a separate system), thus forcing managers to look at all measures simultaneously, to reflect on if success in one perspective has had negative consequences in another perspective [4, 5]. The Balanced Scorecard was supposed to bridge the gap that existed in most management systems providing a process to define, implement and receive criticism of the company's strategy [6]. Companies quickly saw the benefits of using the Balanced Scorecard, but it has also been criticized for not necessarily being based on a company's critical success factors, it often becomes complex and that it is usually made by external consultants who know the company not well enough [7].

For defining good performance measurements, it is important to understand what motivates people at work. In general, motivation can be divided into two categories, intrinsic and extrinsic motivation [8]. Intrinsic motivation can be defined as the motivation to perform a task when the task itself is the motivation. Jobs that are interesting and challenging are examples of jobs related to intrinsic motivation [9]. Extrinsic motivation can be defined as the motivation to perform an action or task in order to obtain unrelated result [8]. Extrinsic incentives include recognition for jobs well done, career progression, bonus payments and higher wages [9]. It is very important for managers to understand what motivates their employees to do good work, but it can also explain why the employees behave the way they do [9].

Two types of business metrics have been defined: result indicators and performance measures [15]. Result indicators (RI) and key result indicators (KRI) are measures of a company's success. Success metrics are measured at longer intervals than performance metrics and are best for business owners to see if the business is moving in the right direction at the right pace [15]. Result indicators are not as useful to managers and teams as performance measures, because the information comes too late to make timely changes. Performance measures are usually the responsibility of the CEO. Performance indicators (PI) are measures of success that can be linked to a specific group or team within a company. The performance measures are the responsibility of the team or group to which they belong, thus providing clarity and ownership [15].

Metrics can be used for defining goals, since these are measured regularly, and the result is numerical. It is important that goals are realistic but still challenging [16]. The strategy becomes clear and when and if the goals have been achieved. If teams are involved in choosing or setting the goals, the team is more likely to agree that the goals are realistic and worthy of achieving them [7]. Clear and measurable goals promote better communication within the company and the team. The team's goals should be related to important metrics and thus describe the team's path to the desired results [7].

2.2 Key Performance Indicators

Key performance indicators contain the most important information for a company to assess whether the company is on track, at the right pace to achieve its goals. KPIs are useful in most companies in order to make successful decisions and improve their performance [18]. It is recommended that for a company of 200 people should have 10 key performance indicators, 80 performance or success measures and 10 key result indicators [15]. It is important that companies realize which key performance indicators are most relevant to their strategic goals [15]. All KPIs can have a downside, as they can lead to other, and often negative, performance than was planned for, thus choosing a KPI must be a well-considered matter. An example of a KPI that can have negative effects is the measurement of the number of closed projects for each employee. The goal of the KPI is to motivate employees to finish tasks more frequently. An experienced employee may choose the easy and quick tasks instead of the more complex ones in order to have more finished tasks. Then the less experienced employees are left with more challenging projects and thus fewer finished tasks. The experience of the less experienced is negative as it fails to perform well at work, while the more experienced do not take on challenging tasks and therefore do not grow at work. One method for choosing KPIs carefully is to discuss with selected employees their reaction if a key performance measure is chosen, and by doing so, an attempt would be made to ensure the positive effect of the measures [15].

Key elements must be present for a measure to be a KPI. They need to be [15, 17], non-financial, since as soon as KPIs are related to money, they turn into result performance indicators. They need to be measured regularly, for example daily or weekly, because if the measurements are not carried out often enough, it is not possible to react quickly enough. They also need to be management oriented, because then the manager gives more attention to KPIs through close monitoring. Additionally, they need to be simple, since all employees need to understand the KPIs and the actions to be taken if changes are needed. Furthermore, it needs to be clear who is responsible for KPIs being in order and the KPIs need to be related to the company's strategic goals and have a strong impact on the company's success. Finally, the KPIs need to be carefully considered so that they have the positive and motivating effects that are proposed. Care must be taken to ensure that the key performance measure does not encourage negative work practices. When key performance measures are well prepared, evaluated and it is ensured that their impact on employees is positive, they have a positive impact on performance. To get the best effect, it is important that the results of the measurements are visible to the employees. The manager should monitor and discuss the results with the employees regularly, but the manager's interest shows the importance of the KPIs [15].

2.3 Service of a Software Company

Service can be defined as the act of helping someone or the act of working for someone [19]. It is said that service is work, method and execution. Another definition of service is: "Service indicates that intangibility is a key factor in deciding whether an offer is or is not a service" [1]. Employees are the link between the company and the customers, so it can be said that the employee is the service [1, 11]. Everything that service personnel do and say affects the image of the company and can therefore be said to be the face of their company [1, 20].

Since service work is often demanding and difficult, good teamwork contributes to less stress and stress for the employees, since those that feel supported by their team provide better service [1]. Teamwork is defined by: "values, attitudes, feelings and skills" [10]. Good team works, is when team members work together toward a specific goal through regular, open, and honest communication [10]. Collaboration encourages individuals to work and use their strengths together [10]. Job satisfaction can be defined as "a positive feeling towards a job as a result of an assessment of its characteristics" [7]. Job satisfaction has been extensively studied and it has been shown that happy employees provide better service [1]. There are two popular methods for measuring job satisfaction. One asks employees to rate the statement "I am happy in my job" on a scale of strongly disagree to strongly agree. The other method is to ask a few questions about the key characteristics of the job. The questions can include, among other things, salary, possibilities for development in the job, colleagues and the work itself. The answers are then added together, and one result is obtained. Research shows that there is no significant difference between the results from these two methods, but the second one can indicate what actions can be taken if job satisfaction needs to be improved [7]. Employees who are happy at work come to work and thus increase the productivity of a company. Employee absenteeism increases when they are dissatisfied with their work [11].

Usability is a measure of how easy a system or service is to use. Research has shown that, if the system is not easy to use, and the users do not like a system, they will avoid using it [21]. Software service personnel need to know how customers experience the system and the services provided. Usually, software people only hear about it when systems crash or don't work as they should. The customer's attitude towards the system and service can therefore affect the software company's employees. Usability has been defined as: "the extent to which a system, product or service can be used by particular users to achieve specified goals with effectiveness, efficiency and satisfaction in a specified context of use" [22]. Customers and software companies generally agree that it is necessary to focus on usability, because if the software is easy to use, it sells better and requires less maintenance [23].

3   Methodology

The study consisted of defining performance indicators (PIs), evaluating those with employees' participation, presentations of the evaluation results and conducting a workshop with employees for discussing and choosing the key performance indicators (KPIs) and possible improvements. In this section we describe the case study approach, the case company, the definition of the performance indicators in the study, the evaluation of the performance indicators, the selection of the KPIs and the analysis of the results.

3.1   Case Study Approach

We used a case study approach with the aim of grasping the complex nature of a particular case [24]. Case studies are usually studies of a specific group or incident, but that is the case. The study is carried out during a certain defined period [25]. Case studies usually have various data gathering methods [26]. The focus of a case study is to formulate and answer relevant research questions [27].

The researcher can either be an active participant in the study or observe without directly participating in it. The advantages of case studies include that the research topic can be brought to life and that the person reading a case study should be able to easily compare their own case with the case of the study. It may be difficult to draw general conclusions from the results of case studies, since the results only apply to the case being studied [28].

In this study, the case was an international software company. More specifically, the participant came from team A within the company that works for Icelandic clients. The second author of the paper is part of that team, which had the effect that the researcher knows the case very well, has a good understanding of how the team works and what attitudes its employees have. From the beginning of the study, it was clear that there is a lot of trust in the team towards the researcher. The methods used for data collection in this study are questionnaires and workshops.

3.2 The Case Company

The case company is a software house that was founded in 2001. Its headquarters are in Iceland with around 50 employees, but in addition, the company has offices in almost every continent with over 230 employees. The second largest offices are in Malaysia and England. The company is a partner of Microsoft and works mostly on two major systems. The team participating in the study mostly works on an Enterprise Resource Planning (ERP) system, which includes financial system, warehouse system, inventory system, sales system, purchasing system, human resource system and production system. This system is a popular financial system worldwide. The company's key products are special solutions the ERP system related to the automotive industry. The company has customers in more than 40 countries and has sold software licenses to more than 90 thousand users. The company became Microsoft's best partner in the Automotive industry in the year 2019.

The Icelandic office has several teams, including team A that works for Icelandic clients. Team A included 13 people, who were programmers, consultants and one supervisor. During the research project period, one employee resigned, so the team counted 12 people at the end of the research project. Team A provides advice, implements new functions, and corrects the ERP system at the customer's request. This only refers to services for systems that customers already have, not implementations for new customers. The customers for team A come from various aspects of the business world and include construction products companies, pharmaceutical companies, car dealers, retail companies and energy companies. It is common for the companies' customers in Iceland to have around 100–150 active users. Team A works closely with key users defined by the customers. The number of key users is usually from two to six for each customer company, but there can be exceptions. The key users are often employees in the customer's IT department and in some cases finance managers and executives. In this paper, the key users are called the customers.

3.3 Definition of PIs

One of the company's goals is related to billed hours, which the company wants to maximize. Each team at the company must reach a certain number of billed hours or an employee must reach a certain percentage of billed hours. Employees do not find these goals sufficiently motivating or positive, and these goals do not have significant impact on the employee's daily work. Objectives related to outsourced work can control the prioritization of projects, for example taking on projects for clients rather than internal projects. However, the goals do not have a direct effect on how the staff and customers interact, whether the employees feel good at work or whether they deliver better work. With these goals, there can be the risk that more experienced staff will take on all the easy and quick tasks to increase their percentage of billed hours. This can lead to them not taking the time to help newer or less experienced staff because then their own percentage of billed hours could drop. A good percentage of the billed hours can be used, among other things, in a salary interview as a benefit for the employee.

To get ideas for defining PIs, the main author of this paper studied many references, which can be found in Sect. 2. PIs that were considered suitable for measuring software services and statements that often appear in research studies about job satisfaction, motivation at work, utility, service, and customer satisfaction were selected. A draft of the list of PIs was reviewed by the second author of the paper. Then the PIs were introduced to the CEO of company in Iceland at a meeting. The CEO also suggested additions and changes. A complete draft of the PIs was tested by four colleagues from another team.

3.4 Evaluation of the Usefulness of the PIs

Two groups participated in the study: the employees in team A in Iceland who work in service and the company's customers. Two questionnaires were made to evaluate the usefulness of the PIs. One was directed to Team A and was called a satisfaction survey; the other was directed to customers and was called a service survey. The PIs included in the questionnaires were grouped into seven super categories and set up in a web survey. The questionnaires contained a total of 58 PIs in 14 categories.

The Satisfaction Survey: It contained 36 PIs with a Likert scale in 8 categories, three open-ended questions and two multiple-choice questions. It was sent out twice. First, the survey was sent to all 12 team A members except the researcher, and the response rate was 100%. During the second round of data gathering the survey was sent to 11 team A members, since one team member had resigned, and the response rate was also 100%.

The Service Survey: It contained 22 PIs with a Likert scale in 6 categories, three open-ended questions and four multiple-choice questions. It was sent to six different companies. The survey was sent out twice. First it was sent to 27 key users, where the response rate was 66%. The second time it was sent to 26 key users, where the response rate was 50%. The key users used two versions of the system (Table 1).

The Data Analysis: The answers from the satisfaction survey and service surveys were imported into Microsoft Excel, where the answers to the Likert questions were changed

Table 1. An overview of the number of PIs in each category in the surveys.

Category	Satisfaction survey	Service survey
Answers	3	3
Plans	4	5
Guidelines	3	2
Assistance	5	0
Employees	3	0
Work	7	4
Communication	5	2
Usability	6	6
Total	36	22

to a scale from 1–5 as follows: 1 = strongly disagreed, 2 = disagree, 3 = neutral, 4 = agree, 5 = strongly agree. The alternative Not applicable was not included.

To get the result for each question, all the numbers were added together and divided by the number of answers for each question. This provided an average number for each question. For customers, results were calculated both for all of them, as well as a score was calculated for those using the same version of the system.

The consulting company Capacent, which is in charge of workplace analysis with respect to job satisfaction, has developed criteria that are used to evaluate the result when the average job satisfaction has been calculated. Results are grouped into three categories: 1) intensity interval, 2) functional interval and 3) action interval. If the result is between 4.20 and 5.00 with the same Likert scale as in this study, it is in the strength range and indicates that things are in good order. Results between 3.70 and 4.19 are in the functional range and indicate that things are fine but could be improved to reach the strength range. Finally, results range from 1.00 to 3.69 are in the action range. That gap indicates that improvement is needed, and those results are classified as weaknesses [31].

3.5 Workshop for Selecting KPIs

A workshop was held to evaluate the importance of the metrics and to select key performance metrics. All 11 members of the team were invited to the workshop and six attended.

First the participants in the workshop were asked to fill in a web survey. Two approaches were used to find KPIs. Participants were asked to rank the PIs in each category, in order of importance. They did that both for the PIs for employees and customers. Then they were asked if they would select one or more PIs for the category to be a KPI. Finally, there was one open question asking if there was anything else the participants wanted to convey. All the open-ended responses of the participants were summed up by counting the number of participants who found a certain statement to be a KPI. After the participants answered the web survey, they discussed the KPIs and if they would like to use them in the future.

The survey was sent to the five employees who could not make it to the workshop, and they all responded. With that, all 11 employees of team A answered the survey.

4 Results

In this section we summarize the answers to the research questions.

4.1 The Impact of Performance Measures

The first research question was: *What is the impact of performance measures on staff working in software services and interacting with customers?*

The effect of performance measures seems to be positive. Right from the presentation of the first results among the staff who took part in the surveys, there was a lot of good discussion. The staff analyzed and considered reasons for the customers' responses. Possible corrective actions were discussed due to the leaked items. In particular, there were a lot of debates about plans both times, as that party came out the worst in both measurements. The discussions seemed to show the staff's interest in the results and showed an immediate encouraging response to the measurements. The feedback indicates that it is very useful for the staff to see the opinions of staff and customers in context. In the workshop, the impact of the measures on the staff was discussed. The staff found the measures useful and positive. The metrics were encouraging, both when the result went up and when it went down. The staff thought it was interesting to see that customers were happier than they thought. That conclusion seems to have increased the confidence of the employees, as the results of the software's usefulness from the second measurement were considerably higher than the first.

The results show that the performance measures were important to the staff, and it can be concluded that they were also useful to the customers. If the staff changes their work based on the results of the measurements, the service will be better, and the customers will be happier. However, if customers stop answering the surveys and make suggestions but the service and communication do not change, this can lead to increasing customer dissatisfaction with the service and inevitably lead to a worse image of the service company. The cooperation of the employees towards improvement and the positive experience from improving the results of the measures are important.

4.2 The Selected KPIs

The second research question was: *What key performance measures do employees choose in software services?* The answer to that question can be found in Table 2.

It is important to keep in mind that the cooperation between the company's staff and owners went very well and there was a lot of response from them, but it was not as easy to get responses from the customers. The fact that staff believe that the clients' answers are more meaningful than their own answers may have a major impact on the results of this study. The customers might have been more willing to answer if there had been fewer questions. The staff selected six KPIs for the customers, so it will take the customers less time to answer only for the six selected KPIs.

Table 2. The Selected KPIs

Respondents	Key Performance Indicators (KPIs)
Employees	I answer customers inquiries within an acceptable time
Employees	I will let a client know when I expect to go over a plan
Employees	I will get help from my colleagues when I need it
Customers	The answers I get are usually satisfactory
Customers	Plans usually pass
Customers	Guidelines for changes are satisfactory
Customers	Jobs done for me are done well
Customers	My communication with the company staff is good
Customers	I am generally satisfied with the company's service

4.3 Future Use of the KPIs

The third research question was: *How willing are employees to continue using the key performance measures?*

The answer to that question can be found in the results of the workshop where the continued use of KPIs was discussed. There were only positive staff responses to the continued use of the measures. Employees find the metrics to be positive and motivating in their work, giving them increased confidence in their work. All employees in the workshop wanted to continue using the KPIs. The main result of the workshop and the KPI web survey was that customer responses were more meaningful than staff responses. Therefore, there was a lot of discussion about the response of the customers, but it dropped considerably between measurements. Staff thought that with fewer statements, customers would be more willing to answer and by that the results would be more significant. During the workshop it was discussed how often the web survey should be send out and whether it could be sent more often out to staff than to customers. The conclusion was that it would be best to send the surveys to customers and employees at the same time and that customers should not be asked to answer more than once a month.

The possibility of analyzing customer responses according to companies was discussed. At the beginning of the workshop, many employees thought it was a key point, but after it was discussed, it was believed that customers would not want to answer the questionnaire, if it would be possible to analyze the answers according to the customer companies. It was also concluded that this analysis would not change much for the employees' tasks. Possibly it would results in excuses for bad results at a certain company due to a recent difficult project instead of taking the result to heart and improve the ways of working It was also concluded that if work practices can be improved at one company, it can't hurt to improve the same work practices at the other companies as well. This relates to the fact that the team owns the metrics. The whole team needs to feel responsible for the results, and it doesn't matter if an employee has worked for all the customers or just one. The team must work together to change the way they work, if necessary, otherwise the metrics will not be able to be key performance indicators. If the metrics are not defined as KPIs, they will not have the positive impact that this project was set out to achieve.

5 Discussion and Conclusion

An Icelandic study from 2010 explores work-related motivation in the Icelandic economy [12]. In this study, 110 responses were received from participants, who were Master's or PhD students at the Faculty of Business at University of Iceland. It resulted in the definition of the Icelandic work motivation list and study of the usage of it. The results of the study show that the highest rated motivation from Icelandic employees was to work on interesting projects, but that was ranked in as the third highest in the Work category in our study. The highest rated motivation in our study was that it is easy to get help from colleagues but a similar statement in the other study is "That colleagues are comfortable" is ranked number seven [12].

A study from 2014 deals with work motivation in one of the biggest Icelandic bank branches [13]. In that study, interesting work was the most important by all participants, but a similar statement was only rated as third highest in our study. The study at one of the biggest banks is based on 35 answers [13], but our study had answers from between 11 and 18 participants. The difference of these results could be explained by the fact that the focus of a software services and customers KPIs are different from the KPIs valued in the financial sector. It may also be explained by the number of participants in our study being limited.

The third study from 2018 investigated job satisfaction among employees of one of the bigger pharmaceutical companies in Iceland [14]. The main results of that study are that salary does not have a key effect on job satisfaction, but there was a strong correlation between demanding work and job satisfaction. It was also stated that a good relationship between colleagues and varied work increases job satisfaction [14]. The results of our study indicate the employees are quite satisfied with their work, but the results of the statements about challenging and varied work received a high score.

Various methods exist for measuring job satisfaction, motivating people at work, and evaluating customer satisfaction. The results of the study define key performance indicators that are both motivating and have a positive impact on software services personnel. The definition of key performance measures was conducted in collaboration with colleagues, where both employees and customers participated in the study. One of the contributions is the nine key performance indicators, which were selected in a systematic way by the employees.

A follow-up study gathering data on the experiences of using the defined KPI's is planned for future work.

Acknowledgement. First and foremost, the authors gratefully thank the participants for their time, interest, and valuable answers to the research questions.

References

1. Zeithaml, V., Bitner, M.: Services Marketing, McGraw-Hill Series in Marketing. McGraw-Hill (1996)
2. Drucker, P.: The Practice of Management. Harper & Row (1954)
3. Behn, R.D.: Why measure performance? Different purposes require different measures. Public Adm. Rev. **63**(5), 586–606 (2003)
4. Kaplan, R.S., Norton, D.P.: The balanced scorecard: measures that drive performance. Harv. Bus. Rev. **83**(7), 172 (2005)
5. Niven, P.: Balanced Scorecard Step-by-Step: Maximizing Performance and Maintaining Results. Wiley (2002)
6. Kaplan, R., Norton, D.I.: Books: 24x7, The Balanced Scorecard: Translating Strategy Into Action, BusinessPro Collection. Harvard Business School Press (1996)
7. Robbins S., Judge, T.: Organizational Behavior. Pearson (2015)
8. Ryan, M., Deci, E.L.: Intrinsic and extrinsic motivations: classic definitions and new directions. Contemp. Educ. Psychol. **25**(1), 54–67 (2000)
9. Jones, G., George, J.: Contemporary Management. McGraw-Hill (2018)
10. Berry, L.: On Great Service: A Framework for Action. Simon & Schuster (1995). ISBN: 9781439105269
11. Carrig, K., Wright, P.M.: Building Profit Through Building People: Making Your Workforce the Strongest Link in the Value-profit Chain, Human Resource Management Online. Society for Human Resource (2006). ISBN: 9781586440695
12. Vilhjálmsdóttir, A.: Work-related motivation: what motivates people at work? Masters thesis, University of Iceland, Reykjavík, IS (2010)
13. Halldórsdóttir, S.: Employee motivation in three branches of Íslandsbanki. Bachelor thesis, University of Iceland, Reykjavík, IS (2014)
14. Pétursdóttir, A.: Job satisfaction - main influencing factors on employees. Masters thesis, University of Iceland, Reykjavík, IS (2018)
15. Parmenter, D.: Key Performance Indicators (KPI): Developing, Implementing, and Using Winning KPIs. Wiley (2010)
16. Burkholder, N., Goals, S., Shapiro, J.: Ultimate Performance: Measuring Human Resources at Work. Wiley (2007). ISBN: 9780470130551
17. Warren. J.: Key Performance Indicators (KPIS): Define and act (2019). https://content.atinternet.com/white-paper-kpis-define-and-act/
18. Marr, B.: What Is A KPI? https://www.bernardmarr.com/default.asp?contentID=762
19. Oxford University Press (OUP). Lexico.com Online Dictionary (2019). https://www.lexico.com/en/definition/service
20. Fitzsimmons, J., Fitzsimmons, M., Bordoloi, S.: Service Management: Operations, Strategy, Information Technology, McGraw-Hill/Irwin Series Operations. McGraw-Hill (2014)
21. Nielsen, J., Loranger, H.: Prioritizing Web Usability, Voices That Matter. Pearson Education (2006). ISBN: 9780132798150
22. ISO – International Standardization Office: Ergonomics of human-system interaction – Part 210: Human-centred design process for interactive systems, International Organization for Standardization, Geneva, Switzerland, Standard (2019)
23. Schaffer, E.: Institutionalization of Usability: A Step-by-step Guide. Addison Wesley (2004)
24. Stake, R.: The Art of Case Study Research. SAGE Publications (1995). ISBN: 9780803957671
25. Hancock, D., Algozzine, B.: Doing Case Study Research: A Practical Guide for Beginning Researchers. Teachers College Press (2017). ISBN: 9780807775554
26. Lazar, J., Feng, J., Hochheiser, H.: Research Methods in Human-Computer Interaction. Wiley (2010). ISBN: 9780470723371

27. Yin, R.: Case Study Research: Design and Methods, Applied Social Research Methods. SAGE Publications (2009). ISBN: 9781412960991
28. Jóhannsdóttir, Þ.J.: Case Studies (2009). http://mennta.hi.is/vefir/ust/tjona/tilviksrann.htm

Cognitively Available Cybersecurity: A Systematic Literature Review

Joakim Kävrestad[1]([⊠]) [iD] and Bilal Naqvi[2] [iD]

[1] Jönköping School of Engineering, Jönköping, Sweden
Joakim.kaverestad@ju.se
[2] Lappeenranta University of Technology, Lappeenranta, Finland
Syed.Naqvi@lut.fi

Abstract. Cybersecurity is imperative to safeguard the digital systems on which the world has come to rely. A core part of cybersecurity is users' ability to adopt protective behavior by using security functions and adhering to security policies. Protective behavior requires cognitive effort, and some research suggests that users with cognitive challenges may struggle. There is no cohesive body of knowledge addressing those struggles and that gap is addressed in this research. A systematic literature was conducted to review how cognitive challenges are discussed in relationship to end-users' cybersecurity. The findings reveal that the research on the topic is limited but agrees that adopting protective behavior is cognitively demanding. That hinders both users with cognitive disabilities and neurotypical users from being secure. While addressing cognitive challenges is the cybersecurity domain is identified as an important future challenge, limiting the effort put on users to minimize the required cognitive energy is identified as a starting point.

Keywords: cognition · cognitive disabilities · cybersecurity · usability · usable security

1 Introduction

Today's digital landscape offers a multitude of services which modern society has become reliant on. Continued digitalization is a cornerstone for the for all aspects of society and bring increased ability to communication, improved access to entertainment and improved access to public services [34]. Bringing more parts of our lives to the digital world does, however, also increase the exposure to digital threats [13]. Different threat agents, including hacktivist, adversarial states, and organized criminals leverage the highly digitalized world for ill-doing [42]. Those malicious activities are carried out with various intentions including financial gain, promotion of disinformation, destabilizing of society and more. There are many different ways, called attack vectors, that the treats agents can use and those can be classified as technological, process-oriented or human-oriented [21]. The domain of this research is the human-oriented attack vector which is typically described as the most frequently used [20, 41].

© IFIP International Federation for Information Processing 2024
Published by Springer Nature Switzerland AG 2024
M. K. Lárusdóttir et al. (Eds.): HCSE 2024, LNCS 14793, pp. 160–170, 2024.
https://doi.org/10.1007/978-3-031-64576-1_9

The human attack vector can be described as exploiting users to carry out attacks. In essence, attackers leverage the facts that users are expected to adopt protective behaviors by, for instance, using strong passwords, follow security rules, and correctly distinguish between phishing email and legitimate email but in practice often fail to do so [18]. Explaining why users fail to adopt protective behavior has been a topic of research for a long time. Two main explanations has been lack of user knowledge (e.g. [1, 2]) and lack of usability in cybersecurity tools and rules (e.g. [4, 12]). The lack of user knowledge explanations suggests that users are not informed about the threats posed in the digital world or equipped with the skills needed to mitigate the threats. The usability explanation suggests that the expectations, tools and rules presented to users are inherently difficult to use which discourages users from using them or hinders correct use. A common example is password complexity guidelines which promote long and complex passwords. Those are intended to result in passwords that are difficult to guess, but users often employ coping strategies to remember their pasw3ords which results in the opposite [43].

As part of the usability research in the cybersecurity domain, researchers started to analyze the cognitive effort needed to adopt protective behavior. Many activities included in this protective behavior requires memory (password creation and use), problem solving (captchas, phishing), or learning and therefore require cognitive effort [17, 27, 39]. The current research landscape agrees that users are more likely to adopt protective behavior which requires less cognitive effort. A further, and less studied topic is how users' ability to adopt protective behavior is impacted by cognitive disabilities. While some studies suggest that a cognitive disability may negatively impact a user's ability to adopt a protective behavior (e.g. [23, 32]) the extent of the effect, and how to handle it is unknown. With the intent of enabling a future research agenda on cognitively accessible cybersecurity, this research seeks to summarize how cognitive challenges has been discussed in cybersecurity research so far by answering the research question *How are cognitive challenges discussed in relation to end-user cybersecurity in research?*

A systematic literature review was conducted to identify how cognitive disabilities in relation to end-user cybersecurity have been discussed in the extant literature. The initial search revealed (n = 248) papers that have been published to date, however, only twelve papers satisfied the inclusion criteria set for this research. From the analysis of (n = 12) papers, it was identified that cognitive abilities are acknowledged as a prerequisite for secure end-user behaviour. The included papers demonstrate that differences in cognitive functioning cause differences in the ability to adopt secure behaviour and pinpoint that memory, and attention as problem-solving is paramount for cybersecurity. The research shows that research into the domain is scarce but in agreement that adopting a secure behaviour is cognitively demanding. Furthermore, cybersecurity functions can sometimes exclude users from using services altogether. While solutions are scarce, usable design is described as positive in the analysed literature.

The remainder of the paper is organized as follows: Section 2 presents the background, Sect. 3 presents the research method, Sect. 4 presents the findings from the systematic literature review, Sect. 4.1 presents the findings from the interviews, Sect. 5 presents the discussion, and Sect. 6 concludes the paper.

2 Background

Cognitive abilities involve perception and people's ability to solve problems, plan, and reason [22]. Concentration and memory are also cognitive abilities [33]. Those abilities are important precursors for cybersecurity behavior where users are expected to follow security plans and procedures, reason and make decisions about the legitimacy of emails, create, and memorize passwords, and more. In the cybersecurity domain, Gutzwiller et al. [17] describe cybersecurity as involving cognitively demanding tasks with cybersecurity fatigue as a possible consequence. Similarly, Boyce et al., [7] describe minimizing cognitive workload as an important usability factor for cybersecurity functions and interfaces.

People's cognitive abilities are dynamic and individual and can be impacted on both a temporary and permanent basis [37, 44]. Several conditions can have a permanent impact on a person's cognitive abilities including autism, dyslexia, stroke, brain injury, and dementia [14]. How a certain condition will impact a person's cognitive abilities is highly individual [28]. However, a person with a cognitive disability will experience limitations in one or more of the cognitive abilities. Estimating the prevalence of cognitive disabilities is cumbersome [36]. However, CDC [10] suggests that 12.8% of U.S. adults are affected by a cognitive disability while Gauchard et al., [16] suggested that the prevalence in a French sample was between 3.0% and 4.7% in 2006. Further, Pais et al. [36] found a median prevalence of 19% for cognitive impairment which refers to loss of memory, learning difficulties, and decreased ability to concentrate among the elderly.

Given the prevalence of cognitive disabilities and the individual nature of how they are manifested, a large portion of people with cognitive disabilities are part of the workforce. It is common to have employees with cognitive disabilities without even knowing about them. Subsequently, it is paramount that cybersecurity functions and processes work for users with cognitive disabilities. Previous research demonstrated that cognitive ability impacts a user's ability to detect phishing and use cybersecurity functions such as captchas [6, 45]. Furthermore, users with cognitive disabilities do have difficulties while authenticating using the current range of authentication options available, for instance remembering complex passwords without writing them down can prove to be a cumbersome task for users with cognitive disabilities, similarly, the use of biometrics such as fingerprints can be difficult for a user who has had stroke resulting in disability or paralysis of arms and hands. A pertinent aspect to consider is either to leave cognitively challenged users reliant on their caregivers to perform cybersecurity functions or to develop solutions that consider cognitive factors in the design and development of cybersecurity functions. Consequently, cognitively accessible cybersecurity is an important security matter since it allows all users to efficiently use cybersecurity functions. It is also an equality and inclusivity concern because it works towards equal access to digital technology.

3 Methodology

A systematic literature review (SLR) was conducted to explore the state of the art of how cognitive disabilities have been considered in cybersecurity research. The SLR methodology described by Paré and Kitsiou [38] was adopted for the review. The upcoming sections will elaborate on the search and selection process and the analysis of the included publications.

3.1 Search Protocol

As suggested by Jesson et al., [19], an inclusive search query was developed to capture publications discussing cognitive abilities, disabilities, and disorders in a cybersecurity context. The following query was used:

Cybersecurity AND (cognition OR cognitive) AND (ability OR abilities OR disorder OR function OR functions).

It is important to note that different databases and digital libraries (considered during this SLR) have their specific syntax for the resultant search queries. Therefore, the query above was reformatted (while retaining the meaning) across the following databases and digital libraries:

- ACM
- IEEE
- Scopus
- Science Direct
- Web of Science

3.2 Screening for Inclusion

The criteria for inclusion were defined to retain only the items that align with the goals of the study and help answer the research question. The following inclusion criteria (IC) were defined and applied for this study.

- IC 1: All papers that report any solutions, developmental approach, guidelines, principles, or recommendations for considering cognitive functions/challenges in the development of cybersecurity functions.
- IC 2: The language of the publication is English.
- IC 3: The publication has been published in a peer-reviewed journal or a conference.

The screening process is presented in Figure; it is based on Page et al., [35] and Sarkis-Onofre et al., [40]. Firstly, the search results were scanned based on title and abstract, and irrelevant publications were discarded. The full body of the remaining papers was scanned again. Both scans were conducted independently by two researchers to minimize researcher bias. After scanning titles and abstracts, records kept by at least one researcher were kept for the scanning of the full papers. After the scanning of the full papers, the researchers discussed papers with conflicting judgments until a consensus was reached. Titles and authors of included publications are listed in Table 1. Searching and screening were conducted in two rounds, in October 2022 and in 2024. Figure 1 provides the combined results of both rounds. The rationale for searching in two rounds was that the initial searching yielded limited results and it was decided to pause the study for two years and then try again. The search and screening process in 2022 resulted in 8 publications selected for inclusion and another 4 were added in 2024.

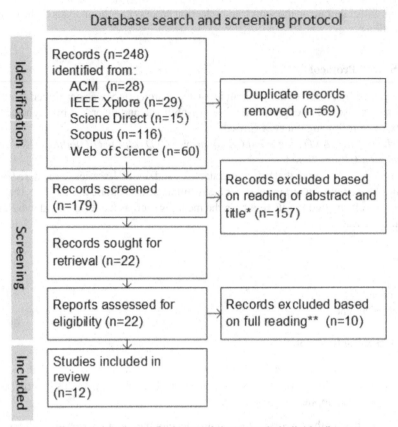

Fig. 1. Screening process for the systematic literature review

4 Results

The twelve included publications was analyzed in a thematic fashion inspired by Braun and Clarke [8]. First, individual concept of relevance for the research question was identified. Those concepts were then combined into three overarching themes. The themes are further described below.

4.1 Cognition is Central to Enable Protective Behaviour

The analysis of the included publications revealed that cognition has a central role to play in making accurate security decisions, may it be detecting and reporting an

Table 1. Titles and authors of included publications

Record title	Authors
An intelligent agent architecture to influence home users' risky behaviours [15]	Foroughi & Luksch, 2019
Neural correlates of gender differences and color in distinguishing security warnings and legitimate websites: A neurosecurity study [3]	Anderson et al., 2015
Leveraging digital intelligence in generation alpha [5]	Avci & Adigüzel, 2020
SOK: young children's cybersecurity knowledge, skills & practice: A systematic literature review [27]	Lamond et al., 2022
Modelling effective cybersecurity training frameworks: A Delphi method-based study [11]	Chowdhury et al., 2022
Cybersecurity as a social phenomenon [29]	McAlaney & Benson, 2019
Usable Privacy and Security from the Perspective of Cognitive Abilities [25]	Kävrestad et al., 2022
Upside and downside risk in online security for older adults with mild cognitive impairment [30]	Mentis et al., 2019
Aging online: Rethinking the aging decision-maker in a digital era [31]	Ebner et al., 2022
An Interdisciplinary Perspective on Mis/Disinformation Control [9]	Caramancion, 2023
Design principles for cognitively accessible cybersecurity training [24]	Kävrestad et al., 2024
Personality and Cognitive Factors in Password Security Behaviors [26]	Kennison & Chan-Tin, 2023

attack, responding to security warnings, or complying with a security policy. Foroughi & Luksch [15] acknowledge cognitive processing as central to users' cybersecurity decision-making. The authors propose a model to support cybersecurity decision-making by gathering information on user actions. While the publication does not explicitly describe how cognitive functioning impacts cybersecurity behavior, it showcases cognition as central to cybersecurity decision-making. Furthermore, Anderson et al., [3] describe that cognitive processing is central to cybersecurity behavior and that many such processes are automatic. Using electroencephalography, [3] examine users' brain activity when subjected to malware warnings and identify an increase in brain activity related to decision-making compared to when users are subjected to benign stimuli. While Anderson et al., focuses on neurotypical users, it demonstrates the importance of cognitive processing in cybersecurity decision-making. A similar perspective is presented by Ebner et al., [31] argue that age-related changes in cognitive functions can lead to poor decision-making online. Kävrestad et al., [24] describe that furthers the discussion by describing cognitive energy as a resource needed for cybersecurity tasks.

Cognitive energy is finite and users with cognitive disabilities may have less cognitive energy than neurotypical users, and cybersecurity tasks are therefore more costly.

In addition, Avci & Adigüzel, [5] describe the concept of digital intelligence as a set of cognitive, meta-cognitive, and socio-emotional skills and argue that users differ in the level of digital intelligence. The authors specifically focus on Generation Alpha as a group that needs to be trained differently from other users because of their life-long exposure to technology. While the paper does not specifically address differences in cognitive abilities, it does highlight cognitive processing as an important part of digital intelligence, and cybersecurity skills as important for digital users. Furthermore, Lamond et al., [27] stipulate that cybersecurity actions require mature cognitive abilities in a study on cybersecurity behavior among children. The paper finds that children often display poor cybersecurity behavior and attributes that, at least in part, to their cognitive functioning is not yet fully developed. Memory, literacy, attention, and problem-solving are described as cognitive functions that are important for cybersecurity activities. Similarly, Kennison & Chan-Tin [26] show that memory is connected to password creation so that users with lower memory ability create weaker passwords.

4.2   Need for Training and Cognitive Heuristics

The current cybersecurity training regime does not consider the abilities, behavioral characteristics, and disabilities people have when developing the training content [24, 25]. Chowdhury et al., [11] Kennison & Chan-Tin [26] and question the effect of many current cybersecurity training programs and suggest that one reason is a lack of consideration of user's cognitive abilities in the development of such programs. Chowdhury et al., [11] then develop a framework for cybersecurity training those accounts for individual differences in different areas, including cognitive abilities. Such training needs to be designed to fortify the cognitive ability of users [9].

Furthermore, McAlaney & Benson, [29] discuss the role of cognitive heuristics in cybersecurity decision-making. Cognitive heuristics can be seen as mental shortcuts taken because cognitive processes require cognitive energy, which is a finite resource. The authors describe that the use of cognitive heuristics is a fundamental human function but that it can lead us to make incorrect cybersecurity decisions.

4.3   Towards Accessible and Inclusive Design

In addition to the findings discussed earlier, the literature identifies the need for using accessible design approaches for inclusivity concerns and addressing the needs of users with cognitive disabilities. This is related to the finding just discussed that cognition is central to cybersecurity decision-making, which means that there is a need to support the cognitively challenged users of security functions thereby also reducing the cybersecurity risks. Kävrestad et al., [24] present an interview study that aims to research usability requirements important for users with cognitive challenges. The main conclusion was that users with cognitive challenges face similar challenges as neurotypical users but often perceive the challenges as significantly more severe. The authors stress that cybersecurity tasks require energy, and that energy is a finite resource. Consequently, cybersecurity functions should strive to be as effortless as possible to use. The paper concludes that using accessible design and easy-to-follow instructions are important for users with cognitive challenges and beneficial for all user groups. Furthermore, Mentis et al., [30] studied how older users with mild cognitive impairments (MCI) are addressing cybersecurity concerns by interviewing users with MCI and their caregivers. They acknowledge that users with MCI may be more susceptible to cyber risks but describe that removing access to online services is also problematic since it reduces autonomy. The authors discuss using systems where a user's activity may be reviewed or monitored by a caregiver as one option, although such a solution would also reduce autonomy. The authors also discuss that services need to be designed to be secure and privacy-preserving without elaborating on how.

In conclusion, the SLR demonstrates that while research on cognitive abilities in relation to cybersecurity is scarce, the existing research does support the notion of cybersecurity activities as cognitively demanding. A few studies further demonstrate that users with cognitive challenges face difficulties when asked to engage in cybersecurity activities. Consequently, not accounting for cognitive challenges when developing cybersecurity functions and routines risks excluding users with cognitive challenges from being secure or using the services altogether.

5 Discussion

This research aimed to review how cognitive challenges in relation to cybersecurity are considered in current state-of-the-art research. The research comprised a systematic literature review to find out how cognitive disabilities are accounted for in cybersecurity research. Briefly, the result shows that academia acknowledge that cognitive disabilities are important to consider in relation to cybersecurity. However, the extent to which they have been considered so far is limited. Although the set of included publications is limited, it is notable that more than half the included publications are published from 2022 and onwards which could suggest an increasing research interest in the topic.

The SLR resulted in a limited set of included publications (n = 12) which was quite surprising given that the initial searches generated 248 hits. However, many of those publications discussed cognitive aspects related to the cybersecurity workforce rather than end-user activities, or cognitive modeling as a computerized model which simulates human behavior. The twelve included publications show a distinctive pattern where most of them (seven) acknowledge cognitive processing or functioning as imperative for cybersecurity behavior. Five papers further showed that differences in cognitive functioning result in different abilities to carry out cybersecurity activities. Only two papers provides insights on how to account for cognitive challenges in the development of cybersecurity routines and functions and suggest ease of use as the most important factor.

Cognitively accessible cybersecurity is important for users who suffer from cognitive disabilities. As discussed earlier, the cognitive ability of neurotypical users may be negatively impacted by temporary conditions such as 'burnout'. Even stress and weariness can cause a person's cognitive abilities to be temporarily lowered. Consequently, cognitively accessible cybersecurity functions can be beneficial for all users.

6 Conclusions

This research shows that cognitive accessibility is important for making all users able to use cybersecurity functions. However, it also shows that research in the domain is limited. While explored research identifies that cognitive accessibility lowers the bar for the adoption of cybersecurity functions, how to do that remains unknown. A suggestion, considering this research, is that decision-makers and standardization bodies include cognitive accessibility into governing documents,

This research shows that cognitive accessibility is an important cybersecurity topic and reveals that both research and practitioner insight are scarce. Consequently, there are several avenues for further research. One such avenue would be to focus on the cognitive energy required to engage with cybersecurity functions. Being able to measure how much energy a certain tool or process requires would be beneficial and developing such a metric could be a direction for future work. Another possibility is to focus on the needs of the industry by researching the industry's preparedness to include cognitive accessibility in cybersecurity practices.

Disclosure of Interests. The authors have no competing interests to declare that are relevant to the content of this article.

References

1. Al-Daeef, M.M., et al.: Security awareness training: a review. In: Proceedings of the World Congress on Engineering, pp. 5–7 (2017)
2. Aldawood, H., Skinner, G.: Educating and raising awareness on cyber security social engineering: a literature review. In: Proceedings of 2018 IEEE International Conference on Teaching, Assessment, and Learning for Engineering, pp. 62–68 IEEE (2018). https://doi.org/10.1109/TALE.2018.8615162
3. Anderson, B.B., et al.: Neural correlates of gender differences and color in distinguishing security warnings and legitimate websites: a neurosecurity study. J. Cybersecur. 1(1), 109–120 (2015). https://doi.org/10.1093/cybsec/tyv005
4. Atwater, E., et al.: Leading Johnny to water: designing for usability and trust. Presented at the Eleventh Symposium on Usable Privacy and Security (SOUPS) (2015)
5. Avci, H., Adigüzel, T.: Leveraging digital intelligence in generation alpha. In: The Teacher of Generation Alpha, pp. 119–132 (2020)
6. Belk, M., et al.: Do human cognitive differences in information processing affect preference and performance of CAPTCHA? Int. J. Hum. Comput. Stud. **84**, 1–18 (2015)
7. Boyce, M.W., et al.: Human performance in cybersecurity: a research agenda. Presented at the Proceedings of the Human Factors and Ergonomics Society Annual Meeting (2011)
8. Braun, V., Clarke, V.: Using thematic analysis in psychology. Qual. Res. Psychol. **3**(2), 77–101 (2006). https://doi.org/10.1191/1478088706qp063oa
9. Caramancion, K.M.: An interdisciplinary perspective on Mis/Disinformation control. In: 2023 3rd International Conference on Electrical, Computer, Communications and Mechatronics Engineering (ICECCME), pp. 1–6 (2023). https://doi.org/10.1109/ICECCME57830.2023.10253252
10. CDC: Disability Impacts All of Us. https://www.cdc.gov/ncbddd/disabilityandhealth/infographic-disability-impacts-all.html

11. Chowdhury, N., et al.: Modeling effective cybersecurity training frameworks: a Delphi method-based study. Comput. Secur. **113**, 102551 (2022). https://doi.org/10.1016/j.cose.2021.102551
12. Das, S., et al.: A qualitative study on usability and acceptability of Yubico security key. Presented at the Proceedings of the 7th Workshop on Socio-Technical Aspects in Security and Trust (2018)
13. ENISA: ENISA Threat Landscape 2023. https://www.enisa.europa.eu/publications/enisa-threat-landscape-2023. Accessed 7 Dec 2023
14. FCC: Cognitive Disabilities. https://www.fcc.gov/cognitive-disabilities
15. Foroughi, F., Luksch, P.: An intelligent agent architecture to influence home users' risky behaviours. Adv. Intell. Syst. Comput. **797**, 883–892 (2019). https://doi.org/10.1007/978-981-13-1165-9_79
16. Gauchard, G.C., et al.: Prevalence of sensory and cognitive disabilities and falls, and their relationships: a community-based study. Neuroepidemiology **26**(2), 108–118 (2006)
17. Gutzwiller, R., et al.: Gaps and opportunities in situational awareness for cybersecurity. Digit. Threats Res. Pract. **1**(3), 1–6 (2020). https://doi.org/10.1145/3384471
18. Hadlington, L.: Human factors in cybersecurity; examining the link between Internet addiction, impulsivity, attitudes towards cybersecurity, and risky cybersecurity behaviours. Heliyon **3**, 7 (2017). https://doi.org/10.1016/j.heliyon.2017.e00346
19. Jesson, J., et al.: Doing Your Literature Review: Traditional and Systematic Techniques. Sage (2011)
20. Joinson, A., van Steen, T.: Human aspects of cyber security: behaviour or culture change? Cyber Secur. Peer-Reviewed J. **1**(4), 351–360 (2018)
21. Juliadotter, N.V., Choo, K.-K.R.: Cloud attack and risk assessment taxonomy. IEEE Cloud Comput. **2**(1), 14–20 (2015). https://doi.org/10.1109/MCC.2015.2
22. Karwowski, M., Kaufman, J.C.: The Creative Self: Effect of Beliefs, Self-Efficacy, Mindset, and Identity. Academic Press (2017)
23. Katsini, C., et al.: Eye gaze-driven prediction of cognitive differences during graphical password composition (2018). https://doi.org/10.1145/3172944.3172996
24. Kävrestad, J., et al.: Design principles for cognitively accessible cybersecurity training. Comput. Secur. **137**, 103630 (2024). https://doi.org/10.1016/j.cose.2023.103630
25. Kävrestad, J., Hagberg, A., Roos, R., Rambusch, J., Nohlberg, M.: Usable privacy and security from the perspective of cognitive abilities. In: Friedewald, M., Krenn, S., Schiering, I., Schiffner, S. (eds.) Privacy and Identity Management. Between Data Protection and Security. IAICT, vol. 644, pp. 105–121. Springer, Cham (2022). https://doi.org/10.1007/978-3-030-99100-5_9
26. Kennison, S.M., Chan-Tin, D.E.: Personality and cognitive factors in password security behaviors. N. Am. J. Psychol. **25**(3), 599 (2023)
27. Lamond, M., et al.: SOK: young children's cybersecurity knowledge, skills & practice: a systematic literature review. Presented at the Proceedings of the 2022 European Symposium on Usable Security (2022)
28. Lundin, L., et al.: Psykiska funktionshinder: stöd och hjälp vid kognitiva funktionsnedsättningar. Studentlitteratur (2012)
29. McAlaney, J., Benson, V.: Cybersecurity as a social phenomenon. In: Cyber Influence and Cognitive Threats, pp. 1–8 (2019). https://doi.org/10.1016/B978-0-12-819204-7.00001-4
30. Mentis, H.M., et al.: Upside and downside risk in online security for older adults with mild cognitive impairment. In: Proceedings of the 2019 CHI Conference on Human Factors in Computing Systems, pp. 1–13 (2019)
31. Ebner, N., et al.: Aging online: rethinking the aging decision-maker in a digital era. In: A Fresh Look at Fraud. Routledge (2022)

32. Nobles, C.: Stress, burnout, and security fatigue in cybersecurity: a human factors problem. HOLISTICA–J. Bus. Public Adm. **13**(1), 49–72 (2022)
33. Oberauer, K., et al.: Working memory capacity—facets of a cognitive ability construct. Personality Individ. Differ. **29**(6), 1017–1045 (2000)
34. OECD: How's Life in the Digital Age? (2019)
35. Page, M.J., et al.: The PRISMA 2020 statement: an updated guideline for reporting systematic reviews. Int. J. Surg. **88**, 105906 (2021)
36. Pais, R., et al.: Global cognitive impairment prevalence and incidence in community dwelling older adults—a systematic review. Geriatrics **5**(4), 84 (2020)
37. Palmer, L.: The relationship between stress, fatigue, and cognitive functioning. Coll. Stud. J. **47**(2), 312–325 (2013)
38. Paré, G., Kitsiou, S.: Methods for literature reviews. In: Handbook of eHealth Evaluation: An Evidence-based Approach [Internet]. University of Victoria (2017)
39. Reeves, A., et al.: Get a red-hot poker and open up my eyes, it's so boring 1: employee perceptions of cybersecurity training. Comput. Secur. (2021)
40. Sarkis-Onofre, R., et al.: How to properly use the PRISMA statement. Syst. Rev. **10**(1), 1–3 (2021)
41. Soare, B.: Vectors of attack. https://heimdalsecurity.com/blog/vectors-of-attack/
42. Stankovska, A.: Cyber threat actors and cyber threat management. Entrepreneurship **4**(1), 174–185 (2016)
43. Ur, B., et al.: I added '!'at the end to make it secure: observing password creation in the lab. Presented at the Proc. SOUPS (2015)
44. Verhagen, S.J., et al.: Measuring within-day cognitive performance using the experience sampling method: a pilot study in a healthy population. PloS One **14**(12), e0226409 (2019)
45. Vishwanath, A., et al.: Suspicion, cognition, and automaticity model of phishing susceptibility. Commun. Res. **45**(8), 1146–1166 (2018)

Evaluating Learning Experiences-Comparison of Two Student Feedback Methods

Marta Lárusdóttir[1]([⊠]) [iD] and Virpi Roto[2] [iD]

[1] Reykjavik University, Menntavegur 1, 102, Reykjavik, Iceland
marta@ru.is
[2] Aalto University, Otaniementie 14, 02150 Espoo, Finland

Abstract. Student feedback is crucial for the development of HCI learning experiences. Still, there is little research on how suitable the feedback methods are for gathering learning experiences and especially how the usage of the methods is experienced by the students. Hence, we have collected feedback using two different methods during an international two-week intensive course to understand the students' experiences and to be able to compare the results. The methods were: the Retrospective Hand method and the Intensive Project Course Evaluation (IPCE) questionnaire method. Feedback was collected both during the course and on the last day of the course. By analyzing the feedback, we were able to iterate the course structure and content accordingly to meet the students' needs. In this paper we describe the two methods and compare the results from both methods. We analyze the findings, discuss how these methods differ and discuss the usefulness of the feedback. Additionally, we advise how the two methods could be used in other courses for extending the communication between course teachers and students for improving the learning experiences.

Keywords: Student feedback methods · HCI education · HCI learning experience

1 Introduction

Student feedback is essential for improving HCI learning experiences of students. Globally, higher education students are commonly requested to rate things like their experiences, engagement, or satisfaction levels with teaching, teachers, and institutions [1, 2] and the student feedback collected has had a significant role in the quality assurance process at many universities [3]. Student feedback forms an increasingly important metric that has been assimilated as a vital measure of quality for evaluating individual, institutional and even system-level performativity [4]. Still, there is little research on how suitable the feedback methods are for gathering learning experiences and especially how the usage of the methods is experienced by the students.

There has been constant criticism on the integrity, reliability, and validity of student ratings through the years, but still, it remains internationally a dominant approach to

© IFIP International Federation for Information Processing 2024
Published by Springer Nature Switzerland AG 2024
M. K. Lárusdóttir et al. (Eds.): HCSE 2024, LNCS 14793, pp. 171–180, 2024.
https://doi.org/10.1007/978-3-031-64576-1_10

evaluate teaching [5]. A study conducted on student feedback survey data at one university showed that there was no evidence that the use of the questionnaire was making any contribution to improving the overall quality of teaching and learning of the departments, at least as perceived by the students [6].

It is vitally important that the purpose of the feedback gathering is defined, that the feedback is used appropriately and that there is an agreement on the overall objective of the feedback collection [7]. The primary purpose of gathering feedback from students can be grouped in four categories [8, 9, 10], including: a) Formative and diagnostic feedback mechanism (for example, used for efforts to improve teaching and courses); b) Summative feedback mechanism (for example, used in personnel and administrative decision-making); c) Source of information for prospective students when selecting course units and teachers; and d) Source of data for research on teaching. In decision making, the input from student feedback has been recommended on an international level both with a formative and summative purpose [11–13].

A recent study states that student ratings have developed through three objectives: a) an originating democratic improvement imperative; b) a dominating quality assurance assimilation and c) the emerging focus of satisfying the students as consumers motivation [4]. The underlying motivation is using the student ratings for decision making on improving the unit of analysis whether it is a unit of a course, the whole course, a study program or the whole curricula of a study program. But using only student ratings for decision making on improving teaching has four significant limitations: a) Students' limited qualifications as raters; b) Technical inadequacy and bias; c) Misuse of scales and misinterpretation of ratings; and d) Inadequate source of evidence for decision making [5]. Feedback can be collected from students at a certain level on various subjects such as: on a professor's knowledge and content expertise, learning outcomes, teaching methods, course design and organization, use of technology, quality of course materials, assessment instruments, and grading practices. But it will take colleagues and other qualified professionals to rate those skills in depth [5]. Feedback from students should only be collected on those items that are directly within their purview of expertise and behaviors they have observed or experienced throughout the course.

This paper contributes to the above presented research area through adding the dimension of comparing different course evaluation methods. More specifically we are interested in the positive and negative aspects of different course evaluation methods. Hence, in this paper, we describe our experience using two feedback collecting methods in an intensive international User-Centred Design (UCD) course.

Notably, we state the following research question:

What are the positive and negative aspects of gathering feedback during an intensive course with the Retrospective Hand method and the Intensive Project Course Evaluation method?

Particularly, we want to understand what characterizes each of the methods and how the students experience the usage of the methods.

2   The Intensive User Centred Design Course

Over three years, we developed a course on User-Centred Design for university-level students. All editions of the course were delivered in two weeks as a 4 ECTS intensive course. We gave the course for the first time in 2017 at Tallinn University with 18 participants from four countries [14]. Based on the student feedback from the first edition, we redesigned the course, and introduced it to a new group of 19 international students at Reykjavik University in 2018 [15]. Again, we redesigned the course and introduced it for the third time at Aalto University in 2019 [16] to a group of 24 students.

The learning objectives upon completion of the course were that higher education students and professionals should be able to conceptualize and prototype digital artefacts ranging from simple web-based services to mobile applications. The students acquired an understanding of what design is and how the entire cycle of the design process is conducted. The students worked in groups on a design assignment using both user-centred design (UCD) methods and the Google Design sprint (GDS) process. Our goal in all three editions of the course has been to provide a learning environment for interaction design that would be useful for the students for the design assignment and for their future jobs and studies.

3   The Two Student Feedback Methods

This section describes the two methods used for collecting student feedback in the course: The Retrospective Hand method and the IPCE questionnaire. Additionally, we describe the data analysis of the feedback gathered. These two methods were chosen for the feedback gathering, because of the different styles in data gathering, the Retrospective Hand being informal and sketchy, and the IPCE questionnaire being more traditional.

3.1   Retrospective Hand

For giving feedback with the Retrospective Hand method, first, students are given an A4 sheet of paper and a black permanent marker. They are asked to draw their right hand on the paper. In the thumb space, they are asked to write; what was good on the course (hence the like finger), in the index finger's space, they are asked to write anything they would like to point out, which could be either positive or negative. In the space for the middle finger, they are asked to write anything they think was not so good in the course (hence, the f*** finger); in the space for the ring finger, they are asked to write what they take home from the course and finally in the area for the pinky, they are asked what they would like more off in the course. An illustration of the instructions is in Fig. 1. We asked the students to fill in the Retrospective Hand at the end of each of the two weeks in all three occasions of the course. Typically, it takes students around 10 min to provide feedback on this form. We usually ask the students to deliver the sheet of paper to a box somewhere in the room to keep anonymity. After collecting the student feedback, we had open discussions between students and teachers for about 15 min so they could share their feedback with the other students and us.

The Retrospective Hand is a free form in that sense that the students can pick topics on the course content, course structure, the fellow students or whatever they want to give feedback on. The students are not restricted in any way of what they choose to write as the positive aspect, the topic they want to point out, the not so good topic, the take home message, nor what they would like more of.

The feedback gathering results after the first week in the first occasion of the course showed that students were not happy that the course description did not match the course content and course during the first week [14]. This was a mistake that we were not aware of, and it was excellent to discuss that with the students. We could not change the course content much, but we could arrange a lab visit to make up for the students' disappointment.

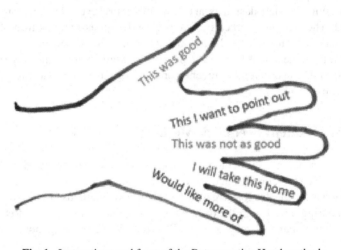

Fig. 1. Instructions and form of the Retrospective Hand method

3.2 Intensive Project Course Evaluation (IPCE) Questionnaire

The Intensive Project Course Evaluation (IPCE) questionnaire was developed by two of the authors based on a student feedback analysis scheme by Steyn et al. [17] and by analyzing the student feedback gathered by the Retrospective Hand method during the previous editions of our course.

The IPCE questionnaire contains questions about 11 aspects of the course, hereafter called IPCE categories, which are: 1. Course content, 2. Teaching methods, 3. Course structure, 4. Soft skills, 5. The learning environment, 6. Learning support, 7. Course administration, 8. Staff quality, 9. People, 10. Experience (overall course experience), 11. Feedback collection. Each aspect was explained with one sentence; for example, Item 3, Course structure, was described as: Structure and scheduling of the activities, days, and the whole course. The students were asked to rate these aspects from 1 (very bad) to 7 (Very good). The students were given the space to freely comment on each aspect, meaning that both quantitative and qualitative data was collected via this method.

Since we wanted to understand how the students experienced these two different course evaluation methods, the students were also asked to compare the usage of the IPCE questionnaire and the Retrospective Hand method. See Fig. 2 for the layout of all these parts. The questionnaire continued with two pages about the specific content of our course, results of which are reported elsewhere [15].

Fig. 2. Snapshot of the IPCE questionnaire

3.3 Data Analysis

To compare the two student feedback collection methods above, we analyzed if the methods are comparable with regards to the topics covered in the student feedback. Most importantly, we wanted to study if the IPCE categories (defined in Sect. 3.2) cover the more freeform feedback topics reported with the Retrospective Hand method. In other words, we wanted to analyze if the students feedback covers the same categories when given an open scheme like the Retrospective Hand as when given a more structured scheme like the IPCE questionnaire.

The students' comments collected with the Retrospective Hand method were first processed into data items containing one topic each. This resulted in 271 individual data items from 23 students at the end of the first week of the course and 22 students at the end of the second week. One of the authors mapped each data item to one of the IPCE categories. The topics that were difficult to categorize were discussed with another author to find consensus.

In the IPCE questionnaire, the students were asked to state if they agreed, were neutral or did not agree to 5 statements about their experience of using the two feedback collection methods. This was to measure their experiences of using both methods. The statements were: 1. Is easy to understand; 2. Is easy to fill in; 3. Is fun to fill in; 4. Is comprehensive; and 5. Allows expressing key issues. The response options were No =

−1, Neutral = 0, and Yes = 1. An average rating was calculated, so an average above 0 means that the students are generally positive towards the aspect. Additionally, the students were asked to give an overall rating for each method with the 7 ratings from Very bad = 1, Neutral = 4, Very good = 7. These ratings are reported as the percentage of the ratings where rating 2 and 3 are reported together as Bad, and rating 5 and 6 are reported together as Good.

The qualitative data from Retrospective Hand and IPCE questionnaire methods were categorized as Positive, Negative, and Suggestions. It proved difficult to categorize the items in the 'I will take this home' section in Retrospective Hand to positive or negative, as it was often unclear if the comment was negative or positive (e.g. "Be clear on design questions", "Experience in working with people that have different backgrounds", "Pencil"). Excluding the Take Home category left us with 217 data items from the Retrospective Hand. From the IPCE questionnaire, we categorised 67 data items into Positive, Negative, and Suggestion items.

4   Results and Discussion

The student feedback collection yielded 271 data items from the Retrospective Hand method (collected twice during the course), while from IPCE questionnaire we collected 241 numeric ratings and 67 comments. In this section we report and discuss results on the qualitative student feedback and the numerical results on the students experiences of the using the two methods.

4.1   Content of the Student Feedback

Most of the student feedback data items collected using the Retrospective Hand fell under the IPCE category called: Course content (26%) and under the IPCE category called: Course structure (20%). These two categories almost covered half of all the student feedback data items from the students (46%). The IPCE categories: Soft skills, Learning support, and Course administration incorporated 9–10% of the Retrospective Hand data items each. Seven data items were too vague to be categorised, for example the comment "Everything" was hard to comprehend. All other data items mapped to the IPCE categories, which indicates that the IPCE categories cover very well the data items mentioned by the students using the Retrospective Hand method in an intensive course such as ours. In other words, using only the Retrospective Hand method to gather feedback from students in a similar course as ours, should cover most of the topics covered using the more structured IPCE questionnaire, but an additional measure of urgency is gained by using the Retrospective Hand, since the frequency of data items in each IPCE category, can be counted. Asking about all the IPCE categories like done in the IPCE questionnaire, does not give the teachers the same understanding of what the students want to point out as being essential feedback.

The results in Table 1 show the percentage of positive and negative comments from students collected with both methods. Additionally, the percentage of suggestions is shown. Note that only qualitative comments from students are analysed, but in the IPCE questionnaire, the students were asked to give both numerical rating and write comments.

Table 1. The percentages of data items collected

Questionnaire	Positive	Negative	Suggestions
Retrospective Hand	42%	28%	30%
IPCE Questionnaire	19%	55%	26%

The results depicted in Table 1 show striking differences in the percentage of positive and negative comments in the different feedback collection methods. The rate of positive topics in the Retrospective Hand method was more than two times higher than IPCE (42% vs 19%), while IPCE provided proportionally two times more negative items than the Retrospective Hand method (55% vs 28%). However, when students were asked to rate the IPCE categories with numerical scores, these were largely positive, with only 19 scores on the negative side, while 202 were on the positive side and 20 scores were neutral. Hence, the topics introduced in the Retrospective Hand method were triggering more positive comments than comments provided by using the IPCE questionnaire. When using the IPCE questionnaire, the students tended to explain the negative numerical scores but rarely commented on the positive scores.

4.2   Student Feedback on Using the Two Methods

Students were asked to rate both their overall experience of providing feedback via the methods and to give feedback on 5 statements regarding the usage of the methods. The results from students of the overall experience of using the methods are shown in Table 2.

Table 2. The overall experience ratings

Questionnaire	Very good	Good	Neutral	Bad	Very bad	No answer
Retrospective Hand	32%	55%	5%	5%	5%	0%
IPCE Questionnaire	23%	68%	0%	0%	0%	5%

According to a Wilcoxon matched-pairs signed-ranks test, there is no significant difference in the two methods' overall ranking, $p < 0.05$. Still, it can be seen that the Retrospective Hand method has more divided opinions, with some negative scores and a higher number of very good ratings.

Table 3 shows the results from 22 students rating 5 statements about the usage of the methods. In general, students were positive towards both methods. Sixteen students say that the IPCE questionnaire is more comprehensive than the Retrospective Hand method. According to a Wilcoxon matched-pairs signed-ranks test, this is a statistically significant difference ($p < 0.05$). The IPCE questionnaire can thus provide a more comprehensive picture of students' experience of the course, which was its original purpose. Even though the Retrospective Hand method got higher scores for being fun and IPCE higher for being easy to fill in, the differences are not statistically significant.

Table 3. Average scores on statements describing the usage the two feedback methods

Heading level	Hand method Average rating	IPCE questionnaire Average rating
Easy to understand	0.77*	0.91
Easy to fill in	0.46	0.82
Fun to fill in	0.41	0.09
Comprehensive	0.09	0.68
Allows expressing key issues	0.55	0.59

* -1 = No, 0 = Neutral, 1 = Very good.

4.3 Experiences on Retrospective Hand Method

One of the difficulties in being a teacher is establishing a learning environment where the students receive relevant learning opportunities for the specific course, the students' education in general, and for their future. Many teachers have experienced that students are more comfortable in traditional learning environments than in more innovative approaches [18]. In our study the Retrospective Hand method is more of an innovation than the IPCE questionnaire, and this also affects the student feedback on it.

We have used the Retrospective Hand in several classes and found the Retrospective Hand method valuable for identifying the essential topics to be noted in teaching. Without specific guidance on particular topic areas, the students report the most burning issues when prompted to state something good or not so good. The importance of each aspect of student feedback may be hard for teachers to identify from more structured questionnaires such as the IPCE questionnaire. Hence, one of the strengths of the Retrospective Hand method is that the teachers get a good overview of the topics that students want to emphasise.

Another valuable aspect of Retrospective Hand method is that it engages all students to give feedback. Whenever we have used the method during class, all the students have given their feedback. Additionally, since the Retrospective Hand method does not ask about various topics, it can be used early on in a course to check students' experiences and react to them early. We have also experienced that students are generally happy to give their feedback in such an agile way of only writing a few sentences to explain their experiences, especially if being told that some of the issues will be addressed.

Feedback from students is typically gathered by the learning services at universities. This is done rather late in the course or even after the course is finished. Therefore, it is hard for the teachers to adjust the course to the feedback until the next version of the course. If the students realize this, they can be more hesitant to give feedback, because it does not improve their own experiences. Additionally, typically only a fraction of the students give their feedback, so it is hard to know how reliable the results are.

5 Conclusion

This paper reported a comparison study of two student feedback questionnaires targeted for evaluating students' experience of an intensive project course. While the feedback in both methods covered the same topics, the two sets of feedback communicated a different picture of the course. Both questionnaires showed that the students were positive about the course. Still, the Retrospective Hand's qualitative results explained why the students gave positive feedback, while there were only a few comments in IPCE explaining the positive scores. For continuous improvement of the course, teachers need to know also what works well, and for that purpose, the Retrospective Hand method provides more extensive feedback. For summative evaluation, the IPCE questionnaire works better since it provides scores for a comprehensive set of topics on this kind of course.

If teachers want to gather formative feedback from students during a course to be able to improve it, we recommend using the Retrospective Hand method. It is an efficient way to get an overview of the student experiences, since it takes the students not more than 10 min to fill in, and the teachers can quickly get a good overview of the student experiences, both positive and negative, after reading their condensed feedback. If teachers want to get more comprehensive feedback covering particular subject areas, the IPCE questionnaire is recommended.

References

1. Chalmers, D.: A review of Australian and international quality systems and indicators of learning and teaching. Strawberry Hills: The Carrick Institute for Learning and Teaching in Higher Education (2007)
2. Hammonds, F., Mariano, G.J., Ammons, G., Chambers, S.: Student evaluations of teaching: improving teaching quality in higher education. Perspect. Policy Pract. High. Educ. (2017). https://doi.org/10.1080/13603108.2016.1227388
3. Leckey, J., Neill, N.: Quantifying quality: the importance of student feedback. Qual. High. Educ. 7(1), 19–32 (2001)
4. Darwin, S.: From the local fringe to market centre: analysing the transforming social function of student ratings in higher education. Stud. High. Educ. (2020). https://doi.org/10.1080/030 75079.2020.1712690
5. Berk, R.A.: Start spreading the news: use multiple sources of evidence to evaluate teaching. J. Fac. De. 32(1), 73–81 (2018)
6. Kember, D., Leung, D.Y., Kwan, K.: Does the use of student feedback questionnaires improve the overall quality of teaching? Assess. Eval. High. Educ. 27(5), 411–425 (2002)
7. Keane, E., Labhrainn, I.M.: Obtaining student feedback on teaching & course quality. Brie ing Paper 2, 1–19 (2005)
8. Marsh, H., Dunkin, M.: Students' evaluations of university teaching: a multidimensional perspective. In: Smart, J. (ed.) Higher Education: Handbook of Theory and Research, pp. 143–223. Agathon, New York (1992)
9. Richardson, J.: Instruments for obtaining student feedback: a review of the literature. Assess. Eval. High. Educ. 30(4), 387–415 (2005)
10. Chen, Y., Hoshower, L.B.: Student evaluation of teaching effectiveness: an assessment of student perception and motivation. Assess. Eval. High. Educ. 28(1), 71–88 (2003)
11. Griffin, A., Cook, V.: Acting on evaluation: twelve tips from a national conference on student evaluations. Med. Teach. 31, 101–104 (2009)

12. Strategy Group: National strategy for higher education to 2030 (Report of the Strategy Group). Department of Education and Skills, Government Publications Office, Dublin, Ireland (2011). http://www.hea.ie/files/files/DES_Higher_Ed_Main_Report.pdf

13. Surgenor, P.W.G.: Obstacles and opportunities: addressing the growing pains of summative student evaluation of teaching. Assess. Eval. High. Educ., 1–14 (2011). iFirst Article. https://doi.org/10.1080/02602938.2011.635247

14. Larusdottir, M., Roto, V., Stage, J., Lucero, A.: Get realistic! - UCD course design and evaluation. In: Bogdan, C., Kuusinen, K., Lárusdóttir, M.K., Palanque, P., Winckler, M. (eds.) Human-Centered Software Engineering. LNCS, vol. 11262, pp. 15–30. Springer, Cham (2019). https://doi.org/10.1007/978-3-030-05909-5_2

15. Larusdottir, M., Roto, V., Stage, J., Lucero, A., Šmorgun, I.: Balance talking and doing! Using google design sprint to enhance an intensive UCD course. In: Lamas, D., Loizides, F., Nacke, L., Petrie, H., Winckler, M., Zaphiris, P. (eds.) Human-Computer Interaction – INTERACT 2019. LNCS, vol. 11747, pp. 95–113. Springer, Cham (2019). https://doi.org/10.1007/978-3-030-29384-0_6

16. Roto, V., Larusdottir, M., Lucero, A., Stage, J., Šmorgun, I.: Focus, structure, reflection! Integrating user-centred design and design sprint. In: Ardito, C., et al. (eds.) Human-Computer Interaction – INTERACT 2021. LNCS, vol. 12933, pp. 239–258. Springer, Cham (2021). https://doi.org/10.1007/978-3-030-85616-8_15

17. Steyn, C., Davies, C., Sambo, A.: Eliciting student feedback for course development: the application of a qualitative course evaluation tool among business research students. Assess. Eval. High. Educ. 44(1), 11–24 (2019)

18. Byers, T., Imms, W., Hartnell-Young, E.: Comparative analysis of the impact of traditional versus innovative learning environment on student attitudes and learning outcomes. Stud. Educ. Eval. 58 (2018). https://doi.org/10.1016/j.stueduc.2018.07.003

Interaction Techniques for Remote Maintenance in an AR Shared Environment

Sarah Claudia Krings$^{(\boxtimes)}$ ⓘ, Kai Biermeier$^{(\boxtimes)}$ ⓘ, and Enes Yigitbas$^{(\boxtimes)}$ ⓘ

Paderborn University, Warburger Street 100, 33098 Paderborn, Germany
{sarah.claudia.krings,kai.biermeier,enes.yigitbas}@uni-paderborn.de
https://www.uni-paderborn.de/

Abstract. In today's world, the importance of remote collaboration for maintenance scenarios is strongly increasing. Especially in the industrial context where machinery and other objects have to be maintained, traditional collaboration tools such as video conferencing systems are not helpful enough to communicate and interact about situation-specific spatial information. In this work, we identify and discuss current challenges in enhancing communication and interaction for mobile augmented reality (AR) based collaboration approaches. To address the identified challenges we introduce a mobile AR solution that integrates various features like voice communication, text chat, screen share, AR annotations, and AR animations to enhance the task of remote collaboration between an on-site technician and a remote expert. Based on a coffee machine maintenance example scenario we have conducted a user study and compared the benefits and drawbacks of different interaction techniques in our mobile AR collaboration solution.

Keywords: mixed reality collaboration · augmented reality · virtual reality · maintenance · usability

1 Introduction

In current times, remote collaboration has become increasingly important. While traditional collaboration tools (chat, phone, video conferencing) offer many options and are a great solution for many circumstances, these approaches are limited, especially when trying to convey abstract information or describing interactions with the real world. It can be very difficult to explain something to someone only using a telephone as it is not easily possible to grasp the situation of the other person, the object of discussion, or the environment without being able to see or experience it. Video conferencing tools add a bit more visibility, but they still limit communication [8]. For example, it is hard to impossible to point out specific components or objects on the other person's side, since it is not possible to interact with them. This can lead to misunderstandings and mistakes and makes the whole interaction quite complicated. A case in which

© IFIP International Federation for Information Processing 2024
Published by Springer Nature Switzerland AG 2024
M. K. Lárusdóttir et al. (Eds.): HCSE 2024, LNCS 14793, pp. 181–193, 2024.
https://doi.org/10.1007/978-3-031-64576-1_11

remote collaboration gains a lot of importance is maintenance [17]. Since maintenance is necessary for nearly all industrial contexts, it is a common field of interest. Usually, maintenance has to be done on location, since it requires physical interaction with the object or machine to be maintained. In this context, especially the other person's three-dimensional surroundings, including the state of the machine that is to be maintained, have to be well understood. Since interaction with 3D space over video streams is difficult, Augmented Reality (AR) [1] is a promising technology to enhance the way of communication and interaction during a remote collaboration task. It can be used on either a specialized headset or a smartphone to display virtual contents in the real space. Especially AR on smartphones (mobile AR) could be interesting for enhancing remote collaboration, since no new equipment needs to be acquired to use it. We have identified two challenges which we want to tackle with mobile AR remote collaboration. The first challenge consists of transferring knowledge about the spatial context of the maintained machine that covers the machine itself and its environment. This challenge focuses on the problem that it is difficult and impractical to get an impression of a remote space and machine through only a description. The second challenge is that it is difficult to describe concrete actions and positions using traditional communication channels as they do not offer good possibilities for describing three-dimensional targets or actions. For example, describing the exact rotation and position in which a part has to be placed is difficult and might lead to a relatively long discussion. An important in the success and user-friendliness of AR remote collaboration solutions are the functionalities that allow users to interact with contents in AR. Even though many ideas for AR remote collaboration exist, most approaches are limited or focused on a few specific collaboration functionalities. Therefore, it is difficult to determine how well the different features work in comparison. Additionally, multiple options for communicating and interacting with persons should be integrated into a remote collaboration solution to provide different alternatives for various context-of-use situations. In some situations, certain features might not be usable (for example loud noise makes voice chats difficult). In that case, it is very helpful to have alternatives to make a solution usable in diverse contexts [12]. To gain more insight into this domain, we want to compare different interaction techniques and their reception.

The rest of the paper is structured as follows: In Sect. 2, we briefly discuss the related work, and in Sect. 3, the architecture of the repository is presented. To show the feasibility of our approach, in Sect. 4, we present an application example where the developed repository was used in a prototyping scenario, followed by our evaluation in section Sect. 5. In the end, in Sect. 6, we conclude our work and give an outlook on future work.

2   Related Work

Using AR in remote collaboration to support maintenance tasks is a well-studied topic in research and industry. For example, Bottecchia et al. [2] aim to combine remote collaboration and industrial maintenance. Their T.A.C. (Télé-Assistance-Collaborative) approach enables the remote expert to see the on-site expert's view as recorded by their AR goggles. The expert is further able to interact in the on-site technician's action space by three basic operations: picking, outlining, and adding. The approach does not consider the features of a text chat. Also, Coupry et al. [4] present several works in their literature review that use the combination of digital twins with AR remote collaboration to support maintenance procedures. For example, Utzig et al. [15], present aircraft maintenance supported by head-mounted AR annotations on a virtual model of the plane and Damgrave et al. [5] present a smart industry testbed that supports inter-collaborative product development and maintenance through AR and VR. However, the focus of these works does not lie on interaction techniques.

There are also more interaction-focused approaches to remote collaboration in mobile AR. In [10], Masino et al. present an approach for remote collaboration using AR. While this approach is similar to ours, it does not support voice chat and animations to enhance collaboration through AR. In [11], Mourtzis et al. present an approach to support collaborative maintenance through a cloud system. It serves the same goal as our approach but works asynchronously. In asynchronous collaboration, the participants do not use the application at the same time, so direct interaction is not possible. In the approach by Mourtzis et al., the on-site technician does not work directly with the remote expert, but they share maintenance data through AR. Marques et al. [9] also offer remote collaboration, but only the on-site technician uses mobile AR, while the remote expert adds annotations to screenshots of the on-site user's view via a computer. The on-site user can then manually add the annotations to their AR view, but there is no direct interaction between the two users happening in AR. In [6], Gauglitz et al. present a framework for remote collaboration in previously unknown environments. They build a marker- and model-less approach for demonstrating different tasks. It is a mobile solution as it is considered to be executable on a smartphone. It has no capability to talk about the task at hand. The authors allowed the participants to communicate by voice. This is possible as the participants were not collaborating remotely but stayed in the same room. In the explanation of the theoretical framework, the authors define multiple annotations usable by the remote expert. These include 3D annotations as well as drawings, etc. The approach does not include support for animations probably due to its priory unknown target environment. Venerella et al. [16] present an approach combining mobile AR with mobile virtual reality (VR), where they eliminate the need for a machine model by using the AR client to create a 3D scan of the environment for the VR client. This is a very promising option in cases where models are not available. They also offered a range of features, including prebuilt and drawn annotations, as well as the possibility to share the AR user's gaze in VR. However, the 3D scan technique did not support animations on models and the possibility of voice chat was not mentioned. The authors also did not compare the different interaction features but proposed an additional user study.

Commercial approaches like Sphere[1], Streem[2], or Microsoft Dynamics 365[3] provide similar features to our approach. However, most of the commercial approaches do not support (controllable) animations on devices for enhancing remote collaboration.

In summary, related approaches do often not cover the integration of various communication and interaction features in a mobile AR-based remote collaboration solution. We therefore want to implement such an integrated solution to help us assess their benefits and drawbacks for the remote maintenance task and to compare them to each other.

3   Solution Concept

In this section, we present the solution concept to tackle the above-mentioned challenges. Our remote collaboration approach combines the traditional, already known communication features like text and voice chat, as well as screen sharing, with the benefits of AR. In our remote collaboration approach for *M*aintenance, users can work in an *AR SH*ared environment (thus, the application name *MARSH*) with a model of the object they want to interact with. Since we focus on maintenance, this object of shared interest will most likely be a machine that needs to be maintained. In this section, we will describe the architecture and implementation of the MARSH application, which is also illustrated in Fig. 1. We use so-called marker-based AR for creating the AR space (to the right in Fig. 1). We decided against using object recognition or object tracking, since

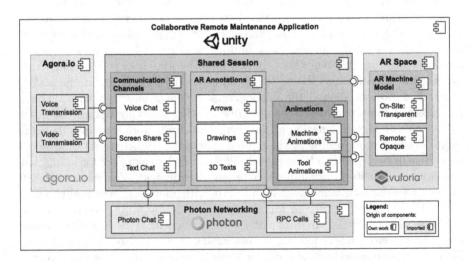

Fig. 1. The architecture of the MARSH framework

---

[1] https://sphere.tech/.

[2] https://www.streem.com.

[3] https://dynamics.microsoft.com/de-de/mixed-reality/overview.

these techniques are not reliable enough yet, neither on smartphones (see Ariano et al. [14]), nor on head-mounted devices like the HoloLens 2 (see Quere et al. [13]). To implement the marker-based tracking, we used the image tracking offered by the Vuforia SDK[4]. The machine model displayed in AR becomes transparent if the local user is an on-site technician. This makes it possible to display the virtual machine over the real machine to show things on it. If the user is entering the session remotely and therefore does not have the machine, they get shown an opaque and realistic model of the real machine. This is supposed to make it easier to keep the structure and parts of the machine in mind, even though the remote expert cannot physically access it. Every person's AR machine model is their local version and is in general not influenced by other users. However, there are different animations available that can be triggered by any user and will be displayed synchronously for all users on their respective machine models (see Fig. 1: "*Animations*"). To achieve this synchronization, the Photon PUN 2[5] networking framework for Unity was used. It makes it possible to send predefined commands (RPC calls) to all users in a room (where our "*Shared Session*" is in) to trigger actions. In this case, each animation gets its own command so it can be triggered by one person for them and all others. Animations can either happen on the AR machine model ("*Machine Animations*") itself (for example opening a flap or moving parts), but there are also "*Tool Animations*". These animate how to use other objects in connection with the machine (for example entering a consumable part or using a screw). In the shared session, all users can add "*AR Annotations*" (Fig. 1, middle), such as "*Arrows*", "*Drawings*", or "*3D Texts*". These annotations will be placed relative to the machine model and are visible in the same relative position for all users. The annotations can be moved, scaled, and rotated to illustrate descriptions and convey information. They should especially offer the possibility to convey positions or simple directions more clearly. Just like the animations, the AR annotations rely on Photon to transmit the underlying commands for the 3D object synchronization. Here, it is also necessary to spawn the objects created by one user in the other users' AR environment so they all have the same information. For the drawings, the exact meshes have to be serialized and distributed to the other users so everyone can see the same drawing on their device. The position, scale, and rotation of all spawned AR annotations are also constantly synchronized across the network. The rate of synchronization is high enough that other users can see the movement and direction of objects while a user is moving them around, making it also possible to show movements to other users. When in the shared session, the users can choose between different communication channels (Fig. 1, middle left). There is a possibility to use a "*Voice Chat*", to share the screen ("*Screen Share*"), and to use a "*Text Chat*". The voice chat and screen share features were implemented based on Agora.io[6], while the text that makes use of Photon. These

---

[4] https://www.ptc.com/en/products/vuforia/vuforia-engine, Accessed: 26.02.24.

[5] https://www.photonengine.com/pun, Accessed: 26.02.24.

[6] https://www.agora.io/en/unity, Accessed: 26.02.24.

communication channels are not mutually exclusive; therefore, it is possible to communicate via multiple channels at once.

4   Application Example

To show the benefit of our remote collaboration approach in practice, we used it to create a remote shared maintenance application that focuses on a coffee machine. The users should be able to use it to communicate about the different steps of using the machine while one person is with the machine and the other person is somewhere else, without access to the coffee machine.

Fig. 2. The shown 3D models differ according to user role

In the following, we will present the application using a typical workflow as an example. The people communicating will be the on-site technician (or user), who is at the coffee machine's location but does not know how to proceed with it, as well as the remote expert. The remote expert is a person who does not have access to the machine but knows what has to be done. In the first step, both people have to log into a so-called "room". After that, both users have to scan the marker and a realistic 3D model of the coffee machine appears (Fig. 2, left). This way, the remote expert can have her own machine (model) to look for machine details, but also to know where to put annotations in later steps. The on-site technician, however, already has a real coffee machine. An opaque 3D model placed over it would just make it difficult to see the original machine (which they have to interact with). Therefore, the on-site technician is shown a transparent machine model (Fig. 2, right). Once both users have joined the room, they might want to establish some communication first. They can use the text chat (Fig. 3, left) to discuss what the general problem is and whether both sides can activate features like voice chat and screen sharing. The voice chat offers the possibility of natural, direct communication without having to type things in first. The screen share feature enables the users to easily see the state of the other person's environment (see Fig. 3, right). The screen sharing is especially important for the remote expert evaluating the on-site technician's situation,

Fig. 3. Supported text chat (left) and screen share (right)

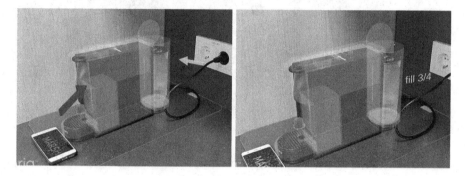

Fig. 4. Supported arrows (left) and 3D text annotations (right)

making it possible to see details about the machine that a non-experienced person might not notice. Thereby, it prevents the on-site technician from having to try and describe everything they see in detail. Once the base communication lines are   established, the actual work can begin firstly, the water tank of the machine has to be refilled. The expert can indicate its position by placing a 3D arrow pointing towards it on the coffee machine model (see Fig. 4, left). The arrows, as well as all annotations we will cover later on, can be created and moved by both users. The annotation's color indicates the person who created the animation to avoid confusion. In Fig. 4, the blue arrow was created by the on-site technician and therefore has a different color to the remote expert's yellow arrow. The remote expert can also place a 3D text with key information to a part of the machine. Here, this is used to explain how much water has to be filled in the tank (Fig. 4, right). This way, the information stays present at the location of the machine part it refers to. When the tank is filled, the machine must be turned on. To indicate the two buttons that have to be pressed for that, the remote expert can just circle them using the drawing tool (Fig. 5, left). This creates a three-dimensional drawing that appears on the location it was drawn and which can, just as the other annotations, be moved around and scaled. Once the machine is on, the coffee capsule has to be inserted. For this, it is very important to insert it in the correct rotation. Since this is difficult to explain, the remote expert can use animation to demonstrate the insertion process. The animation can be started by clicking on the object that should be animated (the capsule) and clicking the appearing arrow to trigger the animation. In Fig. 5, we can see the capsule animation ongoing, as well as the lid of the real and the model machine pointing upwards, which (on the model) is also part of an animation. The arrows for triggering those animations are visible as well. In addition to the animation, the expert can of course also use the screen share to check if the on-site technician is inserting the capsule correctly.

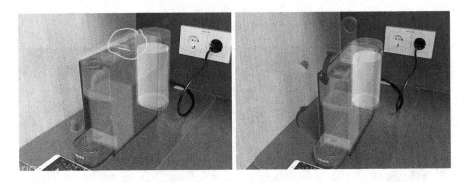

Fig. 5. Supported feature 3D drawing (left) and the animations (right)

5   Evaluation

To evaluate the benefits and drawbacks of MARSH, we conducted a usability study with 8 pairs (16 participants in total). We recruited participants in mailing lists, mostly male (14 male, 1 female, 1 N/A) participants with ages between 18 and 34 (6 18–24, 10 24–34). All participants had at least some knowledge of AR (on average 3,6 on a scale from 1–5). For the usability task, one participant was assigned to the role of the remote expert and the other one had the role of the on-site technician. The remote expert was introduced to the coffee machine

| | On-Site Participants | | | | | | | | | Remote Participants | | | | | | | | |
| | Participants' Answers | | | | | | | | | Participants' Answers | | | | | | | | |
Survey Questions	1	2	3	4	5	6	7	8	Average	1	2	3	4	5	6	7	8	Average
1 I think that I would like to use the application frequently.	3	3	1	3	4	3	2	4	2,9	2	2	3	0	3	3	3	2	2,3
2 I found the application unnecessarily complex.	4	3	2	3	3	4	3	3	3,1	4	3	3	1	4	4	4	4	3,4
3 I thought the application was easy to use.	3	3	3	3	4	4	3	1	3	4	2	4	1	4	4	3	3	3,1
4 I think that I would need the support of a technical person to be able to use the application.	4	3	4	4	3	2	1	3	3	4	2	4	4	4	4	4	4	3,8
5 I found the various functions in the application were well integrated.	3	3	2	3	3	3	3	4	3	2	3	3	2	3	4	3	3	2,9
6 I thought there was too much inconsistency in the application.	4	4	3	4	4	4	4		3,9	4	4	2	4	4	3	3		3,6
7 I would imagine that most people would learn to use the application very quickly.	3	3	3	3	4	3	3	3	3,1	4	3	3	2	4	4	4	3	3,3
8 I found the application very cumbersome (awkward) to use.	4	3	2	3	4	4	3	3	3,3	4	3	2	1	4	4	3	3	3
9 I felt very confident using the application.	4	2	2	4	4	4	2	3	3,1	4	3	4	2	3	4	3	3	3
10 I needed to learn a lot of things before I could get going with the application.	4	3	0	4	2	4	3	3	2,9	4	3	4	2	3	4	4	4	3,5
Resulting Scores:	90	75	55	85	87,5	90	70	72,5	78,1	85	70	80	40	92,5	97,5	85	82,5	79,1

Fig. 6. SUS Questionnaire Results (adjusted so higher values are always positive)

and the task of making coffee. We described this task in detail in the previous section. Both participants were supplied with Android smartphones with our application on it, as well as marker images they could scan to display the virtual model for the collaborative maintenance. Thereafter, both participants were asked to pursue the described task of making a coffee with the help of the remote expert. After the task was fulfilled, the participants were asked to fill out a questionnaire. The questionnaire was composed of the SUS questionnaire [3], the TLX questionnaire [7], and additional questions regarding the collaboration features. There were also free text fields for the participants to give feedback. In the following description and interpretation, we inverted the scale for negatively formulated questions. By this means, a high number always marks a high acceptance and vice versa. As can be seen in Fig. 6, many participants voted on the SUS questions with a rating of 3 or 4 (5-point Likert scale with possible answers between 0-strongly disagree and 4-strongly agree). This is the case for both the remote participants, where MARSH received an average SUS score of 79,1 and the on-site participants, where the average was 78,1. This indicates good usability for both groups. The results were normally distributed according to a Shapiro-Wilk test and an independent samples t-test ($\alpha = 0.05$) showed that there is no significant difference between MARSH's reception by both groups.

Looking at Fig. 7, it is visible the overall average TLX score is 24,2, with the on-site participants rating MARSH at 25 and the remote participants rating it at 23,3. Most single answers also lie around in this range. Again, the results were normally distributed according to a Shapiro-Wilk test and an independent samples t-test ($\alpha = 0.05$) found no significant difference between the remote and the on-site user group.

Survey Questions		On-Site Participants Participants' Answers									Remote Participants Participants' Answers								
		1	2	3	4	5	6	7	8	Average	1	2	3	4	5	6	7	8	Average
1	How mentally demanding was the task?	15	35	20	25	20	25	30	15	23,1	10	65	20	30	15	15	65	20	30,0
2	How physically demanding was the task?	15	15	20	30	15	10	30	40	21,9	5	5	50	15	15	10	40	20	20,0
3	How hurried or rushed was the pace of the task?	20	25	85	10	20	40	20	20	30,0	10	10	15	35	10	15	55	45	24,4
4	How successful were you in accomplishing what you were asked to do?	35	40	20	50	5	30	10	15	25,6	10	20	10	25	5	10	15	15	13,8
5	How hard did you have to work to accomplish your level of performance?	15	40	15	25	25	10	15		21,3	15	55	25	35	10	25	30	20	26,9
6	How insecure, discouraged, irritated, stressed, and annoyed were you?	15	15	5	50	5	25	65	45	28,1	15	65	55	20	5	5	10	25	25,0
Resulting Scores:		19,2	28,3	27,5	31,7	15,0	25,8	27,5	25,0	25	10,8	36,7	29,2	26,7	10,0	13,3	35,8	24,2	23,3

Fig. 7. TLX Questionnaire Results (adjusted so higher values are always positive)

Considering our additional questions (Fig. 8), we find many good ratings on all of our features which is stable for most participants. On average, our features were rated between 2.1 (acceptance: medium+) and 4.0 (acceptance: very high). The results were normally distributed according to a Shapiro-Wilk test and an independent samples t-test ($\alpha = 0.05$) found no significant difference between the remote and the on-site user group when looking at the whole set of features. The highest score was given to the voice chat feature, which all participants voted as very useful (avg. 4.0/4 by both user groups). The screen share feature was also very well received, with most participants voting it as very useful and the others voting it as useful (avg. 3.8/4 by both user groups). Both features reached

Survey Questions		On-Site Participants Participants' Answers									Remote Participants Participants' Answers								
		1	2	3	4	5	6	7	8	Average	1	2	3	4	5	6	7	8	Average
1	I felt the application was well suited for remote shared maintenance.	4	4	3	3	4	2	3	3	3,3	3	3	3	2	3	4	4	4	3,3
2	I had major problems communicating via the application.	4	4	4	4	3	4	3	3	3,6	4	4	3	4	4	4	3		3,6
3	I could easily understand what the other person was trying to tell and show me via the application.	4	3	4	3	3	3	2	3	3,1	0	3	4	2	3	4	4	3	2,9
4	I found the possibility of drawing on the screen useful.	2	4	3	2	3	1	1	4	2,5	3	3	4	0	3	3	2	3	2,6
5	I found the screenshare option useful.	4	4	3	4	4	3	4	4	3,8	3	4	4	3	4	4	4	4	3,8
6	I found the voice chat useful.	4	4	4	4	4	4	4	4	4,0	4	4	4	4	4	4	4	4	4,0
7	I found the 3D arrows useful.	2	2	2	2	3	1	2	4	2,3	3	4	2	2	4	3	4	3	3,1
8	I found the possibility to place texts in the 3D space useful.	2	3	1	3	2	1	2		2,0	4	2	0	3	3	3	0	2	2,1
9	I found the animations useful.	3	4	2	2	2	4	3	2	2,8	3	4	2	2	4	4	3	4	3,25
10	I would have wished for more/different functions in the application.	4	2	3	4	1	2	2	3	2,6	4	3	4	2	2	4	3	4	3,3

Fig. 8. Additional questionnaire results (adjusted so higher values are always positive)

nearly identical values with the two user groups. The other features received more mixed, but mostly positive feedback. The animations were perceived as useful, but with a slightly bigger difference between the user groups (On-site: 2.8/4; Remote: 3.3/4). The drawing feature was perceived as useful with 2.5/4 by the on-site users and 2.6/4 by the remote users. The 3D arrows were perceived as moderately useful by the on-site users (2.3/4) and as useful by the remote users (3.1/4) and the 3D texts were seen as neutral to moderately useful by both groups (On-site: 2.0/4; Remote: 2.1/4).

When asked for positive points in free text fields, several participants described the application as "easy to use" and especially praised the screen share and voice chat for making communication easy. The other features, such as drawings, arrows, and animations, were also mentioned positively. Several participants did, however, suggest making the on-site machine model less opaque to make it easier to see the real machine. A common point of critique was also the size of the screen share window and the screen in general. One user also suggested the option to put the screen share video in AR space. Some users also expressed difficulties in moving the 3D objects in space (e.g. arrows and texts). Another issue was the sound feedback from the voice chat coming out of the smartphone speakers.

Looking at the results, we can say that MARSH was well accepted by users independent of their role. Since there was no significant difference between the roles on any Likert item, we can say that the application seems to support both user groups equally well. Regarding the features, we saw that the "traditional" remote communication features (voice and screen share) were very well received and also seen as very important. We would argue that these features are an important base for any communication. Additionally, they might be intuitive for most users, since they likely used such features in other applications before. The positive reception of the drawings supports our hypothesis that three-dimensional interactions as ways of communication are important for these tasks. We suspect that the arrows and texts fell back behind the drawings (and the animations) because some participants had issues with moving/placing these items (as mentioned in the text feedback), while the drawing feature and animations work more intuitively. To use the drawings, the users could just draw on the screen as they would in a 2D application and for the animations, they only had to tap the machine part to animate and then start the animation with another tap. To move arrows and texts to the correct position, the users had to rotate them with a two-finger gesture and move them through space using swiping motions by moving their phones. Here, it might be helpful to lower the complexity of the interaction to improve reception. However, for moving objects in 3D, the technical limitations of a smartphone (which only has a 2D screen) could be an issue. Adding hand-tracking software (which would still have the issue of users having to hold the phone with one hand and interact with the other) or using an AR headset could help here. When looking at options for improvement within MARSH, it could help to look for different interaction techniques for 3D movement (e.g. only moving on a plane and offering a slider for vertical movement).

Regarding the feature-independent user feedback, smaller changes like making the on-site machine model more transparent, as requested by some users, or even switching to a wireframe model, could also help with visibility. Some other issues that were mentioned are more technical and could be fixed by different hardware, such as redoing the study on tablets instead of smartphones to improve the screen size and by using headphones or software with better noise cancelling to reduce audio feedback.

6   Conclusion and Future Work

In this paper, we have presented a mobile AR-based remote collaboration approach for enhancing the communication and interaction between an on-site technician and a remote expert. Our remote collaboration approach integrates various communication and interaction features to improve the sharing of situation-specific spatial information about the maintained machine or other real-world objects. Based on a user study, we have shown the benefit of our remote collaboration approach which was accepted by most of the participants. Furthermore, we have discussed the advantages and disadvantages of our implemented AR-based collaboration features for remote maintenance scenarios. We showed that some traditional communication features (voice chat, screen share) are also of high importance for AR-based remote collaboration, but that novel features are also important and well received. Additionally, we suggest novel features should have as little complexity as possible for a positive reaction.

In future work, we would like to conduct a larger user study to gain more diverse feedback and even stronger results. Additionally, we plan to extend and apply our remote collaboration approach in further domains where remote maintenance is crucial. We also plan to look in more detail into different interaction techniques for moving objects three-dimensionally using smartphone-based AR to further optimize the user experience.

References

1. Azuma, R.T.: A survey of augmented reality. Presence Teleoper. Virtual Environ. **6**(4), 355–385 (1997)
2. Bottecchia, S., Cieutat, J.M., Jessel, J.P.: TAC: augmented reality system for collaborative tele-assistance in the field of maintenance through internet. In: Proceedings of the 1st Augmented Human International Conference, pp. 1–7 (2010)
3. Brooke, J.: SUS: a "quick and dirty' usability. Usability Eval. Ind. **189**, 4–7 (1996)
4. Coupry, C., Noblecourt, S., Richard, P., Baudry, D., Bigaud, D.: BIM-based digital twin and XR devices to improve maintenance procedures in smart buildings: a literature review. Appl. Sci. **11**(15), 6810 (2021). https://doi.org/10.3390/app11156810
5. Damgrave, R., Lutters, E.: Smart industry testbed. Procedia CIRP **84**, 387–392 (2019). https://doi.org/10.1016/j.procir.2019.04.215
6. Gauglitz, S., Lee, C., Turk, M., Höllerer, T.: Integrating the physical environment into mobile remote collaboration. In: Proceedings of the 14th International Conference on Human-Computer Interaction with Mobile Devices and Services, MobileHCI 2012, pp. 241–250. Association for Computing Machinery, New York (2012). https://doi.org/10.1145/2371574.2371610
7. Hart, S.G., Staveland, L.E.: Development of NASA-TLX (task load index): results of empirical and theoretical research. In: Advances in Psychology, vol. 52, pp. 139–183. Elsevier (1988)
8. Ichino, J., et al.: How gaze visualization facilitates initiation of informal communication in 3D virtual spaces. ACM Trans. Comput.-Hum. Interact. **31**(1), 1–32 (2023). https://doi.org/10.1145/3617368
9. Marques, B., Silva, S., Rocha, A., Dias, P., Santos, B.S.: Remote asynchronous collaboration in maintenance scenarios using augmented reality and annotations. In: 2021 IEEE Conference on Virtual Reality and 3D User Interfaces Abstracts and Workshops (VRW), pp. 567–568 (2021). https://doi.org/10.1109/VRW52623.2021.00166
10. Masoni, R., et al.: Supporting remote maintenance in industry 4.0 through augmented reality. Procedia Manufact. **11**, 1296–1302 (2017)
11. Mourtzis, D., Zogopoulos, V., Vlachou, E.: Augmented reality application to support remote maintenance as a service in the robotics industry. Procedia CIRP **63**, 46–51 (2017)
12. Oviatt, S.: Multimodal system processing in mobile environments. In: Proceedings of the 13th Annual ACM Symposium on User Interface Software and Technology, UIST 2000, pp. 21–30. Association for Computing Machinery, New York (2000). https://doi.org/10.1145/354401.354408
13. Quere, C., Menin, A., Julien, R., Wu, H.Y., Winckler, M.: HandyNotes: using the hands to create semantic representations of contextually aware real-world objects. In: IEEE VR 2024 - The 31st IEEE Conference on Virtual Reality and 3D User Interfaces. Orlando, Florida, United States (2024). https://inria.hal.science/hal-04425616
14. Ariano, R., Manca, M., Paternó, F., Santoro, C.: Smartphone-based augmented reality for end-user creation of home automations. Behav. Inf. Technol. **42**(1), 124–140 (2023). https://doi.org/10.1080/0144929X.2021.2017482
15. Utzig, S., Kaps, R., Azeem, S.M., Gerndt, A.: Augmented reality for remote collaboration in aircraft maintenance tasks. In: 2019 IEEE Aerospace Conference, pp. 1–10 (2019). https://doi.org/10.1109/AERO.2019.8742228

16. Venerella, J., Franklin, T., Sherpa, L., Tang, H., Zhu, Z.: Integrating AR and VR for mobile remote collaboration. In: 2019 IEEE International Symposium on Mixed and Augmented Reality Adjunct (ISMAR-Adjunct), pp. 104–108 (2019). https://doi.org/10.1109/ISMAR-Adjunct.2019.00041

17. Wang, P., et al.: AR/MR remote collaboration on physical tasks: a review. Robot. Comput.-Integr. Manuf. **72**, 102071 (2021). https://doi.org/10.1016/j.rcim.2020.102071

PhD Student Discussion Forum

A Critical Examination of UCD4D Studies

Abdulwahed Bin Mothana[✉] and Anke Dittmar[✉]

University of Rostock, Albert-Einstein-Straße 22, 18059 Rostock, Germany
{abdulwahed.mothana,anke.dittmar}@uni-rostock.de

Abstract. User-centred design (UCD) has been developed as a useful and effective design approach for designing interactive systems. However, some researchers point out that UCD methods created for the developed world imply assumptions that make them difficult to use in the developing world. The paper presents a systematic literature review focused on user-centered design initiatives for development in rural areas. A comprehensive analysis of 190 publications was conducted in order to systematically and critically examine existing design studies. The results support results from previous reviews and provide deeper insights into existing challenges and underlying assumptions and attitudes.

Keywords: user-centred design for development · UCD4D · human-computer interaction for development · HCI4D · systematic literature review

1 Introduction

The field of information and communication technologies (ICT) provides unparalleled opportunities for developing countries to improve education systems, formulate and implement policies, and increase opportunities for businesses and the disadvantaged [7]. However, the still existing digital divide between different countries and cultures is a major limiting factor for socio-economic growth in all areas [6]. Recent years have seen the advent of an interdisciplinary, international research body on the design of ICT and systems that meet the specific user and infrastructure requirements for international development (ICT4D). Human-computer interaction for development (HCI4D) is "a subfield of ICT4D that focuses on understanding how people and computers interact in developing regions, and on designing systems and products specifically for these contexts" [8]. According to [10], common user-centred design approaches may not be valid in a HCI4D context and need to be adapted. Our design study in [2] confirms this observation but it also shows that based solely on a categorization of "developed" and "developing" countries or regions, design situations can easily be lumped together in a useless or even harmful way.

This paper presents a systematic literature review (SLR) to thoroughly examine existing user-centred design for development (UCD4D) practices. It comprehensively enhance the preliminary review in [3]. The focus of the paper is on UCD4D initiatives in rural areas. The results of the SLR confirm results from previous reviews regarding the

M. K. Lárusdóttir et al. (Eds.): HCSE 2024, LNCS 14793, pp. 197–223, 2024.
https://doi.org/10.1007/978-3-031-64576-1_12

where, why, how, and who of UCD4D studies and provide deeper insights into existing challenges and the positionality of the authors of the reviewed studies.

The paper is structured as follows. Section 2 provides an overview of related reviews to identify common themes and gaps in the analysis. Section 3 presents the SLR (research questions, search and screening, analysis and some of the results). The paper ends with a discussion and conclusion section.

2 Related Work

There exist only a few reviews on HCI4D studies, which are briefly described below. Van Biljon and Renaud [11] analyse in their systematic literature review 176 HCI4D publications (published between 2009 and 2019) and categorize their findings into four dimensions: *When* (annual publication levels), *Where* (research and author locations), *Why* (research domains), and *How* (research designs and data collection methods). The authors emphasize the importance of their review as a reflection on the progress made in HCI4D over the past decade. Three types of publications could be identified: 1) foundational publications about understanding the users' needs and context of use, 2) design and intervention publications, and 3) abstraction or theorization publications. 67% of the publications belong to the second category describing aspects of the design, implementation, and evaluation of applications. The focus of the present work is exclusively on design studies.

Dell and Kumar [5] apply a mixed methods approach to understand the landscape of HCI4D research between 2009 and 2014, synthesizing insights from both literature surveys (259 publications from 11 well-known venues) and qualitative interviews with expert researchers. The results show annual trends, geographical distribution, target users, thematic areas, and methodological approaches employed in the analysed studies.

Anokwa et al. [1] utilize a combination of qualitative and quantitative instruments to collect and synthesize their own experiences and challenges they encountered across diverse research locations. Five themes are identified and described: 1) challenges encountered during user studies, 2) managing expectations, 3) choosing users, 4) developing content, and 5) deployment of technology. The significance of comprehending and navigating the distinct challenges posed by cultural, linguistic, and socioeconomic differences in HCI4D research is stressed.

Ho et al. [8] explore the historical background and delve into key issues within HCI4D by conducting a literature review. A pivotal question they pose is "How does designing for and with underserved communities differ from interaction design with reasonably affluent users in the industrialized world?" The authors emphasize the need for reflexivity, documentation of design knowledge, affordability in computing solutions, and collaboration to enhance HCI capacity in developing regions.

Table 1 provides an overview of themes that were considered in the above reviews. While challenges in HCI4D research were mentioned at a general level, it becomes also evident that this theme needs to be examined more systematically. More research is also needed on existing assumptions and attitudes in a HCI4D context.

Table 1. Themes in reviews on HCI4D research.

theme	van Biljon & Renaud [11]	Dell & Kumar [5]	Anokwa et al. [1]	Ho et al. [8]
Where (geographical distribution)	x	x	x	–
When (annual publication levels)	x	x	–	–
Why (focus area/domain)	x	x	–	–
How (research/design methods)	x	x	x	x
Who (target user)	–	x	x	–
Who (researcher/designer)	x	–	x	–
Challenges	(x)	(x)	(x)	(x)

3   The Systematic Literature Review

The present SLR investigates UCD4D design studies with HCI4D researchers and designers and with participants from rural communities in developing regions. We follow in our SLR the steps as recommended, for example, in [4, 9]: 1) define research questions, 2) identify the data sources, 3) establish criteria for includes and excludes of publications, 4) screening, 5) analysis, and 6) presentation of the results and discussion. The following research questions guide our review.

RQ1: Can the trends reported in previous reviews be replicated?
RQ2: What are the challenges and risks that arise with the UCD4D case studies? How do the researchers and designers address and overcome these challenges?
RQ3: What are the assumptions and attitudes of the researchers, designers and participants?

RQ1 addresses the Where, When, Why, How, and Who of the UCD4D case studies to be reviewed (see Table 1). RQ2 aims at identifying and classifying reported challenges. RQ3 arises from our own experiences in [2] and aims to uncover underlying beliefs and perspectives that influence the design studies.

3.1   Search Process, Screening, and Analysis

Peer-reviewed journal articles and conference papers published between 2000 and 2021 were reviewed. The search was carried out in August 2021 using Google Scholar, ACM Digital Library and Scopus as data sources. Search criteria included AND combinations of terms from two sets: 1) user cent(e)red design, UCD4D, UCD4Dev, human computer interaction for development, user centred design for development, HCI4D, and 2) developing world, developing country(ies), developing region(s), rural area(s), rural development, Global South.

A Zotero database was used for iterative screening. First, 1085 duplicate publications were identified and removed. We then excluded publications that did not meet the criteria of being either journal articles or conference papers, as well as those originating from unrelated venues (e.g., Journal of Ultrasound in Medicine). Following the initial screening steps, a total of 464 articles were selected for the review of their abstracts. We excluded papers that were not related and did not describe a UCD4D process. As a result of this refinement, the number of articles for comprehensive assessment was narrowed down to 231. Out of these 231 articles, 34 were subsequently excluded after thorough review as they were determined to be general articles lacking a specific case study. Additionally, 7 articles were excluded because they pertained to developed countries (see Fig. 1). Ultimately, a selection of 190 publications remained, forming the basis for our analysis (the list of these articles is to be found in the appendix).

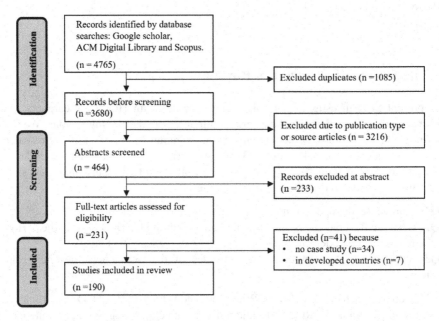

Fig. 1. Flow diagram for the selected publications.

We applied the ATLAS.ti tool and a combined top-down and bottom-up coding to analyse the qualitative data. Themes from existing reviews were employed in the top-down coding process (where, when, why, how, who). Challenges, assumptions and attitudes were identified in a bottom-up manner.

3.2 Results

For reasons of brevity, *only some* of the results can be presented in this paper.

3.2.1 Where and Who (Researcher/designer)

Table 2 shows that the studies mentioned in the analysed publications cover 39 countries. The majority of these studies were carried out in India (n = 77), followed by Kenya (21), Bangladesh (16), Pakistan (15), and South Africa (13).

Table 2. Where and who (researcher/designer).

	Country	no. of studies	#ext. Researcher, diff. Language	#ext. Researcher, same language	#local researcher, same language
1	Angola	1	1	–	–
2	Argentina	1	1	–	1
3	Bangladesh	16	9	9	10
4	Bengal	1	1	–	–
5	Brazil	2	2	–	2
6	Cambodia	1	1	–	1
7	Cameroon	1	–	1	–
8	China	1	–	–	1
9	Congo	1	1	–	–
10	Ecuador	1	1	–	–
11	Egypt	3	1	–	3
12	Ethiopia	3	3	–	3
13	Ghana	4	4	–	2
14	India	77	13	55	41
15	Ivory Coast	2	2	–	2
16	Kazakhstan	2	2	–	1
17	Kenya	21	18	7	6
18	Kyrgyzstan	2	2	–	1
19	Lebanon	1	1	1	–
20	Liberia	1	–	1	–
21	Malawi	1	1	1	–
22	Morocco	1	–	–	1
23	Namibia	5	2	1	3
24	Nepal	1	1	1	–
25	Nigeria	3	–	1	3
26	Pakistan	15	4	8	11
27	Peru	2	2	–	–
28	Philippine	1	–	–	1
29	Rwanda	1	1	–	–
30	South Africa	13	3	3	11
31	Sri Lanka	1	1	–	1
32	Tajikistan	2	2	–	1
33	Tanzania	2	–	2	–

(*continued*)

Table 2. (*continued*)

	Country	no. of studies	#ext. Researcher, diff. Language	#ext. Researcher, same language	#local researcher, same language
34	Thailand	1	1	–	–
35	the Cape Verdean	1	–	–	1
36	U.K	1	1	–	–
37	Uganda	5	2	3	2
38	Uzbekistan	2	2	–	1
39	Zimbabwe	1	–	1	–

Notably, the majority of authors (57%) are currently located in the USA. We categorized the authors into three groups: 1) 'local' researchers located in the same country and with same language as community members, 2) external researchers speaking the same language, and 3) external researchers with different language. In 39 publications, all of the authors are local researchers, in all other cases there are combinations of local and external authors (67) or only external authors (84).

3.2.2 Why, Who (Target User) and How

We identified 22 focus areas with a clear dominance of the following: health domain (n = 50), access to technology (34), mobile system/technology (33), education (23), sustainability (23), culture (18), and assistive technology (16). Accordingly, target user groups include doctors, nurses, health workers and patients, students and teachers, low-literate individuals, farmers, children, families and community members.

In the reviewed studies, 29 UCD methods and techniques were used. The most commonly reported ones are interviews (n = 143), surveys and questionnaires (69), observation (59), prototyping (44), focus groups/group meetings (30), in situ evaluation (22).

3.2.3 Common Challenges

Challenges were identified and classified into six categories, each with two to four sub-categories as to be seen in Table 3. The table also contains example quotes and the number of publications mentioning this type of challenge.

3.2.4 Proposed Solutions

The authors suggest solutions to overcome some of the above mentioned challenges:

– *Select the appropriate technology:* Choosing technology and media according to demographics and user preferences can improve usability and learnability [a25]. For example, the success of the anti-retroviral therapy system in [a25] relies on minimal touchscreen interfaces. Text-free interfaces were recommended for illiterate users in [a10].

- *Involvement of local experts and researchers:* Involving respected local experts can enhance the UCD process [a26]. Local IT professionals can facilitate communication between developers and users, especially in developing economies [a11].
- *Targeting younger participants:* Younger rural participants are noted for their quick learning and high interest in participation [a41].
- *Considering literacy levels:* Literacy level, cultural background, device familiarity, and language beliefs should inform the design process [a19].
- *Utilizing facilitators:* Facilitators and local IT experts can bridge cultural and language gaps between designers and participants [a26], [a11].

Table 3. Categorisation of challenges (references are to be found in the appendix).

Main category	Sub-category	no. Publ	Example
Technical infrastructure	Unreliable power	23	"The erratic electricity supply is on for about 6 h a day, but not always at the times it is most needed." [a128]
	Mobile networks	11	"With… varying mobile phone network coverage one of the primary ongoing issues in the project is communication between the MA and the HSPs." [a66]
	Internet limitation	21	"Since ASHAs did not have access to WiFi facilities at their homes, we used mobile Internet." [a34]
	No fixed telephone line	2	"the clinic was void of any fixed-line telecommunication and electrical infrastructure." [a22]
Culture and religion	Cultural challenge	26	"we can recognize the influence of users' cultural/historical backgrounds on their actions" [a70]
	Religion	2	"…Religion and Culture are the six major challenges that persuasive games designers need to tackle in order to design a game that will be effective for people living in the Rural African communities." [a27]

(*continued*)

Table 3. (*continued*)

Main category	Sub-category	no. Publ	Example
	Gender discrimination	6	"Women are generally economically dependent on their husbands and their insights are often taken lightly if at all in house-hold decision-making, ownership of properties, and financial planning" [a69]
Education and language	Language barriers	12	"The most prominent examples in our experience are that we rarely share a common language with local people" [a26]
	Illiteracy	15	"The lack of literacy also made it difficult to co-create tangible design artefacts that other PD techniques rely on such as storyboards or paper prototypes…" [a144]
	Computer skills	6	"Low computer skill resulted in long content authoring times. As a result, this limited the frequent authoring of digital content among the Low Proficiency teachers." [a64]
Tensions/ conflicts	Community level	4	"…one person, who feels, on the one hand, a strong wish to protect traditional ways of life and the natural environment that this way of life is entangled with, and on the other hand simultaneously dreams about starting a petrol station in the middle of the community in the forest." [a30]

(*continued*)

Table 3. (*continued*)

Main category	Sub-category	no. Publ	Example
	Ideological hegemony	3	"There is a risk that modern practices of information communication... can sideline communities due to their prioritization of scientific rationality. Such ideological hegemony can complicate interactions with data and computers" [a46]
Security	Privacy	18	"Customers saw cash as a safe and reliable mode of payment for small in-person transactions. They noted that cash transactions (usually) involve only the two relevant parties - customer and merchant..." [a32]
	Theft and damage	13	"The project was confronted with theft of sensor nodes..." [a6]
Economic/ financial challenges	Organization/ government	7	"This wifi gateway approach was abandoned due to the SBC's high cost and its power requirements." [a6]
	Personal (low economy)	11	"In rural settings, technology was not widely used for family coordination because it was too costly" [a41]

– *Using DC power:* Incorporating direct current (DC) power, backed by solar energy, can enhance hardware sustainability and maintainability [a25].

3.2.5 Assumptions and Attitudes of Researchers and Participants

We analysed assumptions and attitudes expressed by the authors. Due to the limited length of the paper, only a few points are mentioned here.

– Generally, researchers share a belief in the transformative potential of technology and often presume potential benefits of technological solutions for specific user needs. For example, the mobile verbal autopsy tool in [a50] is assumed to enhance death recording systems. Participants exhibit curiosity, receptiveness and positive attitudes towards new technological solutions such as in [a5], but there are also skeptical attitudes towards technology benefits as reported, e.g., in [a6].

- The importance of user involvement is often emphasized. For instance, the community health workers' enthusiasm for learning and skill improvement in [a34] contributed to collaborative learning in the project. The participants' attitude towards providing feedback is evident through their active engagement with software prototypes in various instances.
- The researchers generally acknowledge that the specific local context requires attention to find sustainable solutions. This includes socio-cultural factors and technical constraints. For example, participants in [a20] were reluctant to accept advice from individuals younger or without children.

4 Discussion and Future Work

The systematic literature review covered UCD4D studies from a wide range of geographic locations (spanning a total of 39 countries) and with strong involvement of both external and local researchers. These results confirm previous reviews and suggest a global relevance and impact of user-centered design approaches.

The concentration of studies in India shows the active involvement of Indian researchers in the field of HCI. This trend can be attributed to the thriving tech industry and educational institutions in India and to the influence researchers abroad. However, there appears to be an unequal geographical distribution of studies, possibly due to limited representation of researchers from certain regions in the field of HCI. This underscores the need for more research in developing countries to gain a deeper understanding of the suitability of user-centered design methods and tools in diverse cultural and infrastructural contexts. It also emphasizes the importance of recognizing the unique challenges and opportunities that arise in these settings.

A few studies were conducted in U.K., China, and Lebanon, which were described as developing region. This prompts us to inquire about the criteria used to classify countries and regions respectively as "developing" or "developed".

All user-centred design processes include activities to understand and specify the context of use. With regard to UCD4D projects, researchers even more emphasize their unique local context that requires an adaptation of user-centered design methods to address existing challenges (e.g., infrastructure issues, illiteracy and cultural issues). This promotion of local solutions may be valuable not only in a UCD4D context.

In the future, we plan to extend the literature review by deepening the analysis of assumptions and attitudes in UCD4D initiatives. We want to use the experiences gained from our case study reported in [2] and insights from this literature review to develop a UCD framework adapted for use in development contexts.

Appendix: List of Papers

ID	Publication Title
1	*Wyche, Susan. "Considering cultural probes in HCI4D/ICTD research." Interactions 27.1 (2019): 80–83*
2	*Wyche, Susan, George Hope Chidziwisano, Florence Uwimbabazi, and Nightingale Simiyu. "Defamiliarizing the Domestic: Exploring" M-Kopa Solar "and Sustainable Practices in Rural Kenyan Households." In Proceedings of the 1st ACM SIGCAS Conference on Computing and Sustainable Societies, pp. 1–11. 2018*
3	*Pecknold, Kara. "Dialogue through design: visual communication across the cultural divide." Proceedings of the seventh ACM conference on Creativity and cognition. 2009*
4	*Dittoh, Francis, Hans Akkermans, Victor De Boer, Anna Bon, Wendeline Tuyp, and Andre Baart. "Information access for low-resource environments." In Proceedings of the 3rd ACM SIGCAS conference on computing and sustainable societies, pp. 325–326. 2020*
5	*Motahar, T., Farden, M. F., Sarkar, D. P., Islam, M. A., Cabrera, M. E., & Cakmak, M. (2019, October). SHEBA: a low-cost assistive robot for older adults in the developing world. In 2019 28th IEEE International Conference on Robot and Human Interactive Communication (RO-MAN) (pp. 1–8). IEEE*
6	*Knoche, Hendrik, PR Sheshagiri Rao, and Jeffrey Huang. "The missing H in ICTD: Lessons learned from the development of an agricultural decision support tool." Proceedings of Mobile HCI and Technical ICTD: A Methodological Perspective Workshop. 2010*
7	*Talukdar, Neeraj, Avinandan Basu, and Ravi Mokashi Punekar. "Upchar: A medi-kit to ensure adherence to TB treatment in India." Proceedings of the 7th Indian Conference on Human-Computer Interaction. 2015*
8	*Teka, Degif, Yvonne Dittrich, and Mesfin Kifle. "Usability challenges in an Ethiopian software development organization." Proceedings of the 9th International Workshop on Cooperative and Human Aspects of Software Engineering. 2016*
9	*Akinola, Olalekan S., and Adepoju Temilola. "Usability Study of Some Selected Functional Websites in Nigeria." African Journal of Computing & ICT May 5.3 (2012): 57–70*
10	*Medhi, Indrani. "User-centered design for development." interactions 14.4 (2007): 12–14*
11	*Teka, Degif, Yvonne Dittrich, and Mesfin Kifle. "Adapting lightweight user-centered design with the scrum-based development process." Proceedings of the 2018 International Conference on Software Engineering in Africa. 2018*
12	*Coetzer, Jeanne. "Application of HCI design principles in overcoming information illiteracy: case of a m-health application for a rural community in South Africa." 2018 International Conference on Intelligent and Innovative Computing Applications (Iconic). IEEE, 2018*
13	*Ebardo, Ryan A., and Nelson J. Celis. "Barriers to the adoption of electronic medical records in select Philippine hospitals: A case study approach." Proceedings of the 2019 5th International Conference on Computing and Artificial Intelligence. 2019*

(continued)

(continued)

ID	Publication Title
14	*Kolko, Beth E., Emma J. Rose, and Erica J. Johnson. "Communication as information-seeking: the case for mobile social software for developing regions." Proceedings of the 16th international conference on World Wide Web. 2007*
15	*Chaudhry, Sarah, Fakhra Batool, Abdul Hafeez Muhammad, and Ansar Siddique. "Designing an Online Appointment System for Semiliterate Users." Intelligent Automation & Soft Computing 28, no. 2 (2021)*
16	*da Rosa, Isaias Barreto, and David Ribeiro Lamas. "Designing mobile access to DSpace-based digital libraries." Proceedings of the International Working Conference on Advanced Visual Interfaces. 2012*
17	*Dittrich, Y., Vaidyanathan, L., Gonsalves, T. A., & Jhunjhunwala, A. (2017, May). Developing e-banking services for rural India: making use of socio-technical prototypes. In 2017 IEEE/ACM 39th International Conference on Software Engineering Companion (ICSE-C) (pp. 204–206). IEEE*
18	*Kolko, Beth, Cynthia Putnam, Emma Rose, and Erica Johnson. "Reflection on research methodologies for ubicomp in developing contexts." Personal and Ubiquitous Computing 15 (2011): 575–583.*
19	*Di Giovanni, Pasquale, Marco Romano, Monica Sebillo, Genoveffa Tortora, Giuliana Vitiello, Tamara Ginige, Lasanthi De Silva, Jeevani Goonethilaka, Gihan Wikramanayake, and Athula Ginige. "User centered scenario based approach for developing mobile interfaces for Social Life Networks." In 2012 First International Workshop on Usability and Accessibility Focused Requirements Engineering (UsARE), pp. 18–24. IEEE, 2012*
20	*Bekele, Rahel, Iris Groher, Johannes Sametinger, Tesfaye Biru, Christiane Floyd, Gustav Pomberger, and Peter Oppelt. "User-centered design in developing countries: a case study of a sustainable intercultural healthcare platform in Ethiopia." In 2019 IEEE/ACM symposium on software engineering in Africa (SEiA), pp. 11–15. IEEE, 2019*
21	*Mugwanya, Raymond, and Gary Marsden. "Using paper prototyping as a rapid participatory design technique in the design of MLCAT-a lecture podcasting tool." (2011)*
22	*Maunder, Andrew, Gary Marsden, Dominic Gruijters, and Edwin Blake. "Designing interactive systems for the developing world-reflections on user-centred design." In 2007 International Conference on Information and Communication Technologies and Development, pp. 1–8. IEEE, 2007*
23	*Ibtasam, Samia, Lubna Razaq, Haider W. Anwar, Hamid Mehmood, Kushal Shah, Jennifer Webster, Neha Kumar, and Richard Anderson. "Knowledge, access, and decision-making: Women's financial inclusion in Pakistan." In Proceedings of the 1st ACM SIGCAS Conference on Computing and Sustainable Societies, pp. 1–12. 2018*
24	*Perrier, Trevor, Elizabeth K. Harrington, Keshet Ronen, Daniel Matemo, John Kinuthia, Grace John-Stewart, Richard Anderson, and Jennifer A. Unger. "Male partner engagement in family planning SMS conversations at Kenyan health clinics." In Proceedings of the 1st ACM SIGCAS Conference on Computing and Sustainable Societies, pp. 1–11. 2018.*

(continued)

(*continued*)

ID	Publication Title
25	Douglas, Gerald P., Zach Landis-Lewis, and Harry Hochheiser. "Simplicity and usability: lessons from a touchscreen electronic medical record system in Malawi." interactions 18.6 (2011): 50–53
26	Pearson, Jennifer, and Simon Robinson. "Developing our world views." Interactions 20.2 (2013): 68–71
27	Ndulue, Chinenye, and Rita Orji. "Developing persuasive mobile games for African rural audiences: challenges implementing the persuasive techniques." Adjunct Publication of the 27th Conference on User Modeling, Adaptation and Personalization. 2019
28	Luz, Saturnino, and Masood Masoodian. "Involving geographically distributed users in the design of an interactive system." Proceedings of the Fifteenth Australasian User Interface Conference-Volume 150. 2014
29	Sharma, Sumita, Blessin Varkey, Krishnaveni Achary, Jaakko Hakulinen, Markku Turunen, Tomi Heimonen, Saurabh Srivastava, and Nitendra Rajput. "Designing gesture-based applications for individuals with developmental disabilities: guidelines from user studies in India." ACM Transactions on Accessible Computing (TACCESS) 11, no. 1 (2018): 1–27
30	Leal, Débora De Castro, Max Krüger, Vanessa Teles E. Teles, Carlos Antônio Teles E. Teles, Denise Machado Cardoso, Dave Randall, and Volker Wulf. "Digital technology at the edge of capitalism: Experiences from the Brazilian Amazon rainforest." ACM Transactions on Computer-Human Interaction (TOCHI) 28, no. 3 (2021): 1–39.39
31	Karusala, Naveena, Isaac Holeman, and Richard Anderson. "Engaging identity, assets, and constraints in designing for resilience." Proceedings of the ACM on Human-Computer Interaction 3.CSCW (2019): 1–23
32	Vashistha, Aditya, Richard Anderson, and Shrirang Mare. "Examining the use and non-use of mobile payment systems for merchant payments in India." Proceedings of the 2nd ACM SIGCAS Conference on Computing and Sustainable Societies. 2019
33	Nkwo, Makuochi, and Rita Orji. "Socially responsive ecommerce platforms: Design implications for online marketplaces in developing African nation." Adjunct Publication of the 27th Conference on User Modeling, Adaptation and Personalization. 2019
34	Yadav, Deepika, Anushka Bhandari, and Pushpendra Singh. "LEAP: Scaffolding collaborative learning of community health workers in India." Proceedings of the ACM on Human-Computer Interaction 3.CSCW (2019): 1–27
35	Kumar, Neha, Azra Ismail, Samyukta Sherugar, and Rajesh Chandwani. "Restoration work: Responding to everyday challenges of HIV outreach." Proceedings of the ACM on Human-Computer Interaction 3, no. CSCW (2019): 1–26
36	Ahmed, Syed Faiz, Pratyasha Saha, and SM Taiabul Haque. "Technology adoption dynamics of the press workers in Bangladesh." Proceedings of the 3rd ACM SIGCAS Conference on Computing and Sustainable Societies. 2020

(*continued*)

(continued)

ID	Publication Title
37	*Mehmood, Hamid, Tallal Ahmad, Lubna Razaq, Shrirang Mare, Maryem Zafar Usmani, Richard Anderson, and Agha Ali Raza. "Towards digitization of collaborative savings among low-income groups." Proceedings of the ACM on Human-Computer Interaction 3, no. CSCW (2019): 1–30*
38	*Hertzum, Morten, Veerendra Veer Singh, Torkil Clemmensen, Dineshkumar Singh, Stefano Valtolina, José Abdelnour-Nocera, and Xiangang Qin. "A mobile app for supporting sustainable fishing practices in Alibaug." interactions 25, no. 3 (2018): 40–45*
39	*Yu, Sarah, and Samia Ibtasam. "A qualitative exploration of mobile money in Ghana." Proceedings of the 1st ACM SIGCAS Conference on Computing and Sustainable Societies. 2018*
40	*Wyche, Susan P. "Designing for everyday interactions in HCI4D." Interactions 18.2 (2011): 52–56*
41	*Oduor, Erick, Carman Neustaedter, and Kate Hennessy. "The design and evaluation of a photograph-sharing application for rural and urban Kenyan families." Personal and Ubiquitous Computing 20 (2016): 615–633*
42	*Sterling, Sarah Revi, Leslie Dodson, and Hawra Al-Rabaan. "The fog phone: water, women, and HCID." Interactions 21.6 (2014): 42–45*
43	*Kumar, Neha, Naveena Karusala, Aaditeshwar Seth, and Biswajit Patra. "Usability, tested?." interactions 24, no. 4 (2017): 74–77*
44	*Cannanure, Vikram Kamath, Justin Souvenir Niweteto, Yves Thierry Adji, Akpe Y. Hermann, Kaja K. Jasinska, Timothy X. Brown, and Amy Ogan. "I'm fine where I am, but I want to do more: Exploring Teacher Aspirations in Rural Côte d'Ivoire." In Proceedings of the 3rd ACM SIGCAS Conference on Computing and Sustainable Societies, pp. 1–12. 2020*
45	*He, Shengfan, Lijun Jiang, Zhelin Li, and Xi Zhang. "Commucity: A social network system for the non-resident elderly in big cities in China." In Proceedings of the second international symposium of Chinese CHI, pp. 97–102. 2014*
46	*Sultana, Sharifa, Syed Ishtiaque Ahmed, and Jeffrey M. Rzeszotarski. "Seeing in context: Traditional visual communication practices in rural bangladesh." Proceedings of the ACM on Human-Computer Interaction 4.CSCW3 (2021): 1–31*
47	*Somanath, Sowmya, Lora Oehlberg, Janette Hughes, Ehud Sharlin, and Mario Costa Sousa. "'Maker'within constraints: Exploratory study of young learners using Arduino at a high school in India." In Proceedings of the 2017 CHI conference on human factors in computing systems, pp. 96–108. 2017*
48	*Lazem, Shaimaa. "A case study for sensitising Egyptian engineering students to user-experience in technology design." Proceedings of the 7th Annual Symposium on Computing for Development. 2016*
49	*Prasad, Vishnu, Richard Shallam, Alok Sharma, Delvin Varghese, and Devansh Mehta. "A Hybrid Multi-Modal System for Conducting Virtual Workshops Using Interactive Voice Response and the WhatsApp Business API." In Extended Abstracts of the 2021 CHI Conference on Human Factors in Computing Systems, pp. 1–6. 2021*

(continued)

(continued)

ID	Publication Title
50	Bird, Jon, Peter Byass, Kathleen Kahn, Paul Mee, and Edward Fottrell. "A matter of life and death: practical and ethical constraints in the development of a mobile verbal autopsy tool." In Proceedings of the SIGCHI conference on human factors in computing systems, pp. 1489–1498. 2013
51	Dell, Nicola Lee. "A mobile point-of-care diagnostic system for low-resource settings." CHI'14 Extended Abstracts on Human Factors in Computing Systems. 2014. 939–944
52	Kazakos, K., Asthana, S., Balaam, M., Duggal, M., Holden, A., Jamir, L., Kannuri, N.K., Kumar, S., Manindla, A.R., Manikam, S.A. and Murthy, G.V.S., 2016, May. A real-time ivr platform for community radio. In Proceedings of the 2016 CHI Conference on Human Factors in Computing Systems (pp. 343–354).
53	Doerflinger, Joerg, Andy Dearden, and Tom Gross. "A software development methodology for sustainable ICTD solutions." CHI'13 Extended Abstracts on Human Factors in Computing Systems. 2013. 2371–2374
54	Kolko, Beth E., Alexis Hope, Waylon Brunette, Karen Saville, Wayne Gerard, Michael Kawooya, and Robert Nathan. "Adapting collaborative radiological practice to low-resource environments." In Proceedings of the ACM 2012 conference on Computer Supported Cooperative Work, pp. 97–106. 2012
55	Gorman, Trina, Emma Rose, Judith Yaaqoubi, Andrew Bayor, and Beth Kolko. "Adapting usability testing for oral, rural users." In Proceedings of the SIGCHI Conference on Human Factors in Computing Systems, pp. 1437–1440. 2011
56	Gitau, Shikoh, Gary Marsden, and Jonathan Donner. "After access: challenges facing mobile-only internet users in the developing world." Proceedings of the SIGCHI conference on human factors in computing systems. 2010
57	Pal, Joyojeet, Anandhi Viswanathan, Priyank Chandra, Anisha Nazareth, Vaishnav Kameswaran, Hariharan Subramonyam, Aditya Johri, Mark S. Ackerman, and Sile O'Modhrain. "Agency in assistive technology adoption: visual impairment and smartphone use in Bangalore." In Proceedings of the 2017 CHI conference on human factors in computing systems, pp. 5929–5940. 2017.
58	Naseem, Mustafa, Bilal Saleem, Sacha St-Onge Ahmad, Jay Chen, and Agha Ali Raza. "An empirical comparison of technologically mediated advertising in under-connected populations." In Proceedings of the 2020 CHI conference on human factors in computing systems, pp. 1–13. 2020
59	Molapo, Maletsabisa, Melissa Densmore, and Limpho Morie. "Apps and skits: Enabling new forms of village-to-clinic feedback for rural health education." Proceedings of the 7th Annual Symposium on Computing for Development. 2016
60	Sajjad, Umaira Uzma, and Suleman Shahid. "Baby + a mobile application to support pregnant women in Pakistan." Proceedings of the 18th international conference on human-computer interaction with mobile devices and services adjunct. 2016
61	Vashistha, Aditya, Pooja Sethi, and Richard Anderson. "BSpeak: An accessible voice-based crowdsourcing marketplace for low-income blind people." Proceedings of the 2018 CHI conference on human factors in computing systems. 2018

(continued)

(continued)

ID	Publication Title
62	*Densmore, Melissa. "Claim mobile: When to fail a technology." Proceedings of the SIGCHI conference on human factors in computing systems. 2012*
63	*Kotut, Lindah, Neelma Bhatti, Morva Saaty, Derek Haqq, Timothy L. Stelter, and D. Scott McCrickard. "Clash of times: Respectful technology space for integrating community stories in intangible exhibits." In Proceedings of the 2020 CHI Conference on Human Factors in Computing Systems, pp. 1–13. 2020*
64	*Hutchful, David, Akhil Matur, Edward Cutrell, and Apurva Joshi. "Cloze: An authoring tool for teachers with low computer proficiency." In Proceedings of the 4th ACM/IEEE international conference on information and communication technologies and development, pp. 1–10. 2010*
65	*Madaio, Michael A., Evelyn Yarzebinski, Vikram Kamath, Benjamin D. Zinszer, Joelle Hannon-Cropp, Fabrice Tanoh, Yapo Hermann Akpe, Axel Blahoua Seri, Kaja K. Jasińska, and Amy Ogan. "Collective support and independent learning with a voice-based literacy technology in rural communities." In Proceedings of the 2020 CHI Conference on Human Factors in Computing Systems, pp. 1–14. 2020*
66	*Ho, Melissa R. "Communication and computing in health facilities of southwest Uganda." CHI'10 Extended Abstracts on Human Factors in Computing Systems. 2010. 4207–4212*
67	*Ghosh, Ishita. "Contextualizing intermediated use in the developing world: findings from India & Ghana." Proceedings of the 2016 CHI Conference on Human Factors in Computing Systems. 2016*
68	*Wyche, Susan P., Thomas N. Smyth, Marshini Chetty, Paul M. Aoki, and Rebecca E. Grinter. "Deliberate interactions: characterizing technology use in Nairobi, Kenya." In Proceedings of the SIGCHI conference on human factors in computing systems, pp. 2593–2602. 2010*
69	*Sultana, Sharifa, François Guimbretière, Phoebe Sengers, and Nicola Dell. "Design within a patriarchal society: Opportunities and challenges in designing for rural women in bangladesh." In Proceedings of the 2018 CHI conference on human factors in computing systems, pp. 1–13. 2018*
70	*Wong-Villacres, Marisol, Arkadeep Kumar, Aditya Vishwanath, Naveena Karusala, Betsy DiSalvo, and Neha Kumar. "Designing for intersections." In Proceedings of the 2018 Designing Interactive Systems Conference, pp. 45–58. 2018*
71	*Tomico, Oscar, V. O. Winthagen, and M. M. G. Van Heist. "Designing for, with or within: 1st, 2nd and 3rd person points of view on designing for systems." Proceedings of the 7th Nordic Conference on Human-Computer Interaction: Making Sense Through Design. 2012*
72	*Bidwell, Nicola J., Thomas Reitmaier, Gary Marsden, and Susan Hansen. "Designing with mobile digital storytelling in rural Africa." In Proceedings of the SIGCHI conference on human factors in computing systems, pp. 1593–1602. 2010*
73	*Pritchard, Gary W., and John Vines. "Digital apartheid: an ethnographic account of racialised hci in Cape Town hip-hop." Proceedings of the SIGCHI Conference on Human Factors in Computing Systems. 2013*

(continued)

(continued)

ID	Publication Title
74	Pal, Joyojeet, Priyank Chandra, Vaishnav Kameswaran, Aakanksha Parameshwar, Sneha Joshi, and Aditya Johri. "Digital payment and its discontents: Street shops and the Indian government's push for cashless transactions." In Proceedings of the 2018 CHI Conference on Human Factors in Computing Systems, pp. 1–13. 2018
75	DeRenzi, Brian, Neal Lesh, Tapan Parikh, Clayton Sims, Werner Maokla, Mwajuma Chemba, Yuna Hamisi, David S hellenberg, Marc Mitchell, and Gaetano Borriello. "E-IMCI: Improving pediatric health care in low-income countries." In Proceedings of the SIGCHI conference on human factors in computing systems, pp. 753–762. 2008
76	Ahmed, Syed Ishtiaque, Steven J. Jackson, Maruf Zaber, Mehrab Bin Morshed, Md Habibullah Bin Ismail, and Sharmin Afrose. "Ecologies of use and design: individual and social practices of mobile phone use within low-literate rickshawpuller communities in urban Bangladesh." In Proceedings of the 4th Annual Symposium on Computing for Development, pp. 1–10. 2013
77	Weld, Galen, Trevor Perrier, Jenny Aker, Joshua E. Blumenstock, Brian Dillon, Adalbertus Kamanzi, Editha Kokushubira, Jennifer Webster, and Richard J. Anderson. "eKichabi: information access through basic mobile phones in rural Tanzania." In Proceedings of the 2018 CHI conference on human factors in computing systems, pp. 1–12. 2018
78	Poon, Anthony, Sarah Giroux, Parfait Eloundou-Enyegue, François Guimbretière, and Nicola Dell. "Engaging high school students in cameroon with exam practice quizzes via sms and whatsapp." In Proceedings of the 2019 CHI Conference on Human Factors in Computing Systems, pp. 1–13. 2019
79	Perrier, Trevor, Nicola Dell, Brian DeRenzi, Richard Anderson, John Kinuthia, Jennifer Unger, and Grace John-Stewart. "Engaging pregnant women in Kenya with a hybrid computer-human SMS communication system." In Proceedings of the 33rd Annual ACM Conference on Human Factors in Computing Systems, pp. 1429–1438. 2015
80	Ahmed, Syed Ishtiaque, Md Romael Haque, Irtaza Haider, Jay Chen, and Nicola Dell. ""Everyone Has Some Personal Stuff" Designing to Support Digital Privacy with Shared Mobile Phone Use in Bangladesh." In Proceedings of the 2019 CHI Conference on Human Factors in Computing Systems, pp. 1–13. 2019
81	Densmore, Melissa. "Experiences with bulk SMS for health financing in Uganda." CHI'12 Extended Abstracts on Human Factors in Computing Systems. 2012. 383–398
82	Chopra, Manu, Indrani Medhi Thies, Joyojeet Pal, Colin Scott, William Thies, and Vivek Seshadri. "Exploring crowdsourced work in low-resource settings." In Proceedings of the 2019 CHI Conference on Human Factors in Computing Systems, pp. 1–13. 2019
83	Oduor, Erick, Carolyn Pang, Charles Wachira, Rachel KE Bellamy, Timothy Nyota, Sekou L. Remy, Aisha Walcott-Bryant, Wycliffe Omwanda, and Julius Mbeya. "Exploring rural community practices in HIV management for the design of technology for hypertensive patients living with HIV." In Proceedings of the 2019 on Designing Interactive Systems Conference, pp. 1595–1606. 2019

(continued)

(*continued*)

ID	Publication Title
84	Mathur, Akhil, and Sharad Jaiswal. *"Exploring the interplay between community media and mobile web in developing regions." Proceedings of the 15th international conference on Human-computer interaction with mobile devices and services. 2013*
85	Mehta, Devansh, Alok Sharma, Ramaravind K. Kommiya Mothilal, Chiraag, Anurag Shukla, Vishnu Prasad, William Thies, Venkanna U, Colin Scott, and Amit Sharma. *"Facilitating Media Distribution with Monetary Incentives." In Extended Abstracts of the 2020 CHI Conference on Human Factors in Computing Systems, pp. 1–7. 2020*
86	Myllynpää, Ville, Jani Haakana, Julius Virtanen, and Erkki Sutinen. *"Holistic Model for Designing a Climate Service Application on the KaiOS Platform." In Extended Abstracts of the 2020 CHI Conference on Human Factors in Computing Systems, pp. 1–8. 2020.*
87	Wyche, Susan P., Andrea Forte, and Sarita Yardi Schoenebeck. *"Hustling online: understanding consolidated facebook use in an informal settlement in Nairobi." Proceedings of the SIGCHI conference on human factors in computing systems. 2013*
88	Jacobs, Jennifer, and Amit Zoran. *"Hybrid Practice in the Kalahari: Design Collaboration through Digital Tools and Hunter-Gatherer Craft." CHI. Vol. 15. 2015*
89	Yadav, Deepika, Prerna Malik, Kirti Dabas, and Pushpendra Singh. *"Illustrating the Gaps and Needs in the Training Support of Community Health Workers in India." In Proceedings of the 2021 CHI Conference on Human Factors in Computing Systems, pp. 1–16. 2021*
90	Sambasivan, Nithya, and Paul M. Aoki. *"Imagined connectivities: synthesized conceptions of public Wi-Fi in urban India." Proceedings of the 2017 CHI Conference on Human Factors in Computing Systems. 2017*
91	Kumar, Anuj, Pooja Reddy, Anuj Tewari, Rajat Agrawal, and Matthew Kam. *"Improving literacy in developing countries using speech recognition-supported games on mobile devices." In Proceedings of the SIGCHI conference on human Factors in Computing systems, pp. 1149–1158. 2012*
92	Motlhabi, Michael B., William D. Tucker, Mariam B. Parker, and Meryl Glaser. *"Improving usability and correctness of a mobile tool to help a deaf person with pharmaceutical instruction." In Proceedings of the 4th Annual Symposium on Computing for Development, pp. 1–10. 2013*
93	Giglitto, Danilo, Shaimaa Lazem, and Anne Preston. *"In the eye of the student: An intangible cultural heritage experience, with a human-computer interaction twist." Proceedings of the 2018 CHI Conference on Human Factors in Computing Systems. 2018*
94	Chandra, Priyank. *"Informality and invisibility: Traditional technologies as tools for collaboration in an informal market." Proceedings of the 2017 CHI conference on human factors in computing systems. 2017*
95	Sambasivan, Nithya, Ed Cutrell, Kentaro Toyama, and Bonnie Nardi. *"Intermediated technology use in developing communities." In Proceedings of the SIGCHI Conference on Human Factors in Computing Systems, pp. 2583–2592. 2010*

(*continued*)

(continued)

ID	Publication Title
96	Okolo, Chinasa T., Srujana Kamath, Nicola Dell, and Aditya Vashistha. ""It cannot do all of my work": community health worker perceptions of AI-enabled mobile health applications in rural India." In Proceedings of the 2021 CHI Conference on Human Factors in Computing Systems, pp. 1–20. 2021
97	Razaq, Samia, Amna Batool, Umair Ali, Muhammad Salman Khalid, Umar Saif, and Mustafa Naseem. "Iterative Design of an Immunization Information System in Pakistan." In Proceedings of the 7th Annual Symposium on Computing for Development, pp. 1–10. 2016
98	Raza, Agha Ali, Farhan Ul Haq, Zain Tariq, Mansoor Pervaiz, Samia Razaq, Umar Saif, and Roni Rosenfeld. "Job opportunities through entertainment: Virally spread speech-based services for low-literate users." In Proceedings of the SIGCHI conference on human factors in computing systems, pp. 2803–2812. 2013
99	Randhawa, Shan M., Tallal Ahmad, Jay Chen, and Agha Ali Raza. "Karamad: A Voice-based Crowdsourcing Platform for Underserved Populations." In Proceedings of the 2021 CHI Conference on Human Factors in Computing Systems, pp. 1–15. 2021
100	Medhi-Thies, Indrani, Pedro Ferreira, Nakull Gupta, Jacki O'Neill, and Edward Cutrell. "KrishiPustak: a social networking system for low-literate farmers." In Proceedings of the 18th ACM conference on computer supported cooperative work & social computing, pp. 1670–1681. 2015
101	Pendse, Sachin R., Faisal M. Lalani, Munmun De Choudhury, Amit Sharma, and Neha Kumar. ""Like Shock Absorbers": understanding the human infrastructures of technology-mediated mental health support." In Proceedings of the 2020 CHI Conference on Human Factors in Computing Systems, pp. 1–14. 2020
102	Chidziwisano, George Hope, and Susan Wyche. "M-kulinda: Using a sensor-based technology probe to explore domestic security in rural kenya." Proceedings of the 2018 CHI conference on human factors in computing systems. 2018
103	Maunder, Andrew, Gary Marsden, and Richard Harper. "Making the link—providing mobile media for novice communities in the developing world." International Journal of Human-Computer Studies 69.10 (2011): 647–657
104	Chandra, Priyank, Syed Ishtiaque Ahmed, and Joyojeet Pal. "Market practices and the bazaar: Technology consumption in ICT markets in the global south." Proceedings of the 2017 CHI conference on human factors in computing systems. 2017
105	Tuli, Anupriya, Shaan Chopra, Pushpendra Singh, and Neha Kumar. "Menstrual (Im) mobilities and safe spaces." In Proceedings of the 2020 CHI Conference on Human Factors in Computing Systems, pp. 1–15. 2020
106	Wyche, Susan, Nightingale Simiyu, and Martha E. Othieno. "Mobile phones as amplifiers of social inequality among rural Kenyan women." ACM Transactions on Computer-Human Interaction (TOCHI) 23.3 (2016): 1–19
107	Kumar, Neha, and Richard J. Anderson. "Mobile phones for maternal health in rural India." Proceedings of the 33rd annual acm conference on human factors in computing systems. 2015

(continued)

(continued)

ID	Publication Title
108	*Kumar, Neha, and Tapan S. Parikh. "Mobiles, music, and materiality." Proceedings of the SIGCHI conference on human factors in computing systems. 2013*
109	*Therias, Emeline, Jon Bird, and Paul Marshall. "Mas tecnologia, más cambio? investigating an educational technology project in rural peru." Proceedings of the 33rd Annual ACM Conference on Human Factors in Computing Systems. 2015*
110	*Unnikrishnan, R., N. Amrita, Alexander Muir, and Bhavani Rao. "Of elephants and nested loops: How to introduce computing to youth in rural India." In Proceedings of the The 15th International Conference on Interaction Design and Children, pp. 137–146. 2016*
111	*Karusala, Naveena, Aditya Vishwanath, Aditya Vashistha, Sunita Kumar, and Neha Kumar. ""Only if you use English you will get to more things" Using Smartphones to Navigate Multilingualism." In Proceedings of the 2018 CHI Conference on Human Factors in Computing Systems, pp. 1–14. 2018*
112	*Cheng, Karen G., Francisco Ernesto, and Khai N. Truong. "Participant and interviewer attitudes toward handheld computers in the context of HIV/AIDS programs in sub-Saharan Africa." Proceedings of the SIGCHI Conference on Human Factors in Computing Systems. 2008*
113	*Mustafa, Maryam, Amna Batool, Beenish Fatima, Fareeda Nawaz, Kentaro Toyama, and Agha Ali Raza. "Patriarchy, maternal health and spiritual healing: Designing maternal health interventions in Pakistan." In Proceedings of the 2020 CHI Conference on Human Factors in Computing Systems, pp. 1–13. 2020*
114	*Wyche, Susan P., and Laura L. Murphy. "Powering the cellphone revolution: findings from mobile phone charging trials in off-grid Kenya." Proceedings of the SIGCHI Conference on Human Factors in Computing Systems. 2013*
115	*Oduor, Erick, Peninah Waweru, Jonathan Lenchner, and Carman Neustaedter. "Practices and technology needs of a network of farmers in Tharaka Nithi, Kenya." In Proceedings of the 2018 CHI conference on human factors in computing systems, pp. 1–11. 2018*
116	*Kirabo, Lynn, Elizabeth Jeanne Carter, Devon Barry, and Aaron Steinfeld. "Priorities, technology, & power: Co-designing an inclusive transit agenda in Kampala, Uganda." In Proceedings of the 2021 CHI Conference on Human Factors in Computing Systems, pp. 1–11. 2021*
117	*Ahmed, Syed Ishtiaque, Md Romael Haque, Shion Guha, Md Rashidujjaman Rifat, and Nicola Dell. "Privacy, security, and surveillance in the Global South: A study of biometric mobile SIM registration in Bangladesh." In Proceedings of the 2017 CHI Conference on Human Factors in Computing Systems, pp. 906–918. 2017*
118	*Nkwo, Makuochi, Banuchitra Suruliraj, and Rita Orji. "Public Perception of Mental Illness: Opportunity for Community-based Collaborative Intervention." Extended Abstracts of the 2020 CHI Conference on Human Factors in Computing Systems. 2020*

(continued)

(continued)

ID	Publication Title
119	Jensen, Kasper L., Heike Winschiers-Theophilus, Kasper Rodil, Naska Winschiers-Goagoses, Gereon K. Kapuire, and Richard Kamukuenjandje. "Putting it in perspective: designing a 3D visualization to contextualize indigenous knowledge in rural Namibia." In Proceedings of the Designing Interactive Systems Conference, pp. 196–199. 2012
120	Raza, A. A., Razaq, S., Raja, A., Naru, R., Gibran, A., Sabri, A.,... & Saif, U. (2016, November). Real-time Automated Surveys among Low-literate Masses using Voice-based Telephone Services. In Proceedings of the 7th Annual Symposium on Computing for Development (pp. 1–4).2016
121	Vashistha, Aditya, Abhinav Garg, and Richard Anderson. "ReCall: Crowdsourcing on basic phones to financially sustain voice forums." Proceedings of the 2019 CHI conference on human factors in computing systems. 2019
122	Vashistha, Aditya, Pooja Sethi, and Richard Anderson. "Respeak: A voice-based, crowd-powered speech transcription system." Proceedings of the 2017 CHI conference on human factors in computing systems. 2017
123	Robinson, S., Pearson, J., Ahire, S., Ahirwar, R., Bhikne, B., Maravi, N., & Jones, M. (2018, April). Revisiting "hole in the wall" computing: Private smart speakers and public slum settings. In Proceedings of the 2018 CHI conference on human factors in computing systems (pp. 1–11)2018
124	Vashistha, A., Cutrell, E., Borriello, G., & Thies, W. Sangeet swara: A community-moderated voice forum in rural india. In Proceedings of the 33rd annual ACM conference on human factors in computing systems (pp. 417–426).2015
125	Sorcar, P., Strauber, B., Loyalka, P., Kumar, N., & Goldman, S. (2017, May). Sidestepping the elephant in the classroom: Using culturally localized technology to teach around taboos. In Proceedings of the 2017
126	Vashistha, A., Cutrell, E., Dell, N., & Anderson, R). Social media platforms for low-income blind people in India. In Proceedings of the 17th international ACM SIGACCESS conference on computers & accessibility (pp. 259–272). 2015
127	Chandwani, Rajesh, and Neha Kumar. "Stitching infrastructures to facilitate telemedicine for low-resource environments." Proceedings of the 2018 CHI Conference on Human Factors in Computing Systems. 2018
128	Vashistha, Aditya, Edward Cutrell, Gaetano Borriello, and William Thies. "Sangeet swara: A community-moderated voice forum in rural india." In Proceedings of the 33rd annual ACM conference on human factors in computing systems, pp. 417–426. 2015
129	Vitos, Michalis, Julia Altenbuchner, Matthias Stevens, Gillian Conquest, Jerome Lewis, and Muki Haklay. "Supporting collaboration with non-literate forest communities in the congo-basin." In Proceedings of the 2017 ACM Conference on Computer Supported Cooperative Work and Social Computing, pp. 1576–1590. 2017
130	DeRenzi, Brian, Nicola Dell, Jeremy Wacksman, Scott Lee, and Neal Lesh. "Supporting community health workers in India through voice-and web-based feedback." In Proceedings of the 2017 CHI conference on human factors in computing systems, pp. 2770–2781. 2017

(continued)

(continued)

ID	Publication Title
131	Jensen, Kasper L., Heike Winschiers-Theophilus, and Kasper Rodil. "Tapping into local lore: toward scalable local mapping and tagging for rural Africa using mobile devices." Proceedings of the 7th Nordic Conference on Human-Computer Interaction: Making Sense Through Design. 2012
132	Wong-Villacres, Marisol, and Shaowen Bardzell. "Technology-mediated parent-child intimacy: designing for ecuadorian families separated by migration." CHI'11 Extended Abstracts on Human Factors in Computing Systems. 2011. 2215–2220
133	Lomas, Derek, Anuj Kumar, Kishan Patel, Dixie Ching, Meera Lakshmanan, Matthew Kam, and Jodi L. Forlizzi. "The power of play: Design lessons for increasing the lifespan of outdated computers." In Proceedings of the SIGCHI Conference on Human Factors in Computing Systems, pp. 2735–2744. 2013
134	Barbareschi, Giulia, Catherine Holloway, Katherine Arnold, Grace Magomere, Wycliffe Ambeyi Wetende, Gabriel Ngare, and Joyce Olenja. "The social network: How people with visual impairment use mobile phones in kibera, Kenya." In Proceedings of the 2020 CHI conference on human factors in computing systems, pp. 1–15. 2020
135	Vashistha, Aditya, Abhinav Garg, Richard Anderson, and Agha Ali Raza. "Threats, abuses, flirting, and blackmail: Gender inequity in social media voice forums." In Proceedings of the 2019 CHI conference on human factors in computing systems, pp. 1–13. 2019
136	Shroff, Geeta, and Matthew Kam. "Towards a design model for women's empowerment in the developing world." Proceedings of the SIGCHI Conference on Human Factors in Computing Systems. 2011
137	Thakkar, Divy, Neha Kumar, and Nithya Sambasivan. "Towards an AI-powered future that works for vocational workers." proceedings of the 2020 CHI Conference on Human Factors in Computing Systems. 2020
138	Toha, Tarik Reza, Md Moyeen Uddin, MD Nayeem Reza, Md Abdullah Al Maruf, Amit Chakraborty, and ABM Alim Al Islam. "Towards making an anonymous and one-stop online reporting system for third-world countries." In Proceedings of the 7th Annual Symposium on Computing for Development, pp. 1–4. 2016
139	Sambasivan, Nithya, and Edward Cutrell. "Understanding negotiation in airtime sharing in low-income microenterprises." Proceedings of the SIGCHI Conference on Human Factors in Computing Systems. 2012
140	Balestrini, Mara, Jon Bird, Paul Marshall, Alberto Zaro, and Yvonne Rogers. "Understanding sustained community engagement: a case study in heritage preservation in rural Argentina." In Proceedings of the SIGCHI Conference on Human Factors in Computing Systems, pp. 2675–2684. 2014
141	Wyche, Susan. "Using cultural probes in new contexts: exploring the benefits of probes in HCI4D/ICTD." Companion Publication of the 2019 Conference on Computer Supported Cooperative Work and Social Computing. 2019
142	Paruthi, Gaurav, and William Thies. "Utilizing DVD players as low-cost offline internet browsers." Proceedings of the SIGCHI Conference on Human Factors in Computing Systems. 2011

(continued)

(continued)

ID	Publication Title
143	Varghese, Delvin, Jay Rainey, Kyle Montague, Tom Bartindale, Patrick Olivier, and Matt Baillie Smith. "Utilizing Participant Voice in Volunteer Training." In Proceedings of the 2020 CHI Conference on Human Factors in Computing Systems, pp. 1–14. 2020
144	Zeb, Kehkashan, Stephen Lindsay, Suleman Shahid, and Matt Jones. "Verbal design: a participatory design approach with illiterate patient user groups." In Proceedings of the 2018 ACM Conference Companion Publication on Designing Interactive Systems, pp. 271–275. 2018
145	Cuendet, Sebastien, Indrani Medhi, Kalika Bali, and Edward Cutrell. "VideoKheti: Making video content accessible to low-literate and novice users." In Proceedings of the SIGCHI conference on human factors in computing systems, pp. 2833–2842. 2013
146	Sambasivan, Nithya, Ed Cutrell, and Kentaro Toyama. "ViralVCD: Tracing information-diffusion paths with low cost media in developing communities." Proceedings of the SIGCHI Conference on Human Factors in Computing Systems. 2010
147	Raza, Agha Ali, Zain Tariq, Shan Randhawa, Bilal Saleem, Awais Athar, Umar Saif, and Roni Rosenfeld. "Voice-based quizzes for measuring knowledge retention in under-connected populations." In Proceedings of the 2019 CHI conference on human factors in computing systems, pp. 1–14. 2019
148	Lazem, Shaimaa, and Hussein Aly Jad. "We play we learn: Exploring the value of digital educational games in Rural Egypt." Proceedings of the 2017 CHI Conference on Human Factors in Computing Systems. 2017
149	Chandwani, Rajesh, and Vaibhavi Kulkarni. "Who's the Doctor? Physicians' Perception of Internet Informed Patients in India." Proceedings of the 2016 CHI Conference on Human Factors in Computing Systems. 2016
150	Vashistha, Aditya, Fabian Okeke, Richard Anderson, and Nicola Dell. ""You Can Always Do Better!" The Impact of Social Proof on Participant Response Bias." In Proceedings of the 2018 chi conference on human factors in computing systems, pp. 1–13. 2018
151	Dell, Nicola, Vidya Vaidyanathan, Indrani Medhi, Edward Cutrell, and William Thies. "" Yours is better!" participant response bias in HCI." In Proceedings of the sigchi conference on human factors in computing systems, pp. 1321–1330. 2012
152	Rahman, Rifat, Md Rishadur Rahman, Nafis Irtiza Tripto, Mohammed Eunus Ali, Sajid Hasan Apon, and Rifat Shahriyar. "AdolescentBot: Understanding opportunities for chatbots in combating adolescent sexual and reproductive health problems in Bangladesh." In Proceedings of the 2021 CHI Conference on Human Factors in Computing Systems, pp. 1–15. 2021
153	Kapuire, Gereon Koch, Heike Winschiers-Theophilus, and Edwin Blake. "An insider perspective on community gains: A subjective account of a Namibian rural communities' perception of a long-term participatory design project." International Journal of Human-Computer Studies 74 (2015): 124–143

(continued)

(continued)

ID	Publication Title
154	*Thinyane, Hannah, and Karthik S. Bhat. "Apprise: Supporting the critical-agency of victims of human trafficking in Thailand." Proceedings of the 2019 CHI Conference on Human Factors in Computing Systems. 2019*
155	*Raza, Agha Ali, Bilal Saleem, Shan Randhawa, Zain Tariq, Awais Athar, Umar Saif, and Roni Rosenfeld. "Baang: A viral speech-based social platform for under-connected populations." In Proceedings of the 2018 CHI conference on human factors in computing systems, pp. 1–12. 2018*
156	*Ismail, Azra, Naveena Karusala, and Neha Kumar. "Bridging disconnected knowledges for community health." Proceedings of the ACM on Human-Computer Interaction 2.CSCW (2018): 1–27*
157	*Leshed, Gilly, Masha Rosca, Michael Huang, Liza Mansbach, Yicheng Zhu, and Juan Nicolás Hernández-Aguilera. "CalcuCafé: Designing for collaboration among coffee farmers to calculate costs of production." Proceedings of the ACM on Human-Computer Interaction 2, no. CSCW (2018): 1–26*
158	*Karusala, Naveena, Aditya Vishwanath, Arkadeep Kumar, Aman Mangal, and Neha Kumar. "Care as a resource in underserved learning environments." Proceedings of the ACM on Human-Computer Interaction 1, no. CSCW (2017): 1–22*
159	*Arawjo, Ian, Ariam Mogos, Steven J. Jackson, Tapan Parikh, and Kentaro Toyama. "Computing education for intercultural learning: Lessons from the Nairobi play project." Proceedings of the ACM on Human-Computer Interaction 3, no. CSCW (2019): 1–24*
160	*Sambasivan, Nithya, Julie Weber, and Edward Cutrell. "Designing a phone broadcasting system for urban sex workers in India." Proceedings of the SIGCHI conference on human factors in computing systems. 2011*
161	*Ahmed, Syed Ishtiaque, Md Romael Haque, Jay Chen, and Nicola Dell. "Digital privacy challenges with shared mobile phone use in Bangladesh." Proceedings of the ACM on Human-computer Interaction 1, no. CSCW (2017): 1–20*
162	*Ismail, Azra, and Neha Kumar. "Engaging solidarity in data collection practices for community health." Proceedings of the ACM on Human-Computer Interaction 2.CSCW (2018): 1–24*
163	*Vashistha, Aditya, Neha Kumar, Anil Mishra, and Richard Anderson. "Examining localization approaches for community health." In Proceedings of the 2017 Conference on Designing Interactive Systems, pp. 357–368. 2017.*
164	*Wyche, Susan, April Greenwood, and Brian Samuel Geyer. "Exploring Photography in Rural Kenyan Households: Considering" Relational Objects" in CSCW and HCI." Proceedings of the ACM on Human-Computer Interaction 4.CSCW1 (2020): 1–26*
165	*Yadav, Deepika, Prerna Malik, Kirti Dabas, and Pushpendra Singh. "Feedpal: Understanding opportunities for chatbots in breastfeeding education of women in india." Proceedings of the ACM on Human-Computer Interaction 3, no. CSCW (2019): 1–30*

(continued)

(*continued*)

ID	Publication Title
166	Varanasi, Rama Adithya, René F. Kizilcec, and Nicola Dell. "How teachers in india reconfigure their work practices around a teacher-oriented technology intervention." *Proceedings of the ACM on Human-Computer Interaction 3.CSCW* (2019): 1–21
167	Okeke, Fabian, Beatrice Wasunna, Mercy Amulele, Isaac Holeman, and Nicola Dell. "Including the voice of care recipients in community health feedback loops in rural Kenya." *Proceedings of the ACM on Human-Computer Interaction 3, no. CSCW* (2019): 1–20
168	Bhat, Karthik S., Mohit Jain, and Neha Kumar. "Infrastructuring telehealth in (in) formal patient-doctor contexts." *Proceedings of the ACM on Human-Computer Interaction 5.CSCW2 (2021): 1–28*
169	Tuli, Anupriya, Shruti Dalvi, Neha Kumar, and Pushpendra Singh. ""It'sa girl thing" Examining Challenges and Opportunities around Menstrual Health Education in India." *ACM Transactions on Computer-Human Interaction (TOCHI) 26, no. 5 (2019): 1–24*
170	Swaminathan, Saiganesh, Indrani Medhi Thies, Devansh Mehta, Edward Cutrell, Amit Sharma, and William Thies. "Learn2Earn: Using mobile airtime incentives to bolster public awareness campaigns." *Proceedings of the ACM on Human-Computer Interaction 3, no. CSCW (2019): 1–20*
171	Tuli, Anupriya, Shaan Chopra, Neha Kumar, and Pushpendra Singh. "Learning from and with menstrupedia: Towards menstrual health education in India." *Proceedings of the ACM on Human-Computer Interaction 2, no. CSCW (2018): 1–20*
172	Smyth, Thomas N., John Etherton, and Michael L. Best. "MOSES: Exploring new ground in media and post-conflict reconciliation." *Proceedings of the SIGCHI conference on Human Factors in computing systems. 2010*
173	Ibtasam, Samia, Lubna Razaq, Maryam Ayub, Jennifer R. Webster, Syed Ishtiaque Ahmed, and Richard Anderson. ""My cousin bought the phone for me. I never go to mobile shops." The Role of Family in Women's Technological Inclusion in Islamic Culture." *Proceedings of the ACM on Human-Computer Interaction 3, no. CSCW (2019): 1–33*
174	Kandathil, George, and Erica L. Wagner. "Negotiating Absent Practices and Dormant Features: Discourse as a means of shaping the implementation of a global enterprise system to meet local work culture." *Proceedings of the 2017 CHI Conference on Human Factors in Computing Systems. 2017*
175	Haque, SM Taiabul, Pratyasha Saha, Muhammad Sajidur Rahman, and Syed Ishtiaque Ahmed. "Of Ulti,'hajano', and" Matachetar otanetak datam "Exploring Local Practices of Exchanging Confidential and Sensitive Information in Urban Bangladesh." *Proceedings of the ACM on Human-Computer Interaction 3, no. CSCW (2019): 1–22*
176	Sultana, Sharifa, Syed Ishtiaque Ahmed, and Susan R. Fussell. ""Parar-daktar Understands My Problems Better" Disentangling the Challenges to Designing Better Access to Healthcare in Rural Bangladesh." *Proceedings of the ACM on Human-Computer Interaction 3.CSCW (2019): 1–27*

(*continued*)

(continued)

ID	Publication Title
177	Jack, Margaret C., Pang Sovannaroth, and Nicola Dell. ""Privacy is not a concept, but a way of dealing with life" Localization of Transnational Technology Platforms and Liminal Privacy Practices in Cambodia." Proceedings of the ACM on Human-Computer Interaction 3.CSCW (2019): 1–19
178	Ahmed, Syed Ishtiaque, Steven J. Jackson, Nova Ahmed, Hasan Shahid Ferdous, Md Rashidujjaman Rifat, A. S. M. Rizvi, Shamir Ahmed, and Rifat Sabbir Mansur. "Protibadi: A platform for fighting sexual harassment in urban Bangladesh." In Proceedings of the SIGCHI Conference on Human Factors in Computing Systems, pp. 2695–2704. 2014.
179	Gautam, Aakash, Chandani Shrestha, Deborah Tatar, and Steve Harrison. "Social photo-elicitation: The use of communal production of meaning to hear a vulnerable population." Proceedings of the ACM on Human-Computer Interaction 2, no. CSCW (2018): 1–20.
180	El Ali, Abdallah, Khaled Bachour, Wilko Heuten, and Susanne Boll. "Technology literacy in poor infrastructure environments: characterizing wayfinding strategies in Lebanon." In Proceedings of the 18th International Conference on Human-Computer Interaction with Mobile Devices and Services, pp. 266–277. 2016
181	Kumar, Neha, and Nimmi Rangaswamy. "The mobile media actor-network in urban India." Proceedings of the SIGCHI conference on human factors in computing systems. 2013
182	Karusala, Naveena, and Neha Kumar. "Women's safety in public spaces: Examining the efficacy of panic buttons in New Delhi." Proceedings of the 2017 CHI conference on human factors in computing systems. 2017
183	Ismail, Azra, and Neha Kumar. "AI in global health: the view from the front lines." Proceedings of the 2021 CHI Conference on Human Factors in Computing Systems. 2021
184	Varanasi, Rama Adithya, Aditya Vashistha, Rene F. Kizilcec, and Nicola Dell. "Investigating technostress among teachers in low-income Indian schools." Proceedings of the ACM on Human-Computer Interaction 5, no. CSCW2 (2021): 1–29.
185	Varanasi, Rama Adithya, Aditya Vashistha, and Nicola Dell. "Tag a teacher: A qualitative analysis of WhatsApp-based teacher networks in low-income Indian schools." Proceedings of the 2021 CHI Conference on Human Factors in Computing Systems. 2021
186	Ravi, Prerna, Azra Ismail, and Neha Kumar. "The pandemic shift to remote learning under resource constraints." Proceedings of the ACM on Human-Computer Interaction 5.CSCW2 (2021): 1–28
187	Moitra, Aparna, Naeemul Hassan, Manash Kumar Mandal, Mansurul Bhuiyan, and Syed Ishtiaque Ahmed. "Understanding the challenges for bangladeshi women to participate in# metoo movement." Proceedings of the ACM on Human-Computer Interaction 4, no. GROUP (2020): 1–25

(continued)

(*continued*)

ID	Publication Title
188	*Wyche, Susan. "Using cultural probes in HCI4D/ICTD: a design case study from Bungoma, Kenya." Proceedings of the ACM on Human-Computer Interaction 4.CSCW1 (2020): 1–23*
189	*Bidwell, Nicola J., Masbulele Siya, Gary Marsden, William D. Tucker, Mvuso Tshemese, N. Gaven, Senzo Ntlangano, Simon Robinson, and Kristen ALI Eglinton. "Walking and the social life of solar charging in rural Africa." ACM Transactions on Computer-Human Interaction (TOCHI) 20, no. 4 (2013): 1–33*
190	*Sultana, Sharifa, and Syed Ishtiaque Ahmed. "Witchcraft and hci: Morality, modernity, and postcolonial computing in rural bangladesh." Proceedings of the 2019 CHI Conference on Human Factors in Computing Systems. 2019*

References

1. Anokwa, Y., et al.: Stories from the field: reflections on HCI4D experiences. Inf. Technol. Int. Dev. **5**(4), 101 (2009)
2. Bin Mothana, A., Dittmar, A.: Exploring the applicability of user-centred design practices in rural Yemen. In: Rau, P.-L.P. (ed.) HCII 2021. LNCS, vol. 12772, pp. 277–288. Springer, Cham (2021). https://doi.org/10.1007/978-3-030-77077-8_22
3. Bin Mothana, A.: A systematic literature review on UCD4D studies. In Proceedings of the 33rd European Conference on Cognitive Ergonomics, pp. 1–4 (2022)
4. Booth, A., Sutton, A., Papaioannou, D.: Systematic Approaches to a Successful Literature Review, 2nd edn. Sage, Los Angeles (2016)
5. Dell, N., Kumar, N.: The ins and outs of HCI for development. In: Proceedings of the 2016 CHI Conference on Human Factors in Computing Systems, pp. 2220–2232. ACM (2016)
6. Dray, S.M., Siegel, D.A., Kotzé, P.: Indra's Net: HCI in the developing world. Interactions **10**(2), 28–37 (2003)
7. Heeks, R.: Information and communication technologies, poverty and development. SSRN Electron. J. (1999)
8. Ho, M.R., Smyth, T.N., Kam, M., Dearden, A.: Human-computer interaction for development: the past, present, and future. Inf. Technol. Int. Dev. **5**(4), 1 (2009)
9. Kitchenham, B., Charters, S.: Guidelines for performing systematic literature reviews in software engineering. Citeseer (2007)
10. Maunder, A., Marsden, G., Gruijters, D., Blake, E.: Designing interactive systems for the developing world-reflections on user-centred design. In: Information and Communication Technologies and Development 2007 (ICTD 2007), pp. 1–8. IEEE (2007)
11. Van Biljon, J., Renaud, K.: Reviewing a decade of human-computer interaction for development (HCI4D) research, as one of best's "grand challenges." Afr. J. Inf. Commun. **27**, 1–15 (2021)

Urban Walkability: A Digital Twin Approach for Urban Regenerative Development

Viet Hung Pham[1,2]([✉]) [iD], Malte Wagenfeld[2] [iD], and Regina Bernhaupt[1] [iD]

[1] Eindhoven University of Technology, Het Eeuwsel 53, 5612 AZ Eindhoven,
The Netherlands
{v.h.pham,r.bernhaupt}@tue.nl, malte.wagenfeld@rmit.edu.au
[2] RMIT University, 124 La Trobe Street, Melbourne, VIC 3000, Australia

Abstract. Traditional urban planning methods fall short in addressing the complexities of modern urbanization and environmental challenges. By adopting Generative Design, Virtual Reality, and Digital Twins, the aim is to make urban planning more interactive, accessible, and inclusive. The research is grounded in a comprehensive literature review across related fields, including Digital Twins' dynamic modeling capabilities and Virtual Reality's immersive visualization potential. Initial findings from sit-down interviews with Eindhoven residents reveal critical insights into pedestrian preferences. In my next steps in the PhD, I will focus on developing Virtual Reality prototypes to further examine walkability and Generative Design prototypes to generate urban planning aligning with regenerative development toward walkability. At the end of my PhD, the knowledge from previous prototypes is used to create a tool to simplify urban planning, including multiple stakeholders, to improve walkability in an urban context. This innovative approach promises to contribute significantly to the creation of livable, sustainable urban environments by leveraging cutting-edge technologies to address key challenges in urban walkability and planning.

Keywords: Urban Planning · Virtual Reality · Walkability · Generative Design · Digital Twin

1 Introduction

Current urban planning practices rely on traditional methods and lack the flexibility and immediacy needed to address today's rapid urbanization and environmental challenges [10]. Conventional approaches use two-dimensional mapping, physical scale modes, and standard computer-aided design software for design, visualization, and planning. These methods, while useful for basic planning and zoning decisions, fall short of conveying the full scope of urban planning projects to non-experts and dynamically simulating the impacts of urban interventions. They lack real-time interaction and the ability to easily reflect changes based on stakeholder feedback [5].

Published by Springer Nature Switzerland AG 2024
M. K. Lárusdóttir et al. (Eds.): HCSE 2024, LNCS 14793, pp. 224–232, 2024.
https://doi.org/10.1007/978-3-031-64576-1_13

Regenerative design is a new approach in urban planning that goes beyond minimizing negative impacts to actively improve and revitalize the environment. It is an emerging concept in urban development, with walkability as a key focus in this process. My research proposed a shift towards integrating Digital Twin (DT), Virtual Reality (VR), and Generative Design for urban planning that emphasizes walkability and generative development. A digital twin acts as a digital hub for real-time, interconnected replicas of urban areas, allowing for the analysis and simulation of urban dynamics as the input data for generating urban designs.

VR technology is adopted in this research to enable planners and stakeholders to step into 3D simulations of generated urban designs, experiencing, evaluating, and editing design proposals. This immersive approach enhances understanding and facilitates more informed feedback, fostering collaborative decision-making for stakeholders. Generative design in this research uses algorithms to explore the vast array of design possibilities, generating optimal solutions based on pre-determined goals, constraints, and requirements for walkability.

The final goal of my PhD is to create a framework based on knowledge from VR, DT, and Generative Design prototypes to simplify urban planning toward improving and promoting walkability in urban contexts. The approach not only enhances the clarity and communicability of urban design proposals but also enables a more inclusive decision-making process by involving more community members. The framework can also be used as a reference for adopting and combining VR, DT, and Generative Design in a large and complex context similar to urban planning.

2   Related Work

2.1   Digital Twin

Digital Twin merges the physical and digital realms in urban planning, creating dynamic, data-updated virtual models of cities or components like buildings and infrastructure. This evolution from basic 3D models to intricate, data-driven simulations allows for the detailed visualization, analysis, and prediction of urban development impacts [2]. Central to DTs is the integration of diverse data sources, including Internet of Thing sensors and geographic information systems, enhancing urban planning with accurate simulations for informed decision-making [14]. Serving as both collaborative platforms and decision-support tools, DTs foster the development of smart, sustainable cities by improving urban resilience and facilitating regenerative city planning through case studies on urban growth and environmental management [3].

2.2   Virtual Reality

Virtual Reality is a technology that allows users to interact and immerse themselves in computer-generated surroundings. It has gained significant attention in urban planning due to its potential to revolutionize various aspects of the field. VR's immersive capabilities facilitate a nuanced understanding of urban environments, allowing for the simulation of complex scenarios and the visualization of potential interventions in real time. VR technology offers to test urban design principles and aids in the design of urban space [9]. The application of VR technology in urban design has shown promising results in terms of modeling, design innovation, and expression ability [15]. Portman et al. [12] emphasize the use of VR in architecture, landscape architecture, and environmental planning, highlighting its potential in urban design exploration. Meenar & Kitson [11] discuss the integration of immersive VR technologies in participatory planning, stressing the need for further research on the impact of these tools on enhancing public engagement.

2.3 Urban Planning

Urban planning has evolved significantly, integrating architecture, economics, sociology, and environmental science to address challenges like population growth, climate change, and resource scarcity [7,8]. Emphasizing regenerative development, walkable cities, and green infrastructure, the field now leverages advanced technologies like geographic information systems, Big Data, Internet of Things, and smart city solutions to enhance data-driven insights and decision-making [1,13]. These technologies have transformed urban planning by improving assessments of urban dynamics and encouraging participatory processes, making urban planning a continually evolving discipline aimed to tackle contemporary urban challenges with innovative solutions.

2.4 Walkability

Walkability is a complex concept influenced by a variety of factors, including the built environment, transportation infrastructure, land use, and social and economic conditions. The concept of walkability in urban areas has gained significant attention in recent years as cities around the world experienced issues related to urbanization, sustainability, and the well-being of their residents. Walkability plays an important role in promoting active transportation, reducing automobile dependence, and fostering healthier, more sustainable urban communities [4]. Furthermore, studies by Frank et al. [6] emphasize the correlation between walkable urban environments and improved public health outcomes. From the literature review, the gaps and opportunities for further research in the realm of walkability, set the stage for the exploration of innovative solutions, including DT, VR, and Generative Design, to advance urban walkability and foster generative urban development.

3   Research Problem

3.1   Research Method

To develop a tool that streamlines urban planning with an emphasis on walkability, my research commenced with a comprehensive literature review to understand the current advancements in the field. This informed the formulation of critical research questions aimed at exploring the capabilities of DTs in urban environments to enhance walkability and aid urban planning.

Main research question:

How can a Digital Twin be used to model and simulate urban environments to support urban planning processes that focus on walkability?

Sub questions:

1. How can DTs improve stakeholder engagement in walkability-centric urban planning projects?
2. How can the implementation of a framework using Digital Twin, Virtual Reality, and Generative Design tailored to walkability contribute to regenerative development within the context of urban development?
3. How can the integration of Digital Twin, Virtual Reality, and Generative Design enhance urban planning toward walkability?

The research plan centers on enhancing walkability within urban planning. It aims to answer how DTs, integrated with VR and Generative design, can model and simulate urban environments, thereby supporting walkability-focused urban development. Initial studies focus on conducting interviews to gather pedestrian perspectives, providing crucial insights into the important criteria of walkability in urban contexts. For stakeholder engagement, I will use VR prototypes to immerse urban planners and other stakeholders in virtual urban environments, allowing them to experience and modify designs based on walkability considerations and validating VR's ability to visualize and immerse stakeholders in urban planning. Generative Design prototypes will use the insights from the initial interviews and design requirements to generate urban designs focused on walkability. The interactions of the urban planners with these prototypes are tracked and analyzed to assess their engagement levels and preferences for improving the framework, tailoring it to the needs of urban planning. The research also examines the process of integrating DT, VR, and Generative Design into current urban planning workflows by using quantitative and qualitative data analysis, usability testing, and comparative analysis. The result is expected to reveal the challenges and opportunities presented by these technologies and their impact on the efficiency and effectiveness of urban planning processes.

3.2   Previous Works

The previous work, which included two rounds of interviews with residents of Eindhoven, Netherlands, aimed to capture a wide range of pedestrian perspectives on urban walkability. Using a structured guide with open-ended questions, the first round provided reflective insights into walkability, while the second utilized a go-along method for real-time observations. Approved by the Eindhoven University of Technology's Industrial Design Department ERB board, these interviews will lay the groundwork for my forthcoming research.

3.2.1   Sit-Down Interviews

In sit-down interviews with 14 Eindhoven residents, we explored urban walkability, focusing on personal experiences and challenges of walking in the city. The study revealed walking, biking, and public transport as preferred mobility options, with walking appreciated for its convenience and sustainability. Despite this, factors like time constraints and adverse weather often deterred participants from walking. Many were unfamiliar with the term "walkability" indicating a gap in public awareness. Essential elements for walkability identified included well-maintained pathways, safety, and accessible public transportation, with challenges such as space limitations and noise pollution noted. These insights underscore the complexity of enhancing urban walkability and highlight areas for improvement in urban planning to better accommodate pedestrian needs. The findings from these interviews will inform future DT frameworks, aiming to improve urban design and walkability in Eindhoven, emphasizing the critical role of pedestrian experiences in urban development (Fig. 1).

Fig. 1. Participants pointed out good examples of urban facilities.

3.2.2   Go-Along Interviews

To further explore the subtleties of pedestrian experiences, a subsequent round of go-along interviews was conducted, adopting a method that immersed the researcher and participants in the urban environment of interest. This innovative approach allowed for the collection of real-time data, capturing the participants' interactions with their surroundings and providing a window into the lived experience of walkability. The go-along interviews provided real-time insights into pedestrian interactions with their environment, uncovering the importance of climate-resilient infrastructure, green spaces, and quality public transportation in promoting walkability. Participants highlighted the need for pathways that can withstand adverse weather and the role of greenery in enhancing the walking experience. The quality of public transport was also a key factor in encouraging walking, alongside the availability of amenities within accessible distances. The findings contribute to a broader understanding of pedestrian needs, informing future urban development towards more walkable, livable cities.

3.3   Planned Study and Work

This next phase will focus on developing VR, Generative Design, and Digital Twin prototypes designed to enhance urban planning and integrate the detailed pedestrian insights collected from previous interviews, aiming to create more walkable, accessible, and efficiently planned urban environments.

In the forthcoming study, titled "Interactive Urban Walkability in Virtual Reality" I will leverage the knowledge acquired about walkability from previous research to evaluate virtual urban walking experiences. The participants of this study are urban planners. The VR prototypes allow participants to experience the immersive urban environment and interact with facilities for pedestrians while performing navigational tasks. By allowing the participants to experience the urban design in an immersive VR environment, more stakeholders can participate in the urban planning process. The data from eye movement and interaction with facilities are collected to capture their behavior, choices, and feedback for later analysis to assess the effectiveness of using VR to enhance walkability in urban planning. This allows for a detailed assessment of pedestrian interactions, navigational choices, and facility usage, thereby enabling the collection of valuable data on user behavior and preferences which can inform more walkable and user-centric urban design solutions. After interacting with the VR prototypes, participants can provide feedback on their experiences to improve the prototypes in later studies. The study's goals include assessing interactions with VR prototypes and the impact of VR on decision-making and stakeholder collaboration. Additionally, this study will feature a comparative analysis of feedback from stakeholders in Melbourne, Australia, and Eindhoven, the Netherlands.

The next study, "Generative Pedestrian-centric Urban Planning" will explore the integration of Generative Design into urban planning, streamlining design processes and incorporating regenerative development criteria. Using regenerative development criteria as the input for Generative Design allows for assessing the prototypes' ability to align the design outcome with regenerative principles in urban planning. Utilizing insights from prior VR prototype evaluations, participants will interact with generated designs in a VR setting to experience and refine urban planning models. Generative Design prototypes then can rapidly iterate and optimize urban designs based on VR evaluations and stakeholders' feedback. The process of using VR designed urban environment and Generative Design to refine the design can highlight the integration of combining these technologies to enhance urban planning toward walkability. The involvement of stakeholders in creating and refining urban design helps to assess the engagements of multiple stakeholders in the planning processes focused on walkability. Workshops with urban planners will facilitate a comparative analysis between generative and actual urban plans, spotlighting the advantages of generative approaches to urban planning, particularly in enhancing walkability. The study will be conducted in Melbourne, Australia, and Eindhoven, the Netherlands.

The last study, "Pedestrian-friendly Urban Planning Using Digital Twin" aims to utilize a DT framework fed with real-time data to inform the generative urban planning process. Stakeholders will experience the generated urban design via VR, allowing for real-time design feedback. This feedback can also be used as additional input for Generative Design to rapidly iterate urban designs that prioritize walkability. This study seeks to determine DT's efficiency as a comprehensive data hub and act as a part of the framework for urban design. The research will include qualitative feedback from stakeholders' interactions with the framework and quantitative analysis of the DT's environmental, social, and economic impacts. A comparative assessment of design interventions between the DT framework and conventional design tools will be conducted.

These studies will culminate in a proposed framework for urban planning that emphasizes walkability and fosters regenerative development, offering a guideline for adopting and developing these technologies in urban planning beyond walkability enhancement.

4   Conclusion

In summary, my research integrates VR, DT, and Generative Design as innovative tools in urban planning to enhance walkability and support regenerative development. The insights derived from two rounds of interviews in Eindhoven provide a nuanced understanding of pedestrian needs, shaping the development of these technologies. VR allows stakeholders to experience and interact with urban simulations, offering an immersive perspective on potential developments. DT serves as a real-time model, reflecting the current state of urban environments, crucial for accurate planning and simulation. Generative Design automates the creation of varied design solutions, guided by specified criteria related to walkability and generative development. Collectively, these technologies promise to revolutionize urban planning by fostering more effective stakeholder collaboration, enabling participatory decision-making, and ensuring urban environments are adaptable, resilient, and in harmony with human and ecological systems. This research sets the stage for future studies to validate and refine these digital tools, ultimately aiming to provide a comprehensive framework for urban planning that prioritizes walkability and regenerative growth. Furthermore, the process of adopting these technologies provides a valuable guideline for utilizing VR, DT, and Generative Design in broader urban planning contexts beyond walkability improvement.

Acknowledgements. This project has received funding from the European Union's Horizon 2020 research and innovation programme under the Marie Skłodowska-Curie grant agreement No 101034328.

References

1. Babar, M., Arif, F.: Smart urban planning using big data analytics based internet of things. In: Proceedings of the 2017 ACM International Joint Conference on Pervasive and Ubiquitous Computing and Proceedings of the 2017 ACM International Symposium on Wearable Computers, Maui, Hawaii, pp. 397–402. ACM, September 2017. https://doi.org/10.1145/3123024.3124411. https://dl.acm.org/doi/10.1145/3123024.3124411

2. Dembski, F., Wössner, U., Letzgus, M., Ruddat, M., Yamu, C.: Urban digital twins for smart cities and citizens: the case study of Herrenberg, Germany. Sustainability **12**(6), 2307 (2020). https://doi.org/10.3390/su12062307. https://www.mdpi.com/2071-1050/12/6/2307

3. Deren, L., Wenbo, Y., Zhenfeng, S.: Smart city based on digital twins. Comput. Urban Sci. **1**(1), 4 (2021). https://doi.org/10.1007/s43762-021-00005-y. http://link.springer.com/10.1007/s43762-021-00005-y

4. Ewing, R., Cervero, R.: Travel and the built environment: a meta-analysis. J. Am. Plann. Assoc. **76**(3), 265–294 (2010). https://doi.org/10.1080/01944361003766766. Dhttp://www.tandfonline.com/doi/abs/10.1080/01944361003766766

5. Fasth, T., Bohman, S., Larsson, A., Ekenberg, L., Danielson, M.: Portfolio decision analysis for evaluating stakeholder conflicts in land use planning. Group Decis. Negot. **29**(2), 321–343 (2020). https://doi.org/10.1007/s10726-020-09656-4. http://link.springer.com/10.1007/s10726-020-09656-4

6. Frank, L.D., Andresen, M.A., Schmid, T.L.: Obesity relationships with community design, physical activity, and time spent in cars. Am. J. Prev. Med. **27**(2), 87–96 (2004). https://doi.org/10.1016/j.amepre.2004.04.011. https://linkinghub.elsevier.com/retrieve/pii/S074937970400087X

7. Hanzl, M.: Information technology as a tool for public participation in urban planning: a review of experiments and potentials. Des. Stud. **28**(3), 289–307 (2007). https://doi.org/10.1016/j.destud.2007.02.003. https://linkinghub.elsevier.com/retrieve/pii/S0142694X0700021X

8. Howard, T.L.J., Gaborit, N.: Using virtual environment technology to improve public participation in urban planning process. J. Urban Plan. Dev. **133**(4), 233–241   (2007).   https://doi.org/10.1061/(ASCE)0733-9488(2007)133:4(233). https://ascelibrary.org/doi/10.1061/%28ASCE%290733-9488%282007%29133%3A4%28233%29

9. Jamei, E., Mortimer, M., Seyedmahmoudian, M., Horan, B., Stojcevski, A.: Investigating the role of virtual reality in planning for sustainable smart cities. Sustainability **9**(11), 2006 (2017). https://doi.org/10.3390/su9112006. http://www.mdpi.com/2071-1050/9/11/2006

10. Ledo Espinoza, P.J.: Peri-urbanization in Sacaba, Bolivia: challenges to the traditional urban planning approach. Int. Plan. Stud. **26**(3), 286–301 (2021). https://doi.org/10.1080/13563475.2020.1839389. https://www.tandfonline.com/doi/full/10.1080/13563475.2020.1839389

11. Meenar, M., Kitson, J.: Using multi-sensory and multi-dimensional immersive virtual reality in participatory planning. Urban Sci. **4**(3), 34 (2020). https://doi.org/10.3390/urbansci4030034. https://www.mdpi.com/2413-8851/4/3/34

12. Portman, M., Natapov, A., Fisher-Gewirtzman, D.: To go where no man has gone before: virtual reality in architecture, landscape architecture and environmental planning. Comput. Environ. Urban Syst. **54**, 376–384 (2015). https://doi.org/10.1016/j.compenvurbsys.2015.05.001. https://linkinghub.elsevier.com/retrieve/pii/S019897151500054X

13. Rathore, M.M., Ahmad, A., Paul, A., Rho, S.: Urban planning and building smart cities based on the Internet of Things using Big Data analytics. Comput. Netw. **101**, 63–80 (2016). https://doi.org/10.1016/j.comnet.2015.12.023. https://linkinghub.elsevier.com/retrieve/pii/S1389128616000086

14. Schrotter, G., Hürzeler, C.: The digital twin of the city of Zurich for urban planning. PFG J. Photogram. Remote Sens. Geoinf. Sci. **88**(1), 99–112 (2020). https://doi.org/10.1007/s41064-020-00092-2. http://link.springer.com/10.1007/s41064-020-00092-2

15. Zhang, X., Fan, W., Guo, X.: Urban landscape design based on data fusion and computer virtual reality technology. Wirel. Commun. Mob. Comput. **2022**, 1–14 (2022). https://doi.org/10.1155/2022/7207585. https://www.hindawi.com/journals/wcmc/2022/7207585/

User-Centred Design: Experiences from Toolbox-Based Learning

Ioana Visescu(✉) ⬤, Marta Lárusdóttir ⬤, and Anna Sigridur Islind ⬤

Reykjavik University, Menntavegur 1, 102, Reykjavík, Iceland
{ioanad,marta,annasi}@ru.is

Abstract. This doctoral research delves into the domain of User-Centered Design (UCD) skills acquisition among software engineering and computer science students and early professionals. Ground the literature, it addresses the challenges faced by novices in understanding complex problems and empathising with diverse user groups. The proposed publications address structured "toolboxes" comprising various UCD methods tailored to different demographics and design contexts. Through a mixed-methods approach, incorporating qualitative and quantitative data collection methods and iterative process optimisation based on student feedback, the study aims to explore the experiences, benefits, and challenges associated with toolbox-based learning of UCD. Notably, the research has progressed with the dissemination of findings through scholarly publications, showcasing the evolution and application of these toolboxes in educational and professional settings. Four publications detail the iterative refinement and application of the toolboxes proposed. The final dissertation is set to offer insights into UCD skill acquisition and application across diverse educational and professional contexts.

Keywords: User-Centred Design · Human-Computer Interaction · Higher Education

1 Problem Framing and Background

As sufficient previous experience is needed to be able to reflect on and draw connections to external disciplines, students and early professionals are at a disadvantage when addressing complex problems in general (Millar 2016). Their lack of experience is also shown in their approach to design and problem framing, as when encouraged to include users in their processes, students and beginners generally use accessible participants from their circle for practice (Olson and Kellogg, 2016). They find it difficult to assess and address complex problems, as they struggle with framing the problem in the first place, oftentimes omitting key information (MacNeil et al. 2021).

Later in their careers, empathising with users proves challenging for software practitioners, many practitioners facing challenges empathising with users who are different from them, be it in gender, age, or national/ethnic background, as well as working with users where a disproportionate power dynamic exists (Lindsay et al., 2012a; Lindsay

© IFIP International Federation for Information Processing 2024
Published by Springer Nature Switzerland AG 2024
M. K. Lárusdóttir et al. (Eds.): HCSE 2024, LNCS 14793, pp. 233–240, 2024.
https://doi.org/10.1007/978-3-031-64576-1_14

et al., 2012b). Furthermore, while there might be a belief that User Experience (UX) or accessibility experts take responsibility for accessibility, studies such as Yesilada et al. (2013) or Lazar et al. (2004), show a majority of web developers considered themselves at least partially responsible for web accessibility. This leads to a need to introduce Software Engineering and Computer Science students to complex problems during their education, encouraging the early formation of soft skills, and teaching students that are about to enter the work market user centred design (UCD) methods can be beneficial in the long run, not only for the company and the field overall, but also for the employability of the student and the work they are to do in the future.

In order to guide students through the best combination of methods and better prepare them to become young practitioners, many encourage educators to anticipate potential hurdles and offer students a base set of methods to encourage the creation of holistic practices to rely on to foster and cultivate their soft skills (Roldan et al. 2020). Instances of embedding design thinking in education (Beckman and Barry 2007) showed successful outcomes. Introducing design sprints has also proved promising, Arce et al. (2022) showing students benefit from a structured approach. Similarly, Visescu et al. (2023) showed students praise a step-by-step approach, which offers them a structured learning process.

In this light, to teach students how to better frame design problems and better empathise with potential users and develop soft skills, this project proposes the introduction and analysis of several structured, step-by-step processes described under the term "toolboxes", with a combination of UCD methods used in a structured way, in a series of cases. The toolboxes proposed are taught using problem-based approaches, which have shown promising results in enhancing student motivation and active learning (Cantor et al. 2015). The in-class approaches presented to students have many parallels with activities presented in active learning theory (Bonwell and Eison 1991; Brame 2016), continuously engaging the students and allowing them to learn by doing. The toolboxes take as a departure point the UCD Sprint, which was successfully pioneered by researchers in the Nordics (Roto et al. 2021) in 2018, based on constructivist learning theories, and has been presented and used in various courses in the industry and academic setting, and iterated over the course of several years (Roto et al. 2021; Larusdottir et al. 2021; Larusdottir et al. 2023; Visescu et al. 2023). The approach has evolved from relying on the UCD Sprint as a single process to utilizing a diverse toolbox of UCD methods. By assembling these methods in different combinations, the design approaches can be tailored to fit the specific context of the projects. This evolution reflects a deeper understanding of design challenges and acknowledges that no single method fits all situations. Instead, the methods can be adapted to meet the unique needs of each project, showing the dynamic nature of design practice as it evolves to better serve users and stakeholders.

2 Research Questions

The overall research question is:

What are the experiences of learning User Centred Design through toolbox-based learning?

The overall research question is further supported and detailed upon through the following:

- What are the perceived benefits and challenges associated with learning UCD through toolbox-based learning?
- How is the usefulness of the UCD toolboxes perceived within the learning context and in the future?
- How do the UCD toolboxes compare in terms of the suitability for different design contexts, and what insights can be gained from this comparative analysis?
- How do students' experiences with the UCD toolboxes vary based on their level of design experience, and what implications does this have for tailoring educational approaches to meet the needs of diverse learners?

3 Methods and Proposed Solution

Education students in using a step-by-step process is meant to widen their skills in a structured manner while promoting holistic design practices. This can lead to better-prepared students, and in the long run, better software being created. Additionally, utilising a toolbox in educational contexts is meant to encourage an approach that focuses on a diverse pool of users and target audiences, while allowing for adaptability and teaching students to utilise methods fit for the projects they address, encouraging the creation and fostering of soft skills.

The toolboxes presented are introduced in a series of courses, and adapted according to context and the received feedback. In order to ensure a better distribution and diversity of opinion, the students approached are in various stages of their studies. The studies serve as a platform for the building of a coherent, comprehensive and well-grounded set of methods for understanding wicked problems in a structured way. Most students are part of a Computer Science department, but extensions to an Engineering department and industry courses is shown. There is a focus on an international approach, and a variety of settings in order to explore practical needs the toolboxes address. This project delves into the versatility and applicability of a multitude of UCD methods by analysing them in the context of three toolboxes tailored to different student demographics and design contexts. Each toolbox focuses on teaching students how to design software with a strong emphasis on user-centric principles, yet they are adapted to suit the needs and experiences of diverse learners.

The first toolbox– the UCD Sprint, introduces core concepts of UCD through a structured approach, and is fit for novice learners, while still allowing for adaptations. This beginner-friendly process aims to lay a solid foundation for understanding and applying UCD principles effectively, and has been studied and improved over a course of several years (Larusdottir et al. 2021; Roto et al. 2021), in studies with industry and students with a variety of experience levels (Larusdottir et al. 2023; Visescu et al. 2023).

The second toolbox – KokemUX, was designed based on the UCD Sprint, for learners with more design experience, offering a more advanced and nuanced exploration of UCD methodologies. Building upon existing knowledge, this toolbox challenges students to delve deeper into user empathy and problem-framing techniques.

Lastly, the third toolbox– the Game Design Process, focuses on user-centred game design, catering specifically to learners interested in game development. This process combines the methods and structure from UCD Sprint with game design methodologies, emphasising the importance of user experience in gaming.

Despite targeting different demographics and design contexts, all three toolboxes share the common goal of instilling UCD principles in software design education. They incorporate a series of well-known UCD methods, which are applied and adapted based on the specific context and the experience level of the learners. This comparative analysis highlights the versatility of UCD methodologies and underscores their role as adaptable tools for promoting user-centric software design across diverse learning environments.

The course data are collected through large and small-scale quantitative and qualitative data in a mixed methods approach, containing qualitative (questionnaires and interviews) and quantitative (questionnaires) measures. The participants are encouraged to provide formal and informal feedback throughout the learning process. The processes, as well as the collection methods themselves, are optimised and evaluated after each course. The qualitative data is analysed through a thematic analysis in the form of open coding, while the quantitative data follows a descriptive analysis method. As sufficient previous experience is needed to be able to reflect on and draw connections to external disciplines.

4 Publications

The first publication, Visescu et al., 2023, outlines the project's initial objective of investigating the UCD Sprint process in the context of novice learners. It emphasises the project's focus on adapting the UCD Sprint based on student feedback and requirements to enhance UCD proficiency. Over seven weeks, students' perceptions of the UCD Sprint and a digital aid accompanying it were studied. While feedback varied, students generally appreciated the UCD Sprint's structured approach. Suggestions for improving the digital aid included more visual content and better usability. The study emphasised iterative improvements and the importance of active learning methods, highlighting the need for ongoing refinement to meet evolving user needs and educational requirements.

The second publication, Larusdottir et al., 2023, focused on teaching the UCD Sprint methodology to practitioners, addressing the application of user-centred design principles in professional settings. Data was gathered on a four-day course with assigned homework between sessions, looking to assess the existing design processes in the Italian industry and the reluctance of practitioners to engage users due to perceived resource constraints. The findings revealed that user involvement typically occurs only during certain phases of software development, with initial requirements often set by customers or stakeholders. The study further analysed the practitioners' experiences with the UCD Sprint course, highlighting the value they derived from the methods presented. Although some aspects of the course structure were criticised for their pace, practitioners expressed interest in integrating more UCD principles into their design practices. Despite challenges posed by existing company norms, many practitioners recognised the importance of user involvement. They considered the UCD Sprint to be a time- and cost-effective solution that would streamline their design processes.

The third publication (under review) provides a synthesis of various research studies on commonly used User-Centred Design (UCD) practices and their associated limitations. It introduces the UCD Sprint process, which is aimed at addressing these limitations in software development integration. The paper presents findings from interviews with

UCD practitioners regarding their current practices, challenges faced, and perceptions of the UCD Sprint. Despite recognising the importance of user involvement, interviewees highlighted difficulties that might arise from its usage. While all practitioners had employed processes like design sprints, they tailored them to suit their nuanced understanding of UCD practices. While practitioners found the UCD Sprint promising, they highlighted the need for clear objectives and adaptability to their work contexts. They also provided valuable feedback on challenges the UCD Sprint does not fully address.

The upcoming fourth publication will conduct a comparative analysis between the UCD Sprint and KokemUX within the framework of a 12-week course involving third-year students from the Computer Science department. Both processes will be assessed under the same course structure, utilising a mixed-methods data-gathering approach. This approach involves qualitative and quantitative questionnaires aimed at evaluating the structures of the processes and the students' experiences with them, and interviews to delve deeper into their perceptions. A self-perceived skill acquisition questionnaire will also be administered to gauge the students' perceived proficiency gains throughout the course. Through this comprehensive methodology, we aim to provide a holistic understanding of the effectiveness and suitability of both the UCD Sprint and KokemUX in the context of intermediate-level students' learning experiences in user-centred design.

The fifth publication, a collaborative effort with the University of Campinas in Brazil, focuses on the Game Design Process, a toolbox tailored to learners keen on game design and development. Combining the UCD Sprint pillar methods with game design methodologies, this approach underscores the significance of a player-centric experience in gaming. A dedicated publication highlights the innovative approach of the process and its potential. The study involves gathering and analysing data on adapting the UCD Sprint structure and methods to game design, incorporating game design methods and approaches while maintaining a user/player-centric focus. Despite catering to a distinct demographic and design context, the Game Design Process aims to assist beginner game designers in the process of designing a player-centric experience, with UCD principles as a departure point.

These five publications outline the papers the dissertation rests on, and is visually presented in Fig. 1, below. The dissertation defence is set for March 2025.

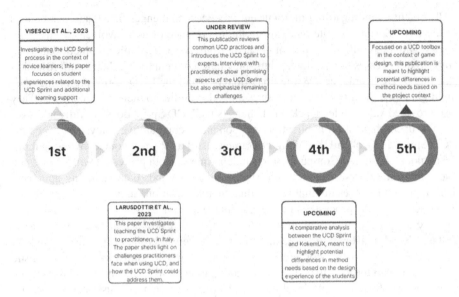

Fig. 1. Publication Outline

5 Progress

The project initially set out with the clear purpose of investigating how the learning and application of the UCD Sprint process influence students' perception of their UCD skills for addressing wicked problems, and to explore avenues for extending these skills further. This involved adapting the UCD Sprint based on student feedback, interactions with the methodology, and industry requirements, with the ultimate aim of enhancing students' UCD proficiency.

However, following feedback from the one-year proposal and two doctoral consortiums, the project's objectives have evolved significantly. The focus has shifted towards a broader analysis of multiple variations of toolboxes, their contextual adaptations, and the various combinations of methods employed within them. Based on this evolution, this thesis aims to show students' preferences and the reception of these toolboxes based on experience levels and to identify essential methods necessary for fostering a productive user-centred design experience. Rather than solely and strictly concentrating on the UCD Sprint process, the project now encompasses an analysis of diverse toolboxes containing methodologies employed in user-centred design education. By studying how these toolboxes are adapted to specific contexts and student demographics, the main contribution of the dissertation is to present insights into effective approaches for teaching UCD skills. Furthermore, by exploring students' experiences and feedback, the project aims to refine and optimise these toolboxes.

6 Focus for the Discussion Forum

The questions to guide the discussion forum discussion are the following:

- What should be the focus of the contribution and framing of the thesis?

  - Analysing the selection of UCD methods in the UCD toolboxes?
  - Or should the focus be on UCD education and skill fostering?
  - Or potentially a balanced combination of the two?

- The UCD toolboxes have been validated through quantitative and qualitative data from questionnaires, and interviews focusing on gathering results on experiences while learning UCD through toolboxes. Can you suggest some alternative ways of method and process validation?

The project initially set out with the clear purpose of investigating how the learning and application of the UCD Sprint process influence students' perception of their UCD skills for addressing wicked problems, and to explore avenues for extending these skills further. This involved adapting the UCD Sprint based on student feedback, interactions with the methodology, and industry requirements, with the ultimate aim of enhancing students' UCD proficiency.

References

Arce, E., Suárez-García, A., López-Vázquez, J.A., Fernández-Ibáñez, M.I.: Design Sprint: enhancing STEAM and engineering education through agile prototyping and testing ideas. Think. Skills Creat., 101039 (2022). https://doi.org/10.1016/j.tsc.2022.101039

Beckman, S.L., Barry, M.: Innovation as a learning process: embedding design thinking. Calif. Manage. Rev. **50**, 25–56 (2007). https://doi.org/10.2307/41166415

Bonwell, C.C., Eison, J.A.: Active Learning: Creating Excitement in the Classroom. Jossey-Bass, San Francisco (1991)

Brame, C.J.: Active learning. In: Vanderbilt University (2016). https://cft.vanderbilt.edu/active-learning. Accessed May 2023

Cantor, A., DeLauer, V., Martin, D., Rogan, J.: Training interdisciplinary "wicked problem" solvers: applying lessons from HERO in community-based research experiences for undergraduates. J. Geogr. High. Educ. **39**, 407–419 (2015). https://doi.org/10.1080/03098265.2015.1048508

Larusdottir, M., Roto, V., Cajander, Å.: Introduction to user-centred design sprint. In: Human-Computer Interaction – INTERACT 2021, pp. 253–256 (2021). https://doi.org/10.1007/978-3-030-85607-6_17

Larusdottir, M.K., Lanzilotti, R., Piccinno, A., et al.: UCD sprint: a fast process to involve users in the design practices of software companies. Int. J. Hum.-Comput. Interact. (2023). https://doi.org/10.1080/10447318.2023.2279816

Lazar, J., Dudley-Sponaugle, A., Greenidge, K.-D.: Improving web accessibility: a study of webmaster perceptions. Comput. Hum. Behav. **20**, 269–288 (2004). https://doi.org/10.1016/j.chb.2003.10.018

Lindsay, S., Brittain, K., Jackson, D., et al.: Empathy, participatory design and people with dementia. In: Proceedings of the 2012 ACM Annual Conference on Human Factors in Computing Systems - CHI 2012 (2012a). https://doi.org/10.1145/2207676.2207749

Lindsay, S., Jackson, D., Schofield, G., Olivier, P.: Engaging older people using participatory design. In: Proceedings of the 2012 ACM annual conference on Human Factors in Computing Systems - CHI 2012 (2012b). https://doi.org/10.1145/2207676.2208570

MacNeil, S., Ding, Z., Quan, K., et al.: Framing Creative Work: Helping Novices Frame Better Problems through Interactive Scaffolding (2021). https://doi.org/10.1145/3450741.3465261

Millar, V.: Interdisciplinary curriculum reform in the changing university. Teach. High. Educ. **21**, 471–483 (2016). https://doi.org/10.1080/13562517.2016.1155549

Olson, J., Kellogg, W. (eds.): Ways of Knowing in HCI. Springer, New York (2016). https://doi.org/10.1007/978-1-4939-0378-8

Roldan, W., Gao, X., Hishikawa, A.M., et al.: Opportunities and challenges in involving users in project-based HCI education. In: Proceedings of the 2020 CHI Conference on Human Factors in Computing Systems (2020). https://doi.org/10.1145/3313831.3376530

Roto, V., Larusdottir, M., Lucero, A., et al.: Focus, structure, reflection! In: Integrating User-Centred Design and Design Sprint. Human-Computer Interaction – INTERACT 2021, pp. 239–258 (2021). https://doi.org/10.1007/978-3-030-85616-8_15

Visescu, I., Larusdottir, M., Islind, A.S.: Supporting active learning in STEM higher education through the UCD Sprint. In: Proceedings of the IEEE Frontiers in Education Conference 2023 (2023). https://doi.org/10.1109/FIE58773.2023.10342978

Yesilada, Y., Brajnik, G., Vigo, M., Harper, S.: Exploring perceptions of web accessibility: a survey approach. Behav. Inf. Technol. **34**, 119–134 (2013). https://doi.org/10.1080/0144929x.2013.848238

Posters

A Survey of Natural Language-Based Editing of Low-Code Applications Using Large Language Models

Simon Cornelius Gorissen[1], Stefan Sauer[2]([⊠]), and Wolf G. Beckmann[1]

[1] TEAM GmbH, Hermann-Löns-Str. 88, 33104 Paderborn, Germany
{sg,wb}@team-pb.de
[2] SICP Software Innovation Lab and Computer Science Department, Paderborn University, Warburger Str. 100, 33098 Paderborn, Germany
sauer@uni-paderborn.de

Abstract. In recent years, Large Language Models (LLMs) have showcased an impressive ability for natural language (NL) understanding, code generation, and logical reasoning. This provides the potential to significantly speed up development times by integrating this technology into software development workflows. Similarly, Low-Code Development Platforms (LCDPs) are already in use for reducing development effort and lowering the entry barrier to who can become a developer in the first place. This poses the question whether these technologies can be combined in order to enable end-users to edit an application via NL while experienced developers can still work on the same app using a regular LCDP and benefit from its advantages. To asses whether this proposal has been realised yet (and if so, to what extend), a literature survey is necessary. This paper presents such a survey, outlining how LLMs have been used to edit low-code applications, and especially Oracle Application Express (APEX) apps. It identifies an open research gap in this direction.

Keywords: Low-Code · Large Language Models · End-User Development · Oracle APEX · Natural Language

1 Introduction

Large Language Models (LLMs) have shown potential to combat the shortage of skilled workers in the software development sector by helping experienced programmers write code and by lowering the entry barrier for end-users to edit their own software. Low-code tools provide similar benefits using more accessible interaction concepts, like drag-and-dropping elements in a visual editor, compared to writing regular source code. This beggs the question whether these two technologies can be combined to reap the added benefits of both of them. Such a combination could, for example, enable end-users to develop a low-code

© IFIP International Federation for Information Processing 2024
Published by Springer Nature Switzerland AG 2024
M. K. Lárusdóttir et al. (Eds.): HCSE 2024, LNCS 14793, pp. 243–254, 2024.
https://doi.org/10.1007/978-3-031-64576-1_15

application using natural language (NL), lowering the entry barrier for software development.

A survey of what research has been published in this direction is needed to assess if and in what capacity such systems already exist. This paper presents such a survey. As an example of a popular low-code tool for creating powerful web-applications, we especially want to focus on Oracle Application Express (APEX). It is a promising candidate for such a combination of low-code and LLMs.

For this literature survey, we have defined the following research questions: *What prior work has been done in using LLMs to create an NL-based editor for low-code apps, especially Oracle APEX?*

To answer this question, it needs to be researched if and in what capacity previous work has already studied systems similar to the one we are proposing. Since Oracle APEX needs SQL queries as the basis of different regions that are shown in APEX applications, like tables and forms, our proposed system will need to generate SQL queries based on users' prompts. Additionally, the Application Programming Interface (API) that can be used to programmatically edit APEX apps consists of PL/SQL procedure calls that change the underlying APEX sources of the application. Therefore, it is also relevant to this research question if and how LLMs have been used in prior work to generate SQL queries and PL/SQL code from NL prompts. This is accounted for in our search queries (see Sect. 2.1) and this is the reason why we specifically report on this aspect in our results (see Sect. 3.1).

Similarly, we also consider high-code (i.e., classic programming) systems that use LLMs. An LLM-based programming system could have significant similarities to a low-code based system that also works with LLMs, e.g. in regards to the user interface design for end-users. This is why we also report on that in our results (see Sect. 3.2).

In the remainder of this paper, Sect. 2 will outline the method used for this literature survey, Sect. 3 will present its results, and Sect. 4 concludes this paper with a discussion on the results' implications.

2   Method

In this section we discuss the methodology we used for this literature survey. We generally followed the approach outlined by Kitchenham [25] for systematic literature reviews. We extended and complemented the search methodology by pre-selecting relevant conferences.

2.1   Data Sources and Search Strategies

We used two different search strategies to generate a list of initial literature that could be relevant. The first one was going through the list of publications from seven scientific conferences. The second was searching different search engines using a defined set of keywords.

For the conferences search, we looked at conferences that were likely to contain relevant literature based on an initial literature search we did. We considered the iterations between and including the years 2020 and 2023. LLMs with their modern capabilities are a fairly new development, so we deemed four years sufficient to find the most relevant literature. The resulting conferences that we searched are the following: (1) IEEE VL/HCC[1], (2) ACM/IEEE MODELS[2], (3) IS-EUD[3], (4) CHI[4], (5) ACM CUI[5], (6) ICCAI[6], and (7) LLM@IJCAI[7].

The list of accepted publications in each of the conferences was taken as the basic corpus of items on which we performed the selection and filtering procedure that will be explained further in Sect. 2.2.

Note that the CHI conference includes several hundred papers on vastly different topics in each of its iterations, therefore we did not consider every single one of them in this review: In its 2021–2023 iterations, the papers are grouped into topics, so we only included the papers that were part of a topic whose title implied possible relevancy. The 2020 iteration did not have these topic headings, so in this case we considered every paper.

We also used a keyword search to find relevant literature. We used the three scientific search engines Google Scholar, IEEE Xplore, and Web of Science. We also used the non-scientific search engine Google Search to find possible systems from the private sector that could be similar to our proposition, but that have not been published in a scientific paper. We searched each of them using the keyword *Large Language Model* in combination with each of the terms *Programming*, *Oracle Apex*, *Citizen Developer*, *Low-Code*, *SQL*, and *PL/SQL* (i.e., the first combined search term was *Large Language Model Programming*). We derived these search terms from our research objective and the topics of relevancy it encompasses, as discussed in Sect. 1. The search using one term in one search engine was continued until ten found items in a row were not relevant anymore. Once we obtained a list of relevant items from the conferences- and the search-engine-based searches via this process, we went through the full text of the most relevant items to see which other works they referenced and again determined if these referenced items were relevant for us.

2.2   Selection and Filtering Procedure

The search strategies described in Sect. 2.1 resulted in a list of items that we needed to check for relevancy. Figure 1 shows an overview of the filtering procedure that we used to determine this relevancy.

---

[1] https://www.computer.org/csdl/proceedings/1001007.
[2] https://conf.researchr.org/series/models.
[3] https://cg3hci.dmi.unica.it/iseud2023/proceedings.html.
[4] https://dl.acm.org/conference/chi/proceedings.
[5] https://dl.acm.org/conference/cui/proceedings.
[6] https://dl.acm.org/conference/iccai/proceedings.
[7] https://bigmodel.ai/llm-ijcai23.

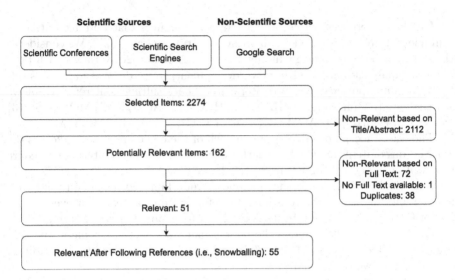

Fig. 1. Overview of this literature survey's selection and filtering procedure including the number of contributions in each group.

First, the title is checked and based on this it is judged whether the item is potentially relevant to the literature research questions. If it is not clear based on the title, the abstract is also read to determine the potential relevancy.

This results in a set of potentially relevant items. For each of these items, the full text of the contribution is used to determine if the item is in fact relevant. Relevancy is always checked against all relevancy criteria and not just the ones specific to the yielding search term.

Thereby, a list of relevant items is created. The main criterion for relevancy is that a contribution helps to answer our research question outlined in Sect. 1 by discussing how LLMs can be integrated in a system that supports a non-IT professional to develop an application through NL prompts, especially when this application is created using a low-code development platform. For this literature research, we are particularly interested in work that *uses* an LLM in a black-box capacity for programming by non-experts as opposed to work that creates a new LLM from scratch, as the former is more in line with the focus of our research proposal.

We specifically excluded work where the full text could not be obtained. We also excluded work that, using an LLM, aimed to educate (student) developers about programming or otherwise reason about code with developers instead of directly generating code that could be used to edit a software program, as the former strays away too far from the focus of our proposal. We also did not include work that discusses how they created a custom LLM without also constructing a system around it that uses that LLM or at least providing an insightful evaluation of the LLM's capabilities. This was done since our focus lies more on the ways in which to use LLM and not their initial creation.

3   Results

The results of this literature survey are presented in this section according to the three primary topics we identified: *SQL and PL/SQL Generation with LLMs*, *Programming with LLMs*, and *Low-Code Development with LLMs*.

3.1   SQL and PL/SQL Generation with LLMs

Generating SQL statements from NL using LLMs has seen a lot of interest recently. Li et al. [28], for example, present a framework where a conversation history concerning a text-to-SQL task is rewritten by an LLM for easier parsing before passing it to the actual RAT-SQL text-to-SQL parser.

Aparicio et al. [2] focus on a similar setting as our proposal: They use an LLM for generating SQL statements based on NL that are meant to be used in a low-code application. However, they train and evaluate a custom-made model and do not integrate this into an actual Low-Code Development Platform (LCDP).

An active line of research is trying to restrict the output of an LLM to valid SQL statements, ensuring the generation of syntactically correct statements. There are multiple variations of such systems that, for example, apply a context-free SQL grammar while parsing [3], incrementally parse the generated output and reject tokens that are not allowed according to custom checks [40], improve the structure awareness of LLMs by inserting special characters into the input [13], or determine similar input tasks to the target one and supply corresponding solutions as examples to the LLM [36].

A different approach for text-to-SQL tasks, that is more focused on prompt design, is the idea to divide the initial NL input into subtasks, that the target SQL statement needs to fulfil. Pourreza et al. [37] and Liu et al. [30] do this by solving these individual subtasks step by step using an LLM. They achieve measurable improvements over a more straightforward method.

Prompt design in general has also been actively researched in the context of text-to-SQL tasks, for example, using chain-of-thought prompting. This aims at improving semantic correctness by letting the LLM describe its *thought process* before giving a final answer [26,30,45,46,51]. Supplying examples in the prompt also improves accuracy [15,34,38] and giving the relevant create-table statements to the LLM proves beneficial for unknown schemas [9,38,50].

Besides new systems being presented, there are also papers that focus on evaluating existing solutions. Liu et al. [29], for example, analysed ChatGPT's out-of-the-box capability for text-to-SQL generation on a variety of benchmarks, including several variants of the Spider benchmark [48]. In their work, Liu et al. provide simple prompts and do not use prompt engineering to improve results. They show that ChatGPT in a zero-shot setting is competitive with other state-of-the-art models and even outperforms some of them in certain benchmarks. Their results suggest that the modern members of the general-purpose GPT family of LLMs already offer good text-to-SQL capabilities out of the box.

There are also some non-scientific contributions available concerning SQL generation using LLMs. The open-source LangChain[8] system, for instance, can be used to generate SQL queries from an Oracle Database [22]. Also, multiple companies offer text-to-SQL systems for usages such as data science [23, 43].

Oracle also presented the *Select AI* feature for Autonomous Databases [16]. It allows users to generate a select-statement for specific tables based on an NL prompt. Yet, they do not evaluate scientifically how well it performs or how it works internally, but focus on how it can be used by developers.

Besides these works on SQL generation, we also tried to find contributions concerning PL/SQL generation using LLMs. However, there seems to be no research on this—possibly as it is more a niche language compared to other examples like Python or plain SQL.

3.2   Programming with LLMs

Like SQL generation, using LLMs for programming is currently an active research field. There are works that focus on general development tasks like configuring software features using NL [1] or specifying software in a human- and LLM-readable format [27]. There is also an approach that translates low-level program descriptions from NL to concrete source code via an LLM [6]. More related to our proposal, however, are systems where the users formulate an *intent* of what the program should do instead of a detailed description of *how* to do it.

Besides general purpose LLMs, like GPT-4, that—especially in their more recent iterations—have the ability to generate code from a user's NL intent description, there have also been works that create LLMs specifically designed for code generation [10, 35]. These works have in common that they do not integrate the LLM into a development workflow. Thus, developers who want to use them still need to copy the generated code and paste it into the appropriate source files in their software project.

There are also different evaluations of how good existing LLMs are for generating code [5, 49]. They find that these models have a rather high accuracy in different programming benchmarks (above 80% in some cases) and that results can be improved when applying fine-tuning.

Other evaluations focus more on users' perspectives [20, 21, 42, 44, 47] instead of benchmarks. In some cases, these works integrate LLM code generation directly into an Integrated Development Environment (IDE) like VisualStudioCode [44], PyCharm [47], and Xcode [42]. These contributions show that LLMs may not be measurably beneficial in terms of saved time yet, but developers still like to use them, and they show great potential, especially as the technology matures over time. These works also serve as examples of how these models can be integrated more directly into development workflows by making them available inside the developer's IDE.

---

[8] https://github.com/langchain-ai/langchain.

Another line of work revolves around improving the correctness of generated code by, for example, letting an LLM debug the code that was already generated by an LLM [11,18,31]. Such contributions can, for example, prompt an LLM to correct possible mistakes in a program generated by another LLM [11] or they execute a program and detect errors, so they can provide the LLM with appropriate error messages for debugging [31].

More similar to our proposal is the work by Kim et al. [24] because they focus on website users instead of programmers as the target audience for their *Stylette* system. It is an LLM-powered browser extension which allows users to input styling goals of a webpage in NL, with an LLM subsequently generating the appropriate CSS code. However, the focus on CSS limits its usefulness in developing or editing fully functional applications.

Calo et al.'s work [8] takes this a step further. Their system can edit HTML and CSS code. In the system prompt, they instruct the LLM to adhere to a certain template format in its responses, so they can directly be used to edit the existing website's code without developer intervention. Here, the focus on only HTML and CSS again prevents creating a production-ready application that would typically need some procedural logic in a language like JavaScript.

The works discussed here show that programming using LLMs is actively researched in a variety of ways. However, to the best of our knowledge, no system has been presented yet that is focused on enabling non-IT professionals to develop a fully featured software product completely through NL. Instead, most systems focus on smaller programming tasks or on assisting experienced developers.

3.3   Low-Code Development with LLMs

As described in Sect. 2, we also searched for contributions that mention citizen developers in the context of LLMs. However, we mainly found opinion pieces and non-scientific articles about how LLMs will transform citizen developers and recommendations for citizen developers about LLM [14,17], or scientific work regarding citizen developers that do not mention LLMs at all.

Low-code development with LLMs in general, on the other hand, has seen more attention in recent years, although often not for directly editing whole applications. There are approaches for using LLMs for prototyping machine learning (ML) functionality [19] and generating business automations in a domain specific language [12]. These basically create domain-specific NL-based LCDPs. Additionally, Lu et al. [32] design an LLM-based system that plans a multi-step solution procedure for a given prompt where each step is realised by one of a given set of modules with specific functionality. They use this for question answering and not for application development, however. Asunis et al. [4] present a chatbot that translates the user's NL input into a rule language that is used to create interactions in a point-and-click game. They also evaluate this in a user study which shows that a conversational interface can make defining such logical specifications easier for users.

There are also some works that more directly integrate LCDPs and LLMs. Rao et al. [39], for instance, present a system and a user study through which users can develop ML pipelines using visual programming and NL prompts.

Cai et al. [7] provide a framework where, based on a user prompt, a planning LLM generates a workflow specification for solving the described task in a diagram. This diagram can then be edited by the user using low-code interaction concepts, such as drag-and-drop, before it is executed by an LLM.

The above contributions have in common that they do not use an LLM in application development—be it through a low-code tool or regular source code. We found two instances of LLMs being used in this way in the low-code context. Skamene [41] discusses how OpenAI's LLMs can be integrated in Oracle APEX applications. They focus on possible usages inside the low-code applications being built and do not use it for creating APEX applications themselves.

In late 2023, Oracle's Mueller et al. [33] presented APEX Assistant, a generative Artificial Intelligence (AI) integrated into the APEX user interface. It enables users to generate SQL statements and add new pages based on NL descriptions. However, it does not seem to have the ability to edit an existing page or component. The system also is not released yet and it is not clear when it will be. Additionally, the system is described as being geared towards experienced APEX developers, whereas our research aims for end-users of apps.

4 Conclusion

This paper has outlined the main related work for our proposal of an NL-based editor for low-code apps. From this, it is clear that there is no such system that enables non-IT professionals to edit fully functional low-code applications without an experienced developer.

We have also outlined that to edit Oracle APEX apps specifically, SQL statements have to be written and edited and that there is a lot of research in regards to how LLMs can be effectively used to do this. Prior research suggests that modern LLMs like GPT-4 have a high degree of accuracy for generating SQL statements as long as they are provided with the necessary schema information.

The closest contribution to our proposal that we found is the one by Calo et al. [8] that enables editing HTML/CSS code of a website purely through NL prompts. However, they directly work on code, leaving the benefits of LCDPs unutilized. Additionally, other work on programming with LLMs can also be a useful foundation for our proposal, for example, in regards to giving the model custom specifications on how to describe necessary change operations in its responses.

There is little work in regards to editing low-code applications directly through NL. Oracle [33] have presented an upcoming feature for APEX that serves as an example of this. However, it is not announced yet when this will be released and what capabilities it will have. Additionally, the feature is intended for experienced APEX developers instead of empowering end-users [33].

Thus, it is fair to say that there is an open research gap here that should be addressed in future work.

Acknowledgment. This research was supported by TEAM GmbH, a software development and consulting company from Paderborn, Germany with a focus on databases and database-centric applications. They have developed multiple applications that incorporate AI features, and especially LLMs (see https://www.team-pb. de/development/individuelle-ki/), and provided both funding and guidance for the realization of this research. For further information about TEAM please visit: https:// www.team-pb.de/

References

1. Acher, M., Duarte, J.G., Jézéquel, J.M.: On programming variability with large language model-based assistant. In: Proceedings of the 27th ACM International Systems and Software Product Line Conference - Volume A. ACM, August 2023. https://doi.org/10.1145/3579027.3608972
2. Aparicio, S., et al.: Natural language to SQL in low-code platforms. ArXiv Preprint, August 2023. https://doi.org/10.48550/ARXIV.2308.15239
3. Arcadinho, S.D., Aparicio, D., Veiga, H., Alegria, A.: T5QL: taming language models for SQL generation. In: Bosselut, A., et al. (eds.) Proceedings of the 2nd Workshop on Natural Language Generation, Evaluation, and Metrics (GEM), pp. 276–286, Abu Dhabi, United Arab Emirates (Hybrid). Association for Computational Linguistics, December 2022. https://doi.org/10.18653/v1/2022.gem-1.23. https://aclanthology.org/2022.gem-1.23
4. Asunis, L., Frau, V., Macis, R., Pireddu, C., Spano, L.D.: PAC-Bot: writing text messages for developing point-and-click games. In: Fogli, D., Tetteroo, D., Barricelli, B.R., Borsci, S., Markopoulos, P., Papadopoulos, G.A. (eds.) IS-EUD 2021. LNCS, vol. 12724, pp. 213–221. Springer, Cham (2021). https://doi.org/10.1007/978-3-030-79840-6_15
5. Austin, J., et al.: Program synthesis with large language models. ArXiv Preprint, August 2021. https://doi.org/10.48550/ARXIV.2108.07732
6. Brummelen, J.V., Weng, K., Lin, P., Yeo, C.: CONVO: what does conversational programming need? In: 2020 IEEE Symposium on Visual Languages and Human-Centric Computing (VL/HCC). IEEE, August 2020. https://doi.org/10.1109/vl/hcc50065.2020.9127277
7. Cai, Y., et al.: Low-code LLM: visual programming over LLMs. ArXiv Preprint, April 2023. https://doi.org/10.48550/ARXIV.2304.08103
8. Calò, T., Russis, L.D.: Leveraging large language models for end-user website generation. In: Spano, L.D., Schmidt, A., Santoro, C., Stumpf, S. (eds.) IS-EUD 2023, vol. 13917, pp. 52–61. Springer, Cham (2023). https://doi.org/10.1007/978-3-031-34433-6_4
9. Chang, S., Fosler-Lussier, E.: How to prompt LLMs for text-to-SQL: a study in zero-shot, single-domain, and cross-domain settings. ArXiv Preprint, May 2023. https://doi.org/10.48550/ARXIV.2305.11853
10. Chen, M., et al.: Evaluating large language models trained on code. ArXiv Preprint, July 2021. https://doi.org/10.48550/ARXIV.2107.03374

11. Chen, X., Lin, M., Schärli, N., Zhou, D.: Teaching large language models to self-debug. ArXiv Preprint, April 2023. https://doi.org/10.48550/ARXIV.2304.05128

12. Desmond, M., Duesterwald, E., Isahagian, V., Muthusamy, V.: A no-code low-code paradigm for authoring business automations using natural language. ArXiv Preprint, July 2022. https://doi.org/10.48550/ARXIV.2207.10648

13. Dou, L., et al.: UniSAr: a unified structure-aware autoregressive language model for text-to-SQL semantic parsing. Int. J. Mach. Learn. Cybern. (2023). https://doi.org/10.1007/s13042-023-01898-3

14. Fitzmaurice, M.: Why citizen development is the wrong model for many enterprises, August 2021. https://venturebeat.com/business/why-citizen-development-is-the-wrong-model-for-many-enterprises/. Accessed 07 Nov 2023

15. Guo, C., et al.: Prompting GPT-3.5 for text-to-SQL with de-semanticization and skeleton retrieval. In: Liu, F., Sadanandan, A.A., Pham, D.N., Mursanto, P., Lukose, D. (eds.) PRICAI 2023: Trends in Artificial Intelligence, vol. 14326, pp. 262–274. Springer, Singapore (2024). https://doi.org/10.1007/978-981-99-7022-3_23

16. Hornick, M.: Introducing select AI - natural language to SQL generation on autonomous database, September 2023. https://blogs.oracle.com/machinelearning/post/introducing-natural-language-to-sql-generation-on-autonomous-database. Accessed 07 Nov 2023

17. Ismael, C.: Tips for new AI citizen developers, June 2023. https://chrispogeek.medium.com/tips-for-new-ai-citizen-developers-ff2dca5e067e, Accessed 07 Nov 2023

18. Jain, N., et al.: Jigsaw: large language models meet program synthesis. In: Proceedings of the 44th International Conference on Software Engineering. ACM, May 2022. https://doi.org/10.1145/3510003.3510203

19. Jiang, E., et al.: PromptMaker: prompt-based prototyping with large language models. In: CHI Conference on Human Factors in Computing Systems Extended Abstracts. ACM, April 2022. https://doi.org/10.1145/3491101.3503564

20. Jiang, E., Toh, E., Molina, A., Donsbach, A., Cai, C.J., Terry, M.: GenLine and GenForm: two tools for interacting with generative language models in a code editor. In: Adjunct Proceedings of the 34th Annual ACM Symposium on User Interface Software and Technology. ACM, October 2021. https://doi.org/10.1145/3474349.3480209

21. Jiang, E., et al.: Discovering the syntax and strategies of natural language programming with generative language models. In: CHI Conference on Human Factors in Computing Systems. ACM, April 2022. https://doi.org/10.1145/3491102.3501870

22. Kam, D.: Leveraging LangChain and LLM for seamless oracle database queries, August 2023. https://www.ateam-oracle.com/post/leveraging-langchain-and-llm-for-seamless-oracle-database-queries. Accessed 07 Nov 2023

23. Kapoor, A.: The end of data analytics - as we know it: large language models, July 2023. https://www.linkedin.com/pulse/end-data-analytics-we-know-large-language-models-anurag-kapoor. Accessed 07 Nov 2023

24. Kim, T.S., Choi, D., Choi, Y., Kim, J.: Stylette: styling the web with natural language. In: CHI Conference on Human Factors in Computing Systems. ACM, April 2022. https://doi.org/10.1145/3491102.3501931

25. Kitchenham, B.: Procedures for performing systematic reviews. Joint Technical Report Software Engineering Group, Keele University, United Kingdom and Empirical Software Engineering, National ICT Australia Ltd, Australia, July 2004

26. Kojima, T., Gu, S.S., Reid, M., Matsuo, Y., Iwasawa, Y.: Large language models are zero-shot reasoners. In: Koyejo, S., Mohamed, S., Agarwal, A., Belgrave, D., Cho, K., Oh, A. (eds.) Advances in Neural Information Processing Systems, vol. 35, pp. 22199–22213. Curran Associates, Inc. (2022)

27. Lee, E., Gong, J., Cao, Q.: Object oriented BDD and executable human-language module specification. In: 2023 26th ACIS International Winter Conference on Software Engineering, Artificial Intelligence, Networking and Parallel/Distributed Computing (SNPD-Winter). IEEE, July 2023. https://doi.org/10.1109/snpd-winter57765.2023.10223873

28. Li, J., et al.: DIR: a large-scale dialogue rewrite dataset for cross-domain conversational text-to-SQL. Appl. Sci. 13(4), 2262 (2023). https://doi.org/10.3390/app13042262

29. Liu, A., Hu, X., Wen, L., Yu, P.S.: A comprehensive evaluation of chatGPT's zero-shot text-to-SQL capability. ArXiv Preprint, March 2023. https://doi.org/10.48550/ARXIV.2303.13547

30. Liu, X., Tan, Z.: Divide and prompt: chain of thought prompting for text-to-SQL. ArXiv Preprint, April 2023. https://doi.org/10.48550/ARXIV.2304.11556

31. Liventsev, V., Grishina, A., Härmä, A., Moonen, L.: Fully autonomous programming with large language models. In: Proceedings of the Genetic and Evolutionary Computation Conference. ACM, July 2023. https://doi.org/10.1145/3583131.3590481

32. Lu, P., et al.: Chameleon: plug-and-play compositional reasoning with large language models. In: Oh, A., Neumann, T., Globerson, A., Saenko, K., Hardt, M., Levine, S. (eds.) Advances in Neural Information Processing Systems, vol. 36, pp. 43447–43478. Curran Associates, Inc. (2023)

33. Mueller, R., Patra, R., Carocari, G., Kareshk, M., Moghadam, H.: Generative AI + oracle apex for low-code application development, September 2023. https://blogs.oracle.com/apex/post/generative-ai-apex-1. Accessed 07 Nov 2023

34. Nan, L., et al.: Enhancing text-to-SQL capabilities of large language models: a study on prompt design strategies. In: Bouamor, H., Pino, J., Bali, K. (eds.) Findings of the Association for Computational Linguistics: EMNLP 2023, pp. 14935–14956. Association for Computational Linguistics, Singapore, December 2023. https://doi.org/10.18653/v1/2023.findings-emnlp.996. https://aclanthology.org/2023.findings-emnlp.996

35. Nijkamp, E., et al.: CodeGen: an open large language model for code with multi-turn program synthesis. In: The Eleventh International Conference on Learning Representations. ICLR 2023, Kigali, Rwanda, May 2023. https://openreview.net/pdf?id=iaYcJKpY2B_

36. Poesia, G., et al.: Synchromesh: reliable code generation from pre-trained language models. In: The Tenth International Conference on Learning Representations. ICLR 2022, Virtual Event, OpenReview.net, April 2022. https://openreview.net/forum?id=KmtVD97J43e

37. Pourreza, M., Rafiei, D.: DIN-SQL: decomposed in-context learning of text-to-SQL with self-correction. In: Oh, A., Neumann, T., Globerson, A., Saenko, K., Hardt, M., Levine, S. (eds.) Advances in Neural Information Processing Systems, vol. 36, pp. 36339–36348. Curran Associates, Inc. (2023)

38. Rajkumar, N., Li, R., Bahdanau, D.: Evaluating the text-to-SQL capabilities of large language models. ArXiv Preprint, March 2022. https://doi.org/10.48550/ARXIV.2204.00498

39. Rao, N., Tsay, J., Kate, K., Hellendoorn, V.J., Hirzel, M.: AI for low-code for AI. ArXiv Preprint, May 2023. https://doi.org/10.48550/ARXIV.2305.20015

40. Scholak, T., Schucher, N., Bahdanau, D.: PICARD: parsing incrementally for constrained auto-regressive decoding from language models. In: Moens, M.F., Huang, X., Specia, L., Yih, S.W.t. (eds.) Proceedings of the 2021 Conference on Empirical Methods in Natural Language Processing, pp. 9895–9901. Association for Computational Linguistics, Online and Punta Cana, Dominican Republic, November 2021. https://doi.org/10.18653/v1/2021.emnlp-main.779. https://aclanthology.org/2021.emnlp-main.779

41. Skamene, M.: Exploring the synergy of openAI's chatGPT and oracle apes: transforming oracle applications. https://www.oatug.org/insight-summer2023/features-archive/exploring-the-synergy. Accessed 07 Nov 2023

42. Tan, C.W., Guo, S., Wong, M.F., Hang, C.N.: Copilot for Xcode: exploring AI-assisted programming by prompting cloud-based large language models. ArXiv Preprint, July 2023. https://doi.org/10.48550/ARXIV.2307.14349

43. Editorial Team of insidebigdata.com: Kinetica launches native large language model for language-to-SQL on enterprise data, September 2023. https://insidebigdata.com/2023/09/18/kinetica-launches-native-large-language-model-for-language-to-sql-on-enterprise-data/. Accessed 07 Nov 2023

44. Vaithilingam, P., Zhang, T., Glassman, E.L.: Expectation vs. experience: evaluating the usability of code generation tools powered by large language models. In: CHI Conference on Human Factors in Computing Systems Extended Abstracts. ACM, April 2022. https://doi.org/10.1145/3491101.3519665

45. Wang, X., et al.: Self-consistency improves chain of thought reasoning in language models. ArXiv Preprint, March 2022. https://doi.org/10.48550/ARXIV.2203.11171

46. Wei, J., et al.: Chain-of-thought prompting elicits reasoning in large language models. ArXiv Preprint, January 2022. https://doi.org/10.48550/ARXIV.2201.11903

47. Xu, F.F., Vasilescu, B., Neubig, G.: In-IDE code generation from natural language: promise and challenges. ACM Trans. Softw. Eng. Methodol. 31(2), 1–47 (2022). https://doi.org/10.1145/3487569

48. Yu, T., et al.: Spider: a large-scale human-labeled dataset for complex and cross-domain semantic parsing and text-to-SQL task. ArXiv Preprint, September 2018. https://doi.org/10.48550/ARXIV.1809.08887

49. Zan, D., et al.: Large language models meet NL2Code: a survey. In: Proceedings of the 61st Annual Meeting of the Association for Computational Linguistics (Volume 1: Long Papers), pp. 7443–7464, Toronto, Canada. Association for Computational Linguistics, July 2023. https://aclanthology.org/2023.acl-long.411

50. Zhang, W., Wang, Y., Fan, M.: Towards robustness of large language models on text-to-SQL task: an adversarial and cross-domain investigation. In: Iliadis, L., Papaleonidas, A., Angelov, P., Jayne, C. (eds.) ICANN 2023, vol. 14258, pp. 181–192. Springer, Cham (2023). https://doi.org/10.1007/978-3-031-44192-9_15

51. Zhou, D., et al.: Least-to-most prompting enables complex reasoning in large language models. In: The Eleventh International Conference on Learning Representations (2023). https://openreview.net/forum?id=WZH7099tgfM

Enhancing Mobile Game Accessibility: Guidelines for Users with Visual and Dexterity Dual Impairments

Chra Abdoulqadir[1]($\boxtimes$)(iD), Fernando Loizides[1]($\boxtimes$)(iD), and Santiago Hoyos[2]

[1] Cardiff University, Cardiff CF24 4AG, United Kingdom
{AbdoulqadirC1,LoizidesF}@cardiff.ac.uk
[2] University of York, York YO10 5DD, United Kingdom
sh3013@york.ac.uk

Abstract. Software accessibility has recently become a legal requirement in most countries. Minimal guidance into the legalities of this matter has been provided, leaving most software engineers to adapt software they write to "skim" the surface of what is acceptable, such as providing simple screen reading capability. Even less information is available for users with two disabilities. In this work, we provide a user-centered designed game example, with a participatory design approach, to address not one but two disabilities, vision and dexterity impairments, concurrently. We show how entertainment and interaction can take priority in the development process while not compromising on the usability and accessibility of the games. We provide the reader with seven guidelines from our findings to create accessible mobile games that can be entertaining for people with dual disabilities and non-disabled individuals equally.

Keywords: Accessibility · Games · Guidelines · Disabilities

1 Introduction and Motivation

As of March 2021, 84% of adults above 16 possess a smartphone [18]. With this widespread of smartphones, mobile gaming is more accessible to a broad audience. However, the current state of game accessibility remains a significant concern, with more than 94.8% of Android applications containing accessibility violations [1]. Research has shown that most developers ignore accessibility guidelines due to two main reasons, the lack of awareness and the lack of tools to support them in the requirement specification and the implementation stages [3].

Researchers have surveyed 836 papers published in ASSETS and CHI venues and have found that only 1% of the published research have targeted users with multiple disabilities [15]. Multiple disabilities involve people with more than one disability in "cognitive, physical and/or functional abilities" [16]. Meanwhile, the majority of accessible games focus on rehabilitation purposes [17,23,28]. In

© IFIP International Federation for Information Processing 2024
Published by Springer Nature Switzerland AG 2024
M. K. Lárusdóttir et al. (Eds.): HCSE 2024, LNCS 14793, pp. 255–263, 2024.
https://doi.org/10.1007/978-3-031-64576-1_16

a recent systematic analysis of video game accessibility, it is concluded that entertainment is not targeted as much and that future research should have more accessible games in the entertainment genre [8]. Indeed, it is important that we target entertainment rather than pure educational, rehabilitation, or therapeutic purposes. There is a clear call for future research projects for users with multiple disabilities or complex needs [24], which highlights the necessity for more inclusive guidelines for mobile application development.

Although specific statistics around users with both vision and dexterity impairments are limited, affected people are more than one could expect. For example, there are an estimated 1.6 million people with complex disabilities in the UK, which is projected to increase to 2 million by 2029 [22]. Complex disabilities involve individuals having two or more sight, hearing, or learning disabilities [21]. Similarly, conditions, such as cerebral palsy, multiple sclerosis, or certain stroke experiences, affect speech and dexterity. 764,000 people have at least one symptom of cerebral palsy in the U.S. [20], and 130,000 adults in the UK [13].

Lazar has proposed a framework for "born-accessible development" [14]. In this approach, "accessibility is considered as a primary design goal from the start, and people with disabilities are included from the start" [14]. Our work aims to develop a framework for mobile game development accessible to users with dual disabilities addressing the need apparent in this area. We utilize Artificial Intelligence (AI) to enhance accessibility and entertainment. This paper presents the initial prototype of our ongoing project focusing on different dual disability combinations. We present one dual disability combination, limited vision and dexterity impairments. We plan on creating new prototypes targeting other dual disability combinations in future projects. We propose seven guidelines for mobile game development to ensure that the game is "born-accessible" for users with limited vision and dexterity. The proposed design guidelines were concluded by developing an accessible mobile game using a user-centered participatory design process. "Cell Escape" is available for anyone to explore and try out suitable for adults with computer literacy.

2   Related Work

WGAG [27] and other guidelines, such as Android Developers [7] and IBM [11] are available for developers. WCAG guidelines cover a range of disabilities, such as vision, hearing, movement, and speech along with combinations of these [27]. For example, part of the guidelines suggested by the UK government include ensuring that the service works with assistive technologies, such as screen readers [26]. Indeed, this guideline helps users with visual and speech dual disabilities, but it would not ensure accessibility for users with vision and movement impairments because screen readers heavily rely on tapping or keyboard use. Guidelines are limited to complex disabilities or less common disabilities.

Similarly, games accessible for dual disabilities are limited. Theil, Buchweitz, et al. have presented one of the first game design recommendations for users with dual sensory loss, particularly deafblind users [25]. They propose user-driven game design recommendations based on different categories, such as timing, turns, instructions, etc. [25]. Nevertheless, they focus on hearing and vision impairments with an ability-based design framework rather than disability.

Binaural sound [4], haptic feedback [12], and audio-based approaches [5] are used effectively in research projects to enhance game accessibility for blind users. Nonetheless, these games are not compatible with users with limited dexterity due to their dependency on tapping and swiping on phones. Similarly, Google has developed the TalkBack feature embedded into the Android platform, a great tool for visually impaired users. Many mobile text-based games using this feature are accessible for the blind, such as the Zork series adventure game [2]. Nevertheless, these games rely on tapping or keyboard keys to play are not applicable to people with limited hand dexterity.

Meanwhile, there are tools and research projects around enhancing accessibility for users with limited dexterity on mobile devices. Google's Voice Access allows users to navigate using voice commands [6], which benefits those with dexterity issues. Yet, it is not accessible for blind users because it numbers the user interface elements requiring users to say the number of the element they want to tap.

The games mentioned rely on visual elements or tapping to move forward. Future endeavors should focus both on technological innovations and ensuring that these advancements contribute to a gaming environment accessible to users with multiple disabilities.

3   Developing the Cell Escape Game Prototype

The Cell Escape Game is a mobile game offering an entertaining experience without the need for tapping on the screen or relying on visual elements. Speech is used as the main input. Sentiment analysis is used for the processing stage and deciding upon where to divert the user. With no visual elements implemented, the game relies on audio files as the main output to communicate with the user. Therefore, the game is accessible for users with both dexterity and visual impairments with speech input and audio output. User input is only taken when the player is asked a question or expected to do a task. It is timed at three seconds because constant consideration of user input is not viable in this instance, as it would result in a disorganized experience due to the nature of the game's input/output process. Figure 1 shows the game's architecture with the devices needed for each operation. The game does not have visual elements as they are not necessary.

In this game, the main character has recently been brought to a prison cell. There is a man in his next cell asking for help to escape. The non-playable character (NPC) gives different options and answers based on what the player says. However, the game story has a linear progression, and the NPC will try to convince the user to help them if the user disagrees to help. This will help and move forward in the game accordingly as shown in Fig. 2. Fixed options

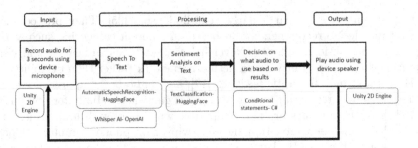

Fig. 1. I/O operations for the game prototype with the technologies used for each process. No visual elements are used.

with no sentiment analysis needed include "start game" and "end game". While "start game" is available only in the introduction scene. The "end game" option is available throughout the game. In the final scene, the story will conclude and the user will be notified that they have reached the end of the prototype. The application will automatically exit afterward. Finally, targeting ethical considerations, permissions are taken from the player to use the microphone from the beginning of the game.

We developed the game using a participatory design approach involving ten user experts, two of whom were legally blind. The experts were user experience and accessibility specialists with extensive professional or academic research backgrounds[1]. The initial requirements were set, and the game went through multiple design iterations. The user experts provided constant participation and support throughout the design and development process. We received comments on the inclusion, entertainment, and efficacy of the accessibility and AI integration in each iteration. This will help with refining the stories and technologies for our upcoming projects. The initial requirements included accessibility for visual and dexterity impairments, entertainment as an essential aspect of the game, and ethical considerations for microphone permissions.

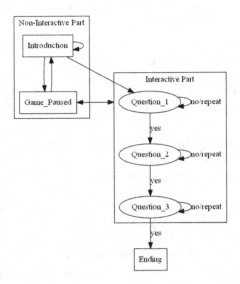

Fig. 2. Linear progression for the first prototype

---

[1] The participants were part of the design and prototyping processes. They do not include the authors.

The game is developed using Unity 2D game engine version 2021.3.2f1. The source code is written in C# (version 7.3). We have used speech-to-text AI libraries. The experimental nature of our prototype led us to employ two distinct AI libraries in separate scripts for a comparative analysis of their efficacy. Whisper [19] is used in the introduction scene and HiggingFace is used in the second and third scenes [9]. Moreover, the TextClassification library [10], developed by the HuggingFace community, is used for sentiment analysis to progress in the game accordingly. Some of the audio files were AI-generated. They were enhanced and edited using Audacity and Logic Pro for binaural effects. The audio files are pre-recorded and edited. They are not generated in real-time. Figure 1 shows the technologies used at each stage.

4   Guidelines

The prototype was developed with constant input from ten user experts, during which we observed their interactions and solicited feedback regarding the game's inclusivity and entertainment. The participants found the game approach feasible for our target disabled users. They also found the game entertaining with positive feedback, highlighting the game's potential. Using participant feedback and developed prototype, we have concluded seven guidelines in Table 1 for developers to follow. These guidelines address accessible games for users with visual and dexterity impairments. The ultimate goal is to encourage inclusion for dual disabilities in mobile games by facilitating developers without compromising the entertainment.

The first guideline listed in Table 1 is concluded from the user's limitation with changing the game's accessibility settings. The game shall be accessible if it is "born-accessible" and not leave it to the user to make it accessible for themselves. The second guideline comes from another input from our expert participants with their uncertainty about what the question or task was in the gameplay. With our audio-based game that takes speech as its main input, we programmed the "repeat" command to repeat the question or task asked. The third guideline shows the significance of letting the user know when input is taken to minimize confusion or unnecessary input. The user cannot see the screen. Audio feedback (a beep sound) was considered an efficient way to communicate when speech input was accepted. The fourth guideline is implemented in the majority of games. It is worth noting that an accessible game shall have these options equally as most players expect them. This is necessary regardless of the length of the game, and users shall have the option to pause the game and get back to it later. Tagging a game with the necessary accessibility tag helps others find their desired accessible games more efficiently and be recognized for its relevant accessibility category. We concluded the sixth guideline with repetitive suggestions from the end user participants for different languages and dialects. It impacts the speech recognition libraries providing the main game input, and it consequently impacts the sentiment analysis. Finally, a limitation we found was the interference of background noise. With binaural sound implemented, the use of headphones provides a more immersive game experience. It also helps minimising background noise captured by the application.

Table 1. Design guidelines for creating mobile games accessible to users with visual and dexterity impairments

ID	Description
1	User shall not be responsible for adjusting their settings only to provide input required for the game
2	The game shall be tolerant enough to repeat the last audio if the user is uncertain of what the task is
3	Feedback shall be given when the voice input starts
4	The pause and resume options shall be available throughout the entire game
5	Published applications must be put in relevant categories with necessary accessibility tags
6	Consider the language preferences and dialects of the target audience for voice input
7	Recommend using a headset if it provides a more immersive experience for the players

5   Conclusions and Future Work

In this paper, we highlighted the need for research targeting multiple or complex disabilities and their impact on society focusing on blind and motor disabilities. We presented our first accessible, working prototype developed using a participatory design process with ten user experts, two legally blind. We also presented our initial guidelines concluded from the process. NLP and sentiment analysis are crucial elements of the prototype to help with accessibility and enhance entertainment. We will explore other technologies for faster and more efficient speech recognition and sentiment analysis. Similarly, we will incorporate the participants' constructive feedback in our future prototypes. With the participants' requests and feedback in mind, future prototypes will focus allowing the user to choose between the stories. Figure 3 shows a sample of the game story progression options we are planning to implement. It allows the story to be more personalized to the answers given by the player with different endings based on sentiment analysis results. This allows a more entertaining experience, which is one of the most essential requirements for creating inclusive games. Further work is necessary to test the game in noisy and quiet environments. More details on observational feedback will be discussed at later stages of the project. Finally, more detailed assessments of current guidelines will be published in the upcoming papers.

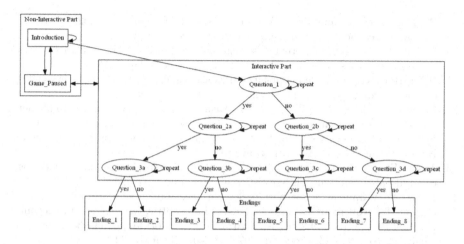

Fig. 3. Proposed future game story progression

Acknowledgements. We extend our gratitude to GOOGLE for their invaluable support and feedback throughout the project. In particular, we appreciate Abhipreeti Chauhan, Karo Caran, Victor Tsaranfor for their guidance, inspiration, and feedback for this work.

References

1. Aguado-Delgado, J., Gutierrez-Martinez, J.M., Hilera, J.R., de Marcos, L., Otón, S.: Accessibility in video games: a systematic review. Univ. Access Inf. Soc. **19**, 169–193 (2020)
2. Anderson, T., Blank, M., Daniels, B., Lebling, D.: Zork - play online at textadventures.co.uk (2023). https://textadventures.co.uk/games/view/5zyoqrsugeopel3ffhz_vq/zork. Accessed 5 Jan 2024
3. Di Gregorio, M., Di Nucci, D., Palomba, F., Vitiello, G.: The making of accessible android applications: an empirical study on the state of the practice. Empir. Softw. Eng. **27**(6), 145 (2022)
4. Drossos, K., Zormpas, N., Giannakopoulos, G., Floros, A.: Accessible games for blind children, empowered by binaural sound. In: Proceedings of the 8th ACM International Conference on Pervasive Technologies Related to Assistive Environments, pp. 1–8 (2015)
5. GMA Games: Your resource for audiogames, games for the blind, games for the visually impaired! (2003). https://audiogames.net/db.php?id=gmatankcommander. Accessed 5 Jan 2024
6. Google: Voice access: Control a device with your voice - android accessibility help (2018). https://support.google.com/accessibility/android/topic/6151842?hl=en&ref_topic=9079844&sjid=17355574717552980440-EU. Accessed 10 Sept 2023
7. Google for Developers: Build more accessible apps (2023). https://developer.android.com/guide/topics/ui/accessibility. Accessed 3 Dec 2023
8. Hassan, L.: Accessibility of games and game-based applications: a systematic literature review and mapping of future directions, p. 14614448231204020. New Media & Society (2023)

9. Hugging Face Community: Automatic speech recognition (2022). https://huggingface.co/docs/transformers/tasks/asr. Accessed 8 Aug 2023

10. Hugging Face Community: Text classification (2022). https://huggingface.co/docs/transformers/tasks/sequence_classification. Accessed 8 Aug 2023

11. IBM: IBM accessibility requirements - IBM accessibility (2023). https://www.ibm.com/able/requirements/requirements/. Accessed 3 Dec 2023

12. Islam, M.N., Inan, T.T., Promi, N.T., Diya, S.Z., Islam, A.: Design, implementation, and evaluation of a mobile game for blind people: toward making mobile fun accessible to everyone. In: Information and Communication Technologies for Humanitarian Services, pp. 291–310 (2020)

13. Jones, E.: Cerebral palsy statistics UK (2023). https://www.jmw.co.uk/blog/cerebral-palsy/cerebral-palsy-statistics-uk. Accessed 1 Apr 2024

14. Lazar, J.: A framework for born-accessible development of software and digital content. In: Abdelnour Nocera, J., Kristín Lárusdóttir, M., Petrie, H., Piccinno, A., Winckler, M. (eds.) INTERACT 2023. IFIP, vol. 14145, pp. 333–338. Springer, Cham (2023). https://doi.org/10.1007/978-3-031-42293-5_32

15. Mack, K., McDonnell, E., Jain, D., Lu Wang, L., E. Froehlich, J., Findlater, L.: What do we mean by "accessibility research"? A literature survey of accessibility papers in chi and assets from 1994 to 2019. In: Proceedings of the 2021 CHI Conference on Human Factors in Computing Systems, pp. 1–18 (2021)

16. Michigan Alliance for Families: Severe multiple impairments (2023). https://www.michiganallianceforfamilies.org/severe-multiple-impairments/#:~:text=Students%20with%20multiple%20impairments%20have. Accessed 23 Jan 2024

17. Nicolaou, K., et al.: Game based learning rehabilitation for children with speech disabilities: presenting two bespoke video games (2023)

18. Office for National Statistics: Percentage of homes and individuals with technological equipment (2022). https://www.ons.gov.uk/aboutus/transparencyandgovernance/freedomofinformationfoi/percentageofhomesandindividualswithtechnologicalequipment. Accessed 16 Oct 2023

19. OpenAI: Introducing whisper (2023). https://openai.com/research/whisper. Accessed 15 Sept 2023

20. Poinsett, P.M.: Cerebral palsy facts and statistics (2024). https://www.cerebralpalsyguidance.com/cerebral-palsy/research/facts-and-statistics/. Accessed 1 Apr 2024

21. Sense: Complex disabilities (2023). https://www.sense.org.uk/information-and-advice/conditions/what-does-complex-disabilities-mean/. Accessed 2 Jan 2024

22. Sense: Complex disabilities in the UK (2024). https://www.sense.org.uk/about-us/statistics/complex-disabilities-overview/. Accessed 2 Jan 2024

23. Szykman, A.G., Gois, J.P., Brandão, A.L.: A perspective of games for people with physical disabilities. In: Proceedings of the Annual Meeting of the Australian Special Interest Group for Computer Human Interaction, pp. 274–283 (2015)

24. Theil, A., Anderton, C., Creed, C., Olson, N., Holt, R.J., Sarcar, S.: Accessibility research and users with multiple disabilities or complex needs. In: Proceedings of the 25th International ACM SIGACCESS Conference on Computers and Accessibility, pp. 1–6 (2023)

25. Theil, A., Buchweitz, L., Schulz, A.S., Korn, O.: Understanding the perceptions and experiences of the deafblind community about digital games. Disabil. Rehabil. Assist. Technol. **18**(8), 1347–1356 (2023)

26. UK Government Digital Service: Understanding WCAG 2.2 (2023). https://www.gov.uk/service-manual/helping-people-to-use-your-service/understanding-wcag. Accessed 2 Apr 2024

27. W3C: Web Content Accessibility Guidelines (WCAG) 2.2 (2023). https://www.w3.org/TR/WCAG22/. Accessed 2 Apr 2024

28. Wästerfors, D., Hansson, K.: Taking ownership of gaming and disability. J. Youth Stud. **20**(9), 1143–1160 (2017)

Exploratory Study on Sustainability in Agile Software Development

Shola Oyedeji[1]([⊠]) [iD], Hatef Shamshiri[1] [iD], Mikhail O. Adisa[1] [iD], Jari Porras[1] [iD], Bilal Naqvi[1] [iD], and Dominic Lammert[2]

[1] LUT University, Lappeenranta, Finland
{shola.oyedeji,hatef.Shamshiri,mikhail.adisa,jari.porras,
Syed.Naqvi}@lut.fi
[2] Hochschule Furtwangen, Furtwangen im Schwarzwald, Germany
dominic.lammert@hfu.eu

Abstract. Sustainability is continuously gaining attention from different software research disciplines and organizations because of the impacts of human activities on the planet aided by software products and services. The process of creating and developing these software products and services through agile has gained significant attention with different guidelines and frameworks proposed to support sustainability. However, there is the challenge of a few concrete illustrations that exemplify how these software sustainability design guidelines and frameworks have been applied in agile practice, specifically Scrum by software development practitioners. This creates no common ground for software development practitioners to understand their role in promoting sustainability during software design and development. This paper explores integrating sustainability into agile software requirement gathering, focusing on the Scrum framework. The outcome presented in this study represents early results from an ongoing case study with an agile development team in the industry.

Keywords: Agile · Scrum · requirement · sustainability · software design · SusAF

1 Introduction

Sustainable development (SD) and sustainability have gained importance in research with continuously increasing populations and decreasing resources [1]. The continuing aim of SD is to maintain the planet's livability for the upcoming generations [2]. A research study involving selected software developers found that only a few considered sustainability as significant, suggesting a need for more awareness regarding the sustainability impacts of software development [3]. In software engineering, sustainability impacts can be viewed from the following dimensions according to Penzenstadler et al. [4]: Environmental (the use and maintenance of natural resources); Economical (maintaining financial capital); Social (factors that affect the interaction between a group of

M. K. Lárusdóttir et al. (Eds.): HCSE 2024, LNCS 14793, pp. 264–272, 2024.
https://doi.org/10.1007/978-3-031-64576-1_17

people such as trust, equality, inclusiveness and diversity); Individual (well-being of individuals and equal access to services); Technical (ensuring that software systems are used for an extended period and can evolve to meet changing requirements).

Research has shown that many software development companies and organizations design their software products and services without considering the sustainability impacts [5]. Instead, most companies focus on economic gains by looking at avenues for cutting development and resource costs to reduce time to deliver software products and services. This led to the wide adoption of agile in software development [6], such as Lean Software Development (LSD), Scrum, and Extreme Programming (XP). Agile methods help detect faulty code, embrace changing requirements, and deliver software products and services quickly [7]. From the lens of sustainability in agile software development, Eckstein and O. Mel [8, 9] explored how agile manifesto can be tailored to support social, economic, and environmental dimensions of sustainability. However, there have been less research exemplifying how this is done in companies. Bambazek et al. [10] investigated the elements of the scrum framework to address sustainability. The study outcome [10] shows software development practitioners see good potential for integrating sustainability impacts into the scrum Framework.

Our study builds on these studies to explore avenues for making software development practitioners (agile development team) aware of sustainability and integrating sustainability impacts into the scrum framework. The rest of the work is structured as follows: background study is in Sect. 2. The study design is detailed in Sect. 3. Results with discussion are presented in Sect. 4 Concluding remarks and suggestions for future work are in Sect. 5.

2 Background

Agile methodology allows for close collaboration with stakeholders during software project, and new requirements may be accepted even later in the project [15]. Despite the flexibility that agile offers for gathering and implementing software requirements, there are fewer tools for sustainability support to agile development teams. The purpose of requirement engineering (RE) is to implement a "system requirements document" to share knowledge, while agile development relies on achieving a similar goal by communicating with customers face-to-face [13]. RE focuses on modeling, conveying, and documenting software system requirements and the environment in which the system operates [14]. However, most applications of RE steps in agile software development do not cover sustainability because of a lack of sustainability knowledge and understanding. This lack of sustainability awareness by software development practitioners and companies is the reason for the development of sustainability awareness framework (SusAF) [16]. SusAF is a question-based tool coving different topics on the five dimensions of sustainability (Table 1) to help software development practitioners identify the potential sustainability impacts of software products and services.

Researchers have shown significant interest in matters relevant to agile software development, which is apparent from many published scientific articles [17]. However, agile practitioners encounter a broad scope of challenges, including sustainability [18]. Sustainability can be seen from two perspectives: sustainable software and sustainability by software. The former concerns the software that is not adversely impacting the

Table 1. Topics covered in each sustainability dimension of SusAF

Dimensions	Topics
Social	Sense of Community, Trust, Inclusiveness and Diversity, Equality, Participation and Communication
Individual	Health, Lifelong learning, Privacy, Safety, Self Awareness and Free will
Environmental	Material and Resources, Soil, Atmospheric and Water Pollution, Energy, Biodiversity and Land Use, Logistics and Transportation
Economic	Value, Customer Relationship Management, Supply chain, Ecosystem, Governance and Processes, Innovation and R&D
Technical	Maintainability, Usability, Extensibility and Adaptability, Security, Scalability

economy, society, or the environment by its deployment and production, while the latter concerns utilizing software to accomplish sustainable goals [19]. This study investigates how to incorporate sustainability impacts in agile software development with a starting point of the scrum product backlog. Product backlogs are lists of tasks (unresolved bugs, user stories, chores, etc.) used by software teams for coordinating work, and developers work on the items at the top of the backlog when developing new features, updating existing features, and fixing bugs [20]. We (authors) concentrated on the scrum product backlog as a starting point because that is the source of requirements for any agile software development within the scrum framework.

3   Study Design

This research details an ongoing case study for a software project (an online marketplace for service seekers and service providers) with software development practitioners (agile development team) in a company (software development company). The goal of the collaboration with the company is to improve the sustainability awareness among software development practitioners in agile software development processes (scrum). The information about the job title and years of experience in software development of the agile development team involved in the case study are detailed in Table 2.

The study process as shown in Fig. 1 begins with a pre-SusAF survey conducted with the agile development team to assess their level of sustainability awareness in software development. Subsequently, SusAF workshop is conducted to help the agile development team identify the potential impacts of the software project. Next, a post-SusAF survey was conducted to identify the changes in sustainability awareness of the agile development team. Thematic analysis is then performed on the pre and post-SusAF survey data to identify emerging themes. Finally, the researchers and agile development team explored ways of integrating sustainability into the agile scrum framework (product backlog) based on results from the SusAF workshop.

Table 2. Agile Team Background

No	Job Title	Years of Experience
1	Product Owner	6
2	Programmer	6
3	UI Specialist	5
4	Software Developer/Architect	6
5	IT Manager	4
6	Team Lead (Scrum Master)	9

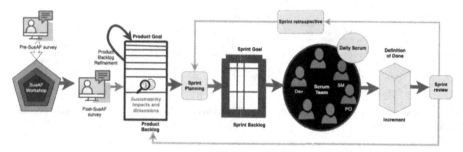

Fig. 1. Overview of the research process

4   Results

The agile team utilized SusAF to identify potential sustainability impacts of the software project as shown in Fig. 2. Figure 2A (red color text: negative impacts, blue color text: positive impacts) highlights how the agile development team grouped all identified impacts based on the likelihood that the impacts will occur with high or low impact. For example, in Fig. 2A SusAF helped the agile development team to identify that potential negative comments from users of the software project could cause other users mental distress (individual dimension), and data gathering within the software project could potentially lead to advertising data manipulation (social dimension).

Figure 2B shows the results of the agile development team prioritization discussion for the identified sustainability impacts across the sustainability dimensions. Some of the key focus covers measure and reduction of CO_2 emissions associated with development of the software project. The agile development also explored accessibility requirements for users, created requirements for a green awareness campaign module to improve user (service providers and service seekers) sustainability awareness and the implementation of content filtering to reduce hate comments on user profile pages.

Subsequently, the agile development team decided to integrate these identified and prioritized sustainability impacts into the scrum product backlog (Fig. 3) to ensure that sustainability is considered during the development process in each sprint. For the purpose of anonymity, Ben was used in Fig. 3 as the product owner. The researchers examined the product backlog (Fig. 3) and discussed them with the agile development team to

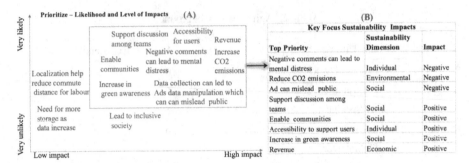

Fig. 2. Identified potential sustainability impacts of the software project (Color figure online)

User Story ID	Title	Description	Impact Indicator	Sustainability Dimension	Iteration	Owner	Legend
1	Register web	As WSP/WSS/WC I want to register	Enable communities	Social	1	Ben	WSS = Web Service Seeker
2	Login web	As WSP/WSS/WC I want to login	Increase in green awareness	Environmental	1	Ben	WSP = Web Service Provider
3	Register mobile	As MSP/MSS/MC I want to register	Enable communities	Social	1	Ben	WC = Web Company
4	Login mobile	As MSP/MSS/MC I want to login	Increase in green awareness	Environmental	1	Ben	MSP= Mobile Service Provider
5	Personal service	As WSP I want to add personal services to profile	Increase in green awareness	Environmental	1	Ben	MSS= Mobile Service Seeker
6	Create team	As WSP I can create team with other members	Enable communities	Social	1	Ben	MC= Mobile Company
7	Join team	As WSP I can join other teams	Support discussion among teams	Social	1	Ben	
8	Hired WSP	As WSP I want to get hired by WSS	Revenue	Economic	2	Ben	
9	Bidding	As WSP I can bid for offers by WSS	Revenue	Economic	2	Ben	
10	Hiring WSS/ WC	As WSS/WC I want to hire team or individual	Revenue	Economic	2	Ben	

Fig. 3. Sustainability impacts and dimensions linked to each item in the software project product backlog

understand the rationale behind linking each sustainability impact to the product backlog items. The agile development team clarified that all sustainability impacts used in the product backlog were based on the results from SusAF analysis (see Fig. 2), which enabled them to focus on high-impact sustainability concerns likely to occur. This process facilitates prioritizing the most critical sustainability impacts during the software development phase.

4.1 Pre and Post-SusAF Survey Results

The results of the pre and post-SusAF survey summarized in Table 3 presents the changes in sustainability awareness of the agile development team. The agile development team were asked to list the top two things that come to mind about sustainability in their work during agile (scrum) software development.

The pre-SusAF survey results with the emerged themes indicated the agile development team's focus on the technical sustainability dimension and traditional indicators of success in Agile development. However, the post-SusAF survey results show a shift in their sustainability perception to include more socially conscious and environmentally friendly considerations such as reducing carbon footprint, inclusiveness and diversity, design for efficiency and reusability. Furthermore, after the post-SusAF survey, the agile development team explained to the researchers some of the decisions and actions influenced by their new understanding of sustainability such as:

- Working with the researchers to create a tool for sustainability in agile software development.

Table 3. Pre and post- SusAF survey data from the agile development team

Pre-SusAF survey		Post-SusAF survey	
First	*Second*	*First*	*Second*
Efficiency	Product success	Efficient product to reduce carbon footprint	Inclusiveness and diversity
Sustainable pace	Working software	Efficient coding	My health and mood at work
Customer satisfaction	Good product	Easy-to-use and maintainable software products	Design for efficiency and reusability
Quality	Good performance based on user requirements	Judicious use of resources and project carbon footprint	Support a sense of community in software product
Good resource allocation	Great products for our customers = Revenue	Design products that are environmentally efficient in resource consumption	The mental well-being of the final users of our products
Usability	Performance	Efficient use of resources among teams	I will now help customers become aware of their CO2 impacts

- Rethink and evaluate their software development process to incorporate the SusAF workflow.
- Find ways to create a guideline that can facilitate better integration of SusAF for their designers

These results indicate a promising future for better sustainability consideration among the agile team during software design and development.

4.2 Discussion

Several sustainability guidelines and frameworks for software requirement elicitation are proposed in different research for software development practitioners to apply in the industry. However, very few concrete examples show how these different sustainability guidelines and frameworks were applied in practice in agile (Scrum) software development of products and services. The early results from the SusAF workshop with the product backlog which includes sustainability impacts and dimensions show there is the potential to consolidate existing research towards transfer of research to practice in agile software development. This can help improve the current state of sustainability practice by software development practitioners.

The collaboration between the researchers and the agile development team during the ongoing case study highlights the issues encountered by software development practitioners when considering sustainability in agile software requirements and development such as a lack of awareness about sustainability and a poor understanding of what sustainability means in software design and development as shown the pre-SusAF survey result (Table 3). This lack of sustainability understanding in software development is also reported in a different study [21]. Another study [22] reported that software development practitioners lack the knowledge and methodological support for acting as facilitators on sustainability issues in their software system.

The SusAF workshop intervention indicated promising results because the sustainability awareness in software development of the agile development team from the post-SusAF survey results showed a transition from a focus on technical sustainability to a holistic view covering the environmental, social and individual sustainability dimensions. Therefore, tool support is required to support and guide software development practitioners for sustainability in agile software development. The results of this study indicate the potential to create sustainability awareness among software development teams in the industry.

4.3 Threat to Validity

The results presented in this research are early results from a case study with one company which can limit the generalization of results. However, this study's outcome in terms of the challenges faced by software development practitioners on sustainability integration into software development is also reported in other studies [22–24].

5   Conclusion

Agile methodologies provide the frameworks for software development practitioners in most ICT companies to design and develop software products and services that have a far-reaching sustainability effect on the users, society, and the environment. Software development practitioners must be empowered to take responsibility for the sustainability impacts of software systems through design decisions in development and deployment. Consequently, it is important to infuse sustainability concerns into agile frameworks such as scrum to promote sustainability awareness among software development practitioners. The results presented in this study are early results from an ongoing case study demonstrating the potential to incorporate sustainability concerns in scrum framework (product backlog). The researchers plan to continuously work with agile development team to create a toolkit covering product backlog and planning, daily scrum, sprint review and retrospective. The aim is to guide software development practitioners in recognizing and improving the sustainability impacts of the different design choices of software systems on sustainability.

References

1. Penzenstadler, B., Fleischmann, A.: Teach sustainability in software engineering? In: 24th IEEE-CS Conference on Software Engineering Education and Training (CSEE&T) (2011). https://doi.org/10.1109/CSEET.2011.5876124
2. Manteuffel, C., Ioakeimidis, S.: A systematic mapping study on sustainable software engineering: a research preview. In: 9th SC RUG 2011–2012, p. 35 (2012)
3. Oyedeji, S., Shamshiri, H., Porras, J., Lammert, D.: Software sustainability: academic understanding and industry perceptions. In: Wang, X., Martini, A., Nguyen-Duc, A., Stray, V. (eds.) ICSOB 2021. LNBIP, vol. 434, pp. 18–34. Springer, Cham (2021). https://doi.org/10.1007/978-3-030-91983-2_3
4. Penzenstadler, B., Femmer, H.: A generic model for sustainability with process- and product-specific instances. In: Proceedings of the 2013 Workshop on Green in/by Software Engineering. In: GIBSE 2013, pp. 3–8. Association for Computing Machinery, New York, March 2013. https://doi.org/10.1145/2451605.2451609
5. Galán, O.A.A., Valdéz, J.L.C., Medina, H.F., Vanegas Contreras, G.A., Sumuano, J.L.S.: Proposal of a sustainable agile model for software deevelopment.pdf. Int. J. Adv. Comput. Sci. Appl. 11(1) (2020)
6. Rashid, N., Khan, S.U.: Developing green and sustainable software using agile methods in global software development: risk factors for vendors. In: ENASE 2016 – Proceedings of the 11th International Conference on Evaluation of Novel Software Approaches to Software Engineering, ENASE, pp. 247–253 (2016). https://doi.org/10.5220/0005913802470253
7. Wrubel, E., Wrubel, J.G.: Contracting for agile software development in the department of defense: an introduction. Technical report. CMUSEI-2015- TN-006 Carneige Mellon Univ. (2015)
8. Eckstein, J., de Melo, C.O.: Sustainability: delivering agility's promise. In: Calero, C., Moraga, M.ªÁ., Piattini, M. (eds.) Software Sustainability, pp. 215–241. Springer, Cham (2021). https://doi.org/10.1007/978-3-030-69970-3_9
9. Melo, CdeO.: Another purpose for agility: sustainability. In: Meirelles, P., Nelson, M.A., Rocha, C. (eds.) WBMA 2019. CCIS, vol. 1106, pp. 3–7. Springer, Cham (2019). https://doi.org/10.1007/978-3-030-36701-5_1
10. Bambazek, P., Groher, I., Seyff, N.: Sustainability in agile software development: a survey study among practitioners. In: 2022 International Conference on ICT for Sustainability (ICT4S), pp. 13–23, June 2022. https://doi.org/10.1109/ICT4S55073.2022.00013
11. Endres, M., Bican, P.M., Wöllner, T.: Sustainability meets agile: using Scrum to develop frugal innovations. J. Clean. Prod. 347, 130871 (2022). https://doi.org/10.1016/j.jclepro.2022.130871
12. Saher, N., Baharom, F., Romli, R.: Identification of Sustainability Characteristics and Sub-Characteristics as Non-Functional Requirement for Requirement Change Management in Agile (2020). https://www.semanticscholar.org/paper/Identification-of-Sustainability-Characteristics-as-Saher-Baharom/f6a38e7bdb6349075f1929bdc37b3f71a6194081. Accessed 05 Apr 2024
13. De Lucia, A., Qusef, A.: Requirements engineering in agile software development. J. Emerg. Technol. Web Intell. 2(3) (2010)
14. Paetsch, F., Maurer, F.: Requirements Engineering and Agile Software Development, pp. 1–6 (2003)
15. Fowler, M., Highsmith, J.: The agile manifesto. Softw. Dev. 9, 28–35 (2001). https://doi.org/10.1177/004057368303900411
16. SusAF - the sustainability awareness framework. Karlskrona Manif. Group (2019)

17. Dingsøyr, T., Nerur, S., Balijepally, V., Moe, N.B.: A decade of agile methodologies: towards explaining agile software development. J. Syst. Softw. **85**(6), 1213–1221 (2012). https://doi.org/10.1016/j.jss.2012.02.033

18. Gregory, P., Barroca, L., Sharp, H., Deshpande, A., Taylor, K.: The challenges that challenge: engaging with agile practitioners' concerns. Inf. Softw. Technol. **77**, 92–104 (2016). https://doi.org/10.1016/j.infsof.2016.04.006

19. Condori-Fernandez, N., Lago, P.: Towards a software sustainability-quality model: insights from a multi-case study. In: 2019 13th International Conference on Research Challenges in Information Science (RCIS), pp. 1–11, May 2019. https://doi.org/10.1109/RCIS.2019.8877084

20. The Product Backlog | IEEE Conference Publication | IEEE Xplore. https://ieeexplore-ieee-org.ezproxy.cc.lut.fi/abstract/document/8812076. Accessed 11 Feb 2024

21. Oyedeji, S., Seffah, A., Penzenstadler, B.: A catalogue supporting software sustainability design. Sustainability **10**(7), 1–30 (2018). https://doi.org/10.3390/su10072296

22. Duboc, L., et al.: Requirements engineering for sustainability: an awareness framework for designing software systems for a better tomorrow. Requir. Eng. **25**(4), 469–492 (2020). https://doi.org/10.1007/s00766-020-00336-y

23. Heldal, R., et al.: Sustainability competencies and skills in software engineering: an Industry perspective. J. Syst. Softw. **211**, 111978 (2024)

24. Betz, S., et al.: Lessons learned from developing a sustainability awareness framework for software engineering using design science. ACM Trans. Softw. Eng. Methodol. **33**(5), 1–39 (2024). https://doi.org/10.1145/3649597

Intuitiveness and Trustworthiness of AI-Powered Interfaces for Neurological Diagnosis - Preliminary Results

Angela Lombardi[1] , Sofia Marzo[1], Eugenio Di Sciascio[1] ,
Tommaso Di Noia[1] , and Carmelo Ardito[2]([✉])

[1] Politecnico di Bari, Bari, Italy
{angela.lombardi,sofia.marzo,eugenio.disciascio,tommaso.dinoia}@poliba.it
[2] Università LUM Giuseppe Degennaro, Casamassima, BA, Italy
ardito@lum.it

Abstract. The work presented in this article is part of a broader research initiative whose focus revolves around the integration of Artificial Intelligence (AI) in diagnosing Mild Cognitive Impairment (MCI), in particular, investigating the reliability and stability of eXplainable AI (XAI) predictions concerning markers of MCI and Alzheimer's Disease. In order to foster neurologists' understanding, confidence and trust in the AI system results, the initial Machine Learning (ML) based analysis pipeline has been now extended to incorporate a graphical user interface (GUI) that would provide "neurologist-centred" explanations. In this article, the focus is on a preliminary study that involved neurology professionals to assess their understanding and confidence in AI-generated diagnoses presented through three alternative plots implemented in the system GUI.

Keywords: Human-Centered Artificial Intelligence (HCAI) ·
Explainable Artificial Intelligence (XAI) · Trustworthiness · Mild
Cognitive Impairment (MCI)

1 Introduction

The integration of Artificial Intelligence (AI) in healthcare, especially in neurology for the diagnosis of conditions such as Mild Cognitive Impairment (MCI), represents a significant advancement in medical diagnostics and patient care [7]. MCI diagnosis, situated at the critical juncture between normal aging and dementia, benefits immensely from early and accurate identification [8]. The complexity inherent in neurological data and decision-making underscores the necessity for interfaces that not only harness the analytical capabilities of AI but also ensure these capabilities are accessible and actionable for clinicians. This highlights the essential role of Human-Computer Interaction (HCI) in the design of medical decision support systems, ensuring that technology aids rather than

© IFIP International Federation for Information Processing 2024
Published by Springer Nature Switzerland AG 2024
M. K. Lárusdóttir et al. (Eds.): HCSE 2024, LNCS 14793, pp. 273–280, 2024.
https://doi.org/10.1007/978-3-031-64576-1_18

complicates the clinician's decision-making process [10]. This synergy is particularly critical in healthcare, where decision accuracy is paramount. Building upon HCI principles, Human-Centered Artificial Intelligence (HCAI) prioritizes the development of AI technologies that adhere to human values and ethics, focusing on transparency and aligning with the end-users' needs and contexts [9]. For neurology and specifically MCI diagnosis, this means developing AI models that are not only accurate but also operate in a manner that is transparent and complementary to clinicians' expertise.

The multidisciplinary interest in Explainable Artificial Intelligence (XAI) reflects a broad recognition of its importance across various fields, from machine learning engineering to cognitive science and HCI. According to Mohseni and others [6], the diversity in definitions and expectations for XAI highlights the need for collaborative research that spans multiple disciplines, acknowledging that different stakeholders have unique requirements and goals [5]. In HCI, the focus is on developing solutions that meet end-user needs, irrespective of the underlying technology. This user-centric approach is vital in ensuring that AI systems, particularly those used in sensitive areas like healthcare, are designed with a clear understanding of the target users' requirements for explainability.

The work presented in this article is part of a broader research initiative whose focus revolves around investigating the reliability and stability of XAI predictions concerning markers of MCI and Alzheimer's Disease.

The AI system introduced in [3] differentiate between healthy individuals and those diagnosed with MCI through the analysis of brain connectivity, utilizing diffusion data from the ADNI database [2]. This analysis allows for the accurate classification of subjects into Healthy Control (HC) and MCI categories based on structural connectivity metrics. In order to foster neurologists' understanding, confidence and trust in the AI system results, it has been extended to incorporate a graphical user interface (GUI) that would provide "neurologist-centred" explanations by means of three alternative plots, based on different explanation visualization techniques.

In Sect. 2, we explore the three visualization techniques and in Sect. 3 we present a preliminary study assessing their effectiveness. As briefly remarked in Sect. 4, this investigation would contribute to the broader discourse on AI, HCI, and healthcare, offering insights into the development of interfaces that effectively bridge human expertise with artificial intelligence.

2   Visualization Techniques for the AI System

Investigating literature and clinicians' knowledge of the specific application domain, it was found that there were two candidate visualisation techniques to be the basis of a graphical user interface for our AI system, namely the Global Tornado Plot [1] and the Brain Connectivity Plot [4], which are largely used in the medical domain as XAI techniques for visualizing AI system results. It was decided to also consider a variant of the former, known as Counterfactual Tornado Plot, because it could be effective for the case at hand. These three visualizations were conceived to present the information in a manner that aligns with different perceptual and cognitive approaches, thereby facilitating a deeper understanding of the XAI outputs.

Global Tornado Plot. This plot, which is represented in Fig. 1, is instrumental in depicting the significance of features as determined by SHAP (SHapley Additive exPlanations) values in our machine learning model. SHAP values are widely used to provide a consistent and objective explanation of the influence of each feature on the model's prediction. Originating from game theory, SHAP values attribute an importance score to every feature within a model, where features with positive SHAP values enhance the prediction, whereas those with negative values detract from it. The size of these values indicates the strength of the impact.

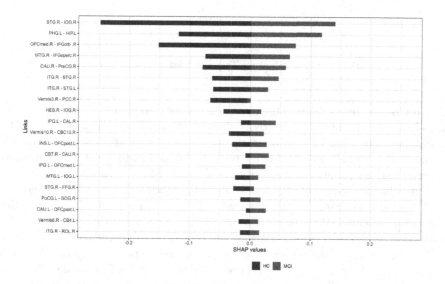

Fig. 1. Global Tornado Plot visualization.

Counterfactual Tornado Plot. This plot, exemplified in Fig. 2, offers insights into the determinants of health classifications, elucidating the impact of various factors on the diagnosis of an individual as either healthy or at risk, and explores hypothetical scenarios where altering certain factors could lead to a different health outcome. Primarily aimed at subjects classified as normal controls, this counterfactual analysis provides healthcare professionals and patients with an understanding of the predictive elements indicating a high risk of disease progression. The plot leverages an AI-generated counterfactual explanation, which proposes an alternate scenario that could have resulted in a different classification outcome.

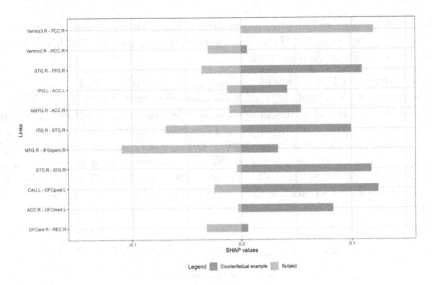

Fig. 2. Counterfactual Tornado Plot visualization.

Brain Connectivity Plot. This visualization, depicted in Fig. 3, leverages a 3D model of brain structural connectivity derived from Diffusion Tensor Imaging to assess the white matter (WM) alterations associated with aging and Alzheimer's Disease. This model, known for its capacity to delineate the microstructural integrity and anatomical connectivity of the brain, plays a crucial role in understanding the progression of MCI and AD by highlighting disease-related effects in WM. By amalgamating SHAP values with detailed brain connectivity data, the plot offers an enriched perspective that merges machine learning insights with neuroscientific knowledge, elucidating how specific features influence outcomes.

For each of these techniques, a static paper prototype representing the data of a possible patient was created and presented to a sample of 3 neurologists in an informal test. After slight modifications and improvements, three final prototypes were implemented to be used in the following phase, i.e. the Neurologist Survey.

3   Neurologist Survey

A preliminary study was carried out as a survey for assessing the effectiveness of the three different plots.

3.1   Participants

A comprehensive cohort of 31 participants was targeted. Regrettably, the response rate fell short of the initial outreach, with only 17 individuals submitting fully completed surveys. Consequently, the ensuing analysis and discussion are exclusively predicated upon the data derived from this subset of participants.

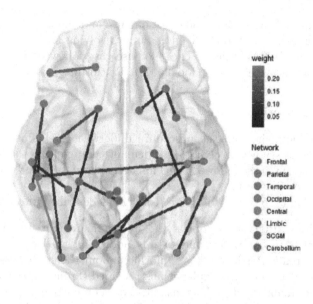

Fig. 3. Brain Connectivity Plot visualization

The demographic profile of the 17 participants who completed the survey is as follows:

- age range: 8 participants in the range 25–35; 5 participants in the range 36–45; 3 participants in the range 46–55; 1 participant in the range 66–70;
- gender distribution: 8 female participants and 9 male participants;
- years of practice as Neurologist: 10 participants declared 1–10 years of practice, 4 participants declared 11–15 years of practice, 2 participants declared 16–25 years of practice, and 1 participant declared 31–40 years of practice.

The geographic distribution of the survey participants spans several key urban and research centers in Italy, namely Bari, Bologna, Lecce, Pavia, Rome, and Florence. All participants reported daily computer usage for work-related activities, with Windows as the predominant operating system. Notably, the majority of participants declared themselves as non-competent in computer usage (58.82%) and non-familiar with AI concepts (82.35%). Additionally, the remaining portion of participants only reported an interaction with ChatGPT.

3.2 Procedure

The survey was conducted remotely and asynchronously. Survey participants received the questionnaire via email. Participants began by clicking the link in the email, and opening the survey on the Lime Survey platform. The first page provided an overview and explained how the survey platform worked, with participants free to quit if they did not consent. Only after giving consent did participants proceed to the main survey. No questions sought information revealing the participant's identity. Both the questionnaire and the procedure underwent preliminary assessment through a pilot study involving two participants competent in the field of Neurology. The pilot use case followed the Think Aloud Strategy and took place via the Google Meet Platform.

3.3 Data Collection

Both the questionnaire and the procedure underwent preliminary assessment through two pilot studies involving a participant competent in the field of Neurology. The pilot use case followed the Think Aloud Strategy and took place via the Google Meet Platform.

The questionnaire consisted of five sections, as described in the following.

1. **Survey introduction**: it opens the questionnaire with an introductory explanation of the AI system under study, addressing the lack of transparency in these systems. Participants are informed about the study's focus on evaluating the effectiveness of explanations provided through various graphs.
2. **Curiosity checklist**: it gathers insightful data on participants' curiosity and motivations toward AI use and for seeking explanations. Participants were presented with a question inquiring, *"Why would you look for an explanation?"*. The question was structured to allow for multiple answer choices, offering participants the opportunity to express their feelings of curiosity.
3. **Comprehension and evaluation**: it is dedicated to providing a comprehensive explanation of each plot. Participants are required to execute some tasks, and to answer, in a 5-point Likert format, questions on satisfaction and trust.
4. **Demographic information**: it collects demographic information and assesses participants' Information Technology knowledge levels.
5. **Survey procedure rating and final thoughts**: it gathers participants comments and ratings of the administered survey.

3.4 Results and Discussions

Curiosity and Engagement. Drawing insights from user opinions on AI usage in Neurology and the responses obtained through the curiosity checklist, clinicians' perspectives unfold with a dual nature. This duality encapsulates both a keen desire to explore AI applications further and, concurrently, a lingering sense of skepticism. Addressing this dual perspective is instrumental in shaping strategies for the third research question. The coexistence of curiosity and skepticism signals an opportunity for targeted interventions in the form of training and education.

Comprehension of Explanations. The highest average rate of correct responses was associated with the interface based on the Global Tornado Plot, achieving a rate of 91%, on par with the Brain Connectivity Plot. Conversely, the Counterfactual Plot ranked lowest with an 84% rate. Participants' varying degrees of success in understanding the explanations provided valuable insights. This task correctness rate unveiled differences across the three visualizations - Global Tornado Plot, Brain Connectivity Plot, and Counterfactual Plot, contributing to our understanding of clinicians' comprehension levels. In particular, it is evident that the visualization garnering the highest average rate of correct responses is associated with the Global Tornado Plot, showing that a quantitative visualization focused on the effects of features discriminating populations, rather than effects on single individuals, is more easily understood by participants.

Comprehension Self-assessment. The Global Tornado Plot maintained the top position, attaining an average rating of 3.71 on a 5-point Likert scale, followed by the Brain Plot and the Counterfactual Plot with average ratings of 3.29 and 3.18, respectively. Participants' self-assessment ratings shed light on their perceived mastery, allowing us to gauge the level of confidence users had in comprehending the intricacies of the explanations. It turned out that while the Tornado Plot was also confirmed in first place in this ranking, participants judged their understanding of Global Plot good, and they also put themselves in a more neutral position concerning the other two plots.

Trust and Satisfaction. The Global Tornado Plot attained a trust sentiment score of 3.32, the Brain Plot scores 3.19, and the Counterfactual Plot scored 3.18, on average. Analyzing trust and satisfaction scores provided a subjective lens into participants' confidence levels. The prevailing neutrality in trust-related responses underscored the delicate nature of establishing trust in AI-related outcomes, presenting a nuanced understanding of clinicians' sentiments. Moreover, while the data ranks the Global Tornado Plot explanation as the most effective across the three metrics, it is imperative to acknowledge that the Counterfactual explanation utilizes the same visualization technique (Tornado Plot). Therefore, it presents opportunities for straightforward improvement. Given the substantial user demand for additional examples, consideration could be given to making them available within the Counterfactual Plot and Brain Plot, coupled with the incorporation of new tasks.

Participant's Feedback. By analyzing the participant feedback on the survey procedure, it emerged that:

- A significant potential for AI is discerned; however, it is underscored that such potential must be concomitantly supported by specialized medical expertise.
- The utility of AI is acknowledged, particularly in the realm of research.
- Emphasis is placed on the prerequisite of specific medical training for physicians concerning the themes, operations, and techniques associated with AI for its effective utilization.
- While the value of AI is recognized, a prevailing sentiment asserts that it cannot replace the indispensable contribution of medical professionals.
- Skepticism towards the application of AI is expressed, primarily stemming from the perceived inadequacy in collaboration with medical practitioners at present.

4   Conclusion

This study serves as a foundational step in an ongoing and open process aimed at designing effective XAI user interfaces tailored for neurological applications, specifically in supporting MCI diagnosis. The insights gleaned from our survey, structured across three levels to answer critical research questions, lay the groundwork for informed decision-making in the development of the XAI system.

The survey results unveiled a notable interest in AI among clinicians, coupled with a reasonable level of confidence in the explainability and interpretability of the XAI tools exploited in this study. However, even with these positive indications, there remains ample room for improvement. The invaluable feedback collected from participants is poised to be a guiding force in refining and optimizing these tools to ensure enhanced user acceptance.

Crucially, this preliminary work suggests that merely relying on user feedback for redesigning the interface might not be sufficient. Instead, it emphasizes the vital need to incorporate targeted training modules. These modules, designed to enhance understanding and trust in AI outputs, are envisioned as integral components for a successful integration of AI into clinical settings.

References

1. Ferraro, A., Galli, A., Moscato, V., Sperlì, G.: Evaluating explainable artificial intelligence tools for hard disk drive predictive maintenance. Artif. Intell. Rev. **56**(7), 7279–7314 (2023)
2. Lella, E., et al.: Communicability characterization of structural DWI subcortical networks in Alzheimer's disease. Entropy **21**(5), 475 (2019)
3. Lombardi, A., et al.: A robust framework to investigate the reliability and stability of explainable artificial intelligence markers of mild cognitive impairment and Alzheimer's disease. Brain Inform. **9**(1), 1–17 (2022)
4. Margulies, D.S., Böttger, J., Watanabe, A., Gorgolewski, K.J.: Visualizing the human connectome. Neuroimage **80**, 445–461 (2013)
5. Miller, T.: Explanation in artificial intelligence: insights from the social sciences. Artif. Intell. **267**, 1–38 (2017). https://api.semanticscholar.org/CorpusID: 36024272
6. Mohseni, S., Zarei, N., Ragan, E.D.: A multidisciplinary survey and framework for design and evaluation of explainable AI systems **11**(3–4) (2021). https://doi.org/10.1145/3387166
7. Patel, U.K., et al.: Artificial intelligence as an emerging technology in the current care of neurological disorders. J. Neurol. **268**, 1623–1642 (2021)
8. Petersen, R.C.: Mild cognitive impairment as a diagnostic entity. J. Intern. Med. **256**(3), 183–194 (2004)
9. Shneiderman, B.: Human-Centered AI. Oxford University Press, Oxford (2022)
10. Topol, E.J.: High-performance medicine: the convergence of human and artificial intelligence. Nat. Med. **25**(1), 44–56 (2019)

Medical-Domain-Expert-Centered AI-Assisted Digitized Histopathology Education Tool

Erika Váczlavová[iD] and Miroslav Laco[(✉)][iD]

Faculty of Informatics and Information Technologies, Slovak University of Technology, Ilkovičova 2, 842 16 Karlova Ves, Bratislava, Slovakia
miroslav.laco@stuba.sk
https://www.fiit.stuba.sk/

Abstract. Education in the medical domain with the help of digitized content using state-of-the-art technology is a current topic, nowadays. In this paper, we are presenting our ongoing research on streamlining the medical domain expert workflow in the field of histopathology by designing a graphical user interface for an artificial-intelligence-powered (AI-powered) assistance educational tool for digitized specimen annotations. We found out that the approach to the presentation of the AI-powered features in the user interface should be built upon the level of expertise of the domain expert. The differences in interactions with the proposed annotation tools were observed in a case study with five participants with different levels of expertise from ongoing research cooperation with medical faculty students and domain experts in the field of histopathology. We discuss the quantitative and qualitative outcomes from the aforementioned case study to serve as a base for maximizing the benefits leveraging from applying AI-powered assistance tools in the field of education in digitized histopathology.

Keywords: Human-AI Interaction · User Experience · Histopathology

1 Introduction

Histopathology specimens are tissue samples obtained during biopsy or surgical procedures and subjected to pathology observation. Specialized scanners are used with whole slide imaging technology (WSI) to digitize these specimens as high-resolution digital images. These types of high-resolution digital images are highly suitable for educational purposes as these are more interactive than the physical specimens examined in the microscope [9]. Moreover, it is easy to share them and to provide the same educative information to each student. Hence, it has naturally been increasingly used in pathology examinations [10,17] since the past decade.

During the examination of a specimen, pathologists carefully observe and interpret the pathological characteristics of the case within the context of clinical information. Through this process, they identify regions of interest, pertinent

Published by Springer Nature Switzerland AG 2024
M. K. Lárusdóttir et al. (Eds.): HCSE 2024, LNCS 14793, pp. 281–290, 2024.
https://doi.org/10.1007/978-3-031-64576-1_19

to the specific cases [19]. The whole process is time-consuming and inefficient when done with a physical specimen using a microscope. Higher accuracy, capability, and efficiency are some of the many reasons why to transform the workflow to a digital one, through the digitization of specimens. The digitized WSI images can be processed using various annotation tools. These tools typically provide a menu of markup shapes including measured lines, polygons, rectangles, circles, and free-form lines, which can be applied in a wide range of colours. Some systems allow text labelling of the annotation [19]. Another method to enhance the efficiency of pathologists' workflow with digitized WSI images is by integrating AI algorithms into the process [5]. These algorithms can automatically identify areas of interest within the images, thereby accelerating the workflow of medical domain experts. Subsequently, experts would review the outputs of the artificial intelligence system [8] and make adjustments as needed. The open research question regarding the aforementioned possibilities is the end-user-centred interface design for the tool capable of mediation of these technologies in the medical education process.

In our work, we aim to leverage the benefits of the assisted digitized image annotation processes incorporated into the education at medical faculties. Our endeavour involves the proposal of a graphical user interface for a specialized educational tool supported by AI-assisted workflows presented accordingly to the target audience. The proposed tool was designed using a custom medical-domain-expert-oriented methodology with respect to state-of-the-art human-centered software design principles.

2 Related Work

The design of AI-infused user interfaces and human-AI interactions poses multifaceted challenges, nowadays. The AI infusion into the applications has a potential for introducing unforeseen errors which can adversely impact both reputation and user experience in collaborative settings. Designing cooperation between humans and the AI is particularly demanding in the case [7, 20].

One of the challenges for user experience designers is setting user expectations regarding AI capabilities. Since the AI lacks the aspect of awareness, there is a concern over the incorrect AI outputs potentially causing frustration to the user in an unexpected way. Additionally, collaborating on the AI applications with the AI experts is challenging for the domain experts due to the distinct domains involved in the collaborative design process. Moreover, it is crucial to design a framework with the correct way of presenting outputs of the AI with the appropriate level of **complexity** and comprehensibility [6, 20] .

While we design the right way of presenting the AI-assisted features in the user interface, we should be also aware of the **understandability** aspect. The understandability is associated with the explainability of the AI black-box nature. The more understandable the AI algorithm and its results are, the deeper the knowledge that humans may benefit from [11] .

Furthermore, various educational and annotation tools for digitized multimodal data can be used for education in the histopathology domain with its own set of advantages and limitations, nowadays. **QuPath** [3] stands as a beacon of open-source ingenuity, offering a versatile platform for the analysis of medical image data. Its ability to handle diverse formats and provide a range of marking tools empowers users to annotate and manipulate areas of interest directly over digital specimens. However, the absence of a comment feature and a somewhat complex user interface may pose challenges, particularly for those with limited computer literacy. Moreover, the usage of the AI algorithms within this tool is a great challenge for an expert in the medical domain. In contrast, **AMBOSS** [1] represents a commercially driven approach, offering an extensive repository of educational materials in a sleek, user-friendly interface. Its virtual library and note-taking functionalities enhance the learning experience, allowing users to create and share annotations with ease. Nonetheless, its closed commercial nature restricts the ability to modify or expand the educational content, limiting its potential for evolving with the dynamic landscape of medical knowledge and innovative AI algorithms. Meanwhile, **The Human Protein Atlas** [2] serves as a valuable supplementary educational resource, providing a wealth of high-resolution images showcasing protein distribution across various human tissues and cell lines. While its predefined pathways and detailed descriptions offer structured learning experiences, the inability to insert custom images or annotate specimens may restrict its utility for interactive teaching and analysis.

In summary, each of the tools possesses distinctive strengths and downsides for educational purposes in the histopathology domain. However, none of the tools is ready to face the ongoing research trends in digitized histopathology to support the education of the next generation of medical domain experts. Nevertheless, understanding and effectively managing individual limitations of these tools is the essential step towards maximizing benefits in the further development of innovative intelligent educational tools in the field of histopathology.

3   AI-Assisted Digitized Histopathology Education Tool

In this paper, we propose the user interface for the AI-Assisted Digitized Histopathology Annotation Tool (AIDHA; see Fig. 2), an annotation tool that will be part of a comprehensive histopathology educational system in cooperation with medical domain experts. The proposed tool focuses on annotating digitized histopathology specimens for educational purposes at the medical faculties using conventional manual annotation methods (see Sect. 2) combined with an AI-assisted approach. The AIDHA tool should serve two identified personas - a histopathology expert teaching histology at the university seeking modern educational methods, and a student as a domain expert with a low level of expertise who seeks hands-on experience in digitized histopathology annotation as a future clinical standard in the field. The proposed user interface for the AIDHA tool is in the form of a high-fidelity prototype designed in the Axure software system with javascript add-ins to enable advanced interactions.

3.1   Medical-Domain-Expert-Centered Design Methodology

Recent studies recommend that for successful designing in the field of medicine and health, it is necessary to adopt specific usability methodologies [14]. We applied modified patient-centred design methodology [14], the medical-domain-expert-centered design methodology (MDEC), to design the user interface of the proposed AIDHA tool. The key components of the proposed methodology can be found in Fig. 1a. During the design process, the role of the MDEC methodology is to ensure that the domain expert provides medical domain knowledge necessary for the technical domain within the system, while the system provides AI outputs to the domain expert in an understandable way. The understandable output presentation is ensured by the user experience designer in the loop. Subsequently, domain knowledge is obtained from the domain expert through intuitive interactions with the AI outputs and translated into technical domain language. Crucial is ensuring that the trust of the domain expert, for whom the system is designed, is gradually established.

The detailed steps of the MDEC design methodology are visualized in Fig. 1b. The very first half of the methodology ends with the understanding of the mental model of the medical domain expert. This phase is preceded by observing domain experts, gradually followed by attending them in their own working environment. Observing the typical working environment helps us better understand the typical flow of activities, while the domain expert appears more confident with their behavioural model undisturbed by various external factors. The second half of the collaboration begins with the trust-building phase. The trust of the domain expert in the field of medicine towards the technical domain expert is crucial due to significant differences in their expertise. With such an approach, the domain expert gains confidence and begins to collaborate with technical domain experts as with colleagues without the need to distinguish or underestimate either side. After gaining trust, it is necessary to reinforce it by involving the domain expert in the design and development process, making it clear that their opinion is important. The involvement of the domain expert may have various forms, from the initial stage of prototype design through the testing and feedback sessions. The final phase of the collaboration is the outcome delivery. The outcome of the collaboration using MDEC design methodology should bring up the benefits for both the medical domain expert side and the technical domain.

3.2   Proposed AI-Assisted Annotation Approach

While designing the user interface for the AIDHA tool, our focus was on deliberating upon the most suitable presentation of AI outputs for the AI-assisted annotation approach. Two principal approaches were considered: automation represented by AI-driven task execution devoid of human intervention and augmentation which entailed AI providing recommendations to the users [18].

We propose the interaction design for the two approaches to AI-assisted annotations aimed at simulating the presentation of the AI outputs using two distinct user interface features. Automation is represented by a tool that automatically

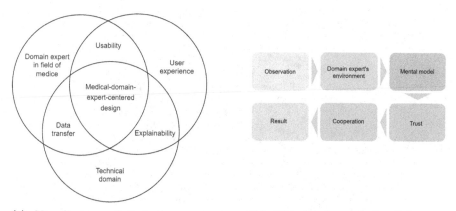

(a) Visualization of 3 key components and their cooperation in the
medical-domain-expert-centered   design (MDEC) methodology. Each area
overlay represents an area to focus on.
Adapted from Meloncon et al. [14]

(b) Visualization of detailed steps
of medical-domain-expert-centered design (MDEC).

Fig. 1. Medical-Domain-Expert-Centered Design Methodology.

highlights all the AI-identified annotations over the digitized specimen upon the
user triggers the workflow. This functionality is depicted in Fig. 2, highlighted
by a green pictogram. Augmentation was represented by a feature gradually
revealing areas of interest in the digitized specimen, requiring user confirmation
or rejection of each annotation within the visual context in the digitized specimen. The snapshot of this functionality is depicted in Fig. 2, highlighted by a
blue pictogram. Our contribution includes comparing the usability and understandability of the AI-assisted annotations by usability testing and evaluating
the user benefits of the proposed approaches for educational purposes.

4   Usability Study

During the usability testing [12] of the AIDHA tool with five domain experts
(more in [15]) representing the two identified personas [13] (see Subsect. 3), we
quantified the task completion rate and time to complete task metrics. Moreover, we collected qualitative data from user feedback during the thinking-aloud
session and user interviews [4]. During the testing phase, we also examined the
understandability of AI-assisted annotations and their proposed presentation
methods.

We designed 3 tasks for the usability testing session with the real digitized
histopathology specimen containing endocardium tissue along with the simulated
AI-assisted annotations based on the ground-truth annotations from domain
experts [16]. The usability testing tasks were designed as follows: manual annotation of the histopathology specimen, AI-assisted annotation using the annota-

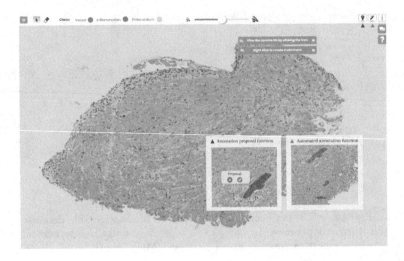

Fig. 2. AI-Assisted Digitized Histopathology Annotation Tool (AIDHA) prototype. The picture contains two proposed AI output presentation features simulating the AI outputs. The augmentation is represented by an Annotation proposal (blue pictogram) and automation by Automated annotations (green pictogram). (Color figure online)

tion proposal presentation approach (augmentation), and AI-assisted annotation using the automation approach. The domain experts annotated the same specimen using all three proposed methods.

4.1   Results and Discussion

Quantitative Results. Regarding the task completion rate metric, participants of the usability testing were able to complete all tasks without any significant assistance from the facilitator of the usability testing. The user interface of the AIDHA tool was proven to be designed as intuitive to early adopters without any deeper experience in the field of information technology. In Table 1, we can observe the trend of user performance within the proposed tool with and without the assistance of AI-powered annotation interactions. As evidenced, tasks involving an AI-assisted annotation approach were completed faster. The limitation of the usability study was introduced by participants gaining experience with the tool and gradually acclimating to its use with each task. Another encountered limitation was of a technical nature introduced by the limited vertical completeness of the designed prototype which did not affect the designed testing scenarios. We claim this bias does not contradict our general research finding that the application of an AI-assisted approach in any form increases work efficiency when introduced in the tool after the user gets familiar with the manual annotation workflow.

Qualitative Results. All participants appreciated the AI-assisted annotation approach using **automation** more than the manual annotation process. Par-

Table 1. Task completion time (seconds) from the usability testing of the AIDHA tool with 5 participants from the medical domain with various levels of expertise.

Participant (Expertise)	Manual annotation (Task 1)	Annotation proposal (Task 2)	Automated annotations (Task 3)
P1 (Low)	145	98	**70**
P2 (Low)	150	80	**60**
P3 (Low)	180	96	**60**
P4 (High)	185	75	**50**
P5 (Low)	180	110	**57**
Average	168	91.8	**59.4**
Std	16.91	12.71	6.43

ticipants with lower levels of expertise stated it would speed up their study workflow and qualify them for their potential future work. Participants with higher levels of expertise exhibit more skepticism towards the automation approach. They were concerned that the system may produce incorrect annotations which they may not have the capability to verify. The **augmentation** was perceived by participants as faster than the manual annotation process, but slower than the automation approach. Participants with lower levels of expertise stated they would benefit mainly from the intuitive orientation in the digitized specimen using this approach. Domain experts with higher levels of expertise claimed it would facilitate their manual and laborious examination of specimens while maintaining control over the annotation workflow. They also leveraged its potential for use in the educational process. In summary, domain experts with lower levels of expertise agreed that automation is more practical and fast. In contrast, domain experts with higher levels of expertise recommend an augmentation approach because of their concerns regarding AI-produced errors.

The level of expertise had an influence on the **trust** towards the AI-assisted annotations. Participants with lower levels of expertise would trust the AI-assisted workflow more only if they had more knowledge in the respective field. Participants with higher levels of expertise stated that the longer the tool is used, the more an expert would know about the potential errors to focus on when validating the AI-assisted annotations. Moreover, domain experts would prefer to have an explainability superstructure over the AI-assisted tool in the form of written decision rules using the medical domain knowledge to support the **understandability** and transparency of the provided AI-assisted annotations.

Generally, we observed a relationship between the expertise level of the medical domain expert and the benefits that can be derived from using AI-assisted tools within the digitized specimen annotation workflow in the means of education. The higher the expertise level, the greater the benefits. This fact originates in the ability of more experienced domain experts to critically validate the AI-assisted outputs and to build up the mental model of the AI-specific errors.

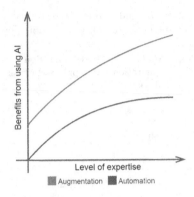

Fig. 3. Visualization of the relationship between the benefits of using AI and levels of expertise in 2 types of AI implementation

There are certain differences between the AI-assisted output presentation approaches and the benefits these methods yield to domain experts with varying levels of expertise (see Fig. 3). The automation approach causes the loss of the crucial part of the learning process for the near-zero domain knowledge users. The magnitude of benefits conferred by automation increases gradually with the accumulation of domain knowledge. The augmentation approach provides higher benefits to the near-zero domain knowledge than the automation approach, indicating that this approach is suitable even in the educational process. The level of benefits increases with the level of expertise, as the domain experts have significant control over the system.

5 Conclusion and Future Work

In this paper, we presented the user interface design for the AI-assisted digitized histopathology annotation tool for educational purposes. We designed the user interface using the proposed medical-domain-expert-centered design approach focusing on the unique aspects of the design of AI-powered interfaces in the specialized medical domain of histopathology. We validated and examined different forms of AI-assisted annotation approaches in a usability testing case study with five domain experts with various levels of expertise. Part of our contribution is the observed and discussed relationship between the AI-assisted annotation approaches and the expertise level of the domain user in the means of benefits that can be derived from using AI-assisted tools.

In our future work, we plan to focus on the extensive long-term testing of the proposed digitized histopathology annotation tool and the proposed AI-assisted annotation approaches at the medical faculties within the ongoing research cooperation. We plan for the medical faculty students to adopt the annotation tool in their education process while evaluating their interactions and organizing regular user interviews and focus groups to derive more insight into the benefits of AI-assisted tools in histopathology education.

Acknowledgements. The authors would like to acknowledge the funding for the financial support of the grant APVV SK-IL-RD-23-0004 and grant for young researchers of the Slovak Technical University in Bratislava 23-07-01-B.

References

1. AMBOSS: medical knowledge platform for doctors and students — amboss.com. https://www.amboss.com/. Accessed 02 Jan 2024
2. Dictionary - normal overview - The Human Protein Atlas — v15.proteinatlas.org. https://v15.proteinatlas.org/learn/dictionary/normal. Accessed 22 Dec 2023
3. Bankhead, P., et al.: QuPath: open source software for digital pathology image analysis. Sci. Rep. **7**(1), 1–7 (2017)
4. Boren, T., Ramey, J.: Thinking aloud: reconciling theory and practice. IEEE Trans. Prof. Commun. **43**(3), 261–278 (2000)
5. Briganti, G., Le Moine, O.: Artificial intelligence in medicine: today and tomorrow. Front. Med. **7**, 509744 (2020)
6. Buckland, M., Gey, F.: The relationship between recall and precision. J. Am. Soc. Inf. Sci. **45**(1), 12–19 (1994)
7. Capel, T., Brereton, M.: What is human-centered about human-centered AI? A map of the research landscape. In: Proceedings of the 2023 CHI Conference on Human Factors in Computing Systems, pp. 1–23 (2023)
8. Dolezal, J.M., et al.: Uncertainty-informed deep learning models enable high-confidence predictions for digital histopathology. Nat. Commun. **13**(1), 6572 (2022)
9. Hamilton, P.W., Wang, Y., McCullough, S.J.: Virtual microscopy and digital pathology in training and education. APMIS **120**(4), 305–315 (2012)
10. Joaquim, D.C., Hortsch, M., Silva, A.S.R.d., David, P.B., Leite, A.C.R.d.M., Girão-Carmona, V.C.C.: Digital information and communication technologies on histology learning: what to expect?–an integrative review. Anatomia Histologia Embryologia **51**(2), 180–188 (2022)
11. Linardatos, P., Papastefanopoulos, V., Kotsiantis, S.: Explainable AI: a review of machine learning interpretability methods. Entropy **23**(1), 18 (2020)
12. Lodhi, A.: Usability heuristics as an assessment parameter: for performing usability testing. In: 2010 2nd International Conference on Software Technology and Engineering, vol. 2, pp. V2–256. IEEE (2010)
13. Märtin, C., Bissinger, B.C., Asta, P.: Optimizing the digital customer journey-improving user experience by exploiting emotions, personas and situations for individualized user interface adaptations. J. Consum. Behav. **22**(5), 1050–1061 (2023)
14. Meloncon, L.K.: Patient experience design: expanding usability methodologies for healthcare. Commun. Des. Q. Rev. **5**(2), 19–28 (2017)
15. Nielsen, J., Landauer, T.K.: A mathematical model of the finding of usability problems. In: Proceedings of the INTERACT 1993 and CHI 1993 Conference on Human Factors in Computing Systems, pp. 206–213 (1993)
16. Panigutti, C., et al.: Co-design of human-centered, explainable AI for clinical decision support. ACM Trans. Interact. Intell. Syst. **13**(4), 1–35 (2023)
17. Pantanowitz, L.: Digital images and the future of digital pathology. J. Pathol. Inform. **1**, 15 (2010)
18. Raisch, S., Krakowski, S.: Artificial intelligence and management: the automation-augmentation paradox. Acad. Manag. Rev. **46**(1), 192–210 (2021)

19. Srinidhi, C.L., Kim, S.W., Chen, F.D., Martel, A.L.: Self-supervised driven consistency training for annotation efficient histopathology image analysis. Med. Image Anal. **75**, 102256 (2022)
20. Yang, Q., Steinfeld, A., Rosé, C., Zimmerman, J.: Re-examining whether, why, and how human-AI interaction is uniquely difficult to design. In: Proceedings of the 2020 CHI Conference on Human Factors in Computing Systems, pp. 1–13 (2020)

Demos

A Preliminary User Interface for Software Vendor Analysis and Selection Tool

Tormod Mork Müller[ID], Anshul Rani[(✉)][ID], and Deepti Mishra[ID]

Norwegian Institute of Science and technology, Gjøvik, Norway
{tormod.m.muller,anshul.rani,deepti.mishra}@ntnu.no

Abstract. In software ecosystems, the decision-making process for vendor selection remains a significant challenge, often worsened by the lack of effective tools that leverage visualization to aid in these decisions. This study aims to bridge this gap by prototyping a tool and hence proposing a user interface for the same, based on a software vendor selection framework, enhancing decision-making through intuitive visualizations and a user-friendly interface. Our research methodology combined a semi-structured literature review, preliminary user interface development, and expert feedback to ensure the tool's practicality and effectiveness. The prototype testing of the user interface design, informed by expert feedback, indicates a positive impact on decision-making processes, demonstrating the prototype's ability to streamline vendor analysis and selection. The proposed tool significantly contributes to reducing the complexity and subjectivity of vendor selection, offering a more structured and data-driven approach.

Keywords: Software Ecosystem · Decision-making · User interface · Tool · Software Vendor Selection · Visualization

1 Introduction

The term Software Ecosystems (SECO) is used for groups of businesses, software service providers, customers and organisations, etc., which come together to develop software of mutual interest [15]. This approach emphasizes cooperative efforts on a common platform, aiming to tackle obstacles and achieve collective objectives [1,9]. Rani et al. [10] categorised the entities participating in software ecosystems as: Company (outsourcing the software development), End User (generating demand for software), and Service provider/vendors (providing their services to the company) which are also called as collaborators. Choosing the most suitable vendor is challenging due to the availability of multiple vendors in a software ecosystem [9]. Typically, the decision-making task is carried out by company personnel termed as decision-makers (DMs) [7,10,11]. The decision-making process becomes complex because decision-makers need to consider how each vendor fits into the company's strategic and architectural goals [10]. Making

© IFIP International Federation for Information Processing 2024
Published by Springer Nature Switzerland AG 2024
M. K. Lárusdóttir et al. (Eds.): HCSE 2024, LNCS 14793, pp. 293–302, 2024.
https://doi.org/10.1007/978-3-031-64576-1_20

the wrong choice can result in serious consequences for the organization. Not only that, but the pressure intensifies further due to the ad-hoc and manual nature of today's decision-making processes [10], making them time-consuming and error-prone. Assisting decision-makers through these processes has been a large focus in the literature; however, limited research has been conducted on how information visualization and automated tools can support to increase the adaptability and usability of the underlying methods. Multiple studies [2,4,5,9,14] attempt to automate and aid decision-makers, however, they often overlook the importance of adaptability and user-friendliness in their approaches.

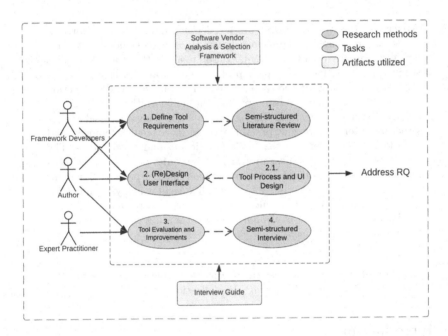

Fig. 1. Research methodology

The clarity of requirements to be outsourced and the shared understanding among decision-makers and stakeholders is crucial due to the subjective nature of the task. DMs and stakeholders often oversee this, and transparency in communicating these requirements and vendor information is crucial in effective decision-making. Further, more than one decision-makers are involved in the decision-making process [13] generally, which further hinders the ease of reaching a common consensus of deciding on one vendor out of many. Considering these challenges of decision-makers in the software vendor selection process, integrating user interfaces and gathering information within one tool proves promising in helping decision-makers through these intricate processes. However, existing literature, instead of providing decision-makers with user interfaces, visual aids or automating the process, typically focuses solely on algorithms and methods.

Considering this research gap, the objective of this study is to expose a preliminary user interface of the tool to a practitioner. Hence, this paper evaluates the proposed user interface of the tool which supports decision-makers to gather and visualize vendor's data in one place in order to make informed decisions.

The foundation of the presented user interface is based on the framework by Rani et al. [9]. Hence, it is built in close collaboration with its authors to ensure its alignment with the framework. Further, it is tested and evaluated by a practitioner at the preliminary stage. Figure 1 shows the methodology consisting of various tasks performed to achieve the set objective, along with the research method employed to complete these tasks. Additionally, it shows the actors involved in completing tasks along with the required artefacts to conduct the study.

2   Tool Processes

After gaining a comprehensive understanding of the underlying framework and defining the tool's requirements including a strategy to consolidate essential data into a unified platform using minimalist design and sensible visualizations, we advanced to detail the tool's workflow. This effort laid the groundwork for how users would engage with the tool, steering the creation of a functional and intuitive interface.

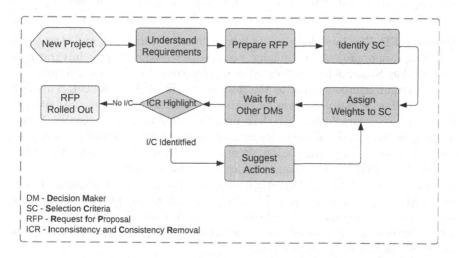

Fig. 2. Process flow of the tool for vendor analysis and selection (before RFP is rolled out)

Figures 2 and 4, illustrates the workflow of the tool through methodically designed steps and through methodically designed steps and thoughtful pause points. Aligned with the framework proposed by Rani et al. [9], it provides a

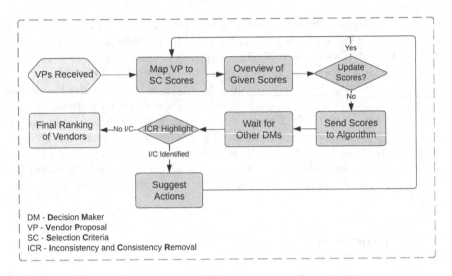

Fig. 3. Process flow of the tool for vendor analysis and selection (after VPs are received)

systematic method from project initiation to RFP release, evaluation of VPs to vendor selection and recommendations. The process is methodically segmented into *Before RFP* and *After Receiving VPs* stages, as depicted in the respective figures, ensuring a streamlined path through the decision-making process.

Before RFP: The intended process flow is illustrated in Fig. 2, and starts with initiating a new project, recognizing the need for outsourcing or integrating a new vendor. Stakeholders and decision-makers convene to define the project's specific requirements, leading to the drafting of the RFP document. This document outlines selection criteria for evaluating vendors, encompassing both primary and secondary factors for clear understanding among all parties. Subsequently, decision-makers assign weights to these criteria, indicating their relative importance. This crucial step, completed individually, precedes the use of an algorithm to check for inconsistencies or conflicts through the Inconsistency and Conflict Removal (ICR) method upon completion by all decision-makers. Detected issues prompt suggested resolutions, such as weight adjustments, discussions or other company procedures, ensuring consistency. This iterative resolution process ensures all conflicts are addressed before distributing the RFP to potential vendors for their proposals.

After Receiving VPs: The process flow of the tool after receiving VPs is illustrated in Fig. 4. After the RFPs are released, vendors submit their proposals, detailing their solutions and alignment with the RFP requirements as a textual document. These VPs are then uploaded to the tool for decision-maker review, where they are evaluated against the selection criteria by assigning scores to each vendor.

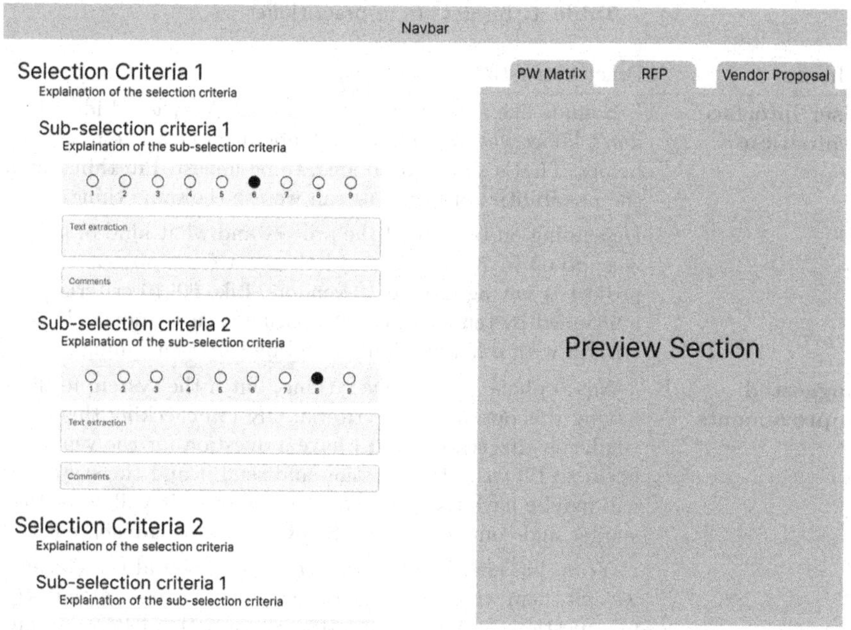

Fig. 4. Example of how to score vendors based on sub-criteria.

Following the scoring, decision-makers receive visualizations summarizing vendor rankings and comparisons, helping to spot any potential scoring errors. They can adjust scores if needed before finalizing their evaluations for algorithmic analysis. The algorithm waits for all decision-makers to submit their scores, then checks for inconsistencies or conflicts in the scoring. If disagreements are identified, resolution steps are taken. Once resolved and no significant disagreements remain, the algorithm proposes the final vendor ranking for decision-makers and stakeholders consideration and action.

3   User Interface Evaluation and Improvement

This section presents some of the insights received from the practitioner (Table 1) so that the original voice of the practitioner can reach to the reader. This is divided into two parts: that is where the practitioner reinstates the need of the tool and the proposed user interface and secondly the additional functionality suggested to add on to the proposed user interface.

3.1   Tool Evaluation

The designed prototype integrates and enhances the framework by Rani et al. [9] for software vendor selection, streamlining project setup to final vendor ranking for decision-makers. It automates tasks and offers a semi-structured approach,

Table 1. Insights from practitioner

Theme	Practitioner (P)
User interface evaluation	'...Sounds like a good idea to be honest. Very good idea. I don't know why we didn't think about an idea like this before. That's a very good idea, to be honest. I'm thinking on the possibilities of like, how can we use the same thing?'
	Depending on the size of the project and what kind of project it is. So 60 to 70 criteria and let's say average size of a project is having around 10 vendors. Like 60–70 criteria multiplied by ten and then comparing each vendor and each criteria with different thing it will be time consuming...
Suggested improvements	...We do phone, emails, everything, but if the system itself is having this option in the criteria, OK I'm checking this vendor in this section and I have a question for the vendor itself, so I'll write the question and send it and the system will maybe have the e-mail of the vendor so it will go to the vendor and come back here. So everything is transparent
	....Yeah, because for like, transparency reason also ... because we call them which is bad... I should just write an e-mail with my question, it should go to the person without knowing my name or I know his name. He just replies me back. Because in our business, we know each other, we shouldn't know who is asking what....
	...This will be helpful because we just write the page number and everything, and the person who wants to check it, they have to do it manually

centralizing information and calculations to overcome the manual and ad-hoc process issues identified by Rani et al. [9,10] in previous studies, as well as by the practitioner (Table 1).

This tool not only simplifies the decision-making journey but also contributes to its overall success by reducing errors, enhancing efficiency, and ensuring a more systematic and data-driven approach which will be addressed next. The tool's development aligns with the research findings of Killen et al. [6], which underscore the value of visualization tools in empowering decision-makers to make more informed and successful choices [3,6]. Consequently, it emerges as a crucial addition to the decision-making process. The tool integrate crucial decision-making data onto a single platform. It originally planned to conduct relative ranking of vendors based on the methodology of Rani et al. [9], which employs AHP [12] as a baseline. However, the practitioner highlighted challenges with this method due to the large volume of VPs (often 10–30) and the extensive selection criteria list (around 60–70) typical in larger projects (Table 1). The necessity for this change caused a reevaluation of the process, ultimately resulting in a solution where decision-makers can evaluate a vendor against the criteria only, while having the option of viewing the pair-wise matrix as a secondary choice. The mapping of scoring will therefore be moved away from the decision-makers and onto the Application Layer and API. A screenshot from the vendor evaluation step can be seen in Fig. 3. After all the vendors are assessed against the selection criteria, a summary screen displays the vendors' scores for the decision-makers to review before submission. The authors of this study believe that employing visualizations in such cases can aid in vendor comparison, as also suggested by Alwi et al. [8]. Consequently, the tool includes a visualization screen after each vendor is evaluated to assist decision-makers in identifying any overlooked details or mistakes when comparing vendors to each other. An example of this visualization page can be seen in Fig. 5. According to the insights received, until now, decision-makers heavily rely on manual and ad-hoc processes for software vendor selection, which involved complicated tasks like writing down page numbers and manually checking each entry. This process is time-consuming and error-prone, making decision-makers wish for a streamlined process from project setup till final vendor ranking. Thus, the tool presented in this study will benefit decision-makers in automating the tasks, and centralize information to overcome these issues. Adding to the processes being labor-intensive, the practitioner also emphasized that in practice, they lack a systematic approach, leading to inefficiencies and potential oversights in the decision-making process. Thus, one of the aids of the proposed tool will be to provide all decision-makers with a similar semi-systematic and data-driven evaluation of software vendors, in the hopes of enhancing decision-making efficiency by reducing errors. Additionally, the practitioner highlighted the significance of consolidating all decision-making data onto a single platform, emphasizing how the proposed tool can simplify the decision-making journey and contribute to its success. Lastly, the practitioner also highlighted that prior practices did not effectively leverage visualizations in the decision-making process. Since the proposed tool carefully integrates visualizations into parts of the decision-making process, this further supports decision-makers in taking more informed decisions, along with easily comparing vendor data at one place.

3.2 Suggestions for Improvement

The practitioner further emphasized that the community is small where many of them know each other and that therefore, providing the tool with an anonymous communication feature will enhance transparency and eliminate bias (Table 1). In a nutshell, following suggestions to improve the user interface further are suggested by the practitioner:

Direct, Anonymous Communication with Vendors: Allowing decision-makers to anonymously get in touch with the vendors to resolve any questions or uncertainties that may arise while conducting the vendor analysis is asked for by the practitioner. This could include functionalities for sending emails or initiating chats. This feature is asked for so that the decision-makers become more informed before making a decision, reducing or removing bias through

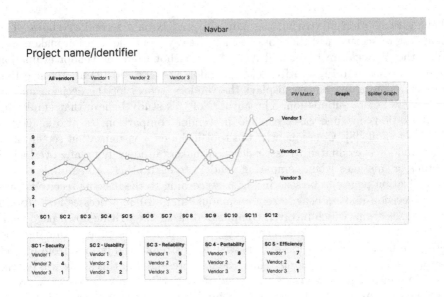

Fig. 5. Example of vendor summary view for a decision maker

anonymous contact, and ensuring a transparent and efficient communication process.

Flexible Scoring System: Furthermore, implementing a flexible scoring system is highlighted as a wanted feature. This is partially included already, but emphasis is put on including and further developing this process. Allowing decision-makers to score both overarching selection criteria as well as granular sub-criteria and questions accommodate the diverse and unique requirements of different projects, allowing for a tailored and nuanced vendor evaluation process. **Text Extraction and Selection Criteria Mapping:** Lastly, developing capabilities to automatically extract and map text from RFPs and VPs to relevant selection criteria scores are asked for by the practitioner. This feature aims to streamline the evaluation process by reducing manual data entry and enhancing the accuracy and efficiency of mapping vendors' offerings to decision-makers' criteria.

4   Conclusion, Limitation and Future Work

This study explored the critical area of software vendor selection in software ecosystems, a domain where decision-making is paramount yet challenging due to the complexity and variety of factors involved. Recognizing the necessity for a robust tool with a reliable user interface for the decision-making process, we proposed user interface sketches and workflow of the potential tool that leverages the power of visualizations to enhance decision-making capabilities. By integrating a user-friendly interface with the underlying methodology of the Rani et al.

[9] framework and the established need of such kind of tool interface, this study paves new paths for investigating the role of user interfaces and visualization in decision-making processes for researchers. It highlights the importance of integrating practical tools with theoretical frameworks to enhance the utility and applicability of research findings. However, the reliance on a limited body of literature and feedback from a single practitioner may affect the generalizability of the findings presented in this work. Hence, this work is at a preliminary stage. In the future, we intend to develop the initial functional prototype and expose it to a variety of practitioners. Additionally, expanding the scope to include more diverse methodologies and integrating advancements in visualization and decision-making theories could further refine and enhance the tool's capabilities.

References

1. Amorim, S., Andrade, S., Mcgregor, J., Almeida, E., Chavez, C.: Tailoring the nfr framework for measuring software ecosystems health, January 2018. https://doi.org/10.17771/PUCRio.wer.inf2018-14
2. Deretarla, Ö., Erdebilli, B., Gündoǎan, M.: An integrated analytic hierarchy process and complex proportional assessment for vendor selection in supply chain management. Decision Anal. J. **6**, 100155 (2023). ISSN 2772-6622. https://doi.org/10.1016/j.dajour.2022.100155. https://www.sciencedirect.com/science/article/pii/S2772662222000868
3. Eberhard, K.: The effects of visualization on judgment and decision-making: a systematic literature review. Manage. Rev. Quart. **73**(1), 167–214 (2023)
4. Gencer, C., Gürpinar, D.: Analytic network process in supplier selection: a case study in an electronic firm. Appl. Math. Modelling **31**(11), 2475–2486 (2007). ISSN 0307-904https://doi.org/10.1016/j.apm.2006.10.002. https://www.sciencedirect.com/science/article/pii/S0307904X06002368
5. Kilincci, O., Aslı Onal, S.: Fuzzy ahp approach for supplier selection in a washing machine company. Expert Syst. Appl. **38**(8), 9656–9664 (2011). ISSN 0957-4174. https://doi.org/10.1016/j.eswa.2011.01.159. https://www.sciencedirect.com/science/article/pii/S0957417411001928
6. Killen, C.P., Geraldi, J., Kock, A.: The role of decision makers' use of visualizations in project portfolio decision making. Int. J. Project Manage. **38**(5), 267–277 (2020). ISSN 0263-7863. https://doi.org/10.1016/j.ijproman.2020.04.002. https://www.sciencedirect.com/science/article/pii/S0263786320300260
7. Kobayashi, H., Osada, H.: Strengthening of collaboration between it vendors and their customer through proposal-based sales. In: 2011 IEEE International Conference on Quality and Reliability, pp. 556–560, September 2011.https://doi.org/10.1109/ICQR.2011.6031601
8. Alwi, N.N.A.N., Hassan, N.H., Baharuden, A.F., Bakar, N.A.A., Maarop, N.: Data visualization of supplier selection using business intelligence dashboard. In: Zaman, H.B., et al. (eds.) Advances in Visual Informatics, pp. 71–81. Springer, Cham (2019). ISBN 978-3-030-34032-2
9. Rani, A., Mishra, D., Omerovic, A.: A framework for software vendor selection by applying inconsistency and conflict removal (icr) method. Int. J. Syst. Assurance Eng. Manage., November 2023. ISSN 0976-4348. https://doi.org/10.1007/s13198-023-02190-x. https://doi.org/10.1007/s13198-023-02190-x

10. Rani, A., Mishra, D., Omerovic, A.: Exploring and extending research in multi-vendor software ecosystem. In: Ben Ahmed, M., et al. (eds.) SCA 2021. LNNS, vol. 393, pp. 379–391. Springer, Cham (2022). https://doi.org/10.1007/978-3-030-94191-8_30

11. Rani, A., Mishra, D., Omerovic, A.: Multi-vendor Software Ecosystem: Challenges from Company' Perspective. In: Rocha, A., Adeli, H., Dzemyda, G., Moreira, F. (eds.) Information Systems and Technologies. WorldCIST 2022. Lecture Notes in Networks and Systems, vol. 470, pp. 382–393. Springer, Cham. https://doi.org/10.1007/978-3-031-04829-6_34

12. Saaty, R.W.: The analytic hierarchy process–what it is and how it is used. Math. Modelling **9**(3), 161–176 (1987). ISSN 0270-0255https://doi.org/10.1016/0270-0255(87)90473-8. https://www.sciencedirect.com/science/article/pii/0270025587904738

13. Saaty, T.L., Vargas, L.G.: Uncertainty and rank order in the analytic hierarchy process. Europ. J. Oper. Res. **32**(1), 107–117 (1987). ISSN 0377-2217. https://doi.org/10.1016/0377-2217(87)90275-X. https://www.sciencedirect.com/science/article/pii/037722178790275X

14. Secundo, G., Magarielli, D., Esposito, E., Passiante, G.: Supporting decision-making in service supplier selection using a hybrid fuzzy extended ahp approach. Bus. Process. Manag. J. **23**(1), 196–222 (2017). https://doi.org/10.1108/bpmj-01-2016-0013

15. Yu, E., Deng, S.: Understanding software ecosystems: a strategic modeling approach. In: Iwseco-2011 Software Ecosystems 2011. Proceedings of the Third International Workshop on Software Ecosystems. Brussels, Belgium, pp. 65–76 (2011)

Developing a VR Factory Walkthrough for Use in Schools

Sarah Claudia Krings(✉)(iD), Enes Yigitbas(✉)(iD), and Stefan Sauer(✉)(iD)

Paderborn University, Warburger Str. 100, 33098 Paderborn, Germany
{sarah.claudia.krings,enes.yigitbas,sauer}@uni-paderborn.de

Abstract. Practical experiences are an important part of the education in vocational schools. In many cases, for example concerning production modes, this experience is gained by excursions to factories. Since the number of such excursions is limited by time and money constraints, and since the current alternative are traditional, less immersive materials such as books or videos, we present a virtual reality (VR) walkthrough of a demonstration factory. We collected requirements that are specific to this situation, built an application, and evaluated it, according to the human-centred design process. From this, we derive an overview of the special precautions and the challenges related to development for use in a school setting.

Keywords: 360° VR Walkthrough · Immersive Learning · Human-Centred Design

1 Introduction

For students in German vocational schools, practical examples are a big part of their lessons. For example, students in many fields have to learn about different modes of production, such as mass, batch, and one-off production. Learning to correctly assess which mode is the best for a product enables commercial trade students to make decisions with the best financial outcome for their (future) companies. Typically, practical context is added through an excursion to a company or a demonstration factory, with the alternative being traditional, less immersive materials like books or videos. However, excursions take time, money and organizational capacities and are therefore only possible a limited number of times. Therefore, an approach to using immersive technologies to enable students to experience production facilities in detail from their classroom is needed. Additionally, institutions or companies could benefit from this since VR-touring their facilities brings the students into contact with the company/institution, increasing its visibility and possibly fostering cooperation or even advertising it. In our use case, we created a virtual reality (VR) walkthrough of a demonstration factory of a technical vocational school, where a Bluetooth speaker box is produced as a demonstration case for one-off production. Since the application offers commercial trade students to experience the factory and learn about the

© IFIP International Federation for Information Processing 2024
Published by Springer Nature Switzerland AG 2024
M. K. Lárusdóttir et al. (Eds.): HCSE 2024, LNCS 14793, pp. 303–311, 2024.
https://doi.org/10.1007/978-3-031-64576-1_21

different production steps from their classroom, it is used in addition to excursions to bring more practical examples to the lessons. These different factors lead us to our research question: How can we create a VR walkthrough that is tailored for use in a school environment?

In this demo paper, we will go into more detail on our solution to this research question and how we achieved it, followed by describing our experiences in several preliminary studies and the lessons we learned from them.

2   Solution

In this section, we will describe the process that brought us to our current version of the VR walkthrough. We followed the human-centred design process as defined by the ISO 9241 standard [2], so we began by assessing the user (student and teacher) context. The results were used to create the requirements formulated below. We then implemented our application based on the requirements, with the end result being described below, along with the decisions we made to fulfil the requirements.

2.1   Requirements

We developed out solution with two target groups in mind: the students and the teachers. Since the teachers should be able to show their students how to use the walkthrough, it is important that they are comfortable with the application too. When developing the VR walkthrough, we had to take several factors into account. An important limitation in the development phase was that there were no 3D models of the different factory rooms or the machines in them available to us. Since 3D modelling is very time-consuming and requires a lot of expertise, designing the whole walkthrough from scratch was not an option. Instead, we needed a solution to immersively display the factory without virtually recreating it by hand (R1: Time-efficient creation of VR environment).

When looking at the actual usage phase of the application, we first had to take the physical surroundings in the vocational school classrooms into account (R2: Practicability in classrooms). Since they followed typical classroom setups with the students being placed at desks positioned in rows or groups, this led to two requirements: Firstly, the walkthrough application had to be usable when seated at a desk (R2.1: Usability in desk setup), which is not necessary given in VR (often a free space without obstacles is required[1]). Secondly, the students had to be able to use the application without excessive hand and arm movement since that could cause them to accidentally hit their neighbours since the real world is not visible while inside the VR application (R2.2: Limitation of hand and arm movement).

Apart from physical measures, we had to ensure that all students were able to use the application well enough to be able to learn about the factory they

---

[1] For example: https://securecdn.oculus.com/sr/oculusquest-warning-english.

visited (R3: Enabling proficient application use). This leads us to several sub-requirements. The application had to be of low complexity so the students as well as the teachers could quickly learn how to interact with it (R3.1: Learnability). Additionally, we noticed in our pilot studies that it is important to make supporting students in the app navigation as easy as possible (R3.2: Supportability), since it is hard to guess from the outside what is happening in VR.

2.2   System Usage

Our 360° VR walkthrough was developed to give the vocational students an overview of the facilities used to produce a Bluetooth speaker in one-off production. We aimed to get an effect as close as possible to a real excursion while keeping the application usable in a classroom.

Fig. 1. A typical view in our VR walkthrough

In the walkthrough, the students can see the factory from many different viewpoints (such as in Fig. 1). In each of these, the students have the same interaction possibilities. Since they are in VR, they can look in every direction to fully take in their surroundings. It is, however, difficult to physically turn very far when sitting on a chair in front of a desk (see R2.1). Therefore, students can also push their right controller's joystick to the left or right to perform a snap rotation, rotating their view by 45°.

To navigate between different viewpoints, there are arrows (Fig. 1, ①) pointing to the different directions where the student could "go". To select one direction, the controller is pointed to the corresponding arrow. The virtual ray being shown in front of the controller snaps to the arrow and changes colour when close enough. This, and a short vibration feedback in the controller, signals to the student that they have successfully selected the arrow. They can then change to the new viewpoint by pressing the trigger button on the controller. We observed the students completing the interaction quite fast since they only had to "point and click" to change their viewpoint.

To give information to the students, we included "Info-Hotspots" (Fig. 1, ②) near interesting features (e.g., machines) in the environment. The hotspots are marked by plus signs which can be selected the same way as the arrows. When a hotspot is selected, it opens a window containing information on the interesting feature. The windows can contain text and, optionally, images or videos (Fig. 1, ③). To keep the windows comfortable to read, its contents are scrollable via "grabbing" it via the trigger button or using the controller joysticks. The contents presented in the hotspot windows contain all the information for the different steps in the production of the Bluetooth speaker box from the lesson example.

With these fundamental controls, the students can "move" through the factory and learn about the machines and tools used in Bluetooth speaker production. There are two modes for them to do so: a guided walk, where the students can only "go" through the different rooms and viewpoints in a fixed order, and free exploration, where the students can explore the factory on their own in any order. The mode can be selected when starting the application in the start menu screen. The selection is again done by pointing the controller and using the trigger button. The start scene also contains pointers instructing the student to turn towards the mode selection in case a student misses it by looking in the wrong direction.

At every viewpoint, it is additionally possible to open a menu (by pressing the "A" button on the controller) that brings the student back to the start screen. This is only to be used in case a student has issues or accidentally starts the walkthrough in the wrong mode and is not introduced to the students otherwise. As an additional support measure, every viewpoint has a number identifying the specific viewpoint shown on the centre of the floor (where the student's feet would be, see Fig. 1, ④). This can be used by the instructors to quickly check where in the walkthrough a student is without complex interaction required by the student, who only has to look downward to see the number.

2.3 Implementation

We tailored our solution to fit our requirements as well as possible. To do so, we chose Unity[2] to develop the walkthrough application, since it is one of the leading VR development environments [3]. We combined it with the Unity XR Interaction Toolkit[3] for VR functionalities to make the application available to a broader range of devices. In the vocational schools, we chose to run the 360° walkthrough application on Meta Quest 3 headsets, since they are standalone devices and can be used flexibly in classrooms (R2.1). They also support VR and AR, futureproofing them for more versatile use at the school and were also significantly less expensive than comparable headsets (e.g. the Meta Quest Pro).

---

[2] https://unity.com/.

[3] https://docs.unity3d.com/Packages/com.unity.xr.interaction.toolkit@3.0/manual/index.html.

To solve R1, we decided to use 360° photographs to give an immersive view of the different rooms. There are specialized cameras that make taking 360° pictures easier. The 360° camera used in our project[4] uses multiple camera lenses to take a complete 360° picture in one shot. We chose this technology since it is easier and reduces the possibility of mistakes (compared to taking several pictures on a single-lens camera and stitching them together). We positioned the camera at different points in the rooms to have pictures from different viewpoints. We used this to enable the students to "walk around" the virtual room, as described above. The 360° pictures also allowed us to depict the factory with all its details (e.g., marks from wear and tear) with significantly less work than modelling would have taken. We then created one Unity scene per perspective/point of view for a clearer development structure. These scenes each contain a large sphere with a skybox material derived from a 360° picture, inside of which the student is going to stand to get the impression of being in the pictured room. Additionally, these scenes contain the movement arrows, hotspots, and the viewpoint number. Any other components, such as the XR interaction setup (the main component for VR in the XR Interaction Toolkit) and the code for switching viewpoints is contained in one base scene into which the "viewpoint scenes" are additively loaded (and unloaded when the viewpoint is switched). This way, we were able to separate the general logic from the viewpoint-specific contents, easing maintenance and making our application extendable to new rooms or even whole new walkthrough locations.

To adjust the application for use in a classroom (R2), we went for an approach where the students themselves would be quite static and interact with the app mainly using their controllers, as described above. To support this, we did several things: Firstly, we did not enable continuous movement (where the user steadily moves around the scene). Continuous movement would break the illusion of being at a viewpoint and seeing the surroundings because the 360° image on the sphere would get distorted instead of moving like a real environment would if the student moved. Additionally, continuous movement in VR without corresponding movement in the real world (since the students sit at their desks, see R2.1) can cause simulator sickness [1], which should be prevented as far as possible to make the application usable for all students.

We also took special care that all interactions were comfortable to reach sitting at a desk to fulfil R2.1. For example, we decided to use straight controller rays instead of the Bezier curve that is often used (especially for teleportation/movement). This way, the students could point at objects from any hand position, while for Bezier curved rays, one sometimes has to raise their hands to select objects far away. We also noticed in pilot studies that straight controller rays seemed to be more intuitive to new VR users (see also "point and click" interaction above). The reduced necessary hand movement and the implementation of the snap turn also represent our approach to solving R2.2 by reducing the need for movement, especially rotation of the body. Since the immersion of VR makes it easier to forget the surroundings, we saw encouraging the students to

---

[4] Insta360 Pro 2 Camera: https://www.insta360.com/de/product/insta360-pro2.

stay in their physical pose and move mainly via the VR controls as a promising way to prevent them from accidentally moving away from their original position and hitting/colliding with other students.

To keep the complexity of using the walkthrough as low as possible, we took several steps. Firstly, we decided to deviate from the typical movement interaction style. Often (e.g., in the Unity XR Interaction toolkit), teleportation movement (where the user instantly moves to a new position) in VR is activated by pressing the right controller joystick forward. Then, the user sees a Bezier curve and a circle at the point where the curve collides with the floor. If they let go of the joystick, they teleport to the position of the circle. As it turned out in pilot studies, this technique was not intuitive to our test users. Therefore, to improve the interactions for teachers and students (R3.1), we decided to use the interaction method described above: there is a limited selection of positions to move to, represented by the arrows. To move to a new position, a user points their controller directly at the target position (visually supported by the straight ray originating from the controller) and confirms using the trigger button. The limitation to only a few positions also harmonizes with the fact that due to us using 360° images, it is not possible to move to any random position or viewpoint, but only to ones that we took pictures of. By limiting the positions selectable for teleportation, we can hide this from the users to keep up the immersion of being "in" the factory. Since the "point and click" interaction worked well in pilot studies, we decided to also use it for other interactions, such as opening the info hotspots and selecting the tour mode. Users can interact with anything in the walkthrough by only pointing their controller and using the trigger button. This way, we were also able to lower the overall number of interactions that users would have to learn. To still offer options for improved comfort, we offer multiple ways of interaction in some cases, for example, the text fields at the info hotspots can be scrolled up and down using the controller joysticks in addition to supporting the "point and click" interaction.

To offer options to support users (R3.2), we tried to find solutions that would be unobtrusive (to prevent distracting users or adding complexity), but easy to access when looking for them. For example, each viewpoint (as well as the main menu) has a unique number on the floor (Fig. 1). The number identifies the user's current position in the walkthrough. If they get lost or need support, it is easy to ask them to look down at their feet and read out the number. This way, an outside helper can quickly determine where they are without having to guess their (virtual) location based on a description of their surroundings. We also added an option that sends the user back to the main menu from any point in the walkthrough. It lets the user select whether they want to return to the main menu via the "point and click" interaction and follows the user so it is always in view. We purposefully implemented it to open when pressing the "A" controller button, which is not used otherwise. This way, inexperienced users are less likely to accidentally open it, but when instructed to, it would be easy to find the button and open the window.

3   Evaluation, Observations, and Lessons Learned

To ensure our VR walkthrough application would fit its purpose, we conducted several stages of pilot studies. In this section, we will describe our procedure and observations from these studies and their influence on the requirements and the development of the next walkthrough iterations.

In the first pilot study, we presented the application to two teachers who were novices in using VR. The tested iteration of the walkthrough application still used typical interaction mechanisms, such as teleportation via joystick (see above). However, in the pilot study, it turned out that some mechanisms were not intuitive enough. The teachers needed one-on-one instructions for using the joystick teleportation interaction and even then, had some issues with using it. This included not letting the stick snap back properly, not pushing it straight up and accidentally rotating, and not finding the joystick on the controller. When trying to explain where to look for certain features of the walkthrough (e.g., arrows and info hotspots), we also faced the problem of not knowing at which viewpoint the teachers were. Since there can be several viewpoints with similar views in one room, asking them to describe the environment did not work as well as we hoped. In this situation, we only had the option to take the headsets away from the teachers to check and, if necessary, fix, the current state by ourselves. Still, the teachers' overall reaction was positive. One teacher expressed excitement with having "such a cool" piece of content to offer their students. From this study, we refined our requirements. R3 was heavily influenced by these observations. The issues with the teleportation led to the current wording of R3.1 and the issues with giving location-based led to the formulation of R3.2. We focused our improvements on these points, adding the "point-and-click" interaction (R3.1) and the viewpoint numbers (R3.2). We then repeated the study, once with the same two teachers, but also with other users who did not use the application before. In both cases, we were able to observe a better success rate of the interactions, and the two teachers clearly preferred the newer version. Also, the new participants learned the interaction more quickly than the two teachers did with the older version. This gave us confidence that we were able to fulfil our requirements R3.1 and R3.2 adequately.

We then conducted our first student study, which took place in a large group (approximately 20 students). Before using the application, we gave a presentation to the group about the use of the application and the headsets in general. The students were quite successful in using the walkthrough and did not mention or show issues with the interaction, suggesting that R3.1 is also fulfilled from the students' perspective. One student criticised that the size of the factory and its machines seemed larger in the VR tour than in real life, which we mitigated by lowering the size of the spheres with the 360° images. Mainly, the students were happy to be able to see the factory in VR. Some students did, however, face difficulties in working with the VR headsets' operating system. Due to the large group size, it was difficult to keep an overview of what students were doing exactly, which made it difficult to gain more in-depth information. Therefore, we changed the structure for the second student pilot study (with a different group of approximately 20 students), where subgroups of 3–6 students were each supervised by a researcher. Due to the smaller group size, we were able to explain the VR operating system and the interaction with the application while the students were actually using it. We gained a clearer picture of the students' behaviour, as well as direct feedback from them. Most became familiar with the walkthrough interactions very quickly. Some struggled with correctly pointing the controller, but with a hint to the ray colour, all students were able to proficiently navigate through the application. The walkthrough was overall quite well received. We also used the smaller groups to let the students try out the teleport interaction. We were able to observe that the students too had more issues with it than they had with our "point and click" interaction. This suggests our approach is easier to learn for both teachers and students. We also did not get any complaints about the look or size of the VR environment; therefore, we see R1 as adequately fulfilled. We did not observe any issues or accidents related to the use of the application while sitting at desks (R2.1) or next to each other (R2.2) in any of the studies. The students sometimes turned around quite far, but they all stayed in their spaces and kept their controllers relatively close, so we see R2 (R2.1 and R2.2) as fulfilled.

From these experiences, we drew several lessons that answer our research question: Firstly, 360° images are a valid and time-effective way to create VR walkthroughs of factories (R1). Secondly, with a suitable interaction design, VR walkthroughs (and VR in general) work well in a classroom setting with desks (R2). Thirdly, in a VR application that will be used with novice groups, it is helpful to lower the complexity of the interactions as far as possible, even if that means traditional interactions are not used (see R3.1). Also, it is difficult to stay aware of what different users/students are doing, so adequate support mechanisms (R3.2) and small groups are helpful.

4   Summary and Outlook

In this demo paper, we presented our approach to creating a VR walkthrough for use in a school environment. We discussed our requirements and solution, as well as the steps we took to preliminarily evaluate and refine our solution. We determined several key points answering our research question: 360° images are a solution for time-effective VR walkthroughs. In development, it is necessary to take physical constraints into account by designing interaction techniques that require little movement. It is also helpful to lower the complexity of interactions where possible, even if this deviates from the more commonly used techniques, and to include support features.

In the future, we plan to conduct a larger, quantitative evaluation of our VR walkthrough, as well as collect more data on the influence of different interaction types. On a development level, the effect of adding gamification elements on the students' motivation and learning success would be interesting. Additionally, a no/low code VR walkthrough creation framework could be of benefit to schools.

Acknowledgments. This work is part of the project "5G-Lernorte OWL", which is funded by the Ministry of Economic Affairs, Industry, Climate Action and Energy of the State of North Rhine-Westphalia.

References

1. Ramaseri Chandra, A.N., El Jamiy, F., Reza, H.: A systematic survey on cybersickness in virtual environments. Computers **11**(4) (2022). https://doi.org/10.3390/computers11040051, https://www.mdpi.com/2073-431X/11/4/51
2. for Standardization, I.O.: Ergonomics of human-system interaction part 210: Human-centred design for interactive systems. Standard, International Organization for Standardization, Geneva, CH (2019)
3. Wang, S., Mao, Z., Zeng, C., Gong, H., Li, S., Chen, B.: A new method of virtual reality based on unity3d. In: 2010 18th International Conference on Geoinformatics. pp. 1–5 (2010) https://doi.org/10.1109/GEOINFORMATICS.2010.5567608

End-User Development of Oracle APEX Low-Code Applications Using Large Language Models

Simon Cornelius Gorissen[1], Stefan Sauer[2(✉)], and Wolf G. Beckmann[1]

[1] TEAM GmbH, Hermann-Löns-Str. 88, 33104 Paderborn, Germany
{sg,wb}@team-pb.de

[2] SICP Software Innovation Lab and Computer Science Department, Paderborn University, Warburger Str. 100, 33098 Paderborn, Germany
sauer@upb.de

Abstract. The natural-language understanding, code generation, and reasoning abilities of Large Language Model (LLMs) have the potential to speed up development times, especially when combined with Low-Code Development Platform (LCDPs). They could also enable end-users to make small to medium-sized changes themselves, while experienced developers can focus on the more complicated development tasks. This paper demos a prototype implementation of this concept. It enables end-users to edit Oracle Application Express (APEX) low-code applications using natural language in a chat-like user interface (UI) powered by the GPT-4 Turbo LLM. We also evaluate this prototype in a qualitative user study with APEX customers from the industry and find that they generally like both the concept and the prototype. The main problem that the study uncovered is a lack of a common vocabulary between the LLM and the users. Participants suggest to solve this by integrating support features like a glossary and an element type and name inspector into the prototype.

Keywords: Low-Code · Large Language Models · End-User Development · Oracle APEX · Natural Language

1 Introduction

There has been a variety of research that incorporates Large Language Model (LLMs) into development workflows, be it SQL generation [2,8,13], source code generation in an Integrated Development Environment (IDE) [10–12], or editing HTML/CSS code using Natural Language (NL) [1,5]. These works highlight that LLMs could be used to speed up development work and lower the entry barrier to developing applications for end-users. However, there has been no work that we are aware of that integrates LLMs with Low-Code Development Platform (LCDPs) to enable end-users to develop fully functional applications using NL.

© IFIP International Federation for Information Processing 2024
Published by Springer Nature Switzerland AG 2024
M. K. Lárusdóttir et al. (Eds.): HCSE 2024, LNCS 14793, pp. 312–320, 2024.
https://doi.org/10.1007/978-3-031-64576-1_22

Such a system could combat the current worker shortage in the software development field by enabling end-users to make small to medium-size changes in their applications themselves, giving experienced developers more time to focus on the more complex changes, that such a system might not be able to perform. The focus on editing low-code applications enables experienced developers to extend applications—that end-users can work on using NL—quickly, due to the speed-up that LCDPs already offer to development processes.

In this paper, we demonstrate that it is possible to realise this concept by presenting a prototype system we have developed. Through this, end-users can describe desired changes in an Oracle Application Express (APEX) low-code Web application to the GPT-4 Turbo LLM (1106 preview) in a chat-like interface. The LLM then performs these changes by generating calls to an internal editing API for Oracle APEX that we have implemented.

Oracle APEX is an LCDP that can be used to create Web applications based on an Oracle database. The applications are directly integrated into such a database and through them, end-users can view and manipulate the data in the database. APEX includes low-code interaction concepts, like a visual editor for the pages of the application under development, and configuration panels for a range of predefined elements that the pages can be populated with. The source code that is present in this low-code framework is mainly SQL and PL/SQL code used for tasks like retrieving from or saving data in the database.

In the remainder of this paper, Sect. 2 will present our conceptual solution and Sect. 3 will discuss its implementation. Section 4 briefly summarises the qualitative user study that we conducted to evaluate the prototype and Sect. 5 concludes this paper with a summary and outlook on future work.

2   Conception

Figure 1 shows an overview of our solution architecture. It outlines that the main system we created communicates with the user, the LLM and the App under Development.

The user interacts with the Natural Language User Interface module. This is a chat-like interface through which the user can communicate with the LLM and inspect the current state of the App under Development. The App under Development is the low-code application that the user wants to change. In order to do that, the user describes change-requests and requirements in the chat of the Natural Language User Interface. The latter sends these messages to the LLM API Manager which forwards the chat messages to the LLM. The LLM can then decide what it needs to do to fulfil the user's requests. It can either respond with a message intended for the user (e.g., a follow-up question) or request an API call that the Application Editing API offers. In the latter case, the LLM API Manager processes this request and forwards it to the Application Editing API. This module is responsible for making the requested changes in the App under Development or returning the requested information about the current state of the app. The result is either textual information or a textual success or error

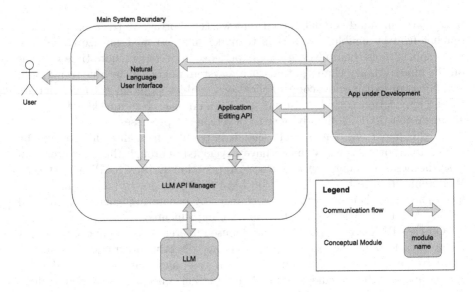

Fig. 1. Overview of our solution architecture.

message that gets returned to the LLM API Manager and forwarded by it to the LLM. Then the LLM decides what it needs to do next. This process can be repeated as long as the LLM decides to call additional API functions. Once it creates a user-facing message instead, this message is forwarded by the LLM API Manager to the Natural Language User Interface which shows the reply to the user. The user can then check the changes made to the App under Development and continue the conversation with the LLM by sending new change-requests in the chat. This way, the user can iteratively develop the low-code application using only natural language.

The LLM is kept outside the system itself and only interacts with the LLM API Manager so it can be treated as a black box similar to how Jain et al. [3] have done it. This has the advantage that the LLM and the rest of the system are properly separated. It enables a "plug-and-play"-style replacement when new and improved model versions are released [3]. This also has the advantage that— when the system has to be migrated to an entirely different LLM—only the LLM API Manager needs to be changed.

There are two central concepts to this solution. The first is the function-calling concept. The LLM is provided with a list of function declarations in each request. These declarations always contain the (1) function's name, (2) its return type, (3) a textual description of what the function will do and return when it is executed, and (4) the definitions of its parameters. Each parameter is defined by (1) its name, (2) its data type, and (3) a textual description of what kind of value needs to be given to this parameter. An example of such a declaration is shown in Fig. 2. It defines the *change_region_title* function that can be called by the LLM to change the title of an element in the application's user interface (UI).

Function declaration of change_region_title

```
function change_region_title returns string: Changes the title of the region with the given region_id on the
    page with the given page_id inside the application with the given app_id
param p_app_id number: the id of the APEX application that the page and region belong to
param p_page_id number: the id of the page on which the region is
param p_region_id number: the id of the region whose title should be changed
param p_new_title string: the new title of the region. Always ask the user what the title should be
```

Fig. 2. An example function declaration that is passed to the LLM by the LLM API Manager.

It is important to understand that the LLM does not execute these functions. It only decides which function(s) to call and what parameters to pass to them. The LLM only serves as the translator between the unstructured natural language from its conversation with the user and the structured function calls. These function calls can be regarded as structured editing descriptions that can be performed without human intervention. They are executed by the LLM API Manager as calls to the Application Editing API. Thus, the function and parameter names in the function declarations that are given to the LLM must match the functions that the Application Editing API actually offers.

The second central concept in this solution is the automatic error correction system. The idea is based on work by Liventsev et al. [6]: The LLM's output is checked through an automated system and if an error is detected, the LLM is provided with a meaningful error message. This message is designed to help the LLM identify and correct its error autonomously. In our system, the functions in the Application Editing API make plausibility checks, for example, on the parameter values provided by the LLM. They also catch any errors that might be thrown during the function's execution. In the case of such an error, they return an appropriate error message to the LLM API Manager—and thereby the LLM. This enables the LLM to correct its own mistakes without the user noticing the error.

The concept of this solution relies on the reasoning abilities of the LLM to decide which functions to call and what parameters to supply to them. The function declarations given to the LLM fall into two types of categories. Both of them are part of the Application Editing API. The first category consists of functions that make changes to the Application under Development. These can be small changes, like changing a title of a text region in the UI, or larger changes, like creating a new table that is shown on a page. The second category of functions consists of information retrieval functions. These can be used by the LLM to obtain information about the current state of the App under Development without having to ask the user for them. This is especially necessary for obtaining technical details, for example, internal IDs of elements like shown in Fig. 2, that the user might not know about.

In our system, the LLM's task is to reason about what functions it needs to call to fulfil the user's request and what information it needs to call these functions. It then has to decide which of these pieces of information it can obtain by calling other functions and which ones it has to ask the user to provide. To do this, it combines its natural-language understanding capabilities with the textual content of the conversation history with the user and the textual descriptions of the functions and their parameters that are provided to it.

3   Implementation

We implemented our prototype as an Oracle APEX application called Oracle Application Express Generative Pretrained Transformer (ApexGPT). It uses a range of PL/SQL packages to realise the Natural Language User Interface, Application Editing API, and LLM API Manager modules shown in Fig. 1. Oracle APEX applications always exist inside an Oracle database inside a container called APEX workspace. The App under Development is also an Oracle APEX application that sits in the same workspace as the ApexGPT app. We use the GPT-4 Turbo LLM (preview 1106) in this prototype. It communicates with the LLM API Manager using the REST API that OpenAI provide for the LLM [7].

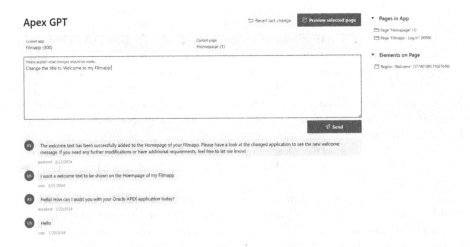

Fig. 3. The user interface of our prototype. Here, the user is currently typing a new message with a change-request for the AI assistant (the LLM). Older messages are shown at the bottom of the conversation history.

Figure 3 shows the UI of our prototype. The prototype is a Web application shown in a browser and has a large input field for the user in the center.

The chat history between the LLM and the user is located below it. Instead of one-shot generation of code snippets, our system aims to enable an iterative development process where users can refine the result of previous requests step by step. This is similar to what Tan et al. [10] and Calo et al. [1] showcase in their solutions. Therefore, we chose to use this chat between the user and the LLM as our primary interface element. To the right of the chat, there are two tree-like visualizations of the pages in the current application and the elements on the current page. Repenning and Ioannidou [9] have argued that end-user development (EUD) environments necessarily involve a learning curve because developing software is conceptually complex—even if the language used for development is simple and natural. Thus, EUD interfaces should support the user in learning the concepts necessary for development [9]. The information panels are meant to achieve this by helping the user identify how the application is structured and how the different elements that exist in it are called. Above the input field are two drop-down lists that define the current app and the current page that are to be edited. They can be changed by the user, but they are also automatically set by the LLM once it performs a change. The *Preview selected page* button opens the current page from the app under development as a dedicated browser tab, so the user can test it and see whether the LLM made the desired changes.

We have recorded a small demo of this prototype being used to edit an application. The demo video can be watched on YouTube[1].

APEX does not provide an easy-to-use API for programmatically editing APEX apps. It only has an internal PL/SQL API that can be used to (re-)create an APEX app with all its elements and configurations in another database. To do this, one needs to create an APEX import file from a given APEX app. This file lists these PL/SQL API calls including all their parameters. It can then be imported in another APEX instance in another database.

To create an editing API usable for our purpose, we utilise these import files. Whenever the LLM requests a function call that needs to make a change to the application, a four step process is followed: (1) The current import file of the application is obtained. (2) The information necessary to make the correct changes in the import file is determined. (3) The import file is changed so its new version represents the application after the changes requested by the LLM are made. (4) The changed import file is re-imported, overwriting the old version of the application. This way, we are able to create a range of API functions that each make specific changes to an import file and thereby provide an easy-to-use editing API for Oracle APEX apps. This is the implementation of the Application Editing API module from Fig. 1. When the necessary changes are limited to a single page, an import file specific to that page is obtained in step (1). This makes it faster to edit and re-import the file because it is significantly smaller compared to one that describes an entire application.

Our current implementation only supports editing an existing APEX application and not creating a new one from scratch. However, this is due to our

---

[1] See https://www.youtube.com/watch?v=8nfifScHESQ.

chosen focus and not a technical limitation of the approach itself. We focused on implementing support for as many different edit operations as possible within our development time, in order to make the prototype's features more useful for our evaluation study. From a technical perspective, it would likely be easy to define a basic import file for an empty application that the LLM can import as a new application via a function call.

4   Evaluation

We evaluated our prototype in a qualitative user study with ten participants (six female, four male). They were recruited by our contacts at TEAM GmbH and are APEX customers, meaning they have little to no experience in editing APEX applications themselves, but are familiar with describing their desired changes to an APEX developer.

We held one study session with each participant that took approximately one hour each. In each session the participant filled out a consent form, and we explained the theoretical concept of our solution to them. Subsequently, we held a semi-structured interview where we asked questions regarding the participant's opinions about this concept. Afterwards, the participant watched a pre-recorded tutorial video for our prototype and subsequently tried out the prototype by solving two given tasks with it. Then, we held another semi-structured interview about the participant's experiences with the prototype, gathering feedback and ideas for its further development. This design of pre- and post-interviews with trying out the prototype in between was adapted from Jiang et al. [4]. In the end, each participant filled out a demographic survey.

The study showed that participants have rather positive opinions in most cases of both the theoretical concept and the prototype itself. While participants did observe some bugs, most of these proved to be easy to resolve after the study. The one major problem that surfaced was a lack of a common vocabulary between the LLM and some users. This may lead the LLM to misunderstand the intent of a user if they describe it in the *wrong* way. Some participants suggested to remedy this by implementing additional support features like a glossary and an inspector that can show the names and types of specific elements in the app that the user is interested in. Overall the study showed that, if developed further, such a system can be very useful for its target audience.

5   Conclusion

This paper has demonstrated that it is possible to create a natural-language-based editor with a chat-like UI for low-code applications using modern LLMs. Our solution builds on the concept of function-calling where function declarations are given to the LLM that generates calls for them. The functions then perform the editing operations that a user requested. The LLM therefore serves as a translator between the unstructured natural language from the chat history with the user and the structured function calls necessary to realise the user's desired changes. Our prototype implementation uses the GPT-4 Turbo LLM from OpenAI and edits Oracle APEX low-code apps. In our prototype, a self-debugging system that returns meaningful error messages to the LLM improves the LLM's reasoning accuracy to the point that it becomes usable for this purpose. In a user study with ten participants from the tool's target audience, we have found that users have largely positive reactions to both the prototype and the theoretical concept. This highlights its potential when developed into a fully featured application.

Future work can iterate on this first contribution by expanding the prototype's capabilities, optimising its performance in time and LLM API usage costs, and by additional qualitative and quantitative user studies to deepen the understanding of the benefits and problems such a system can have for users.

Acknowledgment. This research was supported by TEAM GmbH, a software development and consulting company from Paderborn, Germany with a focus on databases and database-centric applications. They have developed multiple applications that incorporate AI features, and especially LLMs (see https://www.team-pb.de/development/individuelle-ki/), and provided both funding and guidance for the realisation of this research. For further information about TEAM please visit: https://www.team-pb.de/

References

1. Calò, T., Russis, L.D.: Leveraging large language models for end-user website generation. In: End-User Development - 9th International Symposium, IS-EUD 2023, pp. 52–61. Springer, Switzerland, June 2023. https://doi.org/10.1007/978-3-031-34433-6_4

2. Chang, S., Fosler-Lussier, E.: How to prompt llms for text-to-sql: a study in zero-shot, single-domain, and cross-domain settings. ArXiv Preprint, May 2023. https://doi.org/10.48550/ARXIV.2305.11853

3. Jain, N., Vaidyanath, S., Iyer, A., Natarajan, N., Parthasarathy, S., Rajamani, S., Sharma, R.: Jigsaw: Large language models meet program synthesis. In: Proceedings of the 44th International Conference on Software Engineering. ACM, May 2022. https://doi.org/10.1145/3510003.3510203

4. Jiang, E., et al.: Discovering the syntax and strategies of natural language programming with generative language models. In: CHI Conference on Human Factors in Computing Systems. ACM, April 2022. https://doi.org/10.1145/3491102.3501870

5. Kim, T.S., Choi, D., Choi, Y., Kim, J.: Stylette: Styling the web with natural language. In: CHI Conference on Human Factors in Computing Systems. ACM, April 2022. https://doi.org/10.1145/3491102.3501931

6. Liventsev, V., Grishina, A., Härmä, A., Moonen, L.: Fully autonomous programming with large language models. In: Proceedings of the Genetic and Evolutionary Computation Conference. ACM, July 2023. https://doi.org/10.1145/3583131.3590481

7. OpenAI: Chat - api reference. https://platform.openai.com/docs/api-reference/chat. Accessed 07 Mar 2024

8. Rajkumar, N., Li, R., Bahdanau, D.: Evaluating the text-to-sql capabilities of large language models. ArXiv Preprint, March 2022. https://doi.org/10.48550/ARXIV.2204.00498

9. Repenning, A., Ioannidou, A.: What makes end-user development tick? 13 design guidelines. In: Human-Computer Interaction Series, pp. 51–85. Springer Netherlands (2006). https://doi.org/10.1007/1-4020-5386-x_4

10. Tan, C.W., Guo, S., Wong, M.F., Hang, C.N.: Copilot for xcode: exploring ai-assisted programming by prompting cloud-based large language models. ArXiv Preprint, July 2023. https://doi.org/10.48550/ARXIV.2307.14349

11. Vaithilingam, P., Zhang, T., Glassman, E.L.: Expectation vs. experience: Evaluating the usability of code generation tools powered by large language models. In: CHI Conference on Human Factors in Computing Systems Extended Abstracts. ACM, April 2022. https://doi.org/10.1145/3491101.3519665

12. Xu, F.F., Vasilescu, B., Neubig, G.: In-IDE code generation from natural language: promise and challenges. ACM Trans. Softw. Eng. Methodol. 31(2), 1–47 (2022). https://doi.org/10.1145/3487569

13. Zhang, W., Wang, Y., Fan, M.: Towards robustness of large language models on text-to-SQL task: an adversarial and cross-domain investigation. In: Artificial Neural Networks and Machine Learning – ICANN 2023, pp. 181–192. Springer (2023). https://doi.org/10.1007/978-3-031-44192-9_15

InterView: A System to Support Interaction-Driven Visualization Systems Design

Matteo Filosa[1], Alexandra Plexousaki[2], Dario Benvenuti[1], Tiziana Catarci[1], and Marco Angelini[1,3(✉)]

[1] Sapienza Università di Roma, Rome, Italy
{m.filosa,d.benvenuti,catarci,angelini}@diag.uniroma1.it,
m.angelini@unilink.it
[2] ICS-FORTH, University of Crete, Heraklion, Greece
aplex@ics.forth.gr
[3] Link Campus University of Rome, Rome, Italy

Abstract. In the design of a visualization system for exploratory data analysis, a designer faces several issues: *(i)* the recognition of the causes behind excessive latency experienced by end users, who become quickly disengaged in the exploration if the response time is below a desired threshold (i.e., 500 ms); *(ii)* the discovery of portions of the visualization system that are poorly explored or may not work as intended; *(iii)* the lack of precise feedback from the end users who, struggling from excessive latency, become disinterested in the exploration and report high-level feedback that is too broad and generic for the designer to understand and transform into actionable changes to the design. To address these issues and provide more guidance to visualization system designers, we contributed a general framework to model and assess user interactions in big data visualization systems. It models the interaction space of the visualization system with the concept of augmented statecharts that label interactions with their latency thresholds. It is implemented in a system, InterView (the name relates to the collaboration between visualization designers and end users), composed of two software components, one to automatically generate the interaction space of a visualization system using a statechart, and one to replay user traces, reproducing each interaction an end user performed in the interaction log. In this paper, we demonstrate the capabilities of InterView applying it to a well-known crossfilter interface, Falcon, to guide the visualization system designers in discovering the root causes behind excessive latency, coupled with a complete understanding of the interaction space of their visualization system. In such a way, designers can finally acknowledge the problems of their visualization system with higher granularity and precision, giving more context to the feedback received by the end users.

Keywords: Interaction logs · Visualization Systems · User Interaction Modeling

© IFIP International Federation for Information Processing 2024
Published by Springer Nature Switzerland AG 2024
M. K. Lárusdóttir et al. (Eds.): HCSE 2024, LNCS 14793, pp. 321–329, 2024.
https://doi.org/10.1007/978-3-031-64576-1_23

1   Introduction

The analysis and understanding of data are common activities while interacting with a big data visualization system. In this scenario, we identify two types of users: the visualization system designers (VSDs) who actually develop the system, and the end users (EUs) who interact, explore, understand data, and provide feedback to the designers. While designing a visualization system, VSDs have to face various challenges: *(i)* they aim to minimize potential confounding factors in evaluation activities to enhance their effectiveness, with latency being the most problematic factor due to its independence from the system's application domain and its potential to disrupt mental models, or causing user disengagement; *(ii)* VSDs may be in difficult to understand the complete interaction space of the visualization system as they have to define it manually; *(iii)* end users provide "general feedback" without highlighting specific interactions or elements impeding their experience, making it challenging to identify latency-related issues [3,11]. Moreover, these evaluation activities are time-consuming, demanding meticulous design efforts, and their repeated execution may diminish their impact due to factors like memory effects. Indeed, latency, even as low as 500 ms [7,12], can bias the EUs' feedback, disrupting the correct user flow and potentially leading to drop-outs from the system usage. From the point of view of the system, latency can be introduced by: *(i)* Database management systems (DBMS), which can fail to reach desired performance levels when dealing with heavy loads, such as high query rates or large data, as demonstrated by Battle et al. [2]; *(ii)* the heterogeneity of user interactions on a visualization system, that are challenging to model as they are different in their nature and demand different performance needs. Furthermore, looking at the classical visualization pipeline, composed by the *Data-, Visualization- and Interaction-* layers, effective models exist for optimizing the data and visualization layer (e.g., BIRCH [13], DEVise [8]), but no one takes into account optimizations at the interaction layer. Also, no formal approach exists to unify the optimization techniques.

To address these problems and support VSDs, we introduced a conceptual *interaction-driven framework* [3], which proposes a new layer, the *Translation* layer. It enhances the modeling of interactions with augmented statecharts, which label interactions with their latency threshold. They resemble a conceptual directed graph, where nodes denote states and the directed edges' labels represent the interactions that make the state change [5]. To make this layer actionable and to take a step forward in the complete deployment of the framework, we propose InterView, a system composed of two software components: the *Statechart Generator*, that automatically models the interaction space as a statechart for a generic web-based visualization system, labeling the interactions with their latency thresholds, and the *Traces Replayer*, for the automatic replay of user traces, which represent the sequence of all the low-level interactions (e.g., mousemove, click, mousedown, etc.) performed by a user on the visualization system. During the replay, the execution time of each interaction is highlighted, together with the localization of the violations in latency thresholds. Finally, we show the application of InterView to Falcon, a well-known Crossfilter interface [10], showing how it supports VSDs in their tasks while designing, evaluating, and refining their visualization system.

In the proposed demonstration, VSDs automatically get the overview and exploration of the visualization system's complete interaction space, analyze how EUs interact with it, and see which visual component suffered from excessive latency. Moreover, they can understand the usage of their system with more precision, seeing how frequently specific portions of the interaction space are explored, linking such information with the recorded violations in latency thresholds. This allows for optimization strategies in specific portions of the interaction space, reducing response time and enhancing user experience for EUs. Finally, removing excessive latency during the interaction enables EUs to offer more precise and accurate feedback on the system. InterView is available in the following GitHub repository, which also contains a video demonstration: https://github.com/MatteoFilosa/InterView.

2   Method

In the design process of a visualization system, VSDs need to address three tasks. The first, relative to the understanding of the interaction space of the visualization system, needs them to: analyze the states of the system, the available interactions, and the interaction paths (sequence of interactions which act as transitions between states); notice their distribution and topology; discover portions of the interaction space that are poorly used due to their inefficiency, highly explored, or not explored at all (**Task 1**).

Moreover, while EUs interact by completing exploratory tasks on the visualization system, grasping and concretizing their feedback is crucial to having a complete understanding of latency problems affecting the system. It is then necessary for VSDs to link EUs' feedback to the characteristics of the user traces on the modeled interaction space, understanding how latency affects the usage of the system (**Task 2**).

Finally, VSDs need to understand where the violations in latency thresholds happen precisely; identify visual components that cause potentially high latency in the entirety of the visualization system when interacted frequently; highlight portions of the interaction space that are inefficient, after having them related to the frequency of the interactions performed in user traces (**Task 3**).

In the proposed demonstration, we first identify a possible scenario that can arise while VSDs let EUs explore their visualization system, in order to gain high-level feedback on the latency problems encountered in such exploration. We then let the VSDs use InterView to support them in understanding how specific users used the visualization system first, and where latency problems happened, characterizing their gravity and occurrences. We chose the aforementioned Crossfilter interface as an example, based on the exploration of data regarding the U.S. flights dataset [4], containing around 120 million tuples. This interface is particularly suited for this scenario since the interactions performed on it generate a high number of queries (around hundred of queries per second), and they can potentially introduce latency (while EUs expect real-time interaction), as shown by the benchmark conducted by Battle et al. [2].

To better understand how the demonstration works, we propose a use case with a fictional VSD, Daisy: Daisy is a VSD with many years of experience in the fields of visual analytics and human-computer interaction. She wants to collect feedback about the usage of her currently under design visualization system and, for this reason, lets EUs explore it, using brushing and linking techniques [1]. To test her visualization system for exploration, Daisy retrieves an *exploratory task* from the benchmark: "Which factors appear to have the greatest impact on departure delays?". This task is supposed to let the EUs interact with many visual components to answer, evaluating their correlation while brushing. Cameron is a data scientist studying and analyzing flight data distribution in the US, acting as an EU. He is interested in Falcon's crossfilter interface as it supports optimized components for interactive exploration. At Daisy's request, he completes the previously defined exploratory task, brushing over several visual components, triggering a high amount of queries on the visualization system, which struggles to keep real-time performances. Cameron becomes rapidly frustrated, progressively losing interest in the exploration. As a result, the feedback provided to Daisy is too broad and generic, as she struggles to find the real cause of such high latency on the visualization system. In order to have a more in-depth insight into Cameron's interactions, Daisy would need to analyze the sequence of actions performed on the visualization system. Finally, Daisy attempts to investigate potential anomalies (and eventually hypothesize design changes) where the interaction on the visualization system failed.

3   Demonstration

In this section, we illustrate the proposed demonstration. Figure 1 shows the Falcon implementation designed by Daisy. Brushing on the *Distance in Miles* visual component causes the coordinated real-time update of the others. Daisy tests the visualization system through a user study with 50 users [3], collecting 50 user traces. Each trace contains information such as the number and type of interactions performed, the total execution time, and the violations in latency thresholds.

Step 1. Daisy inputs her system's URL to the InterView's interaction space generator to get its complete statechart. It generates the interaction space and lists all the possible interaction events available to a user, exploiting the Puppeteer Node.js library to simulate human actions automatically. It then employs a modified depth-first-search exploration of the interaction space to cover all the possible interaction paths. By leveraging such a process, the generator gives as output the complete statechart, representing the interaction space of the visualization system.

Step 2. Daisy analyzes the generated statechart, representing all the possible interactions on the visualization system. She has already noticed that state 0 is

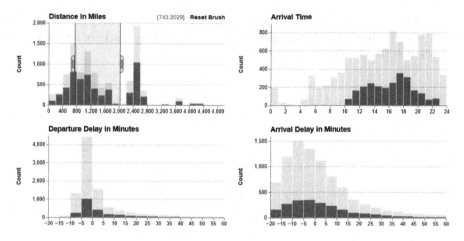

Fig. 1. An end user exploring flight data on Falcon's Crossfilter interface. Brushing on a certain visual component updates the others in real time.

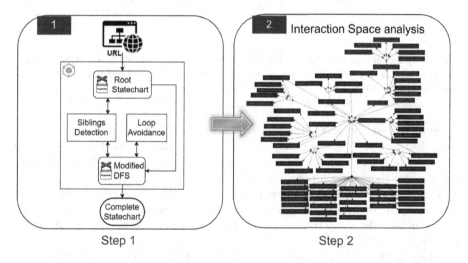

Fig. 2. The first two steps of the intended user flow. The VSDs get an overview of the interaction space of their visualization systems using the generation functionality.

the most important one, as its degree seems to be the highest one with respect to the other states. Looking more in-depth at the statechart's structure, Daisy notices how it presents a hierarchical structure at the bottom, confirming the importance of state 0 (the initial overview of Falcon, acting as the entry point of the system) in the economy of the visualization system. The other states of the statechart are mainly arranged as a star topology. The *mousedown* interactions, representing the start of a brush interaction performed on Falcon's visual components, make state 0 change, following the state related to the visual component where such interaction was recorded. A *mouseup* interaction, confirming the end of the brush, makes the state return to 0 (see Fig. 2 step 2). In such a way, Daisy is supported in exploring and understanding the interaction space composition (thus supporting task 1).

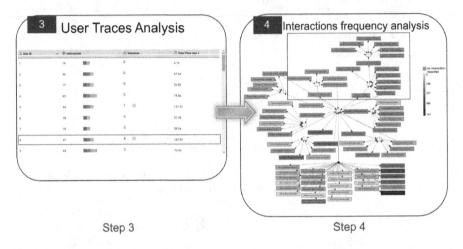

Fig. 3. By inspecting the traces' characteristics, VSDs can notice how frequently specific portions of the interaction space are explored. The highlighted part of the statechart is never explored by EUs.

Step 3. Daisy analyzes the user traces, grouping them and identifying their characteristics, such as the number of interactions, their types, the violations in latency thresholds, and the total execution time recorded for each trace. Daisy can see how they are composed, getting an insight into the type of interactions composing each trace and noticing that some introduced violations while others did not. Daisy remarks that Cameron, the user who reported bad feedback on the system usage, effectively recorded a total of eight violations in latency thresholds (see Fig. 3 user ID 8).

Step 4. Daisy selects the superimposition of user traces data on the statechart. It allows for the frequency of all the possible interactions on the visualization system to be observed. A considerable portion of the interaction space was never explored by any user. This can be because such a portion is not relevant to solving the exploratory tasks the system supports or because it is difficult to reach in the whole interaction space (as the interaction paths are seemingly longer in that portion). On the contrary, the bottom part of the statechart is the most visited by the users. At the end of this phase, Daisy completely fulfills task 1 and is supported in task 2.

Step 5. Carefully analyzing the violations for all the traces, Daisy discovers a portion of the state chart that is causing many violations in latency thresholds (see case 1 in Fig. 4 step 5). Remembering the interaction frequency for the user traces, Daisy notices how that portion of the user trace is also frequently explored by users. Moreover, by repeating such a process, Daisy acknowledges

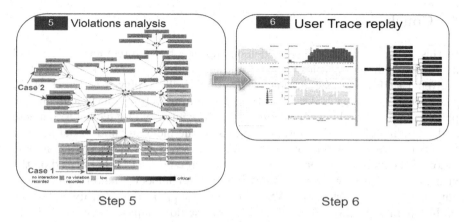

Fig. 4. VSDs can notice the problematic portions of the interaction space, highlighting how paths that are frequently taken record violations in latency thresholds (case 1) or portions that were not as much visited but still record a high number of violations (case 2). Thanks to the replay feature, they can see exactly how EUs interacted.

how specific visual components, such as the *Airtime in minutes* and *Arrival Delay*, are causing severe violations in the system (case 2 in Fig. 4 step 5), even if they were not interacted with as much as other portions of the interaction space like seen for case 1. Combining violations and frequency analyses, Daisy fulfills task 3, identifying two problematic portions of the interaction space.

Step 6. Daisy finally checks for Cameron's specific behavior, having previously identified it as problematic (user 8). She inputs Cameron's user trace to the InterView's replay functionality and analyzes, step by step, the interactions performed in such trace, seeing how they interacted (see Fig. 4 step 6). Daisy can already notice how the many brush interactions are performed very closely in the interaction sequence of the trace, and they are performed on several visual components. The many brush interactions (21) make the system struggle, as the high query rates make updating the visual components increasingly slower. This solves Daisy's doubt that the visualization system suffers from latency when more than 20 brush interactions are performed in a short amount of time (a little more than 10 s), without even allowing the update of the other visual components before performing the next brush interaction. The replay ends, and Daisy now has a clear point of view: Cameron interacted too abruptly within the visualization system, probably frustrated by the increasing latency experienced. This justifies how Cameron's user trace recorded eight violations in latency thresholds in a short amount of time. Finally, Daisy can give more context to Cameron's feedback about the perceived latency on the visualization system, as she analyzed with precision how he interacted (thus fulfilling task 2) and helped confirm the part of the visualization system to focus on for design correction.

4   Conclusion

In this paper, we contributed a demonstration of the InterView system and its two main functionalities that *(i)* automatically generate the statechart of a given visualization system, and *(ii)* automatically replay user traces on it. Their joint use helps VSDs identify and quantitatively evaluate and localize potential latency problems in the means of violations, by also having a complete understanding of how EUs interact thanks to the modeling and visual interactive representation of the interaction space. Moreover, VSDs gain a complete vision of the interaction space, analyzing the interactions EUs performed on the visualization system with fine-grained precision. Thanks to the replay functionality and aggregated statistics, VSDs are better supported in identifying latency problems. Linking this information to the interaction frequency, VSDs can highlight the visual components that need to be optimized, as they more severely impact the responsiveness of the visualization system. Finally, VSDs are supported by projecting users' feedback on specific portions of their visualization system, understanding exactly where and why latency problems were recorded in the user traces. This information guides VSDs to hypothesize design changes to mitigate these problems and get a more responsive visualization system. In future works, we plan to improve the support to the VSD by integrating Artificial Intelligence models to identify potential violations or recommending modifications to the tested system, enriched by their explanation [6]. Additionally, we plan to improve the scalability of the proposed solution by investigating progressive data analysis and visualization techniques for the statechart generator while managing their introduced uncertainty on the VSD [9].

Acknowledgements. This project was supported by the MUR PRIN 2022 Project No. 202248FWFS "Discount quality for responsible data science: Human-in-the-Loop for quality data" within the NextGenerationEU Programme within the NextGenerationEU Programme - M4C2.1.1

References

1. Baeza-Yates, R., et al.: Modern information retrieval, July 1999
2. Battle, L., et al.: Database benchmarking for supporting real-time interactive querying of large data. In: Proceedings of the 2020 ACM SIGMOD International Conference on Management of Data, SIGMOD 2020, pp. 1571–1587. Association for Computing Machinery, New York (2020). https://doi.org/10.1145/3318464.3389732
3. Benvenuti, D., Filosa, M., Catarci, T., Angelini, M.: Modeling and assessing user interaction in big data visualization systems. In: Abdelnour Nocera, J., Kristín Lárusdóttir, M., Petrie, H., Piccinno, A., Winckler, M. (eds.) Human-Computer Interaction - INTERACT 2023, pp. 86–109. Springer Nature Switzerland, Cham (2023)
4. Bureau of Transportation Statistics: On-time performance. https://www.bts.gov/ (nd). Accessed 02 April 2024

5. Harel, D.: Statecharts: a visual formalism for complex systems. Sci. Comput. Program. **8**(3), 231–274 (1987). https://doi.org/10.1016/0167-6423(87)90035-9
6. La Rosa, B., et al.: State of the art of visual analytics for explainable deep learning. Comput. Graph. Forum **42**(1), 319–355 (2023). https://doi.org/10.1111/cgf.14733
7. Liu, Z., Heer, J.: The effects of interactive latency on exploratory visual analysis. IEEE Trans. Visual Comput. Graph. **20**(12), 2122–2131 (2014). https://doi.org/10.1109/TVCG.2014.2346452
8. Livny, M., et al.: Devise: integrated querying and visual exploration of large datasets (demo abstract), vol. 26, pp. 517–520, June 1997
9. Micallef, L., et al.: The human user in progressive visual analytics. In: EuroVis 2019 - Short Papers, pp. 19–23. Eurographics Association (2019). https://doi.org/10.2312/evs.20191164. https://www.eurovis.org/, 21st EG/VGTC Conference on Visualization, EuroVis ; Conference date: 03-06-2019 Through 07-06-2019
10. Moritz, D., Howe, B., Heer, J.: Falcon: balancing interactive latency and resolution sensitivity for scalable linked visualizations, pp. 1–11 (2019). https://doi.org/10.1145/3290605.3300924
11. Shneiderman, B.: Response time and display rate in human performance with computers. ACM Comput. Surv. **16**(3), 265–285 (1984). https://doi.org/10.1145/2514.2517. https://doi.org/10.1145/2514.2517
12. Waloszek, G., Kreichgauer, U.: User-centered evaluation of the responsiveness of applications. In: IFIP Conference on Human-Computer Interaction. pp. 239–242. Springer (2009)
13. Zhang, T., Ramakrishnan, R., Livny, M.: Birch: an efficient data clustering method for very large databases. In: Proceedings of the 1996 ACM SIGMOD International Conference on Management of Data, SIGMOD 1996, pp. 103–114. Association for Computing Machinery, New York (1996).https://doi.org/10.1145/233269.233324

Author Index

© IFIP International Federation for Information Processing 2024
Published by Springer Nature Switzerland AG 2024
M. K. Lárusdóttir et al. (Eds.): HCSE 2024, LNCS 14793, pp. 331–332, 2024.
https://doi.org/10.1007/978-3-031-64576-1